EVIDENCE FOR THE RAPTURE

A BIBLICAL CASE FOR PRETRIBULATIONISM

EVIDENCE FOR THE RAPTURE

A BIBLICAL CASE FOR PRETRIBULATIONISM

JOHN F. HART

GENERAL EDITOR

MOODY PUBLISHERS

CHICAGO

All Scripture quotations, unless otherwise indicated, are taken from the New American Standard Bible®, Copyright ©1960, 1962, 1963, 1968, 1971, 1972, 1973, 1975, 1977, 1995 by The Lockman Foundation. Used by permission. www.Lockman.org

Scripture quotations marked ESV are from The Holy Bible, English Standard Version® (ESV®), copyright © 2001 by Crossway, a publishing ministry of Good News Publishers. Used by permission. All rights reserved.

Scripture quotations marked HCSB are taken from the Holman Christian Standard Bible®. Copyright © 1999, 2000, 2002, 2003, 2009 by Holman Bible Publishers. Used by permission. Holman Christian Standard Bible®, Holman CSB®, and HCSB® are federally registered trademarks of Holman Bible Publishers.

Scripture quotations marked NIV are taken from the Holy Bible, New International Version®, NIV®. Copyright © 1973, 1978, 1984, 2011 by Biblica, Inc.™ Used by permission of Zondervan. All rights reserved worldwide. www.zondervan.com. The "NIV" and "New International Version" are trademarks registered in the United States Patent and Trademark Office by Biblica, Inc.™

Scripture quotations marked KJV are taken from the King James Version.

Scripture quotations marked NET are taken from the NET Bible® copyright ©1996–2006 by Biblical Studies Press, L.L.C. http://netbible.com All rights reserved.

Edited by Jim Vincent
Interior design: Smartt Guys design and Erik M. Peterson
Cover design: Erik M. Peterson
Cover photo of clouds copyright © by Brightside Creative/Lightstock/1947. All rights reserved.

Library of Congress Cataloging-in-Publication Data

Evidence for the rapture : a biblical case for pretribulationism / John F. Hart.
    pages cm
Includes bibliographical references.
ISBN 978-0-8024-1291-1
1. Rapture (Christian eschatology) I. Hart, John F.
BT887.E95 2015
236'.9--dc23
                        2015008124

Moody Publishers
820 N. LaSalle Boulevard
Chicago, IL 60610

1 3 5 7 9 10 8 6 4 2

Printed in the United States of America

IN TRIBUTE

I have chosen to use the outstanding New American Standard Bible as the version for all Scripture citations in this book (unless designated otherwise). One of my purposes for this is to honor the contributions to this translation made by one of our authors, Robert L. Thomas. Dr. Thomas is professor emeritus of The Master's Theological Seminary.

Dr. Thomas was a member of the editorial board of the Lockman Foundation, which produced the New American Standard Bible, and as such participated in the translation of the Greek and Hebrew texts of the NASB. Later, he also became the general editor of the *New American Standard Exhaustive Concordance*. This resource was awarded the Gold Medallion Book Award as the outstanding Bible reference work of 1981–82 by the Evangelical Christian Publishers Association.

CONTENTS

ACKNOWLEDGMENTS

I want to thank Randall Payleitner, editorial director at Moody Publishers, for being so patient as I brought together these ten authors. I also want to thank Greg Thornton, senior vice president of media at Moody Global Ministries, for seeing a vision for this project, and Jim Vincent, Moody Publishers senior editor, for his skills in making final editing decisions with me.

Special thanks go to my wonderful wife, Cindy, who does freelance proofreading for Moody Publishers and has performed a delightful service for this book. Finally, I wish to thank Noah Debaun, one of my students, who read through most of the manuscripts and offered many valuable suggestions.

CONTRIBUTORS

GEORGE A. GUNN, Dean of Admissions and Records, Professor of Bible and Theology, Shasta Bible College and Graduate School | *BA, Shasta Bible College; MDiv, Northwest Baptist Seminary; PhD, Tyndale Theological Seminary*

JOHN F. HART, Professor of Bible, Moody Bible Institute | *BS, West Chester University; ThM, Dallas Theological Seminary; ThD, Grace Theological Seminary*

Dr. Hart has written *50 Things You Need to Know about Heaven* (Bethany), and "John" and "James" in the *Moody Bible Commentary* (Moody).

NATHAN D. HOLSTEEN, Associate Professor of Theological Studies, Dallas Theological Seminary | *BS, Louisiana State University; ThM, Dallas Theological Seminary; PhD, University of Aberdeen*

Dr. Holsteen is coeditor with Dr. Michael Svigel (below) of a three-volume series, *Exploring Christian Theology* (Bethany). He and Dr. Svigel have also coauthored the third volume in the series, *The Church, Spiritual Growth, and the End Times.*

GLENN R. KREIDER, Professor of Theology, Dallas Theological Seminary | *BS, Lancaster Bible College; ThM, PhD, Dallas Theological Seminary*

Dr. Kreider has published two books, including *God with Us: Exploring God's Personal Interactions with His People throughout the Bible* (P&R), and has contributed to several other books, including *The Routledge Encyclopedia of Protestantism* (Routledge), and the *Exploring Christian Theology* series, edited by Dr. Holsteen and Dr. Svigel (two contributors in this book).

MICHAEL A. RYDELNIK, Professor of Jewish Studies, Moody Bible Institute | *BA, Azusa Pacific College; ThM, Dallas Theological Seminary; DMiss, Trinity Evangelical Divinity School*

Dr. Rydelnik is coeditor of the *Moody Bible Commentary* (2014), and has written the Bible commentaries on "Daniel," "Isaiah," and several others for the MBC. He has also written study notes for the *Holman Standard Study Bible* (Broadman Holman), *The Quest Study Bible* (Zondervan), and *The Apologetics Study Bible* (Broadman Holman). He has authored several books, including *The Messianic Hope: Is the Hebrew Bible Messianic?* (Broadman Holman).

MICHAEL J. SVIGEL, Department Chair and Associate Professor of Theological Studies, Dallas Theological Seminary | *BS in Bible, Cairn University; ThM, PhD, Dallas Theological Seminary*

Dr. Svigel is author of *RetroChristianity: Reclaiming the Forgotten Faith* (Crossway) and coeditor with Dr. Holsteen (above) of a three-volume series *Exploring Christian Theology* (Bethany). The third volume in the series is *The Church, Spiritual Growth, and the End Times*. Dr. Svigel has also authored several articles in scholarly journals such as *Trinity Journal* and *Bibliotheca Sacra*.

ROBERT L. THOMAS, Professor Emeritus, The Master's Theological Seminary | *BS, Georgia Institute of Technology; ThM, ThD, Dallas Theological Seminary*

Dr. Thomas has authored *1 Thessalonians and 2 Thessalonians* in the *Expositor's Bible Commentary*, both the original and revised edition (Zondervan). He has also authored *Revelation*, a two-volume exegetical commentary (Moody), and several other books and numerous scholarly articles. He was president of the Evangelical Theological Society, and is the former executive editor of *The Master's Seminary Journal*.

MICHAEL G. VANLANINGHAM, Professor of Bible, Moody Bible Institute | *BA, Nebraska Wesleyan University; MDiv, Talbot Theological Seminary; PhD, Trinity Evangelical Divinity School*

Dr. Vanlaningham is coeditor of the *Moody Bible Commentary* (Moody) and wrote the commentaries on "Matthew" and "Romans." He has also written several articles in *Trinity Journal, The Master's Seminary Journal,* and *Bibliotheca Sacra,* and has authored *Christ, the Savior of Israel* (Peter Lang).

ANDREW M. WOODS, Professor of Bible and Theology, College of Biblical Studies in Houston | *BA, University of Redlands; ThM, Dallas Theological Seminary; PhD, Dallas Theological Seminary; JD, Whittier Law School*

Dr. Woods has authored scholarly articles on Bible prophecy in *Bibliotheca Sacra, Chafer Theological Seminary Journal,* and several others. He has contributed to such books as *The Popular Encyclopedia of Bible Prophecy, The Popular Handbook on the Rapture,* and *The End Times Controversy.* He is senior pastor of the Sugar Land Bible Church, Sugar Land, Texas, and has spoken on prophetic themes at numerous conferences.

KEVIN D. ZUBER, Professor of Theology, Moody Bible Institute | *BA, Grace College; MDiv, ThM, Grace Theological Seminary; PhD, Trinity Evangelical Divinity School*

Dr. Zuber has written commentaries on "Exodus," "1 and 2 Chronicles," "Luke," and "1 and 2 Thessalonians" in the *Moody Bible Commentary.* He is the author of "Metaphor and the Rapture" in *Dispensationalism: Tomorrow and Beyond* (Tyndale Seminary Press).

ABBREVIATIONS

Apoc. Bar   Apocalypse of Baruch

ASV   American Standard Version

BAGD   Bauer, Arndt, Gingrich, and Danker, 2nd ed., rev. F. Wilbur Gingrich and Frederick W. Danker, *Greek–English Lexicon of the New Testament and Other Early Christian Literature*

BDAG   Bauer, Danker, Arndt, and Gingrich 3rd ed., *Greek–English Lexicon of the New Testament and Other Early Christian Literature*

BECNT   Baker Exegetical Commentary on the New Testament

BKC   Bible Knowledge Commentary

BibSac   *Bibliotheca Sacra*

HALOT   Hebrew and Aramaic Lexicon of the Old Testament

ICB   International Children's Bible

ICC   International Critical Commentary

JSNTSS   Journal for the Study of the New Testament Supplement Series

LXX   Septuagint, the Old Testament translation of the Hebrew Bible

NAC   New American Commentary

NICNT   New International Commentary on the New Testament

NRSV   New Revised Standard Version

RSV   Revised Standard Version

TDNT   Theological Dictionary of the New Testament

TVR   *Three Views on the Rapture: Pre, Mid, and Post-Tribulation* Ed. Stanley N. Gundry. Grand Rapids: Zondervan, 1996 .

TVR1   *Three Views on the Rapture: Pretribulation, Prewrath, or Posttribulation.* Alan Hultberg et.al. Grand Rapids: Zondervan, 2010.

WBC   Word Biblical Commentary

WUZNT   Wissenschaftliche Untersuchungen zum Neuen Testament

1QM   The "War Scroll" (Milḥāmāh) of the Dead Sea Scrolls from Qumran Cave 1

Introduction:
Predicting the Rapture

In the past few decades, biblical prophecy has suffered criticism, both from inside and outside the church. Such criticism of the Lord's return reaches its pinnacle when evangelicals mistakenly predict or even suggest a general date or time in which the Lord will return.

In 1970, Hal Lindsey wrote about the pretribulation rapture in his book *The Late Great Planet Earth* (Zondervan). The book aroused intense excitement about the return of Christ and the end of the world. It eventually sold 28 million copies. Despite many accurate interpretations, Lindsay made one primary and serious mistake in the book. It was in how he handled one of the statements by Jesus in His prophecies in the Olivet Discourse (Matt. 24–25; Mark 13; Luke 21). After Jesus had predicted many end-time events (24:4–31), He drew a lesson from the fig tree. "When its branch has already become tender and puts forth its leaves, you know that summer is near; so, you too, when you see all these things, recognize that He is near, right at the door" (vv. 32–33).

Lindsey understood the parable of the budding fig tree to be a reference to the restoration of the nation of Israel to their land. Israel's restoration to their land took place miraculously in 1948 shortly after the holocaust of World War II. Scripture had predicted the reestablishment of Israel in their own land as a nation (cf. Ezek. 36:24; Jer. 16:15, etc.). Now after 2,500 years of governmental rule by several Gentile nations, the Jews were granted the right to establish their own nation again in their own land of Israel.

Following the illustration about the fig tree, Jesus promised, "This generation will not pass away until all these things take place" (Matt. 24:34). Lindsey determined from the Old Testament that a generation was approximately forty years (e.g., Num. 32:14). In Lindsey's understanding of the fig tree parable, "this generation" meant the generation that would see the restoration of Israel to their land. If a generation is forty years, then Jesus had to come back sometime before 1988—forty years after the Jewish people were reestablished in the land.

LINDSEY, WHISENANT, AND OTHERS

Lindsey's book came off the press three years after the completion of the 1967 Six-Day War in Israel. The significant events of that war certainly intensified interest in Bible prophecy and in Lindsey's prediction. During the war Israel recaptured the temple mount, the western wall, and the old city of Jerusalem. But Jesus didn't come back in 1988.

To predict or estimate the day, the month, or the year, or even the decade of Christ's return is fallacious. Jesus Himself said, "But of that day and hour no one knows, not even the angels of heaven, nor the Son, but the Father alone" (Matt. 24:36).

Edgar Whisenant, a retired NASA engineer, published a book in 1988 called *88 Reasons Why the Rapture Will Be in 1988*. The book sold 4.5 million copies. Although he was fully aware of Jesus' statement in Matthew 24:36, Whisenant insisted, "This does not preclude or prevent the faithful from knowing the year, the month, and the week of the Lord's return."[1] In 1997, Ed Dodson, a pastor of an evangelical megachurch in Grand Rapids, wrote *The End: Why Jesus Could Return by A.D. 2000*. Three years later, Harold Camping, a Bible teacher and manager of a Christian radio network, began to publicly teach that the rapture would take place on May 21, 2011, causing a great stir in Christian circles.

This confusion about the timing of the Lord's return points out a fundamental problem in interpreting Bible prophecy about Christ's coming. On the one hand, verses like Matthew 24:36 teach that Jesus' return will be without telltale signs so that no one will be able to know the time of His coming. Jesus warned, "The Son of Man is coming at an hour when you do not think He will" (Matt. 24:44). This statement and similar ones unmistakably imply that no revealing signs or events will precede His coming (cf. Luke 12:35–36, 38–39; 17:26–30; Mark 13:32–37; Rev. 3:3).

On the other hand, numerous prophecies describe observable and predictable signs of His return to earth. Matthew 24:14 states, "This gospel of the kingdom shall be preached in the whole world as a testimony to all the nations, and then the end will come." The Joshua Project identifies 7,052 people groups that are still unreached with the gospel, representing 42 percent of the world population.[2] According to Matthew 24:14, these people groups must be reached before Jesus returns and "the end" takes place (Matt. 24:29–31). Such verses imply that Jesus will come at a predictable time and not at a time when "no one knows" (Matt. 24:36) or when "you do not think He will" (v. 44).

ATTEMPTING TO HARMONIZE BIBLE PROPHECIES

How can these differing prophecies be harmonized and rightly understood? Pretribulationists believe they have the answer. There are two stages to the single, unified "coming" of Christ prophesied in the New Testament. The first stage, called the pretribulation rapture, will occur when Jesus comes down from heaven and will catch up into the sky to be with Him forever all those who believe in Him (1 Thess. 4:17). This "catching up" or rapture has no predictable signs that foretell its coming. It is an imminent event (Matt. 24:43; Luke 12:39). The rapture will precede the "tribulation," i.e., it will precede the divine judgments of the "day of the Lord."

This tribulation is described as a seven-year period divided into two halves (Dan. 9:24–27), i.e., 1,260 days (Rev. 11:3; 12:6) or forty-two months for each half (Rev. 11:2; 13:5). Once a person is living in the tribulation, these and other specific measures of time will make the coming of Christ at the end of the judgments quite predictable.

Those who hold to a pretribulation rapture believe that Jesus will come back for believers of the church before the seven-year tribulation (the day of the Lord) begins. Those who hold to a midtribulation rapture believe the rapture takes Christians from the earth at the middle of this seven-year tribulation. The prewrath rapture view suggests that the rapture occurs about three-fourths through the seven-year tribulation. Finally, the posttribulationist understands the rapture to occur at the end of the seven-year tribulation, shortly before Jesus returns to the earth.

From the pretribulation viewpoint, all other viewpoints of the rapture have a greater difficulty in adequately explaining the passages that teach an imminent, any-moment coming of Jesus. For once the tribulation begins, multiple signs will foretell Christ's coming.

A PREVIEW

This book will explain end-time events described in the Scriptures. Since the teaching of imminence by Jesus and the New Testament authors is so important to understanding Bible prophecy correctly, chapter 1 in *Evidence for the Rapture* is "The Rapture and the Biblical Teaching of Imminency," by Dr. Robert Thomas.

Here's a preview of subsequent chapters. Chapter 2 looks at Jesus, the greatest prophet of all. In "Jesus and the Rapture: Matthew 24" I will propose that Jesus was the originator of the pretribulation rapture, and that all of the other writers of the New Testament Scriptures derive much of their teaching about the rapture from Him.

Some Christians ask, "Why would God want to take Christians out of the world in a pretribulation rapture so that they can be kept from persecution? Persecution is part of the Christian's calling." The answer has to do with the nature of the future "day of the Lord." To understand the nature of the day of the Lord and how it relates to the timing of the rapture, read chapter 3, "The Rapture and the Day of the Lord," by Dr. Glenn Kreider.

In His Upper Room Discourse, Jesus promised His disciples, "I will come again and receive you to Myself, that where I am, there you may be also" (John 14:3). In chapter 4, titled "Jesus and the Rapture: John 14" and written by Dr. George Gunn, readers will discover why pretribulationism best explains the allusions to the Jewish betrothal customs in John 14:1–3.

First Corinthians 15 is sometimes used as a text to substantiate one's position on the rapture. But without the support of other prophetic passages that are harmonized with 1 Corinthians 15, only a few hints can be gained for any rapture position. So in chapter 5, "Paul and the Rapture: 1 Corinthians 15," Dr. Michael Vanlaningham will explain how 1 Corinthians 15 is best understood from a premillennial perspective of prophecy. All pretribulationists are also premillennialists. So a premillennial teaching of prophecy is essential for a pretribulation rapture. For those who are quite unfamiliar with premillennialism, I recommend reading *Christ's Prophetic Plans. A Futuristic Premillennial Primer*, or *Understanding End Time Prophecy* (rev. ed.), both published by Moody Publishers.[3]

Paul's first letter to the Thessalonians contains the central Pauline teaching on the pretribulation rapture. Chapter 6, "Paul and the Rapture: 1 Thessalonians

4–5," by Dr. Kevin Zuber, will give the central reasons why the pretribulation rapture is the best explanation for these two chapters. When these two chapters are read consecutively and with a correct understanding of the occasion for writing, pretribulationism is the unavoidable conclusion. At the same time, Zuber will answer the often-used objection to prophecy, "There is no practical value in debating about the rapture."

Naturally, chapter 7, "Paul and the Rapture: 2 Thessalonians 2," carries on the discussion of the life circumstances at Thessalonica that led to Paul's second letter to this church. Following the way in which we match puzzle pieces to form a puzzle, Dr. Nathan Holsteen describes how the puzzle pieces do not properly fit together unless we explain adequately the false teaching that had reached the Thessalonians. Do you know the nature of that false teaching? Once that is correctly understood, the final piece—a pretribulation rapture—becomes the only reasonable option.

Some Christians question whether the pretribulation rapture is found in the book of Revelation. Two chapters will answer this objection. First, Dr. Andy Woods has written chapter 8, "John and the Rapture: Revelation 2–3." He explains what passages from Revelation 2 and 3 are best interpreted in light of the pretribulation rapture and what passages are not.

Even well-read prophecy advocates have probably not heard anyone interpret Revelation 12:5 as a verse that teaches a pretribulation rapture. But John Nelson Darby (1800–1882), perhaps the first to more clearly expound a pretribulation rapture, used this very passage as his central text. Dr. Michael Svigel will lead the reader through this study in chapter 9, "What Child Is This? A Forgotten Exegetical Argument for the Pretribulation Rapture."

Finally, Dr. Michael Rydelnik, a scholar on Jewish studies, authors chapter 10, "Israel: Why the Church Must Be Raptured before the Tribulation." He will explain why the final coming of Christ to the earth is fully dependent on events that must occur among the Jewish people of the tribulation. Until this happens, Jesus cannot return to earth in His second coming. Additionally, Rydelnik will clarify why the tribulation was designed for Israel and not the church.

The reader will not find in this book complete agreement on all details regarding the pretribulation rapture. But he or she will find a broad conviction that the church is not destined to experience the wrath of the day of the Lord. On the contrary, our hope is a wonderful deliverance from the devastations and judgments of the tribulation. The rapture is not an escape from a world of trials, but a "catching up" to be protected from the future divine judgments that will come on the earth and to join with our Savior and Lord to be with Him forever.

Notes

1. Edgar C. Whisenant, *88 Reasons Why the Rapture Will Be in 1988,* exp. ed. (Nashville: World Bible Society, 1988), 2–3, as cited in Sheryl J. Gregory, "Can the Date of Jesus' Return Be Known?" *BibSac* 169 (January–March 2012): 28.

2. http://joshuaproject.net/global_statistics.

3. *Christ's Prophetic Plans: A Futuristic Premillennial Primer,* ed. John MacArthur and Richard Mayhue (Chicago: Moody, 2012); Paul Benware, *Understanding End Time Prophecy,* rev. ed. (Chicago: Moody, 2006).

1

The Rapture and the Biblical Teaching of Imminency

BY ROBERT L. THOMAS

Be dressed in readiness, and keep your lamps lit. Be like men who are waiting for their master when he returns from the wedding feast, so that they may immediately open the door to him when he comes and knocks.

LUKE 12:35

Imminence is a crucial teaching of Jesus and the apostles related to end-time prophecy. The English word *imminence* means an event that can occur at any time. An imminent danger is a threat that is close at hand and can happen at any moment. There can be no detectable signs that such a danger is about to take place.

When interpreting prophecy, however, some scholars use the word "imminent" less precisely to mean an event that may occur soon, but may also be preceded by specific signs or warnings. Contrary to this, pretribulationists understand the Bible to teach that some prophetic events, such as the rapture and the day of the Lord, will occur at a future time without any preceding signs or events. Therefore, if pretribulationism is the correct New Testament teaching, it must be demonstrated biblically that the rapture will occur without warning and without signs that necessarily indicate its nearness.

The testimony of the ancient fathers, the earliest leaders of the church after the apostles, could perhaps help answer this question. The church fathers
definitely speak of future imminent events. But surprisingly, their testimony
is mixed, sometimes speaking of the imminence of Christ's return and other
times of the imminence of the future time of God's wrath. For example, Clement speaks of the return of Christ as imminent:

> Of a truth, soon and suddenly shall His will be accomplished, as the Scripture
> also bears witness, saying, "Speedily will He come, and will not tarry;" and,
> "The Lord shall suddenly come to His temple, even the Holy One, for whom
> ye look."[1]

Ignatius speaks of the coming of God's wrath on the earth as imminent:

> The last times are come upon us. Let us therefore be of a reverent spirit, and
> fear the long-suffering of God, that it tend not to our condemnation. For let us
> either stand in awe of the wrath to come, or show regard for the grace which is
> at present displayed—one of two things.[2]

But Irenaeus speaks of both as imminent:

> And therefore, when in the end the Church shall be suddenly caught up from
> this, it is said, "There shall be tribulation such as has not been since the begin-
> ning, neither shall be."[3]

Why this apparent ambivalence among early Christian leaders who were
following the same teachings of the New Testament that we follow today? I propose that there is good reason for their teachings that both are imminent. The
return of Christ for His church and the return of Christ to inflict wrath and
tribulation on the world is close at hand and can happen at any moment.

Years ago, I investigated the book of Revelation to substantiate this dual imminence, i.e., that both the coming of Christ and the coming of God's wrath
on the world are imminent.[4] This chapter will focus its attention on Paul's two
epistles to the Thessalonian church, but it first must probe the question of how
the New Testament teaching on imminence originated. The concept of the imminence of these two future happenings interweaves itself into New Testament
teaching from beginning to end, raising the strong probability that the origin
of the teaching was none other than Jesus Himself. Thus the first area to explore
briefly will be some of Jesus' teachings on the subject.

JESUS' EMPHASIS ON IMMINENCE

The Olivet Discourse

In Luke 12:35–48, as part of His later Judean ministry, Jesus instructed His disciples about the need to be ready for His return:

> "Be dressed in readiness, and keep your lamps lit. Be like men who are waiting for their master when he returns from the wedding feast, so that they may immediately open *the door* to him when he comes and knocks. . . .
>
> "But be sure of this, that if the head of the house had known at what hour the thief was coming, he would not have allowed his house to be broken into. "You too, be ready; for the Son of Man is coming at an hour that you do not expect. . . ."
>
> And the Lord said, "Who then is the faithful and sensible steward, whom his master will put in charge of his servants, to give them their rations at the proper time? Blessed is that slave whom his master finds so doing when he comes. Truly I say to you that he will put him in charge of all his possessions. But if that slave says in his heart, 'My master will be a long time in coming,' and begins to beat the slaves, *both* men and women, and to eat and drink and get drunk; the master of that slave will come on a day when he does not expect *him* and at an hour he does not know, and will cut him in pieces, and assign him a place with the unbelievers."

These two parables contain two pictorial expressions that became a vital part of Christian vocabulary throughout the history of the first-century church.[5] The first is that of the master standing at the door and knocking, and the second is that of the unexpected coming of a thief. Both figures are designed to teach the imminence of Christ's return. In each parable the unexpected coming brings blessing to the followers who are prepared, but in the latter parable that coming brings punishment to those who are unprepared.

On Tuesday of His last week on earth, Jesus taught similar lessons regarding the imminence of His return. In Matthew's and Mark's Gospels when giving the parable of the fig tree immediately after speaking of His return in glory to the earth, He derives this application from the parable: "When you see all these things, recognize that He is . . . at the door" (Matt. 24:33). The signs given in Matthew 24:4–28 are within Daniel's Seventieth Week (Dan. 9:24–27) and indicate the nearness of Jesus' return to earth as described in Matthew 24:29–31.[6] These signals of nearness cause this parable to differ from the parable in Luke

12:35–48, which contains no signs of nearness. Neither are there signs available in Luke 17:26–37 where Jesus, with several similar comparisons, predicts the imminent coming of the kingdom of God.

But in Matthew 24:36 Jesus turns the page to speak of the absence of all signs as signals of the beginning of Daniel's Seventieth Week.[7] His words are, "But of that day and hour no one knows, not even the angels of heaven, nor the Son, but the Father alone." Here He indicates the complete unexpectedness of what will overtake the world.[8] He changes attention from the signs that indicate the nearness of His coming to establish the kingdom to speak of events that will have no signals to indicate that they are "at the door."[9] In other words, 24:36 speaks of something different from "all these things" twice referred to in connection with the parable of the fig tree in 24:32–34. After 24:36 Jesus turns to look at the Seventieth-Week events as a whole (the entire future tribulation of seven years) and how the beginning of that week will catch everyone by surprise.[10]

Jesus proceeded to illustrate the complete unexpectedness of the series of events of that week by noting the parallel of His coming to inflict wrath on the world with the way God caught the world by surprise with the flood in Noah's day (24:37–39). The victims did not know until the flood happened. That will be the case when the Son of Man returns. The world will not know until the tribulation period is under way. They will have no warnings such as those alluded to in the parable of the fig tree.

Jesus continued His emphasis on the imminence of His return by describing two workers in the field and two grinders at the mill (24:40–41). In each case, one will be taken in judgment as were those outside of Noah's family, and the other will be left as were the members of Noah's family. The picture presented is that of complete surprise. Outside Noah's immediate family, no one had the faintest idea that a series of cataclysmic events was about to occur. On that basis, Jesus commanded the disciples to watch, because neither they nor anyone else knew or knows on what day their Lord would come (24:42).

At that point Jesus gave the men five parables to enforce His teaching of imminence. The first is in the gospel of Mark and the last four in the gospel of Matthew. The Markan parable tells of a man who left home for a journey and gave his slaves tasks to accomplish while he was gone. He gave special instructions to the doorkeeper to remain on the alert because they had no idea when the master of the house would return (Mark 13:33–37). This parable contains nothing to indicate the master would return within a given timespan, so the slaves were to remain on the alert into the indefinite future.

Matthew's first parable, the second in this series by the Lord, tells of the master of a house who did not know during what watch of the night the thief would come (Matt. 24:43–44). Though not stated explicitly, it is implicit that the master did not know on what given night the thief would come, if he would come at all. As a result, the thief broke into his house because the master was not watching. In light of that comparison, the Lord tells His disciples to be prepared because the Son of Man will come at an hour they do not expect. This marks the Lord's second use of the figure of the unexpected coming of a thief. The parable fixes no limited time frame during which the thief had to come.

Matthew's second parable in this series describes the slave who is faithful and wise and the slave who is wicked (24:45–51). Their master will richly reward the slave whom he finds fulfilling his responsibilities when he returns, but will punish severely that wicked slave who uses the delay in his master's return to abuse the authority given to him. "The master of that slave will come on a day when he [the slave] does not expect him and at an hour which he did not know" (24:50). That slave can expect weeping and gnashing of teeth. The parable fixes no maximum time limit for the master's absence.

The fourth parable in the series, the third in Matthew's gospel, speaks of ten virgins, five of whom were foolish and five wise (25:1–13). When the bridegroom came unexpectedly in the middle of the night, the foolish virgins had no oil for their lamps. By the time they purchased oil, it was too late, and they found themselves locked out of the wedding feast where the wise virgins had been admitted. Neither group knew a fixed period within which the groom would return, but one group was ready, the other was not. The lesson: "Be on the alert then, for you do not know the day nor the hour" (25:13).

The fifth and last parable in the series comes in Matthew 25:14–30, the parable of the talents. Prior to leaving on a journey, the master gave one slave five talents, another two talents, and a third slave one talent. The one with five talents gained five more, and the one with two gained two more. Upon the master's return, they received his commendation with a promise of being given more responsibility. The slave with one talent buried his talent and received the master's rebuke for not investing it to gain more. That slave's destiny was outer darkness. The lesson of this parable is that of serving the Lord responsibly while awaiting His return. Readiness for His return also entails responsible action while He is away.

To synthesize Jesus' teachings: in the flood and sowers-grinders illustrations and in the first four parables, the incontrovertible lesson Jesus teaches is that of the imminence of His return to judge, and therefore, the need for watchfulness and readiness for that return whenever it should occur. It is no wonder that the early church and the church throughout the ages has looked for the imminent return of her Lord. He will return with no prior signals to herald His return. Since nothing remains to occur before His coming, that coming is imminent.

The Upper Room Discourse

On the Mount of Olives, the dominant theme of this Tuesday of Jesus' final week was Christ's return to judge, as He spoke to the disciples as representatives of the nation Israel. On Thursday of that week, He spoke to them in an entirely different role in His discourse in the upper room. This time He addressed them as representatives of a new body to be formed about fifty days later, that body being the church. He injected His imminent return in a more subtle fashion, but He nevertheless made His point. In John 14:3 He said, "If I go and prepare a place for you, I will come again and receive you to Myself, that where I am, there you may be also." Imminence is part of the verb form "I will come," the Greek word being *erchomai*. Used in parallel with the future indicative *paralēmpsomai,* which means "I will receive," the present tense *erchomai* is clearly a futuristic use of the present tense, a use of that tense that strongly implies imminence. The sense is, "I am on my way and may arrive at any moment."

This is a coming for deliverance for the faithful, however, not a coming for judgment. He will retrieve the faithful and take them back to the Father's house with Himself (John 14:2–3). There they will remain with Him until He returns to the earth to establish His earthly kingdom for a thousand years.

We conclude, therefore, that Jesus was the one who initiated the teaching of the imminence of His return both to judge the world and to deliver the faithful. As we proceed, we will see how that teaching caught on with the first-century church. Subsequent books of the New Testament indicate that two figures used by Him to portray that imminence caught the attention and remained in the memories of early Christians. One was the surprise arrival of a thief and the other was the picture of a master standing at the door ready to enter at any moment.

EMPHASIS ON IMMINENCE BY NEW TESTAMENT WRITERS OTHER THAN PAUL

In the late forties of the first century AD, James wrote in his epistle to Jewish believers in the Diaspora (i.e., the dispersion of the Jews) about dual imminence. This dual imminence involved the imminence of judgment on the oppressors of the poor (James 5:1–6) and the imminence of Christ's coming as an incentive for the long-suffering of the faithful (vv. 7–11). James has Christ standing at the door, ready to enter and rectify past injustices (v. 9). That was one of the figures introduced by Jesus in His Olivet Discourse. In the late sixties Peter wrote to believers in what is now north central Asia Minor about the imminent arrival of the day of the Lord (2 Pet. 3:10). Using a later part of that day to represent the whole period, he spoke of the day's coming as a thief, both to encourage mockers to repent and to help the faithful to persevere. That was the second figure used by Jesus on the Mount of Olives. In the last decade of the first century, John wrote to seven churches in first-century Asia to persuade the unrepentant to repent and the faithful to hold fast (Rev. 2–3).[11] One of those churches he exhorted to watchfulness as a thief would in light of Christ's coming (Rev. 3:3).

But our task in the present essay is to examine the writings of a fourth New Testament writer, Paul, and to see how he taught the dual imminence of Christ's return and the day of the Lord, especially in his Thessalonian epistles.

PAUL'S EMPHASIS ON IMMINENCE IN 1 THESSALONIANS

The Day of the Lord in 1 Thessalonians 5

Paul very clearly teaches the imminence of the wrathful phase of the day of the Lord in 1 Thessalonians 5:2–3: "For you yourselves [i.e., the Thessalonian readers] know full well that the day of the Lord will come just like a thief in the night. While they are saying, 'Peace and safety!' then destruction will come upon them suddenly like labor pains upon a woman with child, and they will not escape." The apostle offers further evidence of the widespread impact of Jesus' use of the thief figure to express imminence. He reflects the negative impact of the day of the Lord in speaking of the destruction that will beset earth's inhabitants when it arrives. By comparing the period to the birth pains of a pregnant woman, Paul shows his awareness that the Old Testament and Jesus

Himself used that comparison to depict the time just before Jesus' personal reappearance on earth (Isa. 13:8; 26:17–19; 66:7ff.; Jer. 30:7–8; Mic. 4:9–10; Matt. 24:8).

Later in the paragraph, in discussing the exemption of believers from the horrors of this period, Paul gives indication that the day is a period of wrath: "For God has not destined us for wrath, but for obtaining salvation through our Lord Jesus Christ" (1 Thess. 5:9). This first phase of the day of the Lord (i.e., the tribulation of seven years) will witness the outpouring of God's wrath against a rebellious world.

Regarding 1 Thessalonians 5:2, Hiebert writes, "As a prophetic period, the Day of the Lord is inaugurated with the rapture of the church as described in 4:13–18, covers the time of the Great Tribulation, and involves His return to earth and the establishment of His messianic reign. In this passage Paul is dealing only with the judgment aspect of that day."[12] Regarding the figure of the coming thief, Hiebert continues, "The comparison lies in the suddenness and unexpectedness of both events. The thief comes suddenly and at a time that cannot be predetermined; so the Day of the Lord will come suddenly when people are not expecting it."[13] That is the imminence that Jesus described when He taught His disciples that no one knows the day or the hour when God will begin to vent His wrath against the world. The apostle reminds his readers that they know with exactness that nothing specific regarding the date for the beginning of the day of the Lord can be known. No prior signals will occur to alert people to the proximity of the day, which forces them to respond as though it could begin at any moment.

The Catching Away in 1 Thessalonians 4

The imminence of the day of the Lord in 1 Thessalonians 5 is obvious, but what is the nature of expectation related to the coming of the Lord to catch away His saints in 1 Thessalonians 4? I have expressed elsewhere that the *peri de* ("now concerning" or "now as to") that begins chapter 5 turns to a new subject, but not one completely distinct from the one previously under discussion at the end of chapter 4.[14] The connective phrase marks a shift in thought, but a shift that is not without some connection with chapter 4. Both the previous and the following context of 1 Thessalonians 5:1 relate to the *parousia* ("coming") of Christ. The original readers had an accurate awareness of the unexpectedness of the arrival of the day of the Lord (5:1–2), having received prior instruction from the apostle. But they were ignorant of and therefore perplexed about what would happen to the dead in Christ at the time of Christ's return. Before beginning his review of the imminence of the day of the Lord in 5:1–11, Paul had clarified for them that the dead in Christ will have an equal and even a prior part in the events surrounding Christ's return (4:13–18).

Is that coming for those in Christ described in 1 Thessalonians 4 an imminent coming? The answer to that question is yes and is based on several indicators. One is the writer's use of the first person plural in 4:15, 17: "*we* who are alive and remain until the coming of the Lord . . . *we* who are alive and remain" (italics added). Paul was personally looking forward to the Lord's return. This was not a "pious pretense perpetrated for the good of the church. He sincerely lived and labored in anticipation of the day, but he did not know when it would come."[15] He was setting an example of expectancy for the church of all ages.[16]

> Proper Christian anticipation includes the imminent return of Christ. His coming will be sudden and unexpected, an any-moment possibility. This means that no divinely revealed prophecies remain to be fulfilled before that event. Without setting a deadline, Paul hoped that it would transpire in his own lifetime. Entertaining the possibility of his own death (2 Tim 4:6–8) and not desiring to contravene Christ's teaching about delay (Matt 24:48; 25:5; Luke 19:11–27), Paul, along with all primitive Christianity, reckoned on the prospect of remaining alive till Christ returned (Rom 13:11; 1 Cor 7:26, 29; 10:11; 15:51–52; 16:22; Phil 4:5). A personal hope of this type characterized him throughout his days (2 Cor 5:1–4; Phil 3:20–21; 1 Tim 6:14; 2 Tim 4:8; Tit 2:11–13).[17]

Another indicator of the imminence of Christ's coming for those in Christ lies in the nature of Paul's description in 1 Thessalonians 4:16–17 and its parallel in 1 Corinthians 15. In 1 Thessalonians 4:16–17, Paul taught the Thessalonian believers that the dead in Christ will be the main participants in the first act of the Lord's return since they are resurrected before anything else happens. Then living Christians will suddenly be snatched away, presumably taking on their resurrection bodies without experiencing death. Paul claimed he learned this truth regarding the sudden snatching away of church saints by "the word of the Lord" (1 Thess. 4:15).

In 1 Corinthians 15:51–53, Paul called similar information a "mystery" giving evidence that the two passages treated a parallel subject. In other words,

Paul spoke of the same event described in 1 Thessalonians 4 about four years later when he wrote to the Corinthians:

> Behold, I tell you a mystery; we will not all sleep, but we all will be changed, in a moment, in the twinkling of an eye, at the last trumpet; for the trumpet will sound, and the dead will be raised imperishable, and we will be changed. For this perishable must put on the imperishable, and this mortal must put on immortality.

The additional detail that believers will be changed (resurrected) in a blinking of the eye reveals that the whole process of the rapture will be a momentary happening, not an extended process. Before people know what is happening, it will be over. That again speaks of imminence in that Paul again uses the first person plural ("us" and "we") in 1 Corinthians. He expected to be alive at the parousia.[18] Something that comes and goes that quickly is surely beyond human ability to pinpoint.

How have various prophetic systems with no room for imminence handled this biblical teaching? Notice how Gundry defines imminence: "By common consent imminence means that so far as we know no predicted event will *necessarily* precede the coming of Christ."[19] His definition would be correct if he had omitted "so far as we know" and "*necessarily*" from that sentence. The statement would then read, "By common consent imminence means that no predicted event will precede the coming of Christ." His additions render his definition of imminence totally inaccurate.

He continues, "The concept [of imminence] incorporates three essential elements: suddenness, unexpectedness or incalculability, and a possibility of occurrence at any moment. . . . Imminence would only raise the possibility of pretribulationism on a sliding scale with mid- and posttribulationism." His terms "suddenness," "unexpectedness," and "incalculability" are accurate, as is "a possibility of occurrence at any moment." But raising "the possibility of pretribulationism on a sliding scale with mid- and posttribulationism" is totally inaccurate. If Christ's pretribulation coming is only one possibility among several possibilities (mid- and posttribulationism), the biblical teaching of imminence has disappeared. If a pretribulation rapture is only a possibility, a person who does not prepare for Christ's return has a calculated chance of coming through unscathed after Daniel's Seventieth Week begins. However, Jesus and the other New Testament writers offer no such prospect.

Carson writes regarding imminence, "'The imminent return of Christ' then means Christ may return at any time. But the evangelical writers who use the word divide on whether 'imminent' in the sense of 'at any time' should be pressed to mean 'at any second' or something looser such as 'at any period' or 'in any generation.'"[20] Carson's suggestion of a "looser" meaning of imminence removes the primary force of the word. Trying to understand what he and other representatives of this "not imminent but imminent" group mean by imminence or expectation is extremely difficult. It is almost like trying to adjudicate a "doublespeak" contest.

Carson says, "Yet the terms 'imminent' and 'imminency' retain theological usefulness if they focus attention on the eager expectancy of the Lord's return characteristic of many NT passages, a return that could take place soon, i.e., within a fairly brief period of time, without specifying that the period must be one second or less."[21] Like Gundry, Carson wavers on the meaning of imminent. If imminence means only that Jesus may return at any period or in any generation, it does not match with the New Testament teaching on the subject. Such a looser connotation of the word "imminent" loses contact with what Christ taught and what the rest of the New Testament writers insisted was the proper Christian outlook.

Erickson approaches imminence this way:

> It is one thing to say we do not know when an event will occur; it is another thing to say that we know of no times when it will not occur. If on a time scale we have points 1 to 1,000, we may know that Christ will not come at points 46 and 79, but not know at just what point He will come. The instructions about watchfulness do not mean that Christ may come at any time.[22]

Erickson's reasoning is difficult to follow here. Christ never designated points at which He would not return. He could come at point 46 or 79, contrary to Erickson's assertion. He could come at any point between 1 and 1,000. His failure to come already does not erase the ongoing possibility that He may come at any moment.

Witherington's wording is different: "In short, one cannot conclude that 1 Thessalonians 4:15 clearly means that Paul thought the Lord would definitely return during his lifetime. Possible imminence had to be conjured with, but certain imminence is not affirmed here."[23] From a practical standpoint, possible imminence is tantamount to certain imminence. How Witherington can distinguish between the two defies explanation. *Certain imminence* means Christ could come at any moment; *possible imminence,* unless one offers an alternative of impossible imminence to go with it, also means that Christ could return at any moment. The "impossible-imminence" alternative directly contradicts the possible-imminence teaching and is therefore impossible.

Beker represents an unbiased approach to the text when he clarifies Paul's attitude more accurately than those who cannot fit imminence into their eschatological systems:

> Thus delay of the parousia is not a theological concern for Paul. It is not an embarrassment for him; it does not compel him to shift the center of his attention from apocalyptic imminence to a form of "realized eschatology," that is, to a conviction of the full presence of the kingdom of God in our present history. It is of the essence of his faith in Christ that adjustments in his expectations can occur without a surrender of these expectations (1 Thess. 4:13–18; 1 Cor. 15:15–51; 2 Cor. 5:1–10; Phil. 2:21–24). Indeed, the hope in God's imminent rule through Christ remains the constant in his letters from beginning to end. . . .[24]

The "nonimminence" scholars, who must place Christ's coming for those "in Christ" at the end of Daniel's Seventieth Week, must speak of the unexpectedness of His advent within a limited period of time, because all would agree that events of the tribulation period will be recognizable. Once that period has begun, His coming has to occur within a specified number of years. If that is their meaning, Christ's warnings to watch for His coming are meaningless until that future period arrives. The church need not watch as He commanded. For when that prophetic week arrives, imminence will no longer prevail because His coming will not be totally unexpected. It will have specified events to signal at least approximately, if not exactly, how far away it is.

Saying the New Testament teaching of imminence has become garbled in the systems of prewrath rapturism and posttribulationism is probably not an overstatement. According to different advocates, it may mean at any moment within the last half of the Seventieth Week, at any moment after the Seventieth Week, during any period rather than at any moment, at an unexpected moment with some exceptions, possibly at any moment but not certainly at any moment, or as many other meanings as there are other opponents of a pretribulation rapture.

Other Indications of Imminence in 1 Thessalonians

In 1 Thessalonians 1:9–10 Paul wrote about his readers' turning to God from idols for two purposes: to serve the living and true God and to await His Son from heaven. The second purpose strikes a note that is continuously sounded in his preaching in the city (Acts 17:7) and throughout both Thessalonian epistles (1 Thess. 2:19; 3:13; 4:15; 5:2, 23; 2 Thess. 2:1, 8). Primitive Christianity believed that the resurrected and ascended Christ would return and that His return was near.[25] Paul speaks of Jesus delivering *us* from the coming wrath when He comes from heaven, thereby including himself and his first-century readers among those to be rescued from that future wrath. In this subtle way he again included himself, modeling the proper Christian outlook in expecting a return of Jesus at any moment.

In 1:10 he also speaks of the wrath as "coming" ("who rescues us from the coming wrath," NIV) and uses the present participle *erchomenēs* to qualify the wrath. Though the kind of action—*aktionsart* or aspect—of articular participles is not necessarily stressed in New Testament Greek, the frequent use of the present tense of this verb in a futuristic sense to speak of the imminence of end events probably portrays the imminence of the wrath that is already on its way and hence quite near.[26]

Another statement of Paul in 1 Thessalonians that is best explained as imminence is 1 Thessalonians 2:16b: "But wrath has come upon them to the utmost." These words are the climax of a paragraph in which Paul is uncharacteristically condemning his fellow Jews for their part in the crucifixion of Christ and persecuting the prophets and Paul along with his fellow missionaries. Earlier in verse 16 he speaks of their forbidding the evangelizing of the Gentiles as a part of the divine outcome that they should reach the limit in sinning against God (2:16a).

The wrath for which the Jewish people as well as the rest of the world are destined is the eschatological wrath spoken of already in 1 Thessalonians 1:10, a well-known and expected period—the day of the Lord or Daniel's Seventieth Week—just before the Messiah inaugurates His kingdom. This pronouncement of the arrival of the wrath brings Paul's excursus against the Jews to its logical climax.

Surprisingly, however, Paul does not use a future tense "will come" to speak of the wrath. He uses a past tense, "has come." The Greek expression is *ephthasen epi* ("has come upon"), the same combination used by Jesus in Matthew 12:28 and Luke 11:20 to speak of the arrival of the kingdom. "The kingdom of God has come upon you" were the Lord's words to His listeners. The unique force of the verb in that situation connoted "arrival upon the threshold fulfillment and accessible experience, *not* the entrance into that experience."[27]

The connotation in 1 Thessalonians 2:15 is the same with regard to the wrath. Just as the kingdom reached the covenant people at Christ's first advent without their enjoying "the experience ensuing upon the initial contact,"[28] so the wrath to precede that kingdom has come without the Jews' full experience of it. It is at the threshold. All prerequisites for unleashing this future torrent have been met. God has set conditions in readiness through the first coming and the rejection of the Messiah by His people. A time of trouble awaits Israel just as it does the rest of the world, and the breaking forth of this time is portrayed as an "imminent condemnation" by the combination *ephthasen epi*.[29] Such a potential presence of the wrath accords with the epistle's emphasis on an imminent breaking forth of end-time events, one of which is the time of Israel's trouble just before the Messiah's return.[30]

In light of this brief study of 1 Thessalonians 1:10 and 2:16, it is evident that dual imminence prevails elsewhere in 1 Thessalonians rather than just in chapters 4 and 5.

PAUL'S EMPHASIS ON IMMINENCE IN 2 THESSALONIANS

A major objection to Pauline authorship of 2 Thessalonians has been an eschatological perspective that is allegedly different from what 1 Thessalonians teaches. The theory advanced is that 2 Thessalonians upholds a Christian approach to the doctrine of last things that arose after the destruction of Jerusalem in AD 70.[31] The principal difference cited is that Paul supposedly mentions various signs in 2 Thessalonians that will take place before the arrival of the day of the Lord. That contrasts with the indication in 1 Thessalonians that the day could come at any moment, without any prophesied event(s) to precede it. This proposed difference in teaching, offered as a challenge of the Pauline authorship of 2 Thessalonians, allegedly occurs in 2 Thessalonians 2:1–3.

Imminence of Our Gathering Together and the Day of the Lord (2:1–3)

Since Paul's first epistle to the church at Thessalonica, that church had been beset with false teaching—claims that the day of the Lord had already begun. Believers there must have considered the persecutions and afflictions they were experiencing (2 Thess. 1:4) to be the initial phase of that day, comparable to the pains of a "woman with child" spoken of in the first epistle (1 Thess. 5:3). They could not have had such an impression if Paul had in his first letter led them to believe that Christ's return would be a single event—an event that initiated the day of the Lord. Posttribulationists are at a loss to explain how the first-century readers could have thought themselves to be already in the day of the Lord if that day came concurrently with the coming of Christ. Paul had just written of how God would afflict the unrighteous and reward the faithful in the day of the Lord in the first chapter (2 Thess. 1:5–10). The readers knew that the opening period of that day would be a day of persecution for the saints, so the false teaching had led them to believe that they were already in that period.

To correct this error, Paul first refers to "the coming of our Lord Jesus Christ and our gathering together to Him" (2:1). "Our gathering together to Him" defines which aspect of Jesus' coming the writer has in mind. It reminds the readers of the great event described in 1 Thessalonians 4:14–17, the gathering of those in Christ to meet Him in the air en route to be with the Father in heaven. He wanted to emphasize that the day of the Lord cannot begin on earth until the saints are in heaven with the Father. Since Christ's reappearance to take the saints to heaven had not yet happened, the day of the Lord could not yet have begun. Therefore, the apostle asks them not to be shaken or troubled by the false message they had received (2:2a). The gathering together had not yet occurred; hence the day of the Lord was not yet in progress.

Paul even specifies the nature of the false teaching. It was proposing that "the day of the Lord is present" (2:2b). The rendering of the verb *enestēken* (the perfect tense of *enistēmi*) as "is present" rather than as "has come" or "will come" is very important, because that is the key to interpreting the difficult verse immediately following.

English versions have, for the most part, completely mistranslated the verb *enestēken*. Those with erroneous renderings include the KJV, the RSV, the NASB, the NIV, the ASV, the ESV, and the NKJV. Only three versions consulted render the verb correctly. Darby renders, "the day of the Lord is present," Weymouth has, "the day of the Lord is now here," and the NRSV gives, "the day of the Lord is already here." Any of these captures the intensive force of the perfect tense of *enestēken*. That the perfect tense of *enistēmi* means "is present" cannot be doubted in light of its usage elsewhere in the New Testament (Rom. 8:38; 1 Cor. 3:22; 7:26; Gal. 1:4; Heb. 9:9).[32]

With the nature of the false teaching clearly in mind, as a next step Paul urges, "Let no one in any way deceive you" (2:3a). He then furnishes a reason for knowing that the day of the Lord is not present. The difficulty is Paul's assumption of an unstated main clause to accompany the "unless" clause (i.e., "unless the apostasy comes first, and the man of lawlessness is revealed," 2:3b). As is customary in language usage, Paul chose not to repeat the verb that constitutes the main clause of the conditional sentence, thus requiring readers to substitute the parallel antecedent verb to fill in the blank.[33] We might say, "I am going to the store, then home." In the last clause, we need to supply the verb from the first clause, "then *I am going* home."

The verb to be supplied in 1 Thessalonians 2:3 is, of course, *enestēken* from verse 2. The sense of 2:3b would thus become, "The day of the Lord is not present unless the apostasy comes first and the man of lawlessness is revealed." Unfortunately, no English version consulted renders the suppressed main clause correctly in this verse. Most give the supplied verb a future sense, such as, "The day of the Lord will not come," a change that misses Paul's point. The issue involved in his correction of the false information to which the readers had been exposed is not the future coming of the day of the Lord; it is rather the current non-presence of that day at the time he writes and they read his words. If that day were not present, then they could not be in that day.

For example, suppose I say, "In the northern states, the fall season *will not come* unless first the weather gets colder and the tree leaves change their colors." This sentence might imply that the weather gets colder and the tree leaves change their colors before the fall season comes. But this isn't true. These changes do not occur before the fall but are part of the fall season. But if I say, "The fall season *is not present* (is not here) unless first the weather gets colder and the tree leaves change their colors," this implies something different. The cooler weather happens first, and then the colors of the leaves change. These two factors take place within the fall season and indicate its arrival. They don't occur before the fall season arrives. These examples demonstrate the need for translating 1 Thessalonians 2:3 correctly.

With two small corrections, 2 Thessalonians 2:1–3 of the NASB can be adequately corrected and serve as a guide for further discussion of the passage's meaning [corrections in italics]:

> Now we request you, brethren, with regard to the coming of our Lord Jesus
> Christ and our gathering together to Him, that you not be quickly shaken
> from your composure or be disturbed either by a spirit or a message or a letter
> as if from us, to the effect that the day of the Lord *is now present*. Let no one in
> any way deceive you, for *that day is not present* unless the apostasy comes first,
> and the man of lawlessness is revealed, the son of destruction.

Another vital issue to settle in 2:3b relates to the adverb *prōton* ("first"). In
the preferred translation of 2:3b (i.e., "The day of the Lord is not present unless
the apostasy comes first and the man of lawlessness is revealed"), two meanings
are possible. It can mean that both the coming of the apostasy and the revelation of the man of lawlessness precede the day of the Lord. Or it can mean that
the coming of the apostasy precedes only the revelation of the man of lawlessness and not the day of the Lord.[34]

Typically, prewrath rapturists and posttribulational rapturists opt for the
former possibility, i.e., that the apostasy and the revelation of the man of lawlessness precede the day of the Lord. They base this on the mistranslation of an
implied *enestēken* in various English versions of 2:3b. Robert Gundry typifies
this position and has entitled one of his recent books *First the Antichrist: Why
Christ Won't Come before the Antichrist Does*. He writes, "Paul says not only that
'the Day of the Lord' won't arrive unless that evil figure 'is revealed' but also that
'the rebellion' which he will lead against all divinity except his own (claimed
falsely, of course) 'comes first' (2 Thess. 2:1–4)."[35] Erickson joins Gundry in using
this support for his posttribulational stance when he writes, "Paul also stated
about A.D. 50 that the day of the Lord could not come (II Thess. 2:2) until the
Antichrist and a major apostasy had come (v. 3)."[36] That view is oblivious to the
lexical and grammatical requirements of the Greek text, however, and a brief
survey of syntactical features will show its inadequacy.

A close grammatical parallel to 2 Thessalonians 2:3b occurs in John 7:51,
which uses (1) a present tense verb in a main clause; (2) an "unless" clause (Gr.,
ean mē) with a compound subject (two subjects with an "and"); and (3) the
word "first" (Gr. *prōton)* in the first subject of the compound "unless" clause.[37]
John 7:51 reads: "Our Law does not judge a man unless it first hears from him
and knows what he is doing, does it?" The judicial process (present indicative of
krinei ["judge"]) is not carried out without two parts: hearing from the defendant first and gaining a knowledge of what he is doing. Clearly in this instance,
hearing from the defendant does not precede the judicial process; it is part of it.

But it does precede a knowledge of what the man does. The word "first" (*prōton*) indicates that the first half of the compound "unless" clause is prior to the last half. In the judicial process 1) judges must first hear what a man has to say, and 2) then they can know what he is doing.

So in 2 Thessalonians 2:3, the day of the Lord is not already underway unless two things happen: first, the apostasy must come, and then the man of lawlessness must be revealed. These are two major elements that take place within the day of the Lord, not before it arrives. If the falling leaves are signs within the fall season, they are not signs that precede the fall season.

Another construction that has the same grammatical pattern is Mark 3:27. "No one can enter the strong man's house and plunder his property unless he first [Gr. *prōton*] binds the strong man and then [Gr. *tote*] he will plunder his house." The word "first" in this sentence does not refer to what precedes the "unless" clause, as if it meant that one must first bind a strong man before he can enter his house. Instead, the word "first" shows the priority of what follows: 1) a person enters the strong man's house; 2) he must *first* bind the strong man; 3) and *then* the strong man's house is plundered.[38] The word "first" applies to what follows, as is evident in the word "then" (*tote*) in the final clause of the verse.

Application of these grammatical parallels to 2 Thessalonians 2:3 results in the following: "The day of the Lord is not present unless first in sequence within that day the apostasy comes, and following the apostasy's beginning, the revealing of the man of lawlessness occurs." Rather than the two events preceding the day of the Lord as has often been suggested, these are happenings that comprise conspicuous stages of that day after it has begun. By observing the nonoccurrence of these, the Thessalonian readers could rest assured that the day whose leading events will be so characterized was not yet present.[39]

Assigning this meaning to 2 Thessalonians 2:3 frees Paul from the accusation of contradicting himself. In 1 Thessalonians 5:2 he wrote that the day of the Lord will come as a thief. If that day has precursors, as 2 Thessalonians 2:3 is often alleged to teach, it could hardly come as a thief. Thieves come without advance notice. Neither does the day of the Lord have any prior signals before it arrives.[40] Paul does not contradict that meaning in 2 Thessalonians 2:3. He still clings to the imminence of the wrathful phase of the day of the Lord.

Resulting from all these phenomena, the force of 2:3 is, "The day of the Lord is not present unless first, in sequence within it, the apostasy comes and following the apostasy's beginning comes the revelation of the man of lawlessness."

CONCLUSION

As is clear from the evidence offered above, a dual imminence exists in the teachings of Jesus, Paul, and other New Testament writers. Two prophetic events yet future will take place without any preceding signs or forewarnings of their occurrence: the rapture of the church and the beginning of the day of the Lord. The day of the Lord cannot begin before the rapture. Since both events are imminent, they must coincide with each other, i.e., occur at basically the same moment. That is why Paul can speak about both events as coming like a thief in the night or related expressions (cf. 1 Thess. 1:10; 4:15, 17).[41] Pretribulationism is the only eschatological system that can explain the fact that in the New Testament both the coming rapture and the coming day of the Lord are imminent events on the prophetic calendar.

NOTES

1. The First Epistle of Clement 23.

2. Ignatius, Ephesians 11, shorter version.

3. Irenaeus, *Against Heresies* 5.29.1.

4. Robert L. Thomas, "The 'Comings' of Christ in Revelation 2–3," *The Master's Seminary Journal* 7 (fall 1996):153–81.

5. Marshall notes the recurrence of the picture of the master standing outside the door and knocking in Revelation 3:20, and the recurrence of the metaphor of the thief in 1 Thessalonians 5:2, 4; 2 Peter 3:10; Revelation 3:3; 16:15 in I. Howard Marshall, *The Gospel of Luke: A Commentary on the Greek Text*, NIGTC (Grand Rapids: Eerdmans, 1978), 536, 538. With regard to the thief metaphor, see also Darrell L. Bock, *Luke 9:51–24:53*, BECNT, ed. Moisés Silva (Grand Rapids: Baker, 1996), 1171; and Robert H. Stein, *Luke*, vol. 24, New American Commentary (Nashville: Broadman, 1992), 360.

6. Davies and Allison correctly see "all these things" in verses 33 and 34 as embracing "all the signs and events leading up to the parousia" in W. D. Davies and Dale C. Allison Jr., *A Critical and Exegetical Commentary on the Gospel according to Saint Matthew*, 3 vols., ICC (Edinburgh: T & T Clark, 1997), 366; cf. also 367. Donald A. Hagner agrees that the expression covers "everything spoken of in vv. 4–28," in Hagner, *Matthew 14–28*, WBC, ed. David A. Hubbard and Glenn W. Barker (Dallas: Word, 1995), 715).

7. Davies and Allison take 24:36 as the heading for the section on "Eschatological vigilance" (24:36–25:30) rather than linking it with material that has gone before in the Discourse, and see the entire section as teaching that "one must be ever prepared for what may come at any time" (*Matthew*, 374, cf. also 374 n. 1).

8. Hagner correctly understands "that day and hour" to mean that setting a time for the *parousia* is "beyond human determination altogether, and not just partially, e.g., so that, say, the month or year *could be known*" (*Matthew 14–28*, 716). Blomberg agrees (Craig L. Blomberg, *Matthew*, New American Commentary, ed. David S. Dockery [Nashville: Broadman, 1992], 365).

9. Davies and Allison illustrate the unity of the section begun at verse 36 by citing the repetition of key phrases (e.g., "you do not know" [24:42], "you do not expect" [24:44], "he does not know" [24:50], "you know neither the day nor the hour" [25:13]) and key words (e.g., "know," "day[s]," "hour," "come[s]," "Son of man," "watch") that are repeated throughout (ibid., 377).

10. Davies and Allison understand "that day" in 24:36 to refer to the Old Testament day of the Lord, spoken of in the NT as the *parousia* and, because of a difference in perspective, explain the timing uncertainty of verse 36 not as contradicting the certainty of verse 34 but as interpreting it (ibid., 378; cf. also Blomberg, *Matthew*, 365). They understand "this generation" of verse 34 to refer to Jesus' contemporaries rather than seeing it as a qualitative expression, the view I prefer; cf. Robert L. Thomas, "The Place of Imminence in Two Recent Eschatological Systems," in *Looking into the Future: Evangelical Studies in Eschatology*, ed. David W. Baker (Grand Rapids: Baker, 2001), 201–4. For further delineation of the qualitative view, see Robert H. Gundry, *Matthew: A Commentary on His Handbook for a Mixed Church under Persecution*, 2nd ed. (Grand Rapids: Eerdmans, 1994), 491.

11. See Thomas, "The 'Comings' of Christ," 153–81, for a fuller discussion of dual imminence in that portion of John's writings.

12. D. Edmond Hiebert, *1 & 2 Thessalonians*, rev. ed. (Chicago: Moody, 1992), 227.

13. Ibid.

14. Robert L. Thomas, "1 Thessalonians," in *The Expositor's Bible Commentary*, ed. Frank E. Gaebelein, vol. 11 (Grand Rapids: Zondervan, 1978), 280.

15. Hiebert, *1 & 2 Thessalonians*, 210.

16. J. B. Lightfoot, *Notes on the Epistles of St. Paul* (repr. of 1895 ed.; Grand Rapids: Zondervan, 1957), 67.

17. Thomas, "1 Thessalonians," 11: 278.

18. Gordon D. Fee, *The First Epistle to the Corinthians*, NICNT, ed. Gordon D. Fee (Grand Rapids: Eerdmans, 1987), 800.

19. Robert H. Gundry, *The Church and the Tribulation* (Grand Rapids: Zondervan, 1973), 29.

20. D. A. Carson, "Matthew," *The Expositor's Bible Commentary*, ed. Frank E. Gaebelein (Grand Rapids: Zondervan, 1984), 490.

21. Ibid. Carson's reference to "one second or less" vividly recalls 1 Corinthians 15:52 where Paul prophesies that Christ's coming will be "in a moment [or flash], in the twinkling of an eye."

22. Millard J. Erickson, *A Basic Guide to Eschatology* (Grand Rapids: Baker, 1998), 181.

23. Ben Witherington III, "Transcending Imminence: The Gordian Knot of Pauline Eschatology," *Eschatology in the Bible & Theology* (Downers Grove, IL: InterVarsity, 1997), 174.

24. J. Christiaan Beker, *Paul's Apocalyptic Gospel* (Philadelphia: Fortress, 1982), 49.

25. Ernest Best, *A Commentary on the First and Second Epistles to the Thessalonians* (New York: Harper and Row, 1972), 83.

26. James Everett Frame, *The Epistles of St. Paul to the Thessalonians*, ICC (Edinburgh: T. & T. Clark, 1912), 89.

27. K. W. Clark, "Realized Eschatology," *JBL* 59 (September 1949): 379.

28. Ibid.

29. Ibid., 380.

30. See Best, *First and Second Epistles to the Thessalonians*, 120–21.

31. Willi Marxen, *Introduction to the New Testament*, trans. G. Buswell (Philadelphia: Fortress, 1968), 42; Reginald H. Fuller, *A Critical Introduction to the New Testament* (London: Gerald Duckworth, 1966), 57; Normal Perrin, *The New Testament, An Introduction* (New York: Harcourt Brace Jovanovich, 1974), 120.

32. F. F. Bruce, "1 & 2 Thessalonians," *Word Biblical Commentary*, ed. David A. Hubbard and Glenn W. Barker, vol. 45 (Dallas: Word, 1982), 165; D. Michael Martin, *1, 2 Thessalonians*, *The New American Commentary*, E. Ray Clendenen, vol. 33 (Nashville: Broadman & Holman, 1995), 227–28.

33. Peter Cotterell and Max Turner, *Linguistics & Biblical Interpretation* (Downers Grove, IL: InterVarsity, 1989), 24.

34. Martin (*1, 2 Thessalonians*, 232) notes, "Its [i.e., the adverb *prōton*] placement in the sentence slightly favors the understanding that the apostasy comes 'first' and then the lawless one is revealed," and goes on to say the adverb could possibly indicate the arrival of apostasy and the revelation of the man of lawlessness before the day of the Lord.

35. Robert Gundry, *First the Antichrist* (Grand Rapids: Baker, 1997), 20.

36. Erickson, *Basic Guide to Eschatology*, 175.

37. For a more detailed explanation of the Greek grammar involved, see Robert L. Thomas, "2 Thessalonians," *Ephesians–Philemon*, Expositor's Bible Commentary, vol. 12, ed. Tremper Longman III and David E. Garland, rev. ed. (Grand Rapids: Zondervan, 2006), 467–68.

38. See also Craig A. Blaising, "The Day of the Lord and the Rapture" (part 3 of a four-part series), *BibSac* 169 (July–September 2012): 268–70. Regarding the Mark 3:27 passage, Blaising writes, "In other words, in this example binding the strong man is the first action entailed in entering and plundering the house. For it is likely in this example that the strong man is in the house and thus would first have to be bound" (269).

39. For more details about the context in 2 Thessalonians 2:1–4, such as false reports about the day of the Lord, the time significance of *enestēken*, an implied apodosis of a "present general condition," the role of the adverb *prōton*, see my discussion of the passage in Thomas, "2 Thessalonians," *Ephesians–Philemon*, 461–69.

40. To this effect J. Christiaan Beker writes, "Paul emphasizes the unexpected, the suddenness and surprising character of the final theophany (1 Thess 5:2–10)," in Beker, *Paul's Apocalyptic Gospel*, 48.

41. Thomas, "1 Thessalonians," 2. "Ephesians–Philemon." 12:421

2

Jesus and the Rapture: Matthew 24

BY JOHN F. HART

For the coming of the Son of Man will be just like the days of Noah. For as in those days before the flood they were eating and drinking, marrying and giving in marriage, until the day that Noah entered the ark, and they did not understand until the flood came and took them all away; so will the coming of the Son of Man be. Then there will be two men in the field; one will be taken and one will be left. Two women will be grinding at the mill; one will be taken and one will be left.

MATTHEW 24:37–41

Next to the Sermon on the Mount (Matt. 5–7), the Olivet Discourse in Matthew 24–25 is the second longest uninterrupted message of Jesus in the New Testament. The Discourse, as found in Matthew, is also the second longest prophetic passage in the New Testament next to the book of Revelation. If one adds the fact that the Discourse has extended parallels in Mark 13; Luke 17; and Luke 21, its importance for interpreting prophecy becomes self-evident.

All perspectives of the rapture—pretribulation, midtribulation, prewrath, or posttribulation rapture—have paid close attention to the Discourse in Matthew, especially the nonparabolic material in Matthew 24:1–45. The reason for this is that the special Greek term for the future "coming" of Christ, *parousia*, is found in the Gospels four times—all in Matthew 24 (vv. 3, 27, 37, 39). *Parousia* means "coming, arrival" but also carries the meaning of the "presence" of a person after his or her arrival. The word is used broadly by Bible interpreters as a synonym of Jesus' second coming.

Some opponents of premillennialism understand Matthew 24 as prophesying exclusively the AD 70 destruction of Jerusalem.[1] On the other hand, premillennialism often considers the prophecies of the AD 70 event to prefigure or foreshadow the future coming of Jesus. Luke 21, a parallel passage to Matthew 24, prophesies the second coming of Christ but also predicts the destruction of Jerusalem.[2] But Mathew's presentation of the Discourse is focused more on the future coming of Jesus than on the destruction of Jerusalem in AD 70. Distinguishing between these two prophetic events is sometimes challenging. One can see why Moo concludes, "Most scholars have claimed that the Olivet Discourse is the most difficult portion of the Gospels to interpret."[3]

Posttribulationists argue that the rapture of the church is described in Matthew 24:36–44 (e.g., "one will be taken [i.e., raptured] and one will be left," v. 40). For them, this rapture is the same event as the return of Christ after the tribulation described in verses 29–31: "But immediately after the tribulation of those days . . . . they will see the Son of Man coming" (vv. 29–30). The one who is "taken" in rapture (v. 40) is taken "after the tribulation of those days" (verse 29).[4]

Most pretribulational interpreters have opposed seeing a rapture of any form in Matthew 24.[5] They have insisted that verses 29–31 and verses 36–44 concern the same coming of Christ, and that *neither* passage in Matthew 24 refers to a rapture.[6] The one "taken" in verse 40 refers to the unbeliever being taken to judgment at the second coming, and the one "left" is the believer who is left to go into the millennium. This is a plausible interpretation of the passage. Elsewhere in Matthew when discussing the end of the age (e.g., Matt. 13:30, 49), the unbeliever is judged first; then the believer is given his reward. (This pretribulational perspective is discussed in chapter 3, "The Rapture and the Day of the Lord.")

This chapter will present an alternative pretribulational view. It will suggest that Matthew 24:29–31 refers to the second coming—the return of Christ to the earth. But Matthew 24:36–44 speaks of a pretribulation rapture, and coincides with the sudden onset of the day of the Lord (the future tribulation of seven years). A key Greek transitional marker in verse 36, "Now concerning" (*peri de*), shifts the focus from the second advent to the events that begin the day of the Lord. By observing this transition in verse 36, it will be shown that some arguments used by posttribulationists actually suggest a pretribulation rapture instead. I believe that Jesus was the one who first taught and explained the pretribulation rapture, and that He taught this in both the Discourse and John 14:1–3. Paul, John, and Peter (and perhaps James) have all gained many of their insights into the pretribulation rapture and the day of the Lord from Jesus' teachings in the Discourse.

All pretribulationists must admit that at first glance the reference to one taken from a field or mill while another is "left behind" (24:40–41) sounds unusually similar to the pretribulation rapture described by Paul in 1 Thessalonians 4. Pretribulationists often use the term "left behind" to communicate what happens to the unbeliever at the rapture. Jesus' teaching that no one knows "that day and hour" (24:36) also seems most applicable to the any-moment, pretribulation return of Christ. But since the second coming of Christ in verses 29–31 is mentioned just five verses before Jesus speaks of the ones "taken" (vv. 36–44), pretribulationists have felt compelled by the context to reject a rapture of any kind in verses 36–44.

If the pretribulation rapture is being taught in verses 36–44, the fundamental challenge is to demonstrate contextually how verses 29–31 can refer to the posttribulational second coming of Christ while verses 36–44 can depict the pretribulational rapture of the church seven years earlier. This chapter presents nine reasons for concluding that 24:36–44 speaks of the pretribulation rapture. But prior to that discussion, a brief overview of the Discourse will be considered.

THE STRUCTURE OF THE OLIVET DISCOURSE IN MATTHEW 24

The Occasion

As four of Jesus' disciples (Mark 13:3) were commenting on the beauty of the Jewish temple, Jesus shocked them by predicting its total destruction (Matt. 24:1–3a; Mark 13:2; Luke 21:6). In response, Jesus' disciples raised two questions (v. 3b).[7] Both questions are answered by Jesus,[8] but neither question in the Matthean account concerns the AD 70 destruction of Jerusalem.[9] The two questions are:

1. When will "these things" take place?[10]
2. What will be "the sign of Your coming [Gk. *parousia*], and of the end of the age?"[11]

According to Matthew, Jesus answers these two questions in reverse order. This technique is called a chiasm. A chiasm is a literary structure in which two or more words or concepts are repeated in reverse order.

Chiastic structures in Matthew are quite common.[12] The chiasm in Matthew 24:3–44 is as follows:

> A¹ Question: "When will these things happen?" (v. 3a)
>> B¹ Question: "What will be the sign [Gk. *to sēmeion*] of Your coming and of the end of the age?" (v. 3b)
>> B² Answer: "then the sign [Gk. *to sēmeion*, v. 30] of the Son of Man will appear . . . and they will see the Son of Man coming" (vv. 4–35)
> A² Answer: "But of that day and hour no one knows" (vv. 36–44)

The second question of the disciples is answered first (in B²). This is signaled by the words "the sign" (in the singular with the Greek article *to*), used only at verse 3 and verse 30, which ties these sections together. The first question is answered last at verses 36–44. Beginning in 24:45, the remainder of the Discourse contains four parables (24:45–51; 25:1–13, 14–30, 31–46), naturally dividing the Discourse between verse 44 and verse 45.

Matthew 24:4–31 and Daniel's Seventieth Week

From the inception of the Discourse at 24:4, Matthew depicts the Seventieth Week (or seventieth "seven") described in Daniel 9:24–27. Daniel's Seventieth Week is a future seven-year period often called the tribulation. In the disciples' minds and in the Danielic prophecy, the destruction of the temple and the climax of human history would be fulfilled at the same time. Daniel was the only Old Testament prophet specifically mentioned by name in the entire Olivet Discourse. Jesus instructed the disciples, "when you see the abomination of desolation which was spoken of through Daniel the prophet, standing in the holy place (let the reader understand) . . ." (v. 15). The words "let the reader understand" (v. 15) speak of the reader of Daniel, not the reader of Matthew. Since both Mark (13:14) and Matthew record this statement about the reader gaining understanding, it is more likely a part of the words of Jesus regarding the reading of Daniel than a remark of both Matthew and Mark telling their readers to read their respective Gospels.[13]

It is generally agreed that in the same verse (v. 15) the words "the abomination of desolation" are referencing Daniel 9:27. Jesus is signaling the apostles that Daniel 9:27 is the chronological key to identifying the prophetic events He is describing. Since we are instructed by Jesus to read Daniel, we should anticipate that much more of Jesus' Olivet Discourse has Daniel's Seventieth Week as its background.[14] In addition, the words "let the reader understand" (v. 15) do not concern merely the knowledge of the future but wisdom as well. The book of Daniel is filled with descriptions of Daniel's wisdom and understanding (cf. Dan. 1:4; 2:21; 5:11, 14; 10:12, 14). Jesus was appealing to His disciples to gain prophetic wisdom and understanding from Daniel so as to accurately interpret His teachings in the Discourse. Accurate understanding of prophecy leads to wisdom in life. Therefore, one must interpret the Discourse in light of the understanding and wisdom of Daniel's prophecies.

In Matthew 24:4–14, the Lord surveys the *entire* seven-year tribulation. In verse 8, Jesus uses the term "labor pains" (Gk. *ōdin*), a term frequently used for the future day of the Lord.[15] This supports the interpretation that beginning at 24:4 Daniel's Seventieth Week is the central concern of Jesus' message. In 1 Thessalonians 5 Paul also used the same Greek word, "labor pains" (*ōdin*), to describe the future day of the Lord. Many pretribulationists see the first seal judgment of Revelation paralleling the false Christs of Matthew 24:5. All pretribulationists insist that the second, third, and fourth seal judgments of Revelation (Rev. 6:3–8) clearly depict the first half of the tribulation and parallel the judgments in Matthew 24:5–8.

The clause "Then [Gk. *tote*] they will deliver you to tribulation" (v. 9) is best understood as a transition to the second half of the seven-year tribulation. Verses 9–14 reach the climax of the tribulation as indicated by the phrase "and then the end will come" (v. 14).

By a literary device called "recapitulation" (meaning a repetition with added detail), 24:15 returns to the midpoint of the Seventieth Week of Daniel 9. This technique is like a flashback in time to pick up other details that the author wanted to add. The story of creation does this. Genesis 1:1–2:3 covers the entire creation story. But at Genesis 2:4, the narrative flashes back, returning to the creation of Adam and Eve in order to fill in greater details (e.g., how sin entered the world).

Another example is Luke 17. Verse 24 brings the prophecy to the second coming of Christ: "For just like the lightning, when it flashes out of one part of the sky, shines to the other part of the sky, so will the Son of Man be in His day." But the very next verse (v. 25) returns to the climax of the first coming of Christ. "But *first* He [Christ] must suffer many things and be rejected by this genera- tion" (italics added).

So from Matthew 24:15–28 Jesus gives us a flashback, describing the second half of the tribulation period. But this time He adds other important details. Then at verse 29, Jesus uses the phrase "*immediately after* the tribulation" (ital- ics added). This fixes a very specific time reference for the second coming of Christ described in verses 29–31. With such wording, Jesus declares the second coming of Christ to be highly predictable.

The relationship of Matthew 24:4–31 to the Seventieth Week of Daniel 9 (the tribulation period) is diagrammed in chart 1:

CHART 1

Daniel's Seventieth Week and Matthew 24:4–31

3 ½ YEARS	3 ½ YEARS	
• "the beginning of birth pangs" (v. 8)	• "Then they will deliver you to tribulation" (v. 9)	
• "that is not yet the end" (v. 6)	• "and then the end will come" (v. 14)	
	• "when you see the Abomination of Desolation" (v. 15) • "there will be a great tribulation"(v. 21)	"But immediately after the tribulation of those days" (v. 29)

Verses 32–35 explain how the events of the tribulation are like the springtime budding of the fig tree. As the budding of the fig tree in the spring signals the nearness of summer, so the events that transpire during the Seventieth Week of Daniel give clear evidence of the nearness of the Lord's second coming. In other words, once the tribulation signs begin, the second coming is foreseeable.

PROOFS OF THE PRETRIBULATIONAL
RAPTURE IN MATTHEW 24:36–44

Reason 1: Signs (vv. 4–31) versus No Signs (v. 36)

One of the interpretive challenges of prophecy is that some predictions state clearly that Jesus may come without any preceding visible signs that signal His future return. But other passages mention numerous, well-defined signs that precede and lead up to the precise moment of Jesus' return. Outside of Matthew 24, pretribulationists have insisted that these two types of passages cannot logically refer to the same moment in time. The rapture is an imminent event, i.e., an event that can happen at any time and without signs that precede it. Such an event must be separate from the final return of Jesus to the earth, which is marked out by numerous sequential, observable events. As Thomas correctly reasons, "If signs must occur before His coming, His coming is not imminent."[16]

These two types of prophecies are found in Matthew 24. But pretribulationists have traditionally avoided distinguishing these two types of prophecies in their interpretation of the Discourse. I believe that there is a better option for those who hold to a pretribulation rapture.

Matthew 24:4–35 "contains repeated statements regarding 'warnings' and 'signs.' The whole section is about 'observing things,'" notes Gibbs.[17] In verses 32–35, Jesus commands the disciples to "know" from these signs the nearness of His return. This is possible only if His second coming is predictable.

"when its branch . . . puts forth its leaves, *you know*" (v. 32)
"When you see . . . *you know* that he is near" (v. 33 ESV)

Some signs in 24:3–29 may be dismissed by interpreters as too general and lacking clear value for determining the nearness of the end of the age. Examples include the coming of false Christs (v. 5), wars, famine, and earthquakes (vv. 6–7). Other signs are more precise and clearly identifiable:

1. The gospel of the kingdom must be preached in the whole world, "and then the end will come" (24:14).[18]
2. "When you see the abomination of desolation which was spoken of through Daniel the prophet, standing in the holy place" (24:15).

3. "There will be a great tribulation, such as has not occurred since the be-ginning of the world until now, nor ever will" (24:21).

4. "Unless those days were limited, no one would survive" (24:22 HCSB).[19]

These observable signs stand in obvious contrast to the perspective of 24:36–44. The theme of "not knowing" recurs throughout verses 36–44 (and in 25:13) and is set in full contrast with the fact that the disciples can "know that he is near" (v. 33 ESV).[20] Note these examples:

"But of that day and hour no one knows" (v. 36)
"they did not understand" (v. 39)
"you do not know" (v. 42)
"if the head of the house had known" (v. 43)
"for the Son of Man is coming at an hour when you do not think" (v. 44)

This evidence provides clear support for viewing the rapture in verses 36–44. The latter verses describe the imminent, unpredictable coming of the day of the Lord and the accompanying pretribulational rapture. Therefore, at verse 36, the Lord answers the first question of the disciples (v. 3) about *when* the end-time events will begin. Here Jesus reveals that the inception of the day of the Lord itself and the accompanying pretribulational rapture *cannot be known*.

To explain the seeming contradiction between the signs of verses 4–35 and the imminence portrayed in verses 36–44, posttribulationists, prewrath rap-turists, and even many pretribulationists have reverted to a theory described as "general predictability with specific unpredictability," i.e., the time may be known generally but not precisely.[21] This interpretation is impractical in that it does not really remove the contradiction between knowing and not knowing the time of the Lord's return. Many other commentators criticize such an idea as insufficient to explain the text.[22]

Premillennialists who are posttribulational such as D. A. Carson and Craig Blomberg escape the impasse of verse 36 by suggesting that the events of Mat-thew 24:4–28 span the interadvent age (church age) and have now been suffi-ciently fulfilled. Therefore, the time of Christ's return is incalculable since there are no specific unfulfilled prophecies that precede the posttribulational coming of Jesus.[23]

First, it may be seriously questioned whether the prophecies of Matthew

24:4–28 speak of the church age or have been sufficiently fulfilled. Second, if verses 4–28 describe the church age and not Daniel's Seventieth Week, the words "immediately after" that begin verse 29 ("immediately after the tribulation of those days") become meaningless and unnecessary. Jesus could have simply said, "after the tribulation of those days," avoiding the word "immediately."[24]

But the term "immediately after" signals a precise time, not an event that "no one knows, *not even the angels of heaven*, nor the Son, but the Father alone" (v. 36, italics added). Are none of the angels described in Revelation able to figure out with reasonable precision the time of the Lord's return described in Revelation 19? They probably understand the prophecies described in the book better than we do. Yet in Matthew 24:36, only the Father knows of the time in which Jesus returns and when "that day and hour" will come.

Moo concludes, "There is no basis for any transition from the posttribulational aspect of the Parousia in Matthew 24:31–35 (or –36) to its pretribulational aspect in verses 36ff. Therefore, all interpreters . . . face the difficulty of explaining how an advent heralded by specific signs can yet be one of which it is said, 'no one knows the day and hour.'"[25]

If, on the other hand, it can be shown that a well-defined transition does exist at verse 36, then Jesus may be moving from a posttribulational phase of His coming to a pretribulational phase (i.e., He is carrying the hearer/reader back to a time preceding His visible coming to earth).

No objections can be sustained against a pretribulation rapture on the grounds that the "coming" of Jesus is a single, simplified event. In *all* premillennial schemes, the parousia includes a rapture that takes believers to meet Christ in the clouds, and afterward Christ returns with the saints to the earth. These two stages are separated by an interval of time. The interval is simply confined to a very small portion of the tribulation period in the posttribulational perspective.[26] Prewrath and midtribulational theories have a more extended interval than posttribulationism.[27] Pretribulationism separates the rapture and return of Christ by seven years.

In common usage, the first "coming" of Christ can refer to the thirty-some years of Christ's life, not just His birth. So the thought of "coming" in the Greek word *parousia* carries different shades of meaning involving a span of time—an arrival, and one's presence after arrival. The interpretive issue is the length of this span of time. For many pretribulationists, the parousia of Christ involves His arrival in rapture, His subsequent hidden presence in the world to carry out the judgments of Revelation 4–18, and His final manifestation ("the sign of the Son of Man will appear in the sky," Matt. 24:30) after the great tribulation.[28]

Reason 2: The Greek Phrase "Now Concerning" at Verse 36

"Now concerning that day and hour no one knows—neither the angels in heaven, nor the Son—except the Father only" (v. 36 HCSB). When Jesus said that no one knows that day and hour except the Father alone, Matthew recorded the introduction of the statement with the Greek words *peri de*, "now concerning."[29] When *peri de* stands at the very beginning of a sentence as it does here, it marks a new section of thought that reaches back to previous material, often to resume an unanswered or unspoken question.[30]

In Paul's prophecy of the rapture (1 Thess. 4:13–18) and the coming day of the Lord (1 Thess. 5:1–11), he made a transition between these two related prophetic subjects by using the *peri de* construction at 5:1.[31] Although *peri de* introduces a slightly new subject at 1 Thessalonians 5:1, it carries on the discussion of future things brought out in 4:13–18. This identical perspective is true with the *peri de* of Matthew 24:36.[32]

Blaising, Fruchtenbaum, and Thomas are pretribulationists who have noted this transition with *peri de* at Matthew 24:36.[33] Thomas writes,

> The *de* that begins v. 36 must be transitional because the thirty-sixth verse changes the discussion of signs preceding the coming to emphasize that no signs will precede the *parousia*. *Peri de* is a frequent device for introducing a change from one phase of a subject to another phase of the same subject or from one subject to another. . . .[34]

In other words, because of this major transitional marker, the "coming" mentioned in 24:37 may reference a different phase of the Lord's return (i.e., the pretribulation rapture) than the final return-to-earth phase described in 24:29–31.

In the prophecies of 1 Thessalonians 4–5, Paul was influenced to use *peri de* as a transition marker in 5:1 by the Lord's similar use of the phrase in the Olivet Discourse.[35] In Matthew 24, Jesus transitions from what the disciples can know (24:4–35) to what they cannot know (24:36–44) about the day of the Lord/pretribulation rapture. In 1 Thessalonians 4–5, Paul does the reverse. He transitions with *peri de* from what the Thessalonians do not know to what they do know about the pretribulational rapture/day of the Lord. How *peri de* functions in parallel between Matthew 24:36 and 1 Thessalonians 5:1 is depicted in chart 2. Both show an important transition with *peri de.*

Peri de as a Transition in 1 Thessalonians 5 and Matthew 24

1 THESSALONIANS 4–5	MATTHEW 24
Lack of Knowledge: *What the Thessalonians Do Not Know* (1 Thess. 4:13-18) "But we do not want you to be uninformed, brethren, about those who are asleep" (4:13) Knowledge [*peri de*]: *What the Thessalonians Know* (1 Thess. 5:1-10) "Now concerning [*peri de*] the times and the seasons, brothers, you have no need to have anything written to you" (5:1 ESV)	Knowledge: *What the Disciples Can Know* (Matt. 24:4-31) "but that is not yet the end" (v. 6) "then the end will come" (v. 14) "immediately after the tribulation of those days" (v. 29) "you know that summer is near" (v. 32) "you know that he is near, at the very gates" (v. 33 ESV) Lack of Knowledge [*peri de*]: *What the Disciples Cannot Know* (24:36-44) "But [*peri de*] of that day and hour no one knows" (v. 36) "they knew nothing until the flood came" (v. 39 NET) "if the head of the house had known" (v. 43) "the master . . . will come . . . at an hour which he does not know" (v. 50)

It is difficult to deny that a strong transition exists at verse 36 using *peri de.* The transition sets apart the content of verses 36–44 from the content of the preceding verses, and carries the reader back to the first of the two questions of the disciples, "When will these things take place?"

Reason 3: "That Day and Hour"

The *peri de* ("now concerning") of verse 36 is followed by the phrase "that day and hour." Jesus declared that no one could know about "that day and hour." One should note that up to this point in the Discourse, only the phrase "those days" (plural) has been used (24:19, 22, 29). At verse 36, Jesus changes to "that day" (singular). This helps support the idea that verse 36 is transitional.

Many commentators correctly identify "that day" as the events of the day of the Lord often referred to in the Old Testament prophets (Ezek. 30:3, 9; Joel 3:14, 18; Zeph. 1:7–15). The demonstrative pronoun ("*that* day") confirms the

Old Testament background.[36] "That day" as it relates to the Old Testament day of the Lord portrays an imminent event.[37] Paul uses "day" (Gk. *hēmera*) for the imminent day of the Lord in 1 Thessalonians 5:4. "But you, brethren, are not in darkness, that the day [*hēmera*] would overtake you like a thief." Paul's use of "day" here is likely borrowed from the Lord's use in Matthew 24:36.[38]

If this phrase "that day and hour" refers to the surprise arrival of the day of the Lord as Paul defined it in 1 Thessalonians 5, then the coming of "that day and hour" takes place at the very same time as the pretribulational rapture. This is because both the rapture and the day of the Lord are described as pretribulational and imminent. Both are also illustrated by the thief in the night imagery—an imminent event (Matt. 24:43 and Luke 12:39–40 with 1 Thess. 5:2 and 2 Pet. 3:10).[39]

A similar significance can be attributed to the word "hour" (Gk. *hōra*). In Revelation 3:10, where Jesus tells the Philadelphian church, "I also will keep you from the hour [*hōra*] of testing," "hour" has reference to the future tribulation period of seven years, and therefore to the day of the Lord.

All of these evidences confirm the case that the day of the Lord and the parousia of Jesus are in view in verse 36. Thomas concludes, "In other words, 24:36 speaks of a different arrival from the arrival signaled by 'all these things,' twice referred to in connection with the parable of the fig tree in 24:32–34. After 24:36 Jesus looks at the events of Daniel's seventieth week *as a whole and how the beginning of that week will catch everyone by surprise . . .*" (italics added).[40]

Reason 4: The "Days of Noah" Illustration (vv. 37–39)

In Matthew 24:37–39, Jesus illustrated and elaborated on verse 36. The coming of "that day and hour" will be like the "days of Noah" in which people "were eating and drinking, marrying and giving in marriage, until the day that Noah entered the ark." In a parallel passage, Luke adds a description of the days of Lot when people were also "buying and selling, planting and building" (17:27–28).

Matthew's and Luke's description seem too casual to take place during the second half of the tribulation. During the second half of the tribulation, no buying or selling will be done without the mark of the Beast (Rev. 13:17). The lifestyles depicted in the days of Noah and Lot are those that have existed in every generation since the earliest days of human history. This implies an emphasis on the normalcy and indifference that take place prior to the day of the Lord.[41]

The illustrations that follow verses 37–39 about two men working in the field and two women grinding at the mill (vv. 41–42) also argue for the focus on normalcy. Many commentators simply believe that the ordinary life patterns described in the Noah illustration can coexist with the colossal distresses that run their course prior to Christ's second coming.[42] But this seems unreasonable.

How can a "business-as-usual" attitude toward life exist at the precise time when the twenty-one tribulation judgments of Revelation are being poured out in all their intensity?[43] Instead, the most transparent meaning of the "days of Noah" illustration (vv. 37–39) is that, just as normal but unsuspecting lifestyles existed prior to the great judgment of the flood, so too normal but unsuspecting lifestyles will exist prior to the sudden onslaught of the day-of-the-Lord judgments and the rapture of the church.

In the Noah parallel, the people "knew nothing" (v. 39 NIV, NET) about what was soon to happen until the flood came and took them all away. If the flood judgment illustrates a judgment that takes place at the return of Christ "immediately after the tribulation of those days" (v. 29), can it be said that the world will understand *nothing* of the devastating judgments that have been inflicting them?

At the sixth seal judgment of Revelation, people know fully that the wrath of God has come. They cry out to the rocks, "Fall on us and hide us from the face of Him who sits on the throne, and from the wrath of the Lamb; for the great day of their wrath has come and who is able to stand?" (Rev. 6:16–17). The calamities that precede the second coming of Christ will be so severe that the human race will be close to extinction apart from the Lord's intervention (Matt. 24:22). Would Jesus use a description of casual lifestyles in Matthew 24:37–39 to communicate what the world would be like when "there will be a great tribulation, such as has not occurred since the beginning of the world until now, nor ever will" (Matt. 24:21)? This seems most unlikely. The flood of Noah's day corresponds to the time leading up to the sudden arrival of the day of the Lord, the Seventieth Week of Daniel and the pretribulation rapture.

Reason 5: Harmony of the Olivet Discourse and the Teachings of Paul

Posttribulationists and a few pretribulationists have rightly argued for the interconnection of Paul's teaching on the parousia and that of the Lord's teaching in the Discourse.[44] This interconnection is legitimate for two reasons. First, there is a striking resemblance between one taken from the field or from the mill in

Matthew 24:40–41 with Paul's teaching of the ones taken in rapture in 1 Thessalonians 4:15–18. Second, Christ's illustration about the destruction of the flood in Noah's day and Paul's concept of the surprise arrival of the day of the Lord as bringing destruction on unbelievers in 1 Thessalonians 5 are also parallel.

The similarities of thought are convincing evidence that the source of Paul's prophetic teaching was the Olivet Discourse.[45] First, Paul said, "For you know what commands we gave you *through the Lord Jesus*" (1 Thess. 4:2 NET, italics added). Next, in introducing the subject of the pretribulation rapture, Paul said, "For this we say to you *by the word of the Lord*" (1 Thess. 4:15, italics added). Then in 5:2, Paul states, "you yourselves know full well that the day of the Lord will come just like a thief in the night." The thief analogy can only come from Jesus' teachings, as will be established below. These statements all point to the fact that Paul was drawing on Jesus' teachings as found in the Discourse.[46]

If this is the case, Paul and Jesus must be dealing with the same prophetic events. For Paul, the sudden arrival of the day of the Lord will be preceded by a time of "peace and safety" (1 Thess. 5:1–3). Once the day of the Lord begins, unexpected destruction begins for the unbeliever. The believer will be delivered from that wrath by the rapture (1 Thess. 1:10; 5:9–10).[47]

Pretribulationists appropriately recognize that Paul's teaching of a casual and secure world that precedes the day of the Lord cannot easily be harmonized with John's portrait of the end of the tribulation when the world will gather its armies in war against the coming Christ (Rev. 16:13–16; 19:19). Paul's "peace and safety" is an indicator both of when the day of the Lord will come as well as when the church saints will be delivered from that day by rapture; i.e., both are imminent. Both must be immediately before or at the very inception of the tribulation. If the day of the Lord comes unexpectedly at a time of "peace and safety," then the rapture also comes at a time of "peace and safety."

This Pauline scenario—that the day of the Lord will come suddenly at a time of "peace and safety"—is quite comparable to the descriptions found in Matthew 24:39 ("they were eating and drinking, marrying and giving in marriage"). In the Lord's illustration, the days of Noah were primarily the days before (v. 38) the judgment of the flood when life continued as normal. During the tribulation, the very existence of all life will be in such jeopardy (Matt. 24:22) that the tranquility of life described in Matthew 24:37–39 could hardly take place. Therefore, the Noah illustration taught by Jesus admirably portrays the universal, surprise arrival of the day of the Lord and the rapture as taught by Paul.

Reason 6: Harmony of the Olivet Discourse and the Teachings of Peter

It also seems apparent that the Lord's words in the Discourse have given rise to the 1 and 2 Peter references to Noah. Peter was personally present when Jesus gave His prophecies on the Mount of Olives just days before His death (Mark 13:3). The exact phrase "days of Noah," found in Matthew 24:37 (par. Luke 17:26), also appears in 1 Peter 3:20. The passage reads:

> who [the spirits now in prison] once were disobedient, when the patience of God kept waiting in the days of Noah, during the construction of the ark, in which a few, that is, eight persons, were brought safely through the water. Corresponding [antitypos] to that, baptism now saves you. . . . (1 Pet. 3:20–21a)

In 3:21, the word *antitypos* ("corresponding to, antitype") is used to establish an unquestionable typological view of the flood. For Peter, the flood is a type or foreshadowing of something. The NIV supplies the word "water" in its translation of 3:21, "this water symbolizes baptism that now saves you." The NASB is more in keeping with the vagueness of the Greek, "Corresponding to that [Gk. *ho*], baptism now saves you." The interpretive question is: To what does the relative pronoun "that" (Gk. *ho*) refer? Many commentators are persuaded that "water" in the previous verse is the antecedent. This is grammatically possible.

However, the water did not save Noah and his family but was instead an instrument of divine judgment. The ark saved Noah. Hebrews 11:7 is clear about this: "By faith Noah . . . prepared an ark for the salvation of his household." The relative pronoun in 1 Peter 3:21 makes reference indirectly to the word "ark" in the previous verse, not to the word "water."[48] If the type is the ark[49] and not the water of the flood, then the antitype (*antitypos*) is not water baptism. In context, a strong case can be made that the antitype is better taken as Spirit baptism, which places believers into the invisible church, the body of Christ. In other words, for Peter, Noah's entrance into the ark is a type of the believer's entrance into the invisible church (being "in Christ") by means of Spirit baptism.[50]

Since the apostle Paul declared that the invisible church (i.e., all believers) is delivered by rapture before the tribulation (1 Thess. 5:9–10; cf. Rev. 3:10), and if in Peter's typology the ark represents the church (i.e., everyone who is joined to Christ by Spirit baptism), then the deliverance of Noah and his family in the ark typifies the pretribulational rapture of the church and its deliverance from the future day of the Lord.

Eschatology (i.e., future things) is a major theme in 2 Peter (cf. 1:16–21;

3:3–13). Peter states that he was fully aware of the teachings of Paul's letters (cf. 2 Pet. 3:15–16). Therefore, he understood Paul's teaching on the day of the Lord and the rapture. Immediately preceding the context of his remark about Paul's epistles, Peter himself says that "the day of the Lord will come like a thief" (2 Pet. 3:10). Peter had personally heard Jesus' Olivet Discourse. So undoubtedly, Peter is also drawing from Jesus' teachings in the Discourse as well as Paul's teaching in 1 Thessalonians 4–5.

In 2 Peter 3, the apostle mentions the flood (v. 6). False teachers will ridicule the promise of Christ's return (2 Pet. 3:3–4). Their mocking is based on the fact that life will proceed without any evidence of divine intervention (v. 4). This is similar to Jesus' teachings in the Discourse about the days of Noah (Matt. 24:37–39) and Paul's teaching that peace and safety will precede the sudden destruction of the day of the Lord (1 Thess. 5:3). But Peter informs us that the false teachers have purposefully neglected the flood of Noah's day (2 Pet. 3:5–6). The Greek implies that "they willfully ignore" the truth of the flood (cf. 2 Pet. 3:5 HCSB).

In 2 Peter 2, Peter links the flood to the future judgment of the day of the Lord (2 Pet. 2:4–9). Of interest is the phrase in 2 Peter 2:9 concerning God's rescue of the righteous "from tribulation" (*ek peirasmou*). This phrase suggests the rapture of Revelation 3:10 where believers are kept "from [out of] the hour of trial [tribulation]" (*ek tēs hōras tou peirasmou*). One commentator writes about 2 Peter 2:9 in its context:

> The word Peter uses in v 9 is *peirasmou*, the same word which occurs in Rev. 3:10 . . . . It is clear that "trial," *peirasmou*, does not mean everyday, routine trials. The trials described are the universal flood and the destruction of Sodom and Gomorrah. The flood was a judgment of God on the entire world. It was a physical judgment, not eternal judgment. This parallels the tribulation period and is described by the same term (*peirasmou*). . . . Neither Noah nor Lot went through the trial as did the ungodly. . . . This is not significantly different from the church being in the air with the Lord and possibly over the earth during the tribulation period.[51]

Noah was not in the flood. He did not experience a post-flood, mid-flood, or three-fourths flood rescue but a pre-flood rescue. Lot was not in the fire and sulfur, then rescued out. The deliverance of Noah and Lot can only illustrate the rapture of the church before the day of the Lord. If the day of the Lord is the entire seven years of the tribulation period, then the rescue of believers must be a pretribulational rescue.[52]

In Peter's thinking, then, the judgment of the flood is thoroughly aligned with the time leading up to the imminent arrival of the day of the Lord (the Seventieth Week of Daniel). If 2 Peter 2:9 and 1 Thessalonians 5:9 declare a deliverance from the day of the Lord by a pretribulational rapture for the church, and if Peter and Paul derived their teaching from the Lord in the Discourse, then in Matthew 24:38 Noah's deliverance from the universal judgment of the flood best pictures the church's deliverance by rapture before the great prophetic "flood," the day of the Lord.

Reason 7: The Ones Taken and Those Left Behind (vv. 40–41)

Most pretribulational interpreters understand the word "taken" ("one will be taken," vv. 40–41) to refer to people taken in judgment at the end of the tribulation, not people taken in rapture before the tribulation. They draw this conclusion from the preceding context that says, "the flood came and *took* them all away" (v. 39, italics added). While these interpreters recognize that the Greek word for "took" in verse 39 (*airō*) differs from the Greek word for "taken" in verses 40 and 41 (*paralambanō*), they insist that the "taking" in both cases is the same. The "taking" is for judgment. In their thinking, the only possible rapture in verses 40–41 would be a posttribulational rapture, and a posttribulational rapture must be rejected based on other clear passages of Scripture.[53]

Posttribulationists, on the other hand, have no problem finding a rapture in Matthew 24:40–41. For them, however, the rapture in verses 40–41 must be one and the same with the second coming of Christ in verses 29–31, i.e., a posttribulational rapture. But posttribulational chronology of the Discourse overlooks the transitional nature of the *peri de* ("now concerning") at verse 36. If the transition is allowed, a pretribulational rapture in those verses becomes theologically and exegetically reasonable. The events of verses 36–44 are separated logically and contextually from the events of verses 29–31.

As has been mentioned above, I believe that Paul's teaching on the rapture in 1 Thessalonians 4 originated with Jesus' teaching in the Discourse. Jesus, the greatest prophet of all, was the first to reveal the pretribulation rapture. Besides the brief discussion in John 14:1–3, Matthew 24:37–44 contains the most likely teachings of Jesus from which Paul could have derived his own doctrine about the pretribulational rapture.[54]

In light of the transition at verse 36, some of the exegetical reasons put forward by posttribulationists for seeing a rapture in verses 40–41 can now be turned in support of a pretribulational rapture. Gundry, a posttribulationist, states,

> Two different words appear for the action of taking, *airō* (v. 39) and *paralambanō* (vv. 40, 41). The same word could easily have been employed had an exact parallel between the two takings been intended. Instead we have the employment of another word which only two days later describes the rapture (John 14:3). . . . The apostles would naturally have associated the two expressions. Jesus probably so intended, else He would have drawn a distinction. . . . In light of this, the change from *airō* to *paralambanō* indicates a change in topic and connotation: the former term refers to judgment similar in unexpectedness to the Flood, the latter to reception of the saints at the rapture to be forever with their Lord (Cf. 1 Thess. 4:17; John 14:3).[55]

It is generally agreed that *paralambanō* carries the meaning "to take to or with [oneself]." The thought is always one of accompaniment, and almost always in a positive sense, i.e., for close fellowship. The word is overwhelmingly used in a positive sense.[56] Yet context should be the deciding factor.

Some see the context of Matthew 24:39–41 to be focused on judgment (a negative context). This is only partially correct. The parousia is also mentioned in the context (vv. 37, 39) and either the one taken or the one left could receive judgment. But the Greek word for "left," *aphiēmi* (vv. 40, 41), in Matthew takes on the meaning of "abandon" when its object is a person (Matt. 4:11, 22; 8:15; 13:36; 19:29; 22:22, 25; 26:56, etc.).[57]

If these uses can be allowed to set the pattern, *aphiēmi* could hardly be used of what the Father or the Son do with believers at the final return of Christ to the earth, i.e., to "leave" believers on earth to go into the millennium. Nolland remarks, "The potentially negative nuances of which 'left' (*aphiēmi*) is capable ('left out') make it more likely that being taken off to salvation is intended. . . ."[58] Other than Matthew 24:40–41, there are no other passages in the New Testament that use *aphiēmi* to express what the Lord will do to believers (Jew or Gentile).[59] Just two days after the Discourse, Jesus used *aphiēmi* of what He would *not* do to the disciples: "I will not leave [*aphiēmi*] you as orphans; I will come to you" (John 14:18).

If the one "taken" is taken away for judgment, it is peculiar that a word characterized by personal accompaniment is employed, while the one "left" to enter the kingdom is described with a word frequently used for the forsaken.[60]

If the transitional nature of verse 36 is allowed its full force, the one taken is not taken for salvation at the second coming of Christ. The simplest interpretation is to see "taken" (*paralambanō*) as a reference to the pretribulational rapture of church saints. Two days after Jesus taught His discourse on the Mount of Olives, He used *paralambanō* to depict the taking of believers in a pretribulational rapture (John 14:3).[61] Those abandoned in Matthew 24:40–41 are the unbelievers. The judgments of the day of the Lord come on them and they do not escape (1 Thess. 5:3).

Reason 8: The Thief Imagery

Matthew 24:42–44 contains a short parable concerning the thief (v. 43), framed by two similar exhortations to readiness or watchfulness (vv. 42, 44). Surprisingly, pretribulationists have not been consistent in interpreting the thief analogy in prophetic passages (Matt. 24:43; Luke 12:39; 1 Thess. 5:2, 4; 2 Pet. 3:10; Rev. 3:3; 16:15). Sometimes it is viewed as leading to Christ's second coming (Matt. 24:43; Rev. 16:15) and at other times as announcing the imminent day of the Lord and the pretribulational rapture (2 Pet. 3:10; 1 Thess. 5:2, 4).

Both pretribulationists and posttribulationists have applied the thief passage in Matthew to the second advent.[62] The thief figure is found in several other prophetic passages. The most important are 1 Thessalonians 5:2–4 and 2 Peter 3:10. If the source of Paul's teaching about the day of the Lord and the pretribulational rapture is Jesus' prophetic teachings in the Olivet Discourse, a case for a consistent interpretation of the thief illustration between Matthew 24:42–44 and 1 Thessalonians 5:1–11 is warranted. Both must refer to the same event.

Thomas remarks, "That both [the rapture and the day of the Lord] are any-moment possibilities is why Paul can talk about these two in successive paragraphs [i.e., in 1 Thess. 4 and 5]. This is how the Lord's personal coming as well as the 'day's' coming can be compared to a thief (2 Pet. 3:4, 10; Rev. 3:3, 11; 16:15)."[63]

Concerning the thief analogy in 1 Thessalonians 5, pretribulationist Renald Showers notes, "A thief depends upon the element of surprise for success. He does not give his intended victims a forewarning of his coming. Paul's point— the unsaved will be given no forewarning of the coming of the broad Day of the Lord—rules out any of the seals of Revelation as being forewarnings of the beginning of the broad Day [of the Lord, i.e., Daniel's Seventieth Week]."[64]

The metaphor of the thief does not appear in any prophetic passage of the

Old Testament or of any extrabiblical Jewish literature.[65] This is convincing evidence that Paul in 1 Thessalonians 5:2, 4 is borrowing from Jesus' thief imagery in the Olivet Discourse. He could not have gotten it from anywhere else. Paul, Peter, and John have all based their illustration of the thief on the parable of Jesus in the Discourse.[66]

Since the thief analogy in 1 Thessalonians 5 addresses the imminent (pretribulational) coming of the day of the Lord, the thief analogy in Matthew 24:43 must address the same prophecy. Also, Revelation 3:3 and 16:15 suggest that Christ Himself comes as a thief, while 1 Thessalonians 5:4 makes it clear the day of the Lord comes as a thief. Therefore, the two events are simultaneous.

If we are to honor the surprise element resident in the thief analogy in Matthew 24:43, we must admit that it cannot easily apply to the second coming. A thief never signals his coming (at least willingly), but numerous telltale signs will precede Christ's second coming at the climax of the tribulation.

Reason 9: The Exhortation to "Watch"

In the New Testament, there are twenty-two uses of the verb *grēgoreō*, "to watch, be alert, be awake." It appears first in the New Testament prophecies spoken by Jesus (canonically first in Matt. 24:42, 43; 25:13; chronologically first in Luke 12:37). Over half of the uses (twelve out of twenty-two) are set in prophetic contexts (Matt. 24:42, 43; 25:13; Mark 13:34, 35, 37; Luke 12:37; 1 Thess. 5:6, 10; Rev 3:2, 3; 16:15). Apart from two uses by Paul (1 Thess. 5:6, 10), all uses in prophecy (ten out of twelve) are spoken by Jesus, with seven uses in the Synoptics and three in Revelation. This is strong evidence that Paul borrowed the prophetic use of the Greek term "to watch" (*grēgoreō*) from the Lord.[67]

Eight of the twelve uses of the verb *grēgoreō* in prophecy show up in direct connection contextually with the thief imagery.[68] Imminence appears to be a common accompaniment to the use of "to watch," even apart from prophecy. In the case of the garden of Gethsemane, the disciples needed to stay alert because temptation was imminent ("Behold, the hour is at hand," Matt. 26:45).[69] In Acts 20:31 alertness was essential because Paul predicted that as soon as he would leave, false teachers would begin an attempt to infiltrate the Ephesian elders (vv. 29–30). Peter instructed his readers to watch since Satan may attack at any moment (1 Pet. 5:18). Therefore, there is a suggestion of imminence in most if not all the non-prophetic uses of "to watch" as well. These factors lead to the need for constructing a unified use of the verb "to watch, be alert" (*grēgoreō*) in all twelve prophetic passages.[70]

Since pretribulationists agree that 1 Thessalonians 5:6 and 10 use the verb "to watch" to instruct believers of the New Testament church to "stay alert" for the coming pretribulational rapture, then should we not logically agree that Jesus utilized the same word in the same way in the Discourse? If so, then we may be confident that Paul has brought over Jesus' concern regarding alertness for His imminent (pretribulational) return present in this verb.

The regular use of "to watch" (*grēgoreō*) with the thief imagery and the imminent return of a homeowner in prophetic contexts (Mark 13:35–37) suggests the need for a consistency of interpretation. Since in most contexts and especially prophetic contexts, "to watch" (*grēgoreō*) stresses imminence, the use of "to watch" is most appropriate for the pretribulational rapture of the church, not a posttribulational return of Christ.[71] "Watching" or "alertness" is more fully appropriate for an imminent, pretribulational return of the Lord than for any other premillennial rapture position.[72]

CONCLUSION

The pretribulation rapture is the best exegetical and theological interpretation of Matthew 24:36–44. Other rapture theories do not do justice to the transitional nature of verse 36, to the nature of the Noah illustration, or the imminence resident in the passage as illustrated in the thief imagery and the verb "to be alert" (*grēgoreō*). It should be acknowledged that Jesus was the originator of the pretribulation rapture teaching (both in the Olivet Discourse and John 14:1–3), and that Paul, Peter, and John were dependent upon the Discourse for much of their teaching about the rapture.

The pretribulation rapture teaching does not depend on this perspective of the Discourse. Most pretribulationists have appealed first and foremost to Paul, even though all pretribulationists agree that Jesus speaks of the rapture in John 14. I suggest that the Lord Jesus should be given much more credit for originating and describing the pretribulation rapture—the "blessed hope" of the Lord's imminent return before the coming day of the Lord.

NOTES

1. These interpreters are called preterists. Preterism is a nonpremillennial view that claims that most or all of the Olivet Discourse is fulfilled in AD 70.

2. Some pretribulationists have maintained that the first question of the disciples in Matthew 24:3 concerned the AD 70 event, but is not answered by Jesus. But since the first question asks, "When will *these things* (plural, Gk. *tauta*) be," even this question does not concern AD 70 except by foreshadowing. In the parallel passage, Luke 21:12–24, Jesus did address the AD 70 event. Darrell L. Bock, *Luke 9:51–24:53*, BECNT (Grand Rapids: Baker Academic, 1996), 1,656.

3. Douglas J. Moo, "A Case for the Posttribulation Rapture," *TVR1*, 212.

4. Robert H. Gundry, *The Church and the Tribulation* (Grand Rapids: Zondervan, 1973), 129–39; Douglas J. Moo, "The Case for the Posttribulation Rapture Position," in Gleason L. Archer et al., *TVR*, 190–96.

5. Most pretribulationists have insisted that the group being addressed in the Discourse is Israel, not the church. It is true that the gospel of Matthew is addressed primarily to the Jews. However, it is also the only gospel to mention the "church" (*ekklēsia*, Matt. 16:18; 18:17). The Great Commission in Matthew 28:19–20 is given to the church, not Israel. So, it is not impossible that Matthew and Jesus address the church as well as the Jews in different portions of the Discourse. For a further discussion of these issues, see John F. Hart, "Should Pretribulationists Reconsider the Rapture in Matthew 24:36–44?, Part 3," *Journal of the Grace Theological Society* (autumn 2008): 60–61.

6. Paul D. Feinberg, "The Case for the Pretribulation Rapture Position," *TVR*, 80, 225, 229–31; Charles C. Ryrie, *Come Quickly, Lord Jesus: What You Need to Know about the Rapture* (Eugene, OR: Harvest House, 1996), 94–97; and John F. Walvoord, *The Blessed Hope and the Tribulation* (Grand Rapids: Zondervan, 1976), 85–90.

7. Gibbs rightly argues that the two interrogatives in verse 3 signal just two questions: "When [*tote*] ..., and what [*tis*] ...." Jeffery A. Gibbs, *Jerusalem and Parousia. Jesus' Eschatological Discourse in Matthew's Gospel* (St. Louis: Concordia, 2000), 170. Some writers hold that three questions are addressed. John F. Walvoord, *Matthew: Thy Kingdom Come* (Chicago: Moody, 1974), 182; Ed Glasscock, *Matthew*, Moody Gospel Commentary (Chicago: Moody, 1997), 461, 463.

8. Some dispensationalists maintain that Jesus did not answer the first question since it was about the AD 70 destruction of Jerusalem, e.g., John F. Walvoord, "Christ's Olivet Discourse on the Time of the End. Part II: Prophecies Fulfilled in the Present Age," *BibSac* 128 (July 1971): 207. Hagner (a nondispensationalist) also holds the same view. Donald Hagner, *Matthew 14–28*, WBC, vol. 33b (Nashville: Nelson, 1995), 688. Carson is correct to ask why Matthew retains the first question if Jesus does not answer it. He also argues that Jesus' answer is opaque or even deceptive if He does not interact with the disciples' question. D. A. Carson, "Matthew," Expositor's Bible Commentary, vol. 8, ed. Frank E. Gaebelein (Grand Rapids: Zondervan, 1984), 494–95.

9. Some pretribulationists favor a potential, generic fulfillment (type-antitype) of Matthew 24:4–44 in the AD 70 event. This is highly likely. Cf. Craig Blaising, "A Case for the Pretribulation Rapture," *TVR1*, 51.

10. The NIV unfortunately translates *tauta* ("these things," Gk. pl.) with the singular in 24:3b, "when will *this* happen?" "These things" is much broader than the destruction of Jerusalem.

11. The phrase "the sign of Your coming, and of the end of the age" is just one, single question. However, several scholars wrongly appeal to the Granville Sharp rule of Greek grammar to support this fact: Craig L. Blomberg, *Matthew*, vol. 22, NAC, ed. David S. Dockery (Nashville: Broadman, 1992), 353 n. 37; Hagner, *Matthew 14–28*, 688; and Grant R. Osborne, *Matthew*, Zondervan Exegetical Commentary on the New Testament, ed. Clinton E. Arnold (Grand Rapids: Zondervan, 2010), 869 n. 15. For the correct use of this grammatical rule, see Daniel B. Wallace, *Greek Grammar beyond the Basics: An Exegetical Syntax of the Greek New Testament* (Grand Rapids: Zondervan, 1996), 270–73.

12. Gary W. Derickson, "Matthew's Chiastic Structure and Its Dispensational Implications," *BibSac* 163 (October–December 2006): 423–37.

13. Note also that the Greek verb "to read" (*anaginōskō*) is used elsewhere of reading the Old Testament, even when no text is mentioned (e.g., Mark 2:25). Herman Ridderbos, *The Coming of the Kingdom*, trans. H. de Jongste, ed. Raymond O. Zorn (Philadelphia: P&R, 1962), 532 n. 81.

14. "Matthew 24 is saturated with allusions to Dan. 7–12, including such expressions as 'abomination of desolation' and 'great tribulation,'" notes D. A. Carson, "1–3 John," in *Commentary on the New Testament Use of the Old Testament*, ed. G. K. Beale and D. A. Carson (Grand Rapids: Baker Academic, 2007), 1065. The Discourse also makes an extensive use of the title "Son of Man" (Matt. 24:27, 30, 37, 39, 44; 25:31). A common understanding is to see Daniel 7 as the primary source behind the title "Son of Man." Richard N. Longenecker, "'Son of Man' Imagery: Some Implications for Theology and Discipleship," *Journal of the Evangelical Theological Society* 18 (winter 1975): 10–11.

15. Others who understand the future Seventieth Week of Daniel 9 to be the exclusive purview of Matthew 24:4–28 are Louis A. Barbieri Jr., "Matthew," BKC, vol. 2, ed. John F. Walvoord and Roy B. Zuck (1983; repr., Colorado Springs: Cook, 1996), 76; Paul N. Benware, *Understanding End Times Prophecy: A Comprehensive Approach* (Chicago: Moody, 1995), 318; revised and expanded ed.(2006), 369–72; J. Dwight Pentecost, *Things to Come: A Study of Biblical Eschatology* (Grand Rapids: Zondervan, 1964), 279.

16. Robert L. Thomas, "Imminence in the NT, Especially Paul's Thessalonian Epistles," *The Master's Seminary Journal* 13 (fall 2002): 193. For more detail about imminence, see chapter 1, "The Rapture and the Biblical Teaching of Imminency."

17. Gibbs, *Jesus and Parousia*, 171.

18. Blaising argues, "However, to see it [i.e., the preaching of the NT message of salvation] as a condition for the return of the Lord essentially nullifies the unknown any-moment quality of the parousia, for it effectively ties the timing of the parousia to the modern accomplishment of these goals." Blaising, "Pretribulation Rapture," *TV1*, 37 n. 20.

19. Some make the devastations of 24:21–22 to be devastations throughout the whole church age. Cf. Craig L. Blomberg, "The Posttributionism of the New Testament. Leaving 'Left Behind' Behind," *A Case for Historic Premillennialism*, ed. Craig L. Blomberg and Sung Wook Chung (Grand Rapids: Baker, 2009), 74. Can a time really be found in the church age about which it can be said, "unless those days were limited, no one would survive" (24:22 HCSB; cf. NIV)?

20. Gibbs adds, "In the first half of the discourse, 'the one who is in the field' (24:18) is warned not to turn back to get his cloak. In the second half of the discourse, there will be no warning for the two people in the field (24:40)." Gibbs, *Jesus and Parousia*, 224 n. 21.

21. For posttribulationism, see Gundry, *The Church and the Tribulation*, 42–43. For the prewrath position, see Hultberg, "Prewrath Rapture," *TVR1*, 128. For pretribulationism, see John F. Walvoord, "Christ's Olivet Discourse on the Time of the End: Part IV: How Near Is the Lord's Return?" *BibSac* 129 (January–March 1972): 25.

22. "Hence, Christians who claim they can narrow down the time of Christ's return to a generation or a year or even a few days' period, while still not knowing the literal day or hour, remain singularly ill-informed." Blomberg, *Matthew*, 365. Cf. also Carson, "Matthew," 8:508; Hagner, *Matthew 14–28*, 716; Osborne, *Matthew*, 903 n. 3.

23. Carson, "Matthew," 8:490, 495; Blomberg, *Matthew*, 370.

24. Blomberg says, "Matthew complicates matters by adding the adverb, 'immediately' to modify the phrase, 'after the tribulation of those days.'" Blomberg, "Posttribulationism of the New Testament," 73. But why doesn't "immediately after the tribulation of those days" help clarify matters rather than complicate them? As Hagner states, "It is very difficult to believe that the words 'immediately after the tribulation of those days' refer only to something general in the indeterminate future." Hagner, *Matthew 14–28*, 712.

25. Moo, "Posttribulation Rapture," *TVR1*, 209, 237. Elsewhere, Moo ties the reference to the "great trumpet" (the only eschatological trumpet mentioned by Jesus) in Matthew 24:31, which is clearly post-tribulational, with the "last trumpet" at the rapture described in 1 Corinthians 15:52 and the "trumpet

of God" in 1 Thessalonians 4:16. Interestingly, the only places in the NT or the LXX where the Greek "a great trumpet" is mentioned are in Matthew 24:31 and Isaiah 27:13. Neither 1 Corinthians 15 or 1 Thessalonians 4 (or Revelation) use this term. Both Matthew 24:29–31 and Isaiah 27:13 describe the gathering of Israel ("all the tribes of the earth," Matthew 24:30), not the church. If Paul wanted his readers to recall Isaiah 27:13 or Matthew 24:31, and join either passage about the Jewish restoration to their land with his teaching on the rapture of the church, he could have helped make this identification more clear by describing his trumpet as the "great trumpet."

26. Feinberg, "The Case for the Pretribulation Rapture," in *TVR*, 81.

27. Midtribulationists, like pretribulationists, understand the parousia to involve a span of time. Gleason L. Archer, "Response to the Posttribulation Rapture Position," in *TVR*, 213–18. Prewrath adherents have the same viewpoint. Hultberg, "Prewrath Rapture," *TVRI*, 142–43.

28. Cf. Zane C. Hodges, *Jesus, God's Prophet: His Teaching about the Coming Surprise* (Mesquite, TX: Kerugma, 2006), 26–27, 62–63.

29. This transitional Greek phrase, *peri de* (followed by the genitive case), is also found in the parallel passage in Mark 13:32.

30. "'But about . . .' (*peri de*) occurred similarly in 22:31 to mark a change of subject. . . . Paul uses the same phrase several times in 1 Corinthians (7:1, 25; 8:1; 12:1; 16:1, 12) to move from one of the issues raised by his correspondents to another (cf. also 1 Thess. 4:9; 5:1; Acts 21:25). In each case *peri de* is the rhetorical formula for a new beginning. The analogy with 1 Corinthians indicates that here [Matt. 24:36] the phrase marks the transition from the first of the two questions asked in v. 3 to the second." R. T. France, *The Gospel of Matthew*, NICNT (Grand Rapids: Eerdmans, 2007), 936–37. Unfortunately, France misses the chiastic structure and does not understand the questions are treated in reverse order.

31. Thomas, "1 Thessalonians," 280; D. Michael Martin, *1, 2 Thessalonians*, NAC, ed. E. Ray Clendenen (Accordance electronic ed. Nashville: Broadman & Holman, 1995), 33:133, 156.

32. Verse 36 goes better thematically with the following than with the preceding material, forming a well-knit unit. John Nolland, *The Gospel of Matthew: A Commentary on the Greek Text* (Grand Rapids: Eerdmans, 2005), 990–91, 993; Carson, "Matthew," 8:507.

33. Blaising, "Pretribulation Rapture," *TVR1*, 48; Arnold G. Fruchtenbaum, *The Footsteps of the Messiah: A Study of the Sequence of Prophetic Events*, rev. ed. (San Antonio: Ariel Press, 2011), 640–41.

34. Thomas, "Imminence in the NT," 193–94 n. 8; cf. also M. J. Harris, "Appendix: Prepositions and Theology in the Greek New Testament," *New International Dictionary of New Testament Theology*, ed. Colin Brown (Grand Rapids: Zondervan, 1976), 3:1203.

35. Cf. G. Henry Waterman, "The Source of Paul's Teaching on the 2nd Coming of Christ in 1 and 2 Thessalonians," *Journal of the Evangelical Theological Society* 18 (spring 1975): 109. J. Daniel Hays, J. Scott Duvall, C. Marvin Pate, "Thessalonians, 1 and 2," in *Dictionary of Biblical Prophecy and End Times* (Grand Rapids: Zondervan, 2007), 442.

36. Arthur L. Moore, *The Parousia in the New Testament* (Leiden: Brill, 1966), 99–100.

37. C. Brown, "*hēmera*," NIDNTT, 2:891, where the following references are cited: Isaiah 10:27; 27:1; 29:19; Haggai 2:23; Zechariah 6:10.

38. Waterman, "Source of Paul's Teaching," 109.

39. Some pretribulationists believe that there may be a period of time between the rapture and the inception of Daniel's Seventieth Week. For a brief discussion of this approach, see chapter 8, "John and the Rapture: Revelation 2–3."

40. Thomas, "Imminence in the NT," 194.

41. Bruner comments, "The crime indicated by Jesus in this verse is not *gross sin* (the people of Noah's generation are not doing vicious things in Jesus' description); it *is secular indifference*. The evil here is immersion in the everyday without thought for the Last Day" (italics original). Frederick Dale Bruner, *Matthew, A Commentary*, vol. 2 (Grand Rapids: Eerdmans, 2004), 524. Of course, Genesis records gross sin in Noah's day, specifically that the earth was "filled with violence" (Gen. 6:11, 13).

42. Blomberg, *Matthew,* 366; Carson, "Matthew," 8:509; Hagner, *Matthew 14–28,* 719–20.

43. In a Lukan parallel to Matthew 24 (Luke 21), the verse that immediately precedes the statement that men "will see the Son of Man coming in a cloud with power and great glory" (v. 27), Jesus comments, "men [will be] fainting from fear and the expectation of the things which are coming upon the world" (Luke 21:26). This is not life as usual.

44. Cf. G. K. Beale (an amillennialist), *1–2 Thessalonians,* IVP New Testament Commentary, ed. Grant R. Osborne (Downers Grove, IL: InterVarsity, 2003), 137. Most pretribulationists have argued that Paul received most of his revelation in 1 Thessalonians 4–5 directly from the Lord, and his thoughts are not found in the Gospels. Cf. Robert Dean, Jr. "Three Foundational Rapture Passages," *The Popular Handbook on the Rapture,* ed. Tim LaHaye, Thomas Ice, and Ed Hinson (Eugene, OR: Harvest House, 2011), 93. But Blaising (pretribulational) clearly sees Paul's teaching about the day of the Lord as drawn from Jesus in the Olivet Discourse. Craig A. Blaising, "The Day of the Lord and the Rapture," *BibSac* 169 (July–September 2012): 261–62, 267–68.

45. G. Henry Waterman, "The Source of Paul's Teaching on the 2nd Coming of Christ in 1 and 2 Thessalonians," *Journal of the Evangelical Theological Society* 18 (spring 1975): 106–7. Thomas believes that the origin of all teachings about imminence in the New Testament can be found in Christ. Thomas, "Imminence in the NT," 192, 198. Hodges develops this perspective further, proposing that both Paul (1 Thess. 4–5) and Peter (2 Pet. 3) derived their teaching about the day of the Lord, the thief in the night, and the new revelation of the rapture from the Discourse. Hodges, *Jesus, God's Prophet,* 27–30. Blomberg (*Matthew,* 367) implies that John (Rev. 3:3; 16:15) also picked up his use of the thief imagery from Jesus in Matthew 24.

46. Seyoon Kim, "Jesus, Sayings of," *Dictionary of Paul and His Letters,* ed. Gerald F. Hawthorne and Ralph P. Martin (Downers Grove, IL: InterVarsity, 1993), 477; Gene L. Green, *The Letters to the Thessalonians,* PNTC (Grand Rapids: Eerdmans, 2002), 222. Cf. also Beale, *1–2 Thessalonians,* 135 (footnote on 4:15), 137–38.

47. For more detail on this passage, see chapter 6, "Paul and the Rapture: 1 Thessalonians 4–5."

48. I am following the grammatical conclusions of Bo Reicke, *The Disobedient Spirits and Christian Baptism. A Study of 1 Peter 3:19 and Its Context* (Copenhagen: Munksgaard, 1946), 149–72. Riecke translates "which antitypical baptism now saves you," making *baptisma* the antecedent of *ho.*

49. "Such 'typological' shaping of the Flood narrative by the author of the Pentateuch is remarkably similar to the later reading of this passage in 1 Pet. 3:21. In that passage *the ark* [italics added] is seen to prefigure the saving work of Christ. . . ." John H. Sailhamer, "Genesis," Expositor's Bible Commentary, ed. Frank E. Gaebelein (Grand Rapids: Zondervan, 1984), 2:85.

50. In 1 Peter 3:16, Peter leads into the 3:18–21 context by using Paul's unique term *en christō* ("in Christ"), which takes place only through Spirit baptism. Outside of Paul's seventy-three uses of the term, it is found only in 1 Peter (3:16; 5:10, 14).

51. Thomas R. Edgar, "Robert H. Gundry and Revelation 3:10," *Grace Theological Journal* 3 (spring 1982): 44–45. Greek words in the quotation have been transliterated.

52. Lot's rescue from Sodom is paralleled in Luke 17:26–29 with Noah's rescue from the flood. So Lot's deliverance from destruction also pictures the church's rapture before the destruction of the tribulation period.

53. Many pretribulationists reason that Luke 17:34–36, a parallel to Matthew 24:41–42, confirms their viewpoint that to be "taken" is to be taken in judgment. In Luke 17:37, the disciples ask the brief question "Where, Lord?" Jesus replies with the proverbial statement, "Where the body is, there also the vultures will be gathered." So the disciples' question is understood, "Where are they taken for judgment, Lord?" However, the best solution is that Luke 17:37 refers back to the beginning of the sermon in verse 23 (forming an inclusio), not the immediately preceding context. Cf. I. Howard Marshall, *Commentary on Luke,* New International Greek Testament Commentary, ed. I. Howard Marshall and W. Ward Gasque (Grand Rapids: Eerdmans, 1978), 669; Robert H. Stein, *Luke,* NAC, David S. Dockery gen. ed. (Nashville: Broadman, 1992), 24:441; Joel B. Green, *Gospel of Luke,* NICNT (Accordance electronic ed. Grand Rapids: Eerdmans, 1997), 680 n. 70.

54. In Gundry's view, the Discourse is the central portion of revelation on which his posttribulational doctrine is built. He argues that pretribulationists must look to other passages to demonstrate a pretribulation rapture. Gundry, *The Church and the Tribulation*, 129.

55. Ibid., 138.

56. "The imagery itself lends the most credence to the interpretation that those taken away are taken for salvation." Michael Burer, "Matthew 24:40–41 in the NET Bible Notes: Taken for Salvation or Judgment." https://bible.org/article/matthew-2440-41-net-bible-notes-taken-salvation-or-judgment,. Cf. also Gerhard Delling, "*paralambanō*," *Theological Dictionary of the New Testament*, ed. Gerhard Kittel, trans. Geoffrey W. Bromiley (Grand Rapids: Eerdmans, 1967), 4:13; B. Siede, "*lambanō*," NIDNTT, 3:751.

57. Cf. W. D. Davies and Dale C. Allison Jr., *A Critical and Exegetical Commentary on the Gospel according to Saint Matthew*, ICC, 3 vols. (Edinburgh: T. & T. Clark, 1997), 3:383. Examples of *aphiēmi* outside Matthew express how a spouse might abandon his or her partner (1 Cor. 7:11–13), how the Good Shepherd will not abandon His sheep (John 10:12), and how the Father has certainly not abandoned the Son (John 8:29).

58. Nolland, *Matthew*, 994.

59. *aphiēmi* is repeatedly used of Jesus and God forgiving (*aphiēmi*) the sins of believers. But here the thought is "abandoning" the judgment due our sins, and not abandoning us personally.

60. Brown observes the use of *aphiēmi* in Matthew 23:38 for the judgment of the temple. He concludes that the uses of the word in 24:40–41 serve to warn those who are unprepared like in the days of Noah that they will be forsaken in judgment like the temple. Schuyler Brown, "The Matthean Apocalypse," *Journal for the Study of the New Testament* 4 (1979): 16.

61. Delling links *paralambanō* in Matthew 24:40–41 with John 14:3, taking both uses as an "acceptance into the kingdom of Christ." Delling, "*paralambanō*," TDNT 4:13.

62. Walvoord (pretribulationist), "Christ's Olivet Discourse: Part IV," 28–29; Moo (posttribulationist), "Case for the Posttribulation Rapture, *TVR*, 185; Carson, "Matthew," 8:510.

63. Robert L. Thomas, "1 Thessalonians," Expositor's Bible Commentary, rev. ed., ed. Tremper Longman III and David E. Garland (Accordance electronic ed., Grand Rapids: Zondervan, 2006), 12:421.

64. Renald Showers, *Maranatha: Our Lord Comes!* (Bellmawr, NJ: Friends of Israel, 1995), 60.

65. G. M. Stanton, "Jesus Traditions," *Dictionary of Later New Testament and Its Developments*, ed. Ralph P. Martin and Peter H. Davids (Downers Grove, IL: InterVarsity, 1997), 570.

66. Kim, "Jesus, Sayings of," 476; J. K. Howard, "Our Lord's Teaching concerning His Parousia: A Study in the Gospel of Mark," *Evangelical Quarterly* 38 (1966): 155.

67. Gene L. Green, *The Letters to the Thessalonians*, Pillar New Testament Commentary (Grand Rapids: Eerdmans, 2002), 238.

68. Matthew 24:42–43, "thief" in v. 43; Luke 12:37, "thief" in v. 39; 1 Thessalonians 5:6, 10, "thief" in vv. 2, 4; Revelation 3:2, 3, "thief" in v. 3; Revelation 16:15, "thief" in the same verse. "A connection exists between the imagery of the thief and the idea of watchfulness in the New Testament." Evald Uivestarn Lövestam, *Spiritual Wakefulness in the New Testament* (Lund: CWK Gleerup, 1963), 95.

69. Nolland holds that the intended sense of *grēgoreō* in Matthew 26:38 is the same as that in 24:42, 43; 25:13, i.e., spiritual (not physical) watchfulness. Nolland, *Matthew*, 1098.

70. Ladd faults pretribulationists for sometimes applying the command for watchfulness to the posttribulational second coming (Matt. 24:43), and other times to the church and the rapture (1 Thess. 5). George Eldon Ladd, *The Blessed Hope* (Grand Rapids: Zondervan, 1956), 114–17.

71. Two passages in prophecy that use *grēgoreō* but seem problematic for the pretribulation rapture are Matthew 25:13 and Revelation 16:15. For an explanation of Revelation 16:15 as describing the pretribulation rapture, see Thomas, *Revelation 18–22: An Exegetical Commentary* (Chicago: Moody, 1995), 267. For the pretribulation rapture in Matthew 25:13, see Joseph Dillow, *Final Destiny. The Future Reign of Servant Kings* (Monument, CO: Paniym, 2012), 794–811.

72. For a more extended treatment of *grēgoreō*, see John F. Hart, "Should Pretribulationists Reconsider the Rapture in Matthew 24:36–44? Part 3 of 3," *Journal of the Grace Evangelical Society* 21 (autumn 2008): 53–58.

3

The Rapture and the Day of the Lord

BY GLENN R. KREIDER

Alas, you who are longing for the day of the LORD,
For what purpose will the day of the LORD be to you?
It will be darkness and not light;
As when a man flees from a lion
And a bear meets him,
Or goes home, leans his hand against the wall
And a snake bites him.
Will not the day of the LORD be darkness instead of light,
Even gloom with no brightness in it?

AMOS 5:18–20

In the eighth century BC, God sent the shepherd Amos to the northern kingdom of Israel.[1] To people relishing material prosperity and peace, Amos brought a stern warning. To people who believed their prosperity was a sign of God's blessing, Amos brought a message of judgment.

"For three transgressions . . . and for four" (Amos 1:3, 6, 9, 11; 2:1, 6), Amos announced, judgment from Yahweh is coming to Damascus, Gaza, Tyre, Edom, Moab, Judah, and Israel. That God would judge Israel's enemies and vindicate Israel was consistent with her expectation. That God would also judge Israel, especially in the midst of her prosperity, was a sobering message.

Like many of the other biblical prophets, Amos warned the people of Israel that they had broken the covenant with Yahweh and, unless they repented, they would face divine judgment.[2] Hiers summarizes, "The prophets warned their contemporaries in Israel and Judah that 'the Day of Yahweh' would soon come upon them in the form of cosmic or meteorological catastrophes or of powerful enemy armies which would bring Yahweh's judgment upon them for breaking the covenant requirements of the law."[3]

Amos's jeremiad against Israel included specific sins, among them mistreatment of the poor and needy, injustice, sexual immorality, idolatry, and perverted worship practices (Amos 2:6–8; 5:10–13).[4] In the fifth chapter, Yahweh called Israel to repentance: "Seek Me that you may live" (Amos 5:4) and "Seek good and not evil, that you may live; and thus may the LORD God of hosts be with you, just as you have said!" (Amos 5:14). The implication was clear. God had withdrawn from His people because of their sin. They apparently believed their covenantal relationship with God brought them such privilege that they could sin with impunity. Amos reminded them that the covenant came with responsibilities. Instead of longing for the day of judgment, Israel should pursue justice: "But let justice roll down like waters and righteousness like an ever-flowing stream" (Amos 5:24).

Amos also rebuked the people for their attitude toward the judgment of God and in strong language admonished them to repent (Amos 5:18).[5] They expected the day of the Lord to bring judgment on their enemies and deliverance for them. Amos's prophecy identified Israel as one of the enemies of God.[6] Chisholm explains,

> Amos declared in no uncertain terms that the Northern Kingdom's view of the Day of the Lord was inaccurate. The Lord would indeed intervene in power, but Israel, not her enemies, would be the primary object of His angry judgment. The Day of the Lord would be characterized by darkness (symbolizing judgment), rather than light (symbolizing salvation).[7]

This is the earliest biblical reference to the day of the Lord. According to McComiskey and Longman,

> "The day of the LORD" is an important eschatological concept that runs through the prophetic writings. Amos is the first to mention it, and he assumes that it is already a well-known concept in his culture. The day of the LORD refers to the complex of events surrounding the coming of the Lord in judgment to conquer his foes and to establish his sovereign rule over the world.[8]

Thus, when Amos rebuked Israel's attitude toward this coming judgment, he did so without explaining the term, thereby implying prior understanding.[9] T. H. Jones explains, "The earliest use shows that the phrase was already a standard one in popular phraseology. To the people it meant the day when Yahweh would intervene to put Israel at the head of the nations, irrespective of Israel's faithfulness to him. Amos declares that the Day means judgment for Israel."[10]

What was shocking to Amos's audience was not that the day of judgment was coming; it was that the Lord's judgment would be poured out on them. They expected God to judge the nations. McComiskey and Longman explain, "They regarded their election as the guarantee of the Lord's favor. But their moral vision is blurred. They fail to see the day of the Lord as the time when God will judge all sin, even theirs. They name the name of Yahweh but do not obey his precepts."[11]

The day of the Lord is a day of judgment, a time when God executes just punishment upon rebels and enemies. When this judgment comes, the righteous are not the focus, although the result of the judgment of God's enemies will be peace and blessing for them. The day of the Lord precedes blessing and is even the means by which blessing will come. But the day of the Lord is not blessing itself. It is darkness, not light.[12]

The day of the Lord is not necessarily a twenty-four-hour period, but it is a time of judgment, an era of divine wrath.[13] Throughout the biblical texts, any time of judgment could be designated a day of the Lord, but increasingly, it becomes clear that there is an eschatological day of judgment, a final or ultimate day of the Lord. Kaiser explains, "That final time would be climactic and the sum of all the rest."[14] Thus, the eschatological day of the Lord refers "to the future time of God's decisive action and intervention into human history. Indeed, the prophets frequently telescope all the multifaceted dramatic aspects of the prophetic future—regardless of how long such events may take—into the phrase."[15]

"DAY OF THE LORD" IN THE HEBREW SCRIPTURES

The day of the Lord is a common theme in biblical theology, especially in the Prophets. Blaising asserts that it "is a major unifying theme in the Minor Prophets."[16] He explains that this phrase is found fifteen times in the Hebrew Scriptures, thirteen of which are in the Minor Prophets, in ten different oracles.

But if the "variants of the phrase, such as 'the day of the wrath of Yahweh,' 'on that day,' 'Yahweh (of hosts) has a day,' or 'the day'" are included, the list is much longer.[17] Blaising analyzes and categorizes these texts: Isaiah 2:6–22; 13:1–22; 22:1–25; 24:1–23; 34:1–17; Jeremiah 25:30–38; 46:1–12; Ezekiel 7:1–27; 38:1–39; Joel 1:1–20; 2:1–11, 28–32; 3:1–21; Amos 5:16–27; Obadiah 1:15–21; Nahum 1:1–15; Habakkuk 3:1–16; Zephaniah 1:1–18; 2:1–15; 3:8–13; Zechariah 12:1–9; 14:1–15; and Malachi 3:1–3; 4:1–3.[18] A brief survey of several of these texts should be sufficient to demonstrate the accuracy of Blaising's summary: "The day of the Lord is a well-known theme in the Old Testament Prophets indicating a climactic outpouring of divine wrath. . . . They are days of darkness, dread, and gloom."[19] Imagery similar to Amos 5:18–20, that this is a day of darkness and not light, is common to all these prophetic descriptions.

Day of the Lord in the Major Prophets

The prophet Isaiah promises the house of Jacob (Isa. 2:5–11) that "the LORD of hosts will have a day of reckoning against everyone who is proud and lofty and against everyone who is lifted up" (2:12). On that day, "the idols will completely vanish" (2:18) and "men will go into caves of the rocks and into the holes of the ground before the terror of the LORD" (2:19). This day of God's wrath is a day of judgment on the unrighteous.

Isaiah 13 promises judgment "from the Almighty" (Isa. 13:6) on Babylon (13:1). When this day comes, "they will be terrified, pains and anguish will take hold of them; they will writhe like a woman in labor" (13:8). Isaiah continues, "Behold, the day of the LORD is coming, cruel, with fury and burning anger, to make the land a desolation; and He will exterminate its sinners from it" (13:9). Not only the land and its inhabitants will feel the effects of Yahweh's wrath, but also "the stars of heaven and their constellations will not flash forth their light; the sun will be dark when it rises and the moon will not shed its light" (13:10). The purpose of this judgment is punishment of the wicked: "Thus I will punish the world for its evil and the wicked for their iniquity; . . . Anyone who is found will be thrust through, and anyone who is captured will fall by the sword. Their little ones also will be dashed to pieces before their eyes; their houses will be plundered and their wives ravished" (13:11, 15–16). God wages war against the wicked.[20]

In Isaiah 24, the prophet declares that the day of the Lord will result in the devastation of the earth. "Behold, the LORD lays the earth waste, devastates it, distorts its surface and scatters its inhabitants" (24:1). Also, "The earth will be completely laid waste and completely despoiled, for the LORD has spoken this word" (24:3). The reason for this judgment is that the inhabitants of the earth "transgressed laws, violated statutes, broke the everlasting covenant" (24:5).

It is the nations who will be judged according to Isaiah 34: "For the LORD's indignation is against all the nations, and His wrath against all their armies; He has utterly destroyed them" (34:2). Similarly, according to Jeremiah 25:31, "The LORD has a controversy with the nations. He is entering into judgment with all flesh." God's judgment is inclusive of all wicked people.

In Ezekiel 7, the prophet quotes the Lord God as declaring "a disaster, unique disaster, behold it is coming. . . . Your doom has come to you, O inhabitant of the land. The time has come, the day is near—tumult rather than joyful shouting on the mountains. Now I will shortly pour out My wrath on you and spend My anger against you; judge you according to your ways and bring on you all your abominations" (7:5, 7–8). This predicted judgment had a specific focus, the coming destruction at the hands of the Babylonians.[21] Thus, the judgment of the day of the Lord need not come from the Lord's hand. It is sometimes mediated through human agents, even armies of wicked nations. This apocalyptic language of the destruction of the Babylonian army prefigures the eschatological day of the Lord as well.[22]

Day of the Lord in the Minor Prophets

In addition to Amos, several other minor prophets predict the coming judgment of the Lord. In Joel's prophecy, the devastation will come from locusts (Joel 1:4), but it is still "destruction from the Almighty" (1:15). It will be a day of "darkness and gloom" (2:2). Even the "sun and the moon grow dark and the stars lose their brightness" (2:10). "The day of the LORD is indeed great and very awesome, and who can endure it?" (2:11). But, Joel announces, there is hope: "'Yet even now,' declares the LORD, 'Return to Me with all your heart, and with fasting, weeping and mourning; and rend your heart and not your garments.' Now return to the LORD your God, for He is gracious and compassionate, slow to anger, abounding in lovingkindness and relenting of evil. Who knows whether He will not turn and relent and leave a blessing behind Him" (2:12–14; cf. Ex. 34:6–7). This blessing is not included in the day of the Lord. Rather, as promised in the covenant, if rebellious Israel will repent, the Lord will hear and restore her (Deut. 30:1–5). Blessing comes with repentance and, in response to that repentance, God will relent and withhold His judgment.

Zephaniah similarly promises the possibility of blessing to the wicked, if they will repent and return to God. In that case, the destruction of the day of the Lord will not be poured out on them. He writes, "Near is the great day of the LORD, near and coming very quickly; listen, the day of the LORD! In it the warrior cries out bitterly. A day of wrath is that day, a day of trouble and distress, a day of destruction and desolation, a day of darkness and gloom, a day of clouds and thick darkness, a day of trumpet and battle cry against the fortified cities and the high corner towers. I will bring distress on men so that they will walk like the blind, because they have sinned against the LORD" (Zeph. 1:14–17).

Yet, this is not the end of the story. "Before the decree takes effect . . . Seek the LORD, all you humble of the earth who have carried out His ordinances; seek righteousness, seek humility. Perhaps you will be hidden in the day of the LORD's anger" (2:2–3). In the third chapter of this book, Yahweh again promises judgment: "Therefore wait for Me. . . . for the day when I rise up as a witness. Indeed, My decision is to gather nations, to assemble kingdoms, to pour out on them My indignation, all My burning anger; for all the earth will be devoured by the fire of My zeal" (3:8).

When this day comes, Zephaniah declares, Israel will rejoice and shout in triumph, "The LORD has taken away His judgments against you, He has cleared away your enemies. The King of Israel, the LORD, is in your midst . . . a victorious warrior" (3:15, 17). Even Yahweh will rejoice in that day: "He will exult over you with joy, He will be quiet in His love, He will rejoice over you with shouts of joy" (3:17). This declaration of salvation, deliverance, exultation, and celebration follows the judgment of Yahweh's enemies. Their defeat brings joy to God and His people.[23]

The Old Testament ends with a similar message of hope. Malachi announces, "'For behold, the day is coming, burning like a furnace; and all the arrogant and every evildoer will be chaff; and the day that is coming will set them ablaze,' says the LORD of hosts, 'so that it will leave them neither root nor branch'" (4:1). The destruction is directed toward the wicked, not the righteous: "But for you who fear My name, the sun of righteousness will rise with healing in its wings; and you will go forth and skip about like calves from the stall" (4:2). But there is hope even for the wicked, for the rebellious: "Remember the law of Moses My servant, even the statutes and ordinances which I commanded him in Horeb for all Israel. Behold, I am going to send you Elijah the prophet before the coming of the great and terrible day of the LORD" (4:4–5).

In Amos 5:20, the Lord warns His people not to long for the day of the Lord because it will be a day of darkness, not light. How can people long for blessing that follows the day and not be guilty of violating this prohibition? Malachi provides an answer: Elijah the prophet will come before the day of the Lord, reminding the people of the law of Moses. He will preach a message of repentance: When "you return to the LORD your God and obey Him with all your heart and soul according to all that I command you today, you and your sons, then the LORD your God will restore you from captivity, and have compassion on you . . ." (Deut. 30:2–3). When Elijah comes, if the wicked repent, there is no need for judgment: "He will restore the hearts of the fathers to their children and the hearts of the children to their fathers, so that I will not come and smite the land with a curse" (Mal. 4:6). Thus, the harshness of the devastating judgment of divine wrath can be mitigated through repentance.

The prophets warn that the day is "near" (Isa. 13:6; Zeph. 1:14, Obad. 1:15). This does not necessarily mean that it will come soon, although in the judgment promised by Ezekiel, it did. But it does mean that it could come at any time, and when it does it will come suddenly and without warning. The warning has already been given. No further advance warning is promised and none should be expected.

DAY OF THE LORD IN THE TEACHING OF JESUS

This prophetic understanding of the day of the Lord establishes the background and the context for the teaching of Jesus and the apostles on the day of the Lord.[24] We turn now to the teaching of Jesus in the Olivet Discourse, as recorded in Matthew 24. (The Discourse is also found in Mark 13 and Luke 21.)

Jesus' extended discourse on the Mount of Olives is a response to two questions from His disciples. As Jesus and the disciples exited the temple, the disciples pointed Jesus' attention to the buildings (24:1). In response Jesus predicted the destruction of the buildings: "Not one stone here will be left upon another, which will not be torn down" (24:2). Later, the disciples asked, "Tell us, when will these things happen, and what will be the sign of Your coming, and of the end of the age?" (24:3). They understood the prediction of the destruction of the temple buildings and the return of the Lord to be connected to the end of the age.

Earlier, Jesus had used several parables to explain to His disciples that there would be judgment at the end of the age. In one, He described the judgment using an agricultural metaphor (Matt. 13:24–30, 36–43). It is a parable about a landowner who sowed good seed in his field, but then an enemy sowed tares in the same field. When the servants asked if they should pull the weeds, the master replied, "Allow both to grow together until the harvest; and in the time of the harvest I will say to the reapers, 'First gather up the tares and bind them in bundles to burn them up; but gather the wheat into my barn' " (13:30). In His interpretation of the parable, Jesus explained, "So just as the tares are gathered up and burned with fire, so shall it be at the end of the age. The Son of Man will send forth His angels, and they will gather out of His kingdom all stumbling blocks, and those who commit lawlessness, and will throw them into the furnace of fire; in that place there will be weeping and gnashing of teeth. Then the righteous will shine forth as the sun in the kingdom of their Father . . . " (13:40–43).

In this parable, Jesus prophesies judgment at the end of the age. It is the wicked who will be judged; the righteous are not in focus. Rather, in this day of judgment the evildoers will be cast into the furnace of fire while the righteous will be left behind to shine like the sun—language that comes from Daniel.[25] In the day of the Lord, the wicked are judged and then the righteous are vindicated and blessed. The righteous are left behind to enjoy the blessings of the kingdom.[26] In biblical theology, the distinction between the wicked and the righteous is most clearly seen in judgment, when the wicked are destroyed and the righteous are delivered.

A second parable uses a fishing metaphor (Matt. 13:47–50). Jesus compares the kingdom to a dragnet that gathers fish from the sea. The fishermen then separate the good fish from the bad, which are thrown away. Jesus explains, "So it will be at the end of the age; the angels will come forth and take out the wicked from among the righteous, and will throw them into the furnace of fire; in that place there will be weeping and gnashing of teeth" (13:49–50). The wicked will be taken in judgment. The righteous will be left behind to go into the kingdom. When the wicked are judged in the day of the Lord, the righteous are not judged; they are blessed to enter the kingdom.

In both of these parables, Jesus uses day of the Lord language to describe the day of judgment and in both it is the wicked who face the wrath of God; the righteous are left behind when judgment comes. They remain on the earth to enter the kingdom. The judgment results in a separation between these two groups of people. Jesus predicts that this will occur at the end of the age.

This teaching of Jesus is surely in the minds of the disciples as they hear Him talk about the destruction of the temple. They connect the devastation of the temple buildings to the judgment at the end of the age. They also understand that Jesus' return will be at that time as well. And they ask Him when this will happen and the signs that will accompany the end.

Jesus' response to them begins with a warning not to be misled by false teachers (Matt. 24:4). He describes a period of wars and rumors of wars, of conflict between nations, of famines and earthquakes, of tribulation and persecution; all of these are "merely the beginning of birth pains" (24:8; cf. Isa. 13:8). Later, the apostle Paul will use similar language to describe the earth ever since the fall: "For we know that the whole creation groans and suffers the pains of childbirth together until now. And not only this, but also we ourselves, having the first fruits of the Spirit, even we ourselves groan within ourselves, waiting eagerly for our adoption as sons, the redemption of our body" (Rom. 8:22–23). Creation has been groaning in birth pains ever since the fall. What Jesus describes in Matthew 24:4–14 has always characterized the world in which the righteous have lived as strangers and aliens.

But then His message takes an ominous turn: "Therefore when you see the abomination of desolation which was spoken of through Daniel the prophet . . . flee" (Matt. 24:15–16). The reference is to the vision of seventy weeks decreed for Daniel's people and city (Dan. 9:24–27). The vision includes several time markers; from the issuing of a decree to restore and rebuild Jerusalem until Messiah there are sixty-nine weeks, or 483 years. Then the Messiah will be cut off, the people of the prince who is to come will destroy the city and the sanctuary, and then the end will come. There will be "a firm covenant with the many for one week, but in the middle of the week he will put a stop to sacrifice and grain offering; and on the wing of abominations will come one who makes desolate, even until a complete destruction, one that is decreed, is poured out on the one who makes desolate" (v. 27).[27] The Seventieth Week of Daniel is the tribulation.[28]

According to Jesus, this abomination will be followed by "a great tribulation, such as has not occurred since the beginning of the world until now, nor ever will" (Matt. 24:21; cf. Dan. 12:1). Therefore, abomination is not the end, for more tribulation will come. Jesus uses additional day of the Lord imagery when He says that "the sun will be darkened, and the moon will not give its light, and the stars will fall from the sky, and the powers of the heavens will be shaken" (24:29; cf. Joel 3:15). Then, "The sign of the Son of Man will appear in the sky" (24:30). The disciples had asked for a sign. Here is the sign: "They will see the Son of Man coming on the clouds of the sky with power and great glory" (24:30). The sign of the coming of the Son of Man is the coming of the Son of Man, not the wars, famines, earthquakes, etc. That this is the end of the age is clear: "And He will send forth His angels with a great trumpet and they will gather together His elect from the four winds, from one end of the sky to the other" (24:31; cf. Matt. 13:41–43, 49–50).

But what of the disciples' first question: "When will these things happen?" (24:3). Jesus answers this question clearly and directly: "But of that day and hour no one knows, not even the angels of heaven, nor the Son, but the Father alone" (24:36).[29] As He continues, He compares His coming at the end of the age to the judgment of the flood in the days of Noah. The destruction of the flood came suddenly and unexpectedly: "They did not understand until the flood came and took them all away; so will the coming of the Son of Man be" (24:39).[30] Had they known the date, they would hardly have been without understanding. Later, Jesus says, "Therefore be on the alert, for you do not know which day your Lord is coming" (24:42). Jesus also uses the imagery of a thief, who does not announce his coming in advance. He then makes the application explicit: "For this reason you also must be ready; for the Son of Man is coming at an hour when you do not think He will" (24:44). Finally, another parable, of the ten virgins, ends with this application from Jesus: "Be on the alert then, for you do not know the day nor the hour" (25:13).

The doctrine of imminence of the coming of Christ is the view that His return will occur suddenly, unexpectedly, without warning, and without signs.[31] His coming is near. This understanding of imminence is rooted in the language of Jesus who claims that He does not know when it will be and neither do the angels, that it will be sudden and unexpected as in the days of Noah, that it will be like a thief who comes without warning, and it will be at an unknown and unexpected time. The return of Christ could be at any moment; there are no signs or events that make it possible to predict when it will occur.[32]

According to the chronology Jesus presents in the Olivet Discourse, the day of the Lord will precede His return. This period of time, also known as the tribulation, will be seven years long. The abomination occurs in the midpoint of this week. There are no signs of Jesus' return but there is an obvious sign that great tribulation is coming. When this abomination occurs, Jesus' disciples should flee from the city. But the only sign of the coming of the Son of Man is His coming.

How could there not be a sign of Christ's return if the abomination of desolation precedes the return of Christ by three and a half years? Would not the abomination of desolation make it relatively easy to predict the time of Jesus' return, perhaps even to the day? How can Jesus affirm both a timeline that includes three major events, a covenant at the beginning, an abomination of desolation in the middle, and the return of Christ at the end of the week, and still claim that the time of His return will be sudden, unexpected, without signs, and without warning?

One possible solution is an event prior to the tribulation, which *is* the second coming but is not the entire second coming. If the rapture of the church, in which the saints are removed from the earth, occurs prior to the tribulation, then the pattern that is established in biblical theology is preserved. When judgment comes to the earth, the wicked are taken and the righteous are left. In this event, the pretribulation rapture, the righteous are "left" by being removed from the earth. They are not the focus of divine wrath, so God removes them before the judgment of the day of the Lord is poured out on the wicked. If the rapture happens prior to the covenant of peace and the abomination of desolation, and the rapture could happen at any time, then there are no signs prior to the coming of Christ.

In short, the rapture is the first stage or phase of the second coming. The rapture and second coming are not two separate events.[33] They are two stages of one event.[34] The first stage of the second coming, the rapture, occurs without warning and without signs. The second stage occurs seven years later.[35] One event in two stages preserves both the doctrine of imminency and the chronology of events seen in the Olivet Discourse. The day of the Lord will be bookended by the two stages of the return of Christ. In other words, the day of the Lord begins after the rapture and concludes with the physical return of Christ to the earth to establish the eternal kingdom.

This pattern of two stages continues into the culmination of the work of redemption. The eternal eschatological kingdom also comes in two stages: the millennial stage and then the new heaven and new earth. The millennium and eternity are not two different kingdoms; they are intimately and organically connected. When Christ returns to establish the kingdom, He reigns over the earth from Jerusalem for 1,000 years, and then He continues to reign over the new earth from the heavenly city, which comes down to the earth from heaven (Rev. 22).[36]

The apostles advance our understanding of the relationship between the day of the Lord and the events that precede and follow it. We turn now to the teaching of Paul, Peter, and John.

THE DAY OF THE LORD IN APOSTOLIC TEACHING

The Day of the Lord in Paul's Writings

The central texts for Paul's view of the day of the Lord are his two letters to the Thessalonians. In the first, Paul writes to clarify the relationship between the resurrection of the dead and the glorification of living believers at the return of Christ. He does not assert that believers should not grieve, but that they should grieve well, in hope: "We do not want you to be uninformed . . . about those who are asleep, so that you will not grieve as the rest who have no hope" (1 Thess. 4:13).[37] He reminds these believers of our hope that Jesus will bring with Him those who have died in Him (4:14).[38] He insists that "by the word of the Lord," we know that the living saints will not "precede those who have fallen asleep" (4:15).[39] He concludes, "For the Lord Himself will descend from heaven with a shout, with the voice of the archangel and with the trumpet of God, and the dead in Christ will rise first. Then we who are alive and remain will be caught up together with them in the clouds to meet the Lord in the air, and so we shall always be with the Lord" (4:16–17).[40] This promise of resurrection and glorification sets the context for what Paul writes about the day of the Lord.

In the next chapter, the apostle reminds the believers of what they know about the "times and the epochs," that "the day of the Lord will come just like a thief in the night" (5:1–2). The echoes of Matthew 24:43 are clear. In Jesus' usage of the thief imagery, it is the imminency of His return that is in view. Paul, on the other hand, refers to the imminency of the day of the Lord. The day of the Lord is a time of judgment and it comes suddenly and without warning. Since the day of the Lord precedes the return of Christ, there must be an event that precedes the tribulation in order to preserve the imminency of Christ's return.

Thus, the first stage of the return (the rapture) precedes the day of the Lord. The intertextual link for this association is the thief metaphor. As Paul continues, another image for suddenness and surprise is linked to judgment and destruction: "While they are saying, 'Peace and safety!' then destruction will come upon them suddenly like labor pains upon a woman with child, and they will not escape" (1 Thess. 5:3; cf. Isa. 13:8). The language of destruction is what one would expect from the day of the Lord and the language of suddenness is what one would expect of imminency.

A contrast then is made between "them" (on whom the judgment will fall) and "you," the "brethren."[41] Paul writes, "But you, brethren, are not in darkness, that the day would overtake you like a thief; for you are all sons of light and sons of day" (5:4–5). The day of the Lord is a day of judgment on God's enemies, those who walk in darkness. The righteous, children of light, are not God's enemies and thus will not be the recipients of this judgment.

Later, Paul writes, "For God has not destined us for wrath, but for obtaining salvation through our Lord Jesus Christ" (5:9). This is surely not a promise that believers will never suffer, never face persecution, never experience divine judgment, never endure hardships, never undergo tribulation, and never be oppressed. The Scriptures are replete with promises that the church will suffer (e.g., Matt. 24:9; John 16:33; 2 Tim. 3:12; 1 Pet. 4:12–19). But in this context, the reference to the day of the Lord seems to limit the "wrath of God" to that which is poured out on God's enemies, not on His friends. And the children of light are promised relief from it. In this setting, "Therefore encourage one another and build up one another, just as you also are doing" (1 Thess. 5:11), would not be rooted in the rapture but in the promise that the wrath of God would not be poured out on the righteous.[42]

Paul makes a clear distinction here between "them," on whom the judgment would come, and "you" and "we," who are promised deliverance. This is expected since in the eschatological judgment there is a distinction between the treatment of the wicked and the righteous. Further, Paul elsewhere emphasizes the distinction between darkness and light (Eph. 5:6–13; cf. Matt. 5:14).

The rapture is the means by which the righteous will be protected from the judgment that God pours out on the earth. In the parable of the tares and the wheat in Matthew 13:24–30, the slaves of the landowner are warned not to try to separate the tares from the wheat, "for while you are gathering up the tares, you may uproot the wheat with them" (Matt. 13:29). Instead, "Allow both to grow together until the harvest" and the reapers will separate them (13:30). In His interpretation, Jesus explains that the "Son of Man will send forth His angels, and they will gather out of His kingdom all stumbling blocks, and those who commit lawlessness, and will throw them into the furnace of fire; in that place there will be weeping and gnashing of teeth" (13:41–42). Jesus promises that the wicked will be taken in judgment and the righteous will be left behind to go into the kingdom: "Then the righteous will shine forth as the sun in the kingdom of their Father" (13:43).[43]

In the Olivet Discourse similar language is used. Jesus compares the coming of the Son of Man to the days of Noah: "For as in those days before the flood they were eating and drinking, marrying and giving in marriage, until the day that Noah entered the ark, and they did not understand until the flood came and took them all away . . . " (Matt. 24:38–39). In the judgment of the flood, it is the wicked who were taken and the righteous, who were protected in the ark, who were left behind. Jesus also describes two men in a field and two women at a mill, one will be taken in judgment and the other left behind.

Yet, there are significant differences between the teaching of Jesus in Matthew 13 and 24 and the teaching of Paul in 1 Thessalonians 4–5. In Matthew 13, the day of judgment seems to be final and complete.[44] Similarly in Matthew 24:37–38, the parallel to the flood implies the final judgment. In both cases, there is a cataclysmic judgment followed by the separation of the wicked from the righteous; the wicked are taken and the righteous are left behind. The tone of these texts is ominous, quite consistent with the expectation of judgment and destruction in the day of the Lord.

On the other hand, in the first Thessalonian letter, Paul's message is one of comfort and encouragement (1 Thess. 4:13, 18; 5:11). The subject is resurrection and the focus is the order or the timing of the resurrection of the dead and the glorification of the righteous (4:13–17). Paul explains that the dead are raised and those who are alive are "caught up together with them in the clouds to meet the Lord in the air" (4:17). Paul does not say what happens next; his focus is on the order in which the righteous, dead and the living, are delivered from the "day of the Lord" (5:2). There is no mention of the wicked at all, so the assumption is that they are left behind when the righteous are caught up. Thus, it appears that Paul does not have in mind the same event that Jesus does.[45] Since both the appearance of the Son of Man and the day of the Lord come as a thief (Matt. 24:43; 1 Thess. 5:2), there must be a coming of the Son of Man before the day of the Lord. This is the rapture, the first stage of the second coming, and it precedes the coming of judgment in the day of the Lord.

Blaising summarizes Paul's teaching in 1 Thessalonians 4–5 this way:

> Paul referred to the day of the Lord as informed by Jesus' teaching in the Olivet Discourse, a day of the Lord that is structured as Daniel's seventieth week (Dan. 9:24–27). This day of the Lord will commence suddenly, like labor pains. No one knows when it will begin, but it will result in wrath for unbelievers and salvation for believers, with the dead believers being raised and the living believers caught up together with them to be with Christ.[46]

The means by which the living believers will be saved is the rapture; they will be taken prior to the day of the Lord.[47] The rapture is the first stage of Christ's second coming.

In his second letter to the Thessalonians, Paul corrects a misunderstanding of "the coming of the Lord Jesus Christ and our gathering together to Him" (2 Thess. 2:1). This is the same issue he had addressed in 1 Thessalonians 4–5, the order of resurrection and glorification at the coming of Christ.[48] Apparently some "spirit or a message or a letter" had come to the church with the claim that "the day of the Lord has come" (2:2). Paul warns them about deception and insists that the day of the Lord cannot come "unless the apostasy comes first, and the man of lawlessness is revealed, the son of destruction" (2:3).

Paul's description of the man of lawlessness "who opposes and exalts himself above every so-called god or object of worship, so that he takes his seat in the temple of God, displaying himself as being God" (2:4) appears to be rooted in the language of the little horn of Daniel 7:8–14; 8:9–14; and 9:27.[49] This coming blasphemous one will make a covenant of peace with Israel at the beginning of Daniel's Seventieth Week and be the cause of the abomination of desolation at the midpoint of the week (Dan. 9:27; cf. Matt. 24:15). Thus, if the day of the Lord is the tribulation period (Dan. 9:27), then the day of the Lord cannot have started, or at least cannot be too well underway, without the identity of this blasphemer being widely known.[50] The destiny of this lawless one is clear: he will be killed "with the breath of His [the Lord's] mouth and . . . by the appearance of His coming" (2 Thess. 2:8; cf. Dan. 7:11; 9:27).

Paul does not say anything about the rapture here, explicitly or implicitly.[51] Had he done so, there would be little need for this essay, or for this book. Moo argues that this silence is a compelling argument against pretribulationism:

What is crucial to notice in Paul's response to the Thessalonians' unrest is that he does not say anything about the rapture as a necessary antecedent to the day. If the Thessalonians were to be raptured before the day, we would expect Paul to say something like, "You know that your present sufferings cannot represent the final tribulation, because you will be taken to heaven before then."[52]

Of course, we might have expected Paul to say this and we might even have wished that he did. But he did not. Moo's argument from silence is not compelling. One might just as well say that the reason Paul did not mention the rapture in 2 Thessalonians is because he had already done so in the previous letter. Then in 2 Thessalonians, he provides a second argument for an event that precedes the day of the Lord, an event that comes before the revelation of the man of lawlessness.[53] Since the day cannot begin until the man of lawlessness is revealed, the Thessalonians cannot be in the day of the Lord.

The Day of the Lord in Peter's Writings

In his second letter, Peter identifies and rebukes those who mock the promise of Christ's return (2 Pet. 3:3–4). These people are intentionally ignorant of the words of the prophets and of the Lord Jesus Christ. They insist that things will remain the same as they have always been, ever since the days of creation— that there will be no change. But they forget that things have not always stayed the same. They "deliberately overlook this fact, that the heavens existed long ago, and the earth was formed out of water and through water by the word of God, and that by means of these the world that then existed was deluged with water and perished. But by the same word the heavens and earth that now exist are stored up for fire, being kept until the day of judgment and destruction of the ungodly" (3:5–7 ESV). These "mockers" (3:3; "scoffers" ESV) are ignorant by their own choice, by their deliberate rebellion.[54] Thus, they are culpable for what they know and deliberately reject. Their deliberate ignorance is inexcusable, and it heightens their condemnation. Peter's language here is very similar to Paul's argument about rebellion and God's judgment in Romans 1:18–2:2.[55]

According to Peter, God had judged the earth by water in the past. The present heavens and earth will also be judged, but by fire. The purpose for this is the "destruction of ungodly men" (3:7). This day of judgment is directed toward the unrighteous, not the righteous. Further, that God has delayed sending judgment on the wicked is a sign of His mercy and patience toward the righteous, because He is "patient toward you, not wishing for any to perish but for all to come to repentance" (3:9). [56]

Then Peter writes, "But the day of the Lord will come like a thief, in which the heavens will pass away with a roar and the elements will be destroyed with intense heat, and the earth and its works will be burned up" (v. 10). [57] The day of the Lord is the day of judgment; it is directed toward the ungodly, not the godly. This is consistent with Paul's argument in 2 Thessalonians 2. The day of judgment comes like a thief, which is consistent with Paul's argument in 1 Thessalonians 4 and Jesus' in the Olivet Discourse. But Peter seems to be referring to the final day of reckoning (cf. Rev. 21:1; "the first heaven and earth had passed away"), not the tribulation period. Some dispensational premillennialists have thus understood the day of the Lord to cover the period from the tribulation through the judgment at the end of the millennium. [58] If the day of the Lord is the tribulation period, Daniel's Seventieth Week, how does it relate to this final and ultimate judgment?

If "the day of the Lord" is a period of judgment on God's enemies, then this last and greatest day of judgment would surely deserve to be called such. Blaising shows the intertextual link between Peter's language and Malachi 3, as well as the book of Isaiah (1:21–31; 2:1–4, 19–21; 4:2–6; 66:15–24). [59] The day of the Lord is an extended narrative of judgment, culminating in this final conflagration before the new heaven and new earth. Blaising concludes: "A fire is coming. It is the glory of the Lord Himself who will return to renew His creation and bring His kingdom into fulfillment. It will unfold as a day of trouble for the present order of things as the old separates like dross from the new that will share in His glory. There is no escaping this fire." [60]

As Peter makes clear, this fire of judgment is directed toward the wicked. In particular, it is poured out on the mockers or scoffers who rebel against what they know about God and His promises. In short, the tribulation as the day of the Lord is not the end of God's judgment. A final day of reckoning will occur at the end of the millennium, before the new heavens and the new earth. This judgment on the wicked will strike suddenly and unexpectedly, like the other manifestations of divine wrath.

In this judgment, there will be a clear demarcation between light and darkness, between the righteous and the unrighteous. The enemies of the Messiah will have "surrounded the camp of the saints and the beloved city, and fire [will come] down from heaven and [devour] them" (Rev. 20:9). Blaising describes what Peter predicts this way: "He was speaking of the coming of the Day of the Lord as a movement from the heavens, through the heavenly bodies, to the earth. And this movement is that of a refining fire descending from the heavens, refining the cosmos as it descends, finally bringing that refinement to the earth and the works done on it. The result is a 'new heavens and new earth in which righteousness dwells' (2 Peter 3:13)."[61]

In short, as the rapture and second coming are one event in two stages, so too the day of the Lord is one event in two stages; stage one is the tribulation and the final stage is the climactic judgment of the wicked. The first stage of the day of the Lord is preceded by the rapture and followed by the second coming. The final stage is preceded by the millennium and followed by the eternal new earth.

The Day of the Lord in the Apocalypse

In the final book in the canon of Scripture, John receives "the Revelation of Jesus Christ, which God gave Him to show to His bond-servants, the things which must soon take place" (Rev. 1:1). When John meets Jesus in this vision, Jesus tells him, "Therefore write the things which you have seen, and the things which are, and the things which will take place after these things" (Rev. 1:19).[62] What follows are letters to the seven churches of Asia Minor (Rev. 2–3), a glimpse into heaven (Rev. 4–5), and then the opening of the book with seven seals (Rev. 6–19). The vision ends with the millennium, final judgment, and the new heaven and new earth (Rev. 20–22).

Christians differ in their interpretive approach to this book. Four traditional views have been identified: historicist, preterist, idealist, and futurist.[63] Dispensationalists, because they are premillennial, interpret the book as describing events in the future. Harris summarizes: "The divine judgments described in 6–16 are future events which immediately precede the second coming of Christ. Interpreters of Revelation have often noted a connection between the events related in these chapters and the last seven years of Israel's history prophesied in Daniel 9:27 (the 'seventieth week')."[64]

The imagery and the language used in Revelation 6–18 seem clearly rooted in the Old Testament idea of the day of the Lord. When the seals are opened, and judgment is unleashed on the earth, the inhabitants of the earth hide from the Lord: "Then the kings of the earth and the great men and the commanders and the rich and the strong and every slave and free man hid themselves in the caves and among the rocks of the mountains; and they said to the mountains and to the rocks, 'Fall on us and hide us from the presence of Him who sits on the throne, and from the wrath of the Lamb; for the great day of their wrath has come, and who is able to stand?'" (Rev. 6:15–17; cf. Isa. 2:19). Thomas explains, "The words from earth's unrepentant population, terrified by the cataclysmic upheavals of the sixth-seal judgment, recognize the outpouring of God's wrath in the happenings they are witnessing. They go even further in their identification of the events as part of 'the great day of their wrath' (6:17), none other than 'the day of the LORD' spoken of so frequently in the Old Testament as concomitant of the Messiah's coming in judgment."[65]

This day of the Lord ends with the second advent of the Lord. When He comes, the Beast and False Prophet are thrown into the lake of fire and the wicked are killed by "the sword which came from the mouth of Him who sat on the horse" (Rev. 19:21). Thus, the wicked are taken in judgment and the righteous are left to enter into the millennium (20:1–6).[66] When the millennium comes to an end, with the devil leading a rebellion against the Messiah, the fire of God's judgment destroys him and his followers (20:10). The wicked are not annihilated; they are resurrected and appear before the great white throne (20:11–15).

This is the final and ultimate manifestation of the day of the Lord, for in the new heaven and the new earth, there will "no longer be any curse" (22:3) for sin and all of its effects had been removed; "the first things have passed away" (21:4). All things have been made new.

CONCLUSION

The day of the Lord is a time of judgment. It is directed toward the unrighteous, toward God's enemies. When judgment comes, the wicked are taken from the earth; they are destroyed. Although they are not the focus of the day, the destruction of God's enemies does result in blessing for the righteous. When the wicked are taken, the righteous are left behind to experience the presence and the glory of God in the millennium.

That God has promised a new earth in which He will dwell with the righteous forever implies the removal of the wicked in judgment prior to that kingdom. And that is exactly what God has promised. John records this promise of the resurrected Messiah: "Behold, I am coming quickly, and My reward is with Me, to render to every man according to what he has done. I am the Alpha and the Omega, the first and the last, the beginning and the end" (Rev. 22:12–13). Christ promises a clear distinction between the wicked, who are excluded from the kingdom, and the righteous, who are included. "Blessed are those who wash their robes, so that they may have the right to the tree of life, and may enter by the gates into the city. Outside are the dogs and the sorcerers and the immoral persons and the murderers and the idolaters, and everyone who loves and practices lying" (22:14–15).

John concludes his Apocalypse with these words, which provide a fitting end to this essay: "He who testifies to these things says, 'Yes, I am coming quickly.' Amen. Come, Lord Jesus. The grace of the Lord Jesus be with all. Amen" (22:20–21).

NOTES

1. For an introduction to this book, see Donald R. Sunukjian, "Amos," BKC, vol. 1, ed. John F. Walvoord and Roy B. Zuck (Wheaton: Victor, 1985), 1425–26.

2. McComiskey and Longman explain: "Prophets such as Amos were called into action when Israel broke the covenant. They threatened God's people with covenantal punishments if they did not repent." Thomas E. McComiskey and Tremper Longman III, "Amos," in *The Expositor's Bible Commentary: Daniel–Malachi,* ed. D. E. Garland, rev. ed., vol. 8 (Grand Rapids: Zondervan, 2008), 356,

3. Richard H. Hiers, "Day of the Lord," in *Anchor Bible Dictionary,* ed. David Noel Freedman (New York: Doubleday, 1992), 2:82.

4. Helen Rhee, "Wealth, Poverty, and Eschatology: Pre-Constantine Christian Social Thought and the Hope for the World to Come," in *Reading Patristic Texts on Social Ethics: Issues and Challenges for Twenty-First-Century Christian Social Thought,* ed. Johan Leemans, Brian J. Matz, and Johan Verstraeten (Washington, DC: Catholic University of America Press, 2011), 68–69. Rhee explains, "'In the Day of the Lord,' God would surely bring his judgment upon the rich who violated the core of God's law and the whole people of Israel (Isa 5:8–9; Amos 5:11–13; Mic 6:13–16). . . . Such prophetic oracles can be juxtaposed with the lament psalms in which may be found the Psalmist's self-identification with the poor and needy (e.g., 40:17; 69:30; 86:1; 88:16; 109:22)."

5. "The term *hoy* ('woe') was used when mourning the dead. . . . The prophet here either engages in role playing and mourns the death of the nation in advance or sarcastically taunts those who hold to this misplaced belief." NET Bible note on Amos 5:18, https://bible.org/netbible/, accessed 28 December 2014.

6. This was a "startling and shocking pronouncement to people who expected a totally different kind of divine inbreaking. Instead of reassurance, Amos offered words of warning that God would indeed intervene, but in a way very different from their assumptions." Joan E. Cook, "The Prophetic Message about the Day of the Lord," *Bible Today* 51 (2013): 14.

7. Later, he says, "The coming judgment of the Lord's day would place Israel in the role of her traditional enemies." Robert B. Chisholm Jr., "A Theology of the Minor Prophets," *A Biblical Theology of the Old Testament,* ed. Roy B. Zuck (Chicago: Moody, 1991), 406.

8. McComiskey and Longman, "Amos," 400. Blaising points out, correctly, that reading "the Twelve [i.e., the twelve minor prophets] canonically leads to a different view of the day of the Lord in Amos, for unlike the imagined audience of historical critical reconstruction, the reader of the Twelve comes to Amos informed that the day of the Lord threatens both Yahweh's people and the nations. Amos's words

would then be seen as a reminder rather than a shocking new revelation." Craig A. Blaising, "The Day of the Lord: Theme and Pattern in Biblical Theology," *BibSac* 169 (January–March 2012): 12. But why would the interpreter need to choose between these two approaches? Surely the readings based on canonical order and the historical context of the writings are not in conflict.

9. Von Rad argues that the context for the imagery of the day of the Lord is Israel's holy war tradition. Gerhard von Rad, "The Origin of the Concept of the Day of Yahweh," *Journal of Semitic Studies* 4 (1959): 97–108. For an alternative view, see Meir Weiss, "The Origin of the 'Day of the Lord'—Reconsidered," *Hebrew Union College Annual* 37 (1966): 29–63. Weiss focuses on the descriptions of light and darkness and argues that the imagery is of divine presence and absence.

10. T. H. Jones, "Day of the Lord," in *New Bible Dictionary*, ed. J. D. Douglas, 2nd ed. (Wheaton: Tyndale, 1962), 269. See also the discussion in Blaising, "The Day of the Lord: Theme and Pattern," 8–10.

11. McComiskey and Longman, "Amos," 400.

12. Richard L. Mayhue, "The Bible's Watchword: Day of the Lord," *The Master's Seminary Journal* 22 (spring 2011): 82, writes, "Blessing is subsequent to, not the reason for DOL [day of the Lord]. Blessing can be (but not always) the end, but DOL judgment is the means." Greg A. King disagrees in "The Day of the Lord in Zephaniah," *BibSac* 152 (January–March 1995): 16: "Some past studies have tended to minimize the blessing or salvific aspect of the day of the Lord and have understood the day simply as the Lord's holy war against His enemies. This is unfortunate because many occurrences of 'the day of the Lord' and related expressions refer to a future time of blessing and salvation." That blessing follows the day does not mean that blessing is part of the day. The day of the Lord is a day of darkness (Amos 5:18).

13. Henry Holloman, *Kregel Dictionary of the Bible and Theology* (Grand Rapids: Kregel, 2005), 99, writes, "This is an era rather than a solar day." King, "The Day of the Lord in Zephaniah," 19, notes that "epoch" or "era" might be a better translation than "day."

14. Walter C. Kaiser Jr., *Toward an Old Testament Theology* (Grand Rapids: Zondervan, 1978), 191.

15. J Danny Hays, J. Scott Duvall, and C. Marvin Pate, *Dictionary of Biblical Prophecy and End Times* (Grand Rapids: Zondervan, 2007), 109.

16. Blaising, "Day of the Lord: Theme and Pattern," 11. He cites both the emphasis of the prophets in the language of the texts as well as "interconnections of the day of the Lord type or pattern to other prophetic oracles of judgment" (12).

17. Ibid., 13.

18. Ibid. Blaising discerns a variety of patterns in these texts. He concludes, "These eight patterns show that the day of the Lord can be referenced in both simple and complex descriptions. Furthermore, these patterns are related so that simple descriptions often appear together with extended narratives" (16–17).

19. Craig A. Blaising, "A Case for the Pretribulation Rapture," *TVR1*, 29.

20. See von Rad, "The Origin of the Concept of the Day of Yahweh," 97–108.

21. Eugene H. Merrill, "A Theology of Ezekiel and Daniel," in *A Biblical Theology of the Old Testament*, ed. Roy B. Zuck (Chicago: Moody, 1991), 373. Merrill observes, "This took place, as is well known, in 586 B.C. and was attended by fire, sword, and exile. The human agent of the wrath of God was Nebuchadnezzar, king of Babylon."

22. Ibid. Elsewhere, Merrill writes, "The message of judgment is summarized by Ezekiel in the strongly apocalyptic language of 'the day of the Lord.' Although not developed here as fully as in the writings of other prophets, the idea of that day as a cataclysmic intervention by the Lord is nonetheless unmistakable. The theme finds most lengthy expression in chapter 7" (374).

23. King, "The Day of the Lord in Zephaniah," 29–31, argues that the day of the Lord includes both "cataclysmic, destructive, overwhelming judgment" and "a time of salvation so thrilling and wonderful that Yahweh Himself will burst into songs of rejoicing (3:17)," 29. It is better to see the salvation as an effect of the judgment of the day, not part of that day.

24. Blaising's summary of the Old Testament usage of the day of the Lord seems accurate: "By means of common motifs, shared imagery, and historical typology, the day of the Lord—whether conceptualized simply, holistically, as a catastrophic judgment event, or visualized in complex narrative fashion as unfolding disaster—emerges as a primary theme in prophetic Scripture." Blaising, "Day of the Lord: Theme and Pattern," 19.

25. "Those who have insight will shine brightly like the brightness of the expanse of heaven, and those who lead the many to righteousness, like the stars forever and ever" (Dan. 12:3).

26. As described in Matthew 24:40–41, I am taking the view that those "left behind" are believers who are left to enter the millennial kingdom, and those "taken" are taken in judgment at the second coming. For an alternate view of those "taken" and those "left behind," see chapter 2, "Jesus and the Rapture: Matthew 24."

27. Daniel also refers to the abomination of desolation in Daniel 11:31 and 12:11. In all three cases, the reference seems to be to something devastating that occurs in the temple, which results in an end to the offering of sacrifices. So, Jesus warns, when this happens people in Jerusalem should flee. In Daniel 9, the abomination of desolation occurs after the sixty-nine weeks, after the Messiah is cut off, and after the covenant in the middle of the Seventieth Week.

28. Jesus' use of the language of Daniel, including the specific reference to that prophet, and the details of the vision of Daniel 9, not to mention the reference to tribulation or distress in Daniel 12:1, is the reason to identify this seven-year period as the tribulation period. See Glenn R. Kreider, "Tribulationism," in *The Routledge Encyclopedia of Protestantism*, ed. Hans Hillerbrand (New York: Routledge, 2004), 4:915.

29. It seems best to take Jesus' statement here at face value, that He does not know the time of His return. This ignorance of the future while being fully omniscient is one of the great mysteries of the incarnation, of the two natures in one person.

30. The judgment in the flood in Noah's day resulted in the death of the wicked ("the flood came and took them all away," Matt. 24:39) and Noah and his family, and the animals on the ark, were left behind. Thus, those who are taken at the coming of the Son of Man would be the wicked, taken in judgment (cf. Matt. 24:40–41).

31. It is surprising to read the discussion by Douglas J. Moo, "Posttribulation Rapture Position," in *Three Views on the Rapture: Pre-, Mid-, or Post-tribulational* (Grand Rapids: Zondervan, 1984, 1996), 207–11. Moo quotes a definition of "imminency" from the *Oxford English Dictionary* to argue against the view that imminency means at "any moment" (207). The idea of imminency must be rooted in the biblical language that the term is intended to summarize, not by looking it up in the English dictionary. Further, the word does mean "likely to occur at any moment; impending" (http://dictionary.reference.com/browse/imminent, accessed December 15, 2014). Moo then goes on to evaluate the "many words used to describe the nearness of the Parousia" (208) rather than the word pictures Jesus uses in Matthew 24. This section also appears, with little change, in the updated version of this book. Douglas J. Moo, "A Case for the Posttribulation Rapture," *TVR1*, 235–39.

32. For further details regarding the NT teaching of imminency, refer to chapter 1, "The Rapture and the Biblical Teaching of Imminency."

33. Dispensationalists have sometimes separated the rapture of the church and the second coming of Christ into two events. For example, see J. Dwight Pentecost, who calls them "two separate programs" that "cannot be unified into one event," in *Things to Come: A Study in Biblical Eschatology* (Grand Rapids: Zondervan, 1958), 206–7.

34. Although he rejects this view, Moo says that a "two-stage coming cannot be ruled out a priori" ("A Case for the Posttribulation Rapture," 195).

35. There might be reason to hope that this period will be shortened. Jesus said, "For the sake of the elect those days shall be cut short" (Matt. 24:22). The elect would be those who will come to faith in the Messiah during the tribulation.

36. My teacher, friend, and former colleague at Dallas Theological Seminary, Stanley D. Toussaint, regularly referred to the millennium as the "front porch to eternity." "BE107 Transcript," accessed December 27, 2014, https://community.dts.edu/mobile/transcript.aspx?course=BE107&unit=1&video=8.

37. As I write this paragraph, my father is in the final days of his life. He breathed his final breath around 9:30 a.m. on 20 December 2014. This text is a great comfort to my sisters and me as we, and the rest of his family and friends, grieve his passing and look forward to the resurrection of the dead. Cancer won this battle, but the resurrected Christ will have the final word.

38. Although it is not clear from this text, it seems likely that OT saints are included in this group of believers who accompany Jesus. For a contrary view, that OT saints will be raised at the second coming and not the rapture, see John F. Walvoord, *Major Bible Prophecies: 37 Crucial Prophecies That Affect You Today* (Grand Rapids: Zondervan, 1991), 385.

39. The "word of the Lord" need not be a saying of Jesus that is found in the Gospels, since there does not seem to be such a teaching found there. Paul seems to be reminding the Thessalonians of what he had taught them. On the diversity of views of this phrase, see F. F. Bruce, *1 &2 Thessalonians*, WBC, vol. 45 (Dallas: Word, 2002), 98–99. Thomas L. Constable, "1 Thessalonians," BKC, vol. 2, ed. John F. Walvoord and Roy B. Zuck (Wheaton: Victor Books, 1985), 704, proposes that Paul had received "direct revelation" of this promise.

40. In verse 18 Paul adds, "Therefore comfort one another with these words." This promise of resurrection, the defeat of death, and being present with the Lord forever is a comfort to believers of all eschatological perspectives. This statement should not be used as an argument for a pretribulation rapture. For a contrary position, see John F. Walvoord, *End Times: Understanding Today's World Events in Bible Prophecy* (Nashville: Nelson, 1998), 36–38, 219. Walvoord surely overstates the case when he writes: "While many prophetic truths are of great importance, the Rapture is the most important for believers in Christ" (38).

41. See the discussion of this contrast in Craig A. Blaising, "The Day of the Lord and the Rapture," *BibSac* 169 (July–September 2012): 263–64.

42. Even Christians who interpret this text differently, who do not believe in a pretribulation rapture, should be encouraged by the hope of resurrection.

43. The language here seems to be an allusion to Daniel 12:3; "And those who have insight will shine brightly like the brightness of the expanse of heaven, and those who lead the many to righteousness, like the stars forever and ever."

44. See the discussion of 1 Peter 3 and the Revelation that follows. The day of the Lord is also one event in two stages.

45. The language of 1 Thessalonians does not fit into the biblical pattern of judgment (the wicked are taken and the righteous are left behind). The rapture is not judgment but deliverance from judgment. In the rapture, the righteous are taken prior to the day of the Lord, at the end of which the wicked are taken and the righteous left behind.

46. Blaising, "The Day of the Lord and the Rapture," 264. Earlier in this essay, Blaising writes, "Both wrath and deliverance are features of the day of the Lord" (264). As argued above, it is better to distinguish deliverance from the day of the Lord or blessing as a result of the day from the events of the day itself. There is no light in a day of darkness, no salvation in a day of judgment, nothing good in the destruction of this day. But God's judgment on His enemies does result in blessing for the righteous.

47. Blaising concludes, "In other words, Paul was teaching a pre- or onset day-of-the-Lord rapture, with the day of the Lord being an extended event, as seen in Daniel's seventieth week. Stated more succinctly, the rapture is pretribulational." "The Day of the Lord and the Rapture," 264–65.

48. Blaising says that the phrase "'our being gathered together to him,' is most certainly a reference to the rapture" (ibid., 265). See chapter 7, "Paul and the Rapture: 2 Thessalonians 2" for further support for this interpretation.

49. Pentecost, *Things to Come*, 332–36. See also Moo, "A Case for the Posttribulation Rapture," *TVR1*, 209, who argues similarly for the identity of this ruler, this blasphemous "little horn."

50. Paul's point seems to be that during the day of the Lord, the tribulation, the identify of this blasphemous ruler will be well known.

51. Some defenders of the pretribulation rapture argue that the "restrainer" in 2 Thessalonians 2:6 is the Holy Spirit and the removal of that which restrains would be the removal of the Holy Spirit from the world in the rapture of the church; e.g., Walvoord, *End Times*, 35. In contrast, Thomas L. Constable takes a more cautious approach: "Paul said the Thessalonians knew what it was, but he did not identify it here. Perhaps he had told them in person. Something or Someone is holding back the culmination of lawlessness. Part of the purpose of this restraint is to keep the man of sin from being revealed prematurely." Constable, "2 Thessalonians," BKC, vol. 2, 218.

52. Moo, "A Case for the Posttribulation Rapture," *TVR1*, 210. See Blaising's response in the same book, "A Pretribulation Response," 251–52.

53. Mayhue, "'The Bible's Watchword: Day of the Lord," 73, observes that if the Thessalonians believed that Paul had taught them a posttribulation rapture, they would have been expected to rejoice that the day of the Lord had begun. That would mean their deliverance is near. So their concern about being in the day would seem to indicate that they did not believe in a posttribulation rapture.

54. In 2 Peter 3:5, the NASB footnote reads: "They are willfully ignorant." These false teachers are deliberately ignorant. They know the truth as it has been taught, but they choose to reject it.

55. See the discussion of "Romans 1–3: Humans Rebel against God's Creation," in Douglas K. Blount, Nathan D. Holsteen, Glenn R. Kreider, and Michael J. Svigel, "How Firm a Foundation: Revelation, Scripture, and the Triune God," *Exploring Christian Theology*, vol. 1, ed. Nathan D. Holsteen and Michael J. Svigel (Minneapolis: Bethany, 2014), 1:33–35.

56. That God is merciful and forgiving is a major theme in the biblical story. God's condescension for the sake of His creatures and for all creation is often overlooked in biblical theology. See my *God with Us: Exploring God's Personal Interactions with His People throughout the Bible* (Phillipsburg, NJ: P&R, 2014).

57. In the same way that the destruction of the earth by water did not result in the annihilation of the earth, the fire of the final destruction will be purifying not consuming. See Glenn R. Kreider, "The Flood Is as Bad as It Gets: Never Again Will God Destroy the Earth," *BibSac* 171 (October–December 2014): 162–77.

58. Pentecost identifies several views and concludes that "the Day of the Lord is that extended period of time beginning with God's dealing with Israel after the rapture at the beginning of the tribulation period and extending through the second advent and the millennial age unto the creation of the new heavens and new earth after the millennium" (*Things to Come*, 231). Walvoord, similarly, declares that the day of the Lord "will include the Tribulation, Christ's second coming, and the Millennium" (*End Times*, 150). Since the day of the Lord is a day of judgment, it is hard to see how the millennium could be included in that period. Mayhue, "The Bible's Watchword," 75, critiques Walvoord's view when he writes, "There is minimal biblical evidence to warrant extending DOL [day of the Lord] into the millennium. Because DOL is chiefly a time of judgment, the Millennium is *not* a part of DOL."

59. Craig A. Blaising, "The Day of the Lord Will Come: An Exposition of 2 Peter 3:1–18," *BibSac* 169 (October–December 2012): 399.

60. Ibid., 401.

61. Ibid., 399.

62. John F. Walvoord observes, "This appears to be the divine outline of Revelation," Walvoord, "Revelation," BKC, vol. 2, 931. See also Robert Thomas, "A Classical Dispensationalist View of Revelation," in *Four Views on the Book of Revelation*, ed. C. Marvin Pate (Grand Rapids: Zondervan, 1998), 185.

63. C. Marvin Pate, "Introduction to Revelation," in *Four Views on the Book of Revelation*, ed. C. Marvin Pate (Grand Rapids: Zondervan, 1998), 9–34. See also my summary of the history of interpretation of the book in Glenn R. Kreider, *Jonathan Edwards's Interpretation of Revelation 4:1—8:1* (Lanham, MD: University Press of America, 2004), 37–87.

64. W. Hall Harris, "A Theology of John's Writings," in *A Biblical Theology of the New Testament*, ed. Roy B. Zuck (Chicago: Moody, 1994), 238. I believe chapters 17–18 also describe the events prior to the return of Christ (Rev. 19:11–21).

65. Thomas, "A Classical Dispensationalist View of Revelation," 195–96. Although he does see historical allusions to events in John's day in this vision, Pate argues "the ultimate fulfillment of the prophetic events contained in these chapters [6–18] awaits the time of the Parousia." C. Marvin Pate, "A Progressive Dispensationalist View of Revelation," in *Four Views on the Book of Revelation*, 161.

66. Christ's return is premillennial, i.e., He comes back to the earth (Rev. 19) before the millennium (Rev. 20). For an excellent defense of the premillennial view, see Craig A. Blaising, "Premillennialism," in *Three Views on the Millennium and Beyond*, ed. Darrell L. Bock (Grand Rapids: Zondervan, 1999), 157–227.

4

Jesus and the Rapture: John 14

BY GEORGE A. GUNN

In My Father's house are many dwelling places; if it were not so, I would have told you; for I go to prepare a place for you. If I go and prepare a place for you, I will come again and receive you to Myself, that where I am, there you may be also.

JOHN 14:2–3

The promise of John 14:2–3 that Jesus will come again has been understood by many Christians as a promise of the rapture of the church. As such, it is of significant importance to the pretribulation rapture position. However, many nondispensationalists today are seeking to present this promise as noneschatological and, thus, not a promise of the rapture. Their arguments are based both on their understanding of the context of the Upper Room Discourse (John 13–17) and on the specific language used by Jesus in these verses.

In this chapter I will demonstrate the importance of this promise to the pretribulation rapture position. Then I will defend its eschatological interpretation by examining the history of its interpretation, the context of the saying, and the specific language employed by Jesus.

IMPORTANCE OF JOHN 14:1-3
TO THE PRETRIBULATION RAPTURE

The rapture, though alluded to frequently in the New Testament, is really described in detail in only three passages: John 14:1–3; 1 Corinthians 15:51–54;

and 1 Thessalonians 4:13–18. Each of these passages contributes information about the event, and, taken together, we have a fairly complete description of the rapture. However, the information from all three passages is required in order to piece together a complete picture of the rapture. The event takes place in five distinct movements:

1. The Lord Jesus, along with the spirits of those believers who have died during the church age, descends from heaven to earth's atmosphere.
2. The bodies of believers who have died during the church age are resurrected.
3. Believers who are alive at the time of the rapture are changed to receive glorified bodies.
4. Together, resurrected bodies of dead saints and changed living believers are caught up to the Lord in the atmosphere.
5. The assembled company of all believers from the entire church age ac-company the Lord on His journey from the atmosphere to His next venue.

You'll notice that I have worded the fifth movement in such a way that it could fit the description of either a pretribulation rapture, posttribulation rapture, or other rapture-timing options relative to the tribulation. Essentially, anyone who actually believes in a rapture could agree with this five-movement description. What really divides the pretribulational position from the posttribulational po-sition is the question of the "next venue" for the Lord following the rapture. The two positions, with their five movements, are presented in chart 3.

CHART 3

The Five-Step Movement of the Rapture

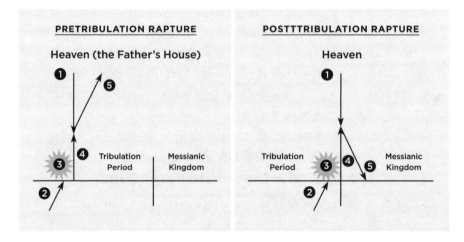

Though we often think of the difference between the pretribulational position and the posttribulational position as being one of *timing*, it might also be conceived as a difference in *venue*, i.e., where do the believer and Jesus go after being caught up into the clouds in the air? Do they go back to heaven or do they go down to earth? Posttribulationist Robert Gundry recognized the importance of venue to the pretribulational position when he stated, "no passage concerning the rapture incorporates a return to heaven."[1] To support his position, Gundry reinterprets John 14:1–3 so as to make it a noneschatological promise. It is because of this issue of venue that John 14:1–3 is so crucial to the pretribulational position.

John 14:1–3 contains specific, detailed, and vital information descriptive of the rapture. The importance of John 14:1–3 for the pretribulational position is further seen in one theologian's statement to a daily Dallas newspaper:

> "I call it [dispensationalism] a theological racket," says Barbara Rossing, an edge in her voice. The Lutheran theologian has little patience for dispensationalism. The basis cited for its concept of the Rapture is just as summarily dealt with. "If you look closely at that passage [1 Thess 4:13–18], Jesus is descending from heaven," Rossing says. "Yes, to be sure, Paul says people will be snatched up in the air to meet Jesus, but *it never says that Jesus turns around, switches direction and goes back up to heaven for seven years*. They have to insert that. They have to make that up because it's not in the text."[2]

Rossing, of course, was restricting her comments solely to 1 Thessalonians 4:13–18 as if that were the only passage dealing with the rapture. If that were the only passage describing the rapture, she would be correct. In fact, with the exception of John 14, no major rapture passage (1 Cor. 15:51–54; Phil. 3:20–21; 1 Thess. 4:13–18) explicitly mentions the return to heaven.[3] Only John 14 specifically describes the return to heaven as the final venue of the rapture event.

Those who hold to a pretribulation rapture tend to agree that John 14:1–3 describes the rapture. Those who do not hold to the pretribulational position generally fall into two broad categories: (1) John 14:1–3 describes the rapture but it is not pretribulational (i.e., it is either posttribulational or occurs in conjunction with either an amillennial or postmillennial second coming); or (2) John 14:1–3 describes a noneschatological coming of Christ (i.e., postresurrection, postascension, or some other "coming" event). If the promise of John 14:1–3 can be shown to be an eschatological coming, I believe the issue of venue forces us to the pretribulational position. The most crucial issues, then, that must be settled are:

1. Is the promise eschatological or noneschatological?[4]
2. What venue is described by the "Father's house" ("mansions," KJV; "dwelling places," NASB, HCSB, NET; "rooms," ESV) and the "place prepared" by Jesus?

Therefore, it is with this reminder of the importance of John 14:1–3 for the pretribulational position, that we focus our attention on this fascinating passage of Scripture.

VARIOUS INTERPRETATIONS OF JOHN 14:1–3

When it comes to John 14:1–3, the challenge confronting the interpreter of Scripture is daunting. In the short span of three verses, differing views by major commentators on the meaning of four different expressions yield no less than seventeen different interpretations! The following is a brief survey of these interpretations.

"Believe . . . Believe," Verse 1

The word "believe" occurs twice in this verse, the form of the original Greek verb being identical for both. Both occurrences could be either a statement of fact, "you believe," or a command, "believe!" This gives the possibility of four different interpretations. Though the differences are noted by most commentaries, they have little bearing on the actual meaning of this verse, at least as it pertains to our discussion of the rapture.

The four interpretations—grammatically—are:

1. *Two Statements.* "You believe in God; you also believe in Me."
2. *Statement Followed by Command.* "You believe in God; believe also in Me."
3. *Command Followed by Statement.* "Believe in God; indeed, you believe in Me."
4. *Two Commands.* "Believe in God; believe also in Me."

My Father's House (oikia), Verse 2

This precise phrase (using the Greek word *oikia* for "house") does not occur elsewhere in John, though a very similar one (using the Greek word *oikos* for "house") occurs one other time in John (2:16), where it is a reference to the temple in Jerusalem. Luke 2:49 is perhaps a similar reference to the temple, but it lacks the word "house" (either *oikos* or *oikia*). Luke 16:27 and Acts 7:20, the only other similar New Testament references, refer to earthly houses of human fathers. This has given rise to at least three interpretations for the phrase, "My Father's house" in John 14:2.

> 5. "My Father's house" describes heaven.[5]
> 6. "My Father's house" describes both heaven and earth.[6]
> 7. "My Father's house" describes the body of Christ as the new temple.[7]

"Dwelling Places" (monai), Verse 2

This Greek noun occurs only one other time in all the New Testament (John 14:23) where it is a reference to Jesus' and the Father's coming to make their dwelling (*monai*) with the believer during the church age. Two interpretations have been given for this noun in verse 2.

> 8. Dwelling places in heaven.[8]
> 9. The believer as God's dwelling place.[9]

"I Will Come Again," Verse 3

Many of the preceding interpretive choices ultimately depend on, or determine, how one interprets this phrase. Because the verb in the original Greek occurs in the present tense ("I am coming"), some have been reluctant to take this as predicting a future event. Others, while admitting that the present tense is "predictive" are unwilling to make it a prediction of a *distant* future event.[10] Thus, at least eight different interpretations have been put forth:[11]

> 10. Christ's return from death at the resurrection and the postresurrection appearances.[12]
> 11. Christ's coming on the day of Pentecost in the Person of the Holy Spirit to bring believers into the body of Christ.[13]
> 12. Christ's coming to the believer at death to receive him to heaven.[14]
> 13. Christ's coming for the church at the pretribulation rapture.[15]
> 14. Christ's coming in power and glory at the posttribulation rapture.[16]
> 15. Christ's coming at the last great judgment.[17]
> 16. Christ's coming to the believer at individual salvation.[18]
> 17. Christ's ever coming into the world and to the church as the risen Lord.[19]

HISTORY OF THE INTERPRETATION OF JOHN 14:1-3

We must exercise caution here. An appeal to the early church fathers is not a sure guide to correct interpretation. The early fathers were clearly wrong on a number of issues (e.g., baptismal regeneration, allegorical hermeneutics, the value of asceticism, etc.).[20] Nevertheless, they were also right on a number of issues, due to the fact that oral transmission of traditional interpretation was still only a generation or two removed from the apostles. At the very least, it would be interesting to see whether the early Christian writers understood John 14:1–3 as being eschatological and the "Father's house" as a reference to heaven.

If the *apostles* had understood the reference to be both eschatological and heavenly, then we would expect the *early fathers* to reflect this understanding. In fact, this is precisely what we do find. At least five ante-Nicene fathers (ca. AD 100–325) make reference to John 14:1–3 in their writings: Papias (ca. 110), Irenaeus (ca. 130–202), Tertullian (ca. 196–212), Origen (ca. 182–251), and Cyprian (d. 258),[21] and they all view it as having a future fulfillment. From the earliest years following the death of the apostle John, through the mid-third century, the promise of John 14:1–3 was seen in terms of a future coming to receive believers to heaven. The ante-Nicene fathers did not think that this promise had been fulfilled either in Christ's own resurrection or in the coming of the Holy Spirit at Pentecost. And since the promise was seen as being fulfilled in connection with the believer's future resurrection, they clearly were not thinking in terms of multiple comings at the individual Christian's death, much less of a spiritual coming at the salvation of each Christian. They were thinking of a future day when all believers will be raised to receive their rewards.[22]

EXEGESIS OF JOHN 14:1-3

The Context

The exegesis of any passage needs to pay close attention to the context. John 14:1–3 is no exception. Those who argue for a noneschatological interpretation of Jesus' promise often point out that matters of eschatology are almost entirely missing from the Upper Room Discourse and are certainly to be found nowhere in the immediate context of our passage. Indeed, John wrote the least eschatological of the four Gospels. Tenney admitted, "I will come back" of verse 3 is "one of the few eschatological allusions in this Gospel."[23] We should therefore raise the question of whether this promise is indeed an eschatological promise.

True, the Upper Room Discourse is not an eschatological discourse *per se* (like the Olivet Discourse or the parables of the kingdom). However, to rule out the possibility of any eschatological reference on this basis is unwarranted. This is not the only place in the gospel of John that an eschatological saying of Jesus occurs in the midst of a noneschatological discourse. See, for example, John 5:25–29; 6:39, 40, 44, 54.[24] A reference in the Upper Room Discourse to His coming back is entirely appropriate to a context dealing with words of comfort given to the disciples He is about to leave. It is true that comfort is offered by means of reference to the coming of the *Paraklete* ("Helper," NASB, ESV; "Advocate," NET), i.e., the Holy Spirit, in John 16:7. But this same *Paraklete* will "comfort" them in part by showing them "what is to come" (16:13). Paul possibly had these words of Christ in mind when he concluded his rapture passage with the statement: "Therefore *comfort* one another with these words" (1 Thess. 4:18).[25]

Two Distinct Contexts

There are two distinct contexts to consider when interpreting this passage: (1) the context of the original saying in the upper room, and (2) the context of the recording of this saying some sixty or more years later.[26] In terms of the recording of the text, we recognize that this discourse was recorded by the apostle John somewhere in the mid- to late nineties to help further his purpose of bringing unbelievers to faith in Jesus (John 20:30–31). On the other hand, when we consider the original saying itself, we have a different time frame and purpose, and thus a different context. We are not only looking at inspired text recorded by the apostle John. We are also looking at the words of Jesus spoken to His disciples for the purpose of giving them the information they will need in order to live a faithful life in the days following His departure from them. Chart 4 displays the differences.

Possibly there was an appropriate eschatological context in the original saying that did not suit John's evangelistic purpose. If so, John would simply have omitted those features that described the eschatological context. Jesus may have had a reason for speaking eschatologically to His disciples, but when John recorded these words for unbelievers, he meant to bring out the evangelistic application. Is there good reason to suppose an original eschatological context? Is there any actual evidence for such a theoretical context? I believe there is such evidence.

CHART 4

The Contexts of John 14:1–3

	THE SPEAKER	THE WRITER
	Original Discourse by Jesus	*Original Writing by John*
TIME FRAME	Early to mid 30s	Mid- to late 90s
AUDIENCE	Disciples	Unbelievers
PURPOSE	Instruction for discipleship	Evangelistic (John 20:31)
CONTEXT	Passover meal and Last Supper	Upper Room Discourse (John 13–16)

Comparing John's gospel with the Synoptic Gospels, we observe some very interesting features. John has the discourse, but the Synoptics do not. On the other hand, the Synoptics have the Lord's Supper, while John does not. We know by comparing certain events of the Upper Room Discourse with the Synoptic Gospel accounts of the Lord's Supper that they occurred at the same time. Edersheim notes, "So far as we can judge, the Institution of the Holy Supper was followed by the Discourse recorded in St. John xiv."[27]

The Lord's Supper itself is an institution that is meaningful for the believer but not necessarily for the unbeliever, and thus was not relevant to John's evangelistic purpose. It seems reasonable, therefore, that John would omit a description of the institution of this ordinance. But it is specifically this "Last Supper context" that provides us with the eschatological setting for Jesus' promise. The Synoptic Gospels inform us that the Supper was instituted with an accompanying eschatological reference when Jesus said, "I will not drink of this fruit of the vine from now on until that day when I drink it new with you in My Father's kingdom" (Matt. 26:29). Furthermore, when we note the progress of the Seder celebration and how it correlates with the discussions in the upper room, we find an additional—and very significant—eschatological setting. Edersheim reconstructs the Last Supper and its correlation with the Upper Room Discourse as shown in chart 5.

If Edersheim is correct in his reconstruction of the events of that night, then John 14 immediately follows the singing of the eschatological Psalm 118. With the refrain of "Blessed is the one who comes in the name of the LORD" (Ps. 118:26) still ringing in the disciples' ears, Jesus comforts their sorrowing hearts with this promise, "I will come again and receive you to Myself . . ." Yes, there is indeed an eschatological context, and the significance of the specific language of Psalm 118:26 will be explored below under the exegesis of verse 3.

CHART 5

Events of the Last Supper and the Upper Room Discourse

PASCHAL SUPPER	UPPER ROOM DISCOURSE
1. The first cup	
2. Head of the company washes his hands	Washing the disciples' feet (13:5-17)
3. Bitter herbs, salt water & karpas	
4. Breaking of the unleavened wafer	(Breaking "the bread" of the Eucharist— Matt. 26:26; Mark 14:22; Luke 22:17; not in John)
5. The second cup is filled	
6. The second cup is elevated three times; Psalms 113 & 114 (beginning of the great hallel) are sung; the cup is drunk	
7. The entire company wash their hands	
8. The "sop" is taken	Prediction of Judas's betrayal (13:18-30) Prediction of Jesus' departure (13:31-35) Prediction of Peter's denial (13:36-38)
9. The third cup is filled	"The cup of blessing" (1 Cor. 10:16) = the Communion cup (Matt. 26:27; Mark 14:23; Luke 22:20; not in John)
10. The fourth cup is filled; Psalms 115-18 are sung	
11.	Discourse of John 14

Chart adapted from Alfred Edersheim, *The Life and Times of Jesus the Messiah*, vol. 2 (New York: Anson D. F. Randolph and Company, 1947), 480–515.

Verse 2

"My Father's House"

Some noneschatological approaches to this passage note that this precise phrase occurs only one other time in the gospel of John (2:16) and is a reference to the temple. Hence, they argue, this reference must be to the new temple, the church (as in Eph. 2:20–22).[28] If John 2:16 were the only other occurrence of the exact same phrase, they would have a point. But John in fact has *not* used precisely the same phrase in 14:2 as he did in 2:16. Instead, he has used a different term for the word "house." John 2:16 uses the masculine noun *oikos*, whereas 14:2 uses the feminine noun *oikia*. Though generally considered as covering the same semantic range, these words originally were "differentiated in meaning."[29] Only the apostle John himself could tell us precisely why he used different words in the two verses. But sound exegesis should inquire into any possible reason for the change of terms, and indeed should caution us against building too much significance on the parallel, when, in fact, different words have been used.

The Greek word *oikos* is the predominant term used in the New Testament, but *oikia* is the predominant term used in John (approximately twice as often as *oikos*).[30] Thus, John's use of *oikos* for the temple in 2:16 appears to be a conscious, definite selection of terminology. This might lead us to suspect that his use of *oikia* in 14:2 is not a reference to temple imagery but rather to heaven as God's abode, i.e., His household as a place where He and His family members abide. The *Theological Dictionary of the New Testament* affirms that the New Testament normally uses *oikos,* not *oikia,* to refer to the temple of God.[31]

It appears, then, that the masculine *oikos* in John 2:16 makes that verse an unsuitable parallel for the feminine *oikia* in 14:2. So, if we should not use John 2:16 as a parallel, how shall we proceed in determining the meaning of the phrase "My Father's house"?

The expression "father's house" actually occurs quite frequently in Scripture, particularly in the Old Testament, and was probably a recognizable phrase with a coherent meaning for first-century Jews. Here we can find some help in determining the meaning of "My Father's house" in John 14:2. Many of these Old Testament occurrences are irrelevant to our context—for example, those that refer to a "father's house" as one's clan or family extended over several generations.

But of particular significance to its use in John 14 are the occurrences where someone either leaves or returns to his father's house. It should be noted that Jesus' coming from heaven and returning to heaven is a significant subtheme of the gospel of John.[32] Thus, if the "Father's house" is a reference to heaven, then Jesus' language here can be seen within the context of this subtheme.

The first of these Old Testament occurrences that have to do with coming from or going to one's father's house is the command to Abraham to leave his father's house (Gen. 12:1). Could there be a parallel between Jesus' use of the phrase "Father's house" and the covenantal command issued to Abraham? Some insight into a first-century understanding of the expression may come from the *Apocalypse of Abraham,* an apocryphal writing usually dated in the first to second century and containing a legendary story of Abraham's conversion from idolatry:

> The story of *Apocalypse of Abraham* begins with Abraham's conversion to the worship of the one God (*Apoc. Abr.* 1–8). While tending to his father's busi-

ness as a carver of idols, Abraham perceives the helplessness of these human artifacts. Stone gods break; wooden gods burn; either may be sunk in the waters of a river or be smashed in a fall. Abraham realizes that rather than being gods to his father, Terah, the idols are his father's creatures. It is Terah who functions as a god in creating the idols. As Abraham ponders the helplessness of his father's idols, he hears the voice of the Mighty One coming to him from heaven and commanding him to leave his father's house. This he does just in time to avoid destruction.[33]

Since Terah himself was, in effect, a false god, Abraham's act of leaving his father's house was an act of faith. Jesus, on the other hand, was the Son of the true God and must return to His Father's house. When Abraham left his father's house—the house of a false god—he remained in the land of his sojourn. But Jesus cannot remain in the land of His sojourn; He must return to His Father's house—the house of the one true God. The noneschatological view of John 14 misses this perspective on the Father's house.

In an example from the Old Testament Scriptures, Rachel leaves her father's house and takes with her the household gods (Gen. 31:30, 34). This indicates that the household of Abraham's father never did forsake its attachment to false worship. Furthermore, Rachel, though leaving in body, remained attached in spirit. Sometime later, God commands Jacob to get rid of these false gods (35:2). Other verses relevant to leaving or returning to one's father's house include the following: Genesis 20:13; 24:7; 28:21; 38:11; 50:22; Leviticus 22:12–13; 1 Samuel 18:1–4; Luke 2:49[34]; 16:27. It seems best, then, to view Jesus' expression, "My Father's house" not as a reference to cultic temple imagery spiritualized as the church but rather as a reference to heaven as the legitimate place of residence for Jesus, a place to which He must return after His sojourn in the world.

"Many Mansions"

The Greek word translated here "mansions" (KJV; "dwelling places," NASB) occurs only twice in the New Testament. The King James translation has given rise to some faulty views. The English "mansion" today generally gives rise to ideas of a spacious and elaborate home. However, the Greek term (*monē*) simply means either "an abode" (without any reference to its size) or "'a place of halt' on a journey, 'an inn.'"[35] The translation "mansion" is from the Vulgate *mansiones*, which in ancient times simply meant "an abode, abiding place." Tyndale first used the English "mansions," following the Vulgate, and he was followed by the

King James and other early English translations.[36]

Some noneschatological approaches to this passage understand these abiding places in terms of the only other New Testament occurrence of the Greek term (*monē*), John 14:23, "If anyone loves Me, he will keep My word; and My Father will love him, and We will come to him and make Our abode [*monē*] with him." Keener states, "The only other place in the New Testament where this term for 'dwelling places' or 'rooms' occurs is in 14:23, where it refers to the believer as God's dwelling place."[37] Therefore, Keener and others understand the dwelling places in 14:2 as being a reference to the many believers who will constitute the habitation for God in the new temple, the church.

Well, what of this? Are we who see an eschatological promise justified in taking *monē* in verse 2 in a different sense than in verse 23? I think we are. At first glance, it may seem like a sound exegetical principle to establish the meaning of *monē* based on its use elsewhere in the same context. However, this is really an overly simplistic view of how language actually works. It is entirely normal for the same word to bear different senses within the same context, even within the same verse. Each occurrence of a word needs to be examined in terms of its usage in the immediate context. For example, in the following totally fictional account, note how the verb "to run" is used a total of five times, with widely different senses:

> I **ran** out of ingredients for the salad, so I decided to make a quick **run** down to the store. While at the store, I left the car engine **running** while I made my purchase, thinking that I would be right out again. However, while I was in the store, I **ran** into my good friend Edward who was **running** for county supervisor.

We have no difficulty distinguishing the different senses of the same word "run" throughout the context of this fictional account. Similarly, when we exegete a scriptural text, we need to examine the sense of each occurrence of a word in terms of its use in the immediate context.

Though verses 2 and 23 occur in the same chapter, John 14, the contexts are quite different. The issue in verse 2 is the disciples' sorrow over Jesus' departure to be with the Father in heaven (see discussion on the expression "I go" below), but the focus changes in verse 15. Verses 15–24 form a distinct unit in the Upper Room Discourse characterized by the believer's love for Jesus as evidenced by the believer's keeping of Jesus' commandments.[38]

One way of seeing this topic shift is by noting that the verb "to love" occurs eight times in verses 15–24, but does not occur once in verses 1–14, and the verb "to keep" occurs four times in verses 15–24, but does not occur once in verses 1–14. At the beginning of this section on loving Jesus and keeping His commandments is the promise that the Holy Spirit would be given to the believer (v. 16). It is by means of the Spirit's indwelling that the believer is: (1) not left as an orphan (v. 18), and (2) empowered to love Jesus and keep His commandments. It is Jesus' sending of the Spirit to indwell believers that makes us understand *monē* ("dwelling place") in verse 23 as located in the believer. On the other hand, in verse 2, the location of the *monē* is fixed by where we understand the "Father's house" to be. Or, as noted by Borchert, "the concept of dwelling is actually focused in two different directions: in the first the disciples are to gain their dwelling in the divine domain, and in the second the persons of the Godhead come to dwell in the disciples."[39]

I have argued above that it is best to see the Father's house as located in heaven. In fact, as Köstenberger notes, the concept of these dwelling places as living quarters attached to the Father's residence in heaven is well suited to the customary imagery of the day:

> In Jesus' day many dwelling units were combined to form an extended household. It was customary for sons to add to their father's house once married, so that the entire estate grew into a large compound centered around a communal courtyard. The image used by Jesus may also have conjured up notions of luxurious Greco-Roman villas, replete with numerous terraces and buildings situated among shady gardens with an abundance of trees and flowing water. Jesus' listeners may have been familiar with this kind of setting from the Herodian palaces in Jerusalem, Tiberias, and Jericho.[40]

Further, as I will argue below, Jesus' statement "I go to prepare a place for you" is best taken as a reference to Jesus' departure from earth at the ascension to begin His activity in heaven. Thus, the *monē* of verse 2 should be seen as a place of abode fixed in heaven where Jesus will one day bring His disciples.

Another erroneous attempt to establish the meaning of *monē* seeks a meaning based on the use of the cognate verb *menō* ("to abide, remain") in John's writings.[41] Standard works on exegesis and hermeneutics caution against such etymologizing.[42] The error here is in trying to define the noun *monē* based on the meaning of the cognate verb *menō*. Though cognates are sometimes related in meaning, this is by no means guaranteed. And when it comes to differentiating nuances of meaning (e.g., "spiritual dwellings" vs. "localized dwellings"), such etymologically based reasoning is tenuous at best, and is certainly not based on sound linguistic principles. The immediate context surrounding John 14:2 calls for a localized sense to the word *monē* as was also true with the expression "the Father's house."

One further note on the sense of *monē* is warranted. Some critics of the pretribulation rapture position have argued that it makes no sense for Jesus to spend two millennia in heaven preparing mansions for believers if those believers will only inhabit these mansions for seven years. This argument is based in part on a misunderstanding of what the term "mansions" represents. Though the term *monē* is capable of bearing a rather wide semantic range of various types of dwelling places, one confirmed sense in classical literature is that of a "stopping-place," a "station,"[43] or even "a hut for watching in a field."[44] Thus, a place for a seven-year stay before the millennium is entirely within the scope of the semantic range for *monē*.[45] If John used *monē* in a sense similar to that found in classical Greek, then he would have Jesus describing the dwelling places in heaven as temporary places of abode where we await Christ's return to earth in power and great glory. Jesus' meaning, then, is simply that there is plenty of room in heaven for all who will believe in Him following His departure from the earth.

"I Go"

What is the intended destination of this departure? At issue here is whether Jesus was referring primarily to His death or to His ascension. Some who express a noneschatological interpretation insist that in the Upper Room Discourse Jesus' departure is a reference to His death by crucifixion.[46] But this seems to be missing the point. Jesus' main point here is not to teach the way to positional righteousness but to show the way of entrance to heaven. To be sure, only those who are positionally justified will find such entrance, but the primary point here is not immediate and personal; rather, it is eschatological and local. To understand Jesus' language of "going" here, it is important to notice that throughout the gospel of John there is a significant subtheme of "coming and going." The general outline of this theme is as follows:

1. In eternity, both Jesus and the Father shared equal glory with each other in heaven (1:1; 8:58; 17:5).

2. At the incarnation, the Father sent Jesus from heaven to the earth to fulfill the Father's will (6:14, 33, 38, 51; 8:14–16, 21–23; 13:3; 16:27–28, 30; 17:8, 18, 23).

3. In the death-resurrection-ascension event, Jesus returns to heaven once again to be glorified in the Father's presence (6:62; 7:33–34; 8:14; 13:1, 3, 33, 36–37; 14:1–7, 12, 28–29; 16:5–7, 28; 17:1, 11, 13, 24).

When John 14:2 is viewed against the backdrop of this prevailing theme, it seems obvious that Jesus was referring not merely to His departure by death, but to His departure from the earth at the ascension and His subsequent arrival in heaven to be glorified once again in the Father's house. If this is so, then His coming cannot be equated with His postresurrection appearances, and His receiving of the disciples to Himself is not a receiving of Christians into the mystical body of Christ but a receiving of Christians to a location apart from the earth—the location where He is being glorified alongside the Father, indeed heaven itself.

"To Prepare"

Sometimes the effort to delocalize the promise takes the form of an argument that shows how an opponent's viewpoint ultimately leads to an absurd conclusion, as when Borchert states, "The Gospel of John is not trying to portray Jesus as being in the construction business of building or renovating rooms. Rather, Jesus was in the business of leading people to God."[47] Well, what *did* Jesus mean when He said that He would prepare a place for the disciples? "To prepare" (*hetoimazō*) does not necessarily mean to build or construct an edifice. The verb is frequently used of making preparations in advance of someone's arrival. Philemon was to prepare a lodging for Paul (Philem. 22). This term was used especially of preparations for a meal (Matt. 22:4; 26:19; Mark 14:16; Luke 17:8; 22:13).[48] In this connection, Neyrey's comment is interesting:

> We may recall how Jesus, the day before (Mark 14:12–16) had sent two of his disciples ahead to secure "a large room upstairs" for the Last Supper. They did not "know the way," but had to follow the owner. Arriving, they found everything "prepared" as Jesus had said. It looks as if here [John 14:2] Jesus has made the disciples' journey of the previous day into a parable of "eternity" in which the upper room foreshadows the home of God with its many habitations.[49]

The idea of God's going before His people to prepare a place of rest for them is not foreign to the Scriptures. In Numbers 10:33, the ark (God's presence) went before the children of Israel to seek out a place of rest for them. In Hebrews 6:20, we are told Jesus, our forerunner, has entered into heaven to serve as our high priest. Thus, the preparations referred to likely include such things as preparing the wedding feast for the bride of the Lamb, and daily intercessory prayers of Christ before the throne of God on behalf of Christians.

"A Place"

Some interpreters who refuse to see this as an eschatological promise of the rapture want to understand the passage in terms of individual salvation.[50] Such attempts to delocalize Jesus' reference to a "place" result in such nonsensical statements as we find in Comfort and Hawley:

> When Jesus said he was going to prepare a place for the disciples in the Father's house, could he not have been suggesting that he himself was that house? Did not the Father live in him and he in the Father? . . . Gundry observed that the many rooms are not "mansions in the sky but spiritual positions in Christ, much as in Pauline theology. . . . Jesus was preparing the way through himself to the Father. The destination is not a place but a Person."[51]

If this were the case, then Jesus' going to prepare a place is merely a "going" to Himself, which is really not a "going" at all, nor is it really to a place! The vocabulary of John 14:1–4 is heavily localized. Note the terms "Father's house," "dwelling places," "a place," "where I am," and "where I am going."[52] Jesus could scarcely have used more specifically localized language. Surely He was referring not to the spiritual sphere of individualized salvation but to a location in heaven where He intended to take His disciples in the great eschatological event we refer to as the rapture.[53]

Verse 3

"I Will Come Again"

One noneschatological approach to this passage understands the coming to be that of Christ to His children at death.[54] This seems unlikely. As Ice has commented, "The Bible never speaks of death as an event in which the Lord comes for a believer; instead, Scripture speaks of Lazarus 'carried away by the angels to Abraham's bosom' (Luke 16:22). In the instance of Stephen the Martyr, he saw 'the heavens opened up and the Son of Man standing at the right hand of God' (Acts 7:56)."[55] Furthermore, the adverb "again" implies that this coming will be a onetime event like the first coming was, not many comings repeated over and over every time a believer dies.[56]

Others have argued that the use of the Greek present tense for "I will come" ("I am coming") suggests a sense of immediacy about this coming, and though it may be a *future* coming, it could not be a *distant* future coming (like 2,000 years).[57] They argue that the present tense fits much better with a coming that was fulfilled either in Christ's postresurrection coming to the disciples, or in His coming at Pentecost in the person of the Holy Spirit.

In the first place, this explanation of the present tense is faulty. The futuristic use of the present does not denote *near* future as opposed to *distant* future. Rather, it presents a future event confidently and vividly without reference to the length of the intervening time. Greek grammarians Blass, DeBrunner, and Funk state that the futuristic use of the present is used "in confident assertions regarding the future."[58] Gromacki puts it this way, "The choice of the present tense rather than the future in a prophetic context probably implies an ever-present possibility of fulfillment, or imminency."[59]

What appears absolutely to rule out both the postresurrection appearances and the coming of the Holy Spirit at Pentecost as fulfillments of Jesus' promise here are two other sayings of Christ. The first is Christ's saying to Peter at the close of the gospel of John, one of the last of the postresurrection appearances. Having just restored Peter to discipleship and predicted his martyrdom (21:15–19), Peter inquires about the future of John. Jesus replies, "If I want him to remain until I come, what is that to you?" (v. 22). The expression "until I come" likewise uses the present tense of the same Greek verb as is used in John 14:3 in reference to a future event. Clearly, this future event cannot be a reference to the postresurrection appearances of Christ, and apparently refers to an event that is future to Peter's martyrdom. This seems to make it clear that the promise of Jesus' coming in the gospel of John refers to a coming well in the future to the day of Pentecost.

Second, approximately sixty years after the crucifixion and resurrection, Jesus still speaks (through a revelation to John) of a future coming, using the exact same present tense verb seven times in the book of Revelation (2:5, 16; 3:11; 16:15; 22:7, 12, 20). In Revelation, with both the resurrection and the coming of the Spirit at Pentecost long past, the promise is clearly *not* referring to a postresurrection appearance or to Pentecost but to an eschatological coming. Since in both the Upper Room Discourse, in Jesus' private words to Peter, and in the book of Revelation, we are dealing with the same author (John) and the same speaker (Jesus), we have good reason to see a parallel between the "I am coming" of John 14:2 with the "I am coming" to Peter and in Revelation.[60]

If we remember that Jesus and the disciples had just finished singing Psalm 118, it would be a reasonable assumption that the present tense ("I come") actually reflects "the one who comes" of Psalm 118:26. Jesus would therefore have been saying something like, "I, the blessed One who is coming in the name of the Lord, will receive you to Myself. . . ." Assuming that "come" refers to Psalm 118:26 also helps to explain the adverb "again" in John 14:3. Psalm 118 ultimately looks to a fulfillment in the day of the Lord and the millennial kingdom.[61] Jesus had come to Israel *offering* the kingdom. The disciples had believed that Jesus was the "coming one," but Jesus had not *delivered* the kingdom. Having come once, Jesus now says that He will come *again*. It is at this next coming that the day of the Lord will be ushered in and the kingdom will surely be set up without further delay.

"Receive You to Myself . . . Where I Am"

Noneschatological views hold that "receive you to Myself" means to receive the believer into the body of Christ. This requires the following sequence:

1. I [Jesus] go to the Father (death, resurrection, ascension)
2. I come again (at salvation or at Pentecost)
3. I receive you unto Myself (Spirit baptism—entrance into the body of Christ)

If this is what Jesus intended, then Jesus receives His followers to a different locale than where He went (He went to heaven, but receives them into the universal church). It also seems to require that the "going away" of verse 4 (*hupagō*, a going to the body of Christ) must be different than the "going away" of verse 2 (*poreuomai*, a going to the Father's house). The change in vocabulary (*poreuomai* to *hupagō*) might appear to justify this change of locus. But an examination of how John uses *hupagō* argues against the position. The most accepted Greek lexicon notes that *hupagō* is used especially of going "home."[62] In the context of John 14, the "home" in view would seem to be the Father's house, and this is borne out by Jesus' earlier usage of *hupagō* in His conversation with the disciples: "Jesus then said, 'I will be with you a little longer, and then I am going [*hupagō*] to him who sent me'" (John 7:33 ESV).[63]

If the "going away" of verse 4 is a going to the Father's house (= heaven), then it must be the same as the "going away" of verse 2, and the change in terms is merely stylistic, not semantic. This being the case, Jesus is promising to take the disciples to the same place where He is departing, viz., the Father's house. Where will He take them? He said He would take them "where I am." Where exactly is that? Brindle answers the question as follows:

> Two clues help answer this question. First, Jesus' double reference to "preparing a place for them" in heaven is irrelevant (even worthless) information if He did not intend to take them there. The foregoing context thus requires the conclusion that He intends to take them to heaven—where He "will be" ([*eimi*] is also a futuristic present here). Second, Jesus then said, "You know the way where I am going" (v. 4). Unless Jesus was being intentionally devious, it must be assumed that He was still speaking of heaven. In fact, following Thomas's question about the way (v. 5), Jesus candidly stated that no one is able to go "to the Father" except through Him (v. 6).[64]

CONCLUSIONS AND IMPLICATIONS

From the earliest period in the history of interpretation, Christians have looked at Jesus' promise in John 14:1–3 as an eschatological promise of Christ's return to take His children to a heavenly home where they would be rewarded. Since the destination points to a venue in heaven, not earth, the promise cannot point to a posttribulation rapture and is most consistent with a pretribulation rapture. In more recent times, however, there have been attempts to "de-eschatologize" this precious promise. If the promise could be shown to be noneschatological, then an important support for the pretribulation rapture would be removed. These noneschatological views have included: Christ's postresurrection appearances, the coming of the Holy Spirit at Pentecost, Christ's coming to the individual believer at salvation, Christ's coming to the individual believer at death, and Christ's coming to the believer at any time of need in answer to prayer.

However, we have shown there are serious problems associated with the various noneschatological views of this promise. The problems with a supposed noneschatological context for the Upper Room Discourse were shown to be irrelevant in light of the clearly eschatological context of the conclusion of the Passover Seder. Also, the specific language of verses 2–3 is entirely consistent with the promise of a pretribulation rapture of the church. So, while some might suggest that the believer has already arrived at the Father's house, our word of encouragement is: No, we're not there yet. Just be patient, we'll be there soon—*"I will come again."*

"Amen. Come, Lord Jesus."

NOTES

1. Robert H. Gundry, *The Church and the Tribulation* (Grand Rapids: Zondervan, 1973), 153.

2. Rick Kennedy, "The End Is Near," *Dallas Observer* (Feb. 9, 2006), page 4. Emphasis mine.

3. By inference, the necessity for the judgment seat of Christ before the marriage supper of the Lamb would seem to require a return to heaven, as would some other arguments based on inference. However, John 14 is the only clear scriptural reference to a specific return to heaven at the rapture.

4. In using the term "eschatological," I am referring to events that are future to our own time. Some theologians hold to a position that has come to be referred to as "realized eschatology" in which the first coming of Jesus is seen as bringing in the eschaton (i.e., the last days), and hence we are presently in eschatological times. I am not using the term "eschatological" in the same sense that a realized eschatology theologian would.

5. Edwin A. Blum, "John," BKC, vol. 2, ed. John F. Walvoord and Roy B. Zuck (Wheaton: Victor Books, 1983), 322. Leon Morris, *The Gospel according to John*, NICNT (Grand Rapids: Eerdmans, 1971), 638.

6. Morris, *John*, 638 n. 5.

7. Philip W. Comfort and Wendell C. Hawley, *Opening the Gospel of John* (Wheaton: Tyndale 1994), 229. See also Craig S. Keener, *The IVP Bible Background Commentary: New Testament* (Downers Grove, IL: InterVarsity, 1993), 298–99.

8. Morris, *John*, 638–39.

9. Keener, *John, IVP Bible Background Commentary*, 298–99.

10. Comfort and Hawley, *John*, 230.

11. B. F. Westcott, *The Gospel according to St. John: Introduction and Notes on the Authorized Version*, ed. B. F. Westcott & A. Westcott (London: J. Murray, 1908), 201.

12. Comfort and Hawley, *John*, 222, 230.

13. Keener, *IVP Bible Background Commentary*, 298–99. See also Frederic Louis Godet, *Commentary on John's Gospel* (Grand Rapids: Kregel, 1978; repr. of 1886 ed.), 830.

14. J. Barton Payne, *The Imminent Appearing of Christ* (Grand Rapids: Eerdmans, 1962), 74. See also Augustus Hopkins Strong, *Systematic Theology* (Bellingham, WA: Logos Research Systems, 2004), 1003; Kenneth Gentry, *The Beast of Revelation* (Tyler, TX: Institute for Christian Economics, 1989), 25–26. This view is also shared by Godet, *John*, 830, and by Grotius, Reuss, Lange, Hengstenberg, and Keil.

15. Blum, "John," BKC, vol. 2, 322.

16. Gundry, *The Church and the Tribulation*, 134. In other places Gundry seems to prefer seeing this as a noneschatological promise.

17. John Calvin, *Calvin's Commentaries*, vol. 12 "John 12–21; Acts 1–13" (Grand Rapids: Zondervan, (2005), 83.

18. Many commentators make reference to this view, but I have been unable to obtain a quote from someone who actually holds the position.

19. Westcott, *John*, 201.

20. Many of the ante-Nicene fathers seem to support a posttribulation rapture. I believe they reasoned, based on their experience, that the imperial Roman persecution they were facing was the eschatological rise of anti-Christian Rome in the tribulation period. Believing they were in the tribulation period, they obviously could not believe in a pretribulation rapture! We might be tempted to think the same thing, were we to have gone through that horrible experience. This is a perfectly good example of the kind of eisegesis that results from interpreting Scripture based on one's experience.

21. See Papias, *Exposition of the Oracles of the Lord*, IV; Irenaeus, *Against Heresies*, Book III, Ch. XIX.3; Tertullia, *On the Resurrection of the Flesh*, XLI and *On Monogamy*, Ch. X; Origen, *Commentary on the Gospel of John*, Tenth Book, 28; Cyprian, Treatise II, *On the Dress of Virgins*. 23. For example, Irenaeus describes the future day of the Christian's resurrection as a day when the believer will be caught up to the mansions in the Father's house in heaven, writing, "As the Head rose from the dead, so also the remaining part of the body—[namely, the body] of every man who is found in life. . . . For there are *many mansions in the Father's house*, inasmuch as there are also many members in the body."

22. References to John 14:1–3 virtually disappear in the writings of the Nicene and post-Nicene fathers (church leaders who lived after the Council of Nicea in AD 325). This is a bit surprising, given the abundance of material in these later writers when compared with the ante-Nicenes. With the rise of Augustinian amillennialism and its optimistic interpretation regarding the present arrival of the kingdom of God, the kind of hope held out in John 14:1–3 apparently ceased to hold relevance.

23. Merrill C. Tenney, "The Gospel of John," *Expositor's Bible Commentary*, ed. J. M. Boice and M. C. Tenney (Grand Rapids: Zondervan, 1981), 143.

24. John T. Carroll et al., *The Return of Jesus in Early Christianity* (Peabody, MA: Hendrickson, 2000), 86–89.

25. Thomas Ice argues convincingly for a tight correspondence between John 14:1–3 and 1 Thessalonians 4:13–18 in "The Rapture and John 14," Pre-Trib Research Center, http://www.pre-trib.org/article-view. php?id=35. The article includes a helpful table illustrating the correspondence of the two Bible passages. Ice also cites the following notable works in support of this position: Renald Showers, *Maranatha: Our Lord Come!* (Bellmawr, NJ: Friends of Israel, 1995), 161–64; J. B. Smith, *A Revelation of Jesus Christ: A Commentary on the Book of Revelation* (Scottdale, PA: Herald Press, 1961), 311–13.

26. Gerald L. Borchert, *John 12–21*, New American Commentary (Nashville: Broadman, 2002), 103.

27. Alfred Edersheim, *The Life and Times of Jesus the Messiah*, vol. 2 (New York: Anson D. F. Randolph, 1947), 513.

28. Keener, *IVP Bible Background Commentary*, 298–99.

29. J. Goetzmann, "*House, Build, Manage, Steward (oikos)*," NIDNTT, ed. Colin Brown (Grand Rapids: Zondervan, 1975), 2:247.

30. *Oikos* occurs 114 times in the New Testament, whereas *oikia* occurs ninety-three times. In John 6 *oikia* occurs five times, and six times in all Johannine literature. In contrast, *oikos* occurs four times in John, one of which (7:53) is textually uncertain, and never again in Johannine literature

31. TDNT, ed. Gerhard Kittel, Geoffrey William Bromiley, and Gerhard Friedrich, vol. 5, electronic ed. (Grand Rapids: Eerdmans, 1967), 121, 132. See also Goetzmann, "House (*oikos*)," NIDNTT, vol. 2, 250.

32. For "coming and going" as a subtheme in the gospel of John, see 1:1; 6:14, 33, 38, 51, 62; 7:33–36; 8:14–16, 21–23, 58; 13:1, 3, 33, 36–37; 14:1–7, 12, 28–29; 16:5–12, 16–18, 27–28, 30; 17:8, 11, 13, 18, 23; 21:22.

33. S. E. Robinson, "Apocalypse of Abraham," ed. S. E. Porter, and C. A. Evans, *Dictionary of New Testament Background* (Downers Grove: InterVarsity, 2000).

34. At the age of twelve, when Jesus was found by His parents at the temple in Jerusalem, He replied, "Did you not know that I had to be in My Father's *house*?" However, "in My Father's house" may not be the

best translation. The term "house" (either *oikos* or *oikia*) is not even used; instead, a plural neuter article ([*tois*] possibly masc.) occurs before *tou patros mou* ("My Father") and may mean something like "about My Father's business," or "among My Father's people."

35. TDNT, vol. 4, 579. Origen took this sense of *monē* to signify "stations or halts in the journey of the soul to God," *De Principiis* II.11.6.

36. Wycliffe used the word "dwellings": "In the hous of my fadir ben many dwellyngis."

37. Keener, *IVP Bible Background Commentary*, 298–99.

38. Borchert, *John 12–21*, 101.

39. Ibid, 106.

40. Andreas J. Köstenberger, *John*, BECNT (Grand Rapids: Baker, 2004), 426.

41. Gundry, *The Church and the Tribulation,* 154–55. Similar is the comment of Gary M. Burge, *John: From Biblical Text to Contemporary Life*, NIV Application Commentary (Grand Rapids: Zondervan, 2000), 390.

42. E.g., Roy B. Zuck, *Basic Bible Interpretation* (Colorado Springs: Chariot Victor, 1991), 100–103; D. A. Carson, *Exegetical Fallacies* (Grand Rapids: Baker, 1996), 26–32; Peter Cotterell and Max Turner, *Linguistics and Biblical Interpretation* (Downers Grove, IL: InterVarsity, 1989), 113–15, 132–33; Grant R. Osborne, *The Hermeneutical Spiral* (Downers Grove, IL: InterVarsity, 1991), 69–71.

43. Henry G. Liddell, Robert Scott, and Henry S. Jones, *A Greek-English Lexicon* (repr., Oxford: Clarendon, 1968), on [*monē*]; Showers, *Maranatha*, 155.

44. NIDNTT, vol. 3, 229.

45. Westcott, *John*, 200. Enns may be correct when he states that "The new Jerusalem is . . . the dwelling place Christ went to prepare (John 14:2)." Paul Enns, *The Moody Handbook of Theology* (Chicago: Moody, 1989), 142, 373. The New Jerusalem is described in Revelation 21:2 as "prepared." However, I suspect that this is improperly mixing the bride metaphor of Revelation 21:2 with the "dwelling-place" metaphor of John 14:2. If the prepared place of John 14:2 is indeed the New Jerusalem, then the *monē* is an individual, permanent dwelling place within that city being prepared for each believer. However, this would require that the city descends from heaven at the beginning of the millennium, rather than at the conclusion of the millennium—a position held by some dispensationalists (e.g., J. Dwight Pentecost, *Things to Come* [Grand Rapids: Zondervan, 1958], 577).

46. James Luther Mays, *Harper's Bible Commentary*, rev. ed. (San Francisco: Harper & Row, 2000), 1978.

47. Borchert, *John 12–21*, 105.

48. BAGD (Chicago: University of Chicago, 1979), 316.

49. Jerome H. Neyrey, *The Gospel of John*, New Cambridge Bible Commentary (New York: Cambridge University Press, 2006), 141.

50. TDNT, vol. 4, 580.

51. Comfort and Hawley, *John*, 230–31. Gundry's statement is as follows: "He is going to prepare for them *spiritual abodes within His own person*. Dwelling in these abiding places they will belong to God's household . . . . the rest of the Upper Room Discourse indicates that [*monē*] and its verbal cognate [*menō*] have to do with a spiritual abode in Christ rather than a material structure in heaven." Gundry, *The Church and the Tribulation*, 154.

52. Brindle follows a similar line of reasoning. Wayne A. Brindle, "Biblical Evidence for the Imminence of the Rapture," *BibSac* 158 (April–June 2001): 140.

53. Walvoord refers to Gundry's reference to "spiritual abodes within His own person" as "spiritualization to an extreme." John F. Walvoord, "Posttribulationism Today, Part VII: Do the Gospels Reveal a Post-tribulational Rapture?" *BibSac* 133 (July–September 1976): 212.

54. See endnote 14.

55. Ice, "The Rapture and John 14," 1–2.

56. Showers, *Maranatha*, 159.

57. Comfort and Hawley, *John*, 230. See similar comments on p. 222.

58. Friedrich Blass, Albert Debrunner, and Robert Walter Funk, *A Greek Grammar of the New Testament and Other Early Christian Literature* (Chicago: University of Chicago Press, 1961), 168.

59. Robert A. Gromacki, "The Imminent Return of Jesus Christ," *Grace Theological Journal* 6 (fall 1965): 18.

60. In addition, it should be remembered that in the upper room, Jesus may have spoken in Aramaic or Hebrew. Neither Aramaic nor Hebrew have a "present tense" per se, only a perfect tense and an imperfect tense. The Greek present would not likely be a translation of an original Aramaic or Hebrew perfect tense. More likely, the Greek present would translate either an original imperfect, which would not have signified any distinction between an immediate future versus a distant future, or a participle, which could have the same implications as the imperfect.

61. This does not necessarily imply a posttribulational rapture. Psalm 118 has in view the entire "day of the Lord" scenario, including both the tribulation period (vv. 10–13) and the millennium (vv. 14–24). His "coming" in this psalm is a coming both to judge (tribulation period) and to deliver (millennium). In John 14, Jesus expands the concept of His "coming" to include a coming for His disciples to bring them to the Father's house, not into the millennial kingdom. In keeping with the mystery character of the rapture, Psalm 118 does not see this particular deliverance, but Jesus reveals it in the context of Psalm 118.

62. BAGD, s.v., [*hypagō*], 1, "esp. *go home* (Epict. 3, 22, 108) Mt 8:13; 19:21; 20:14; Mk 2:9 v. l; 7:29; 10:52."

63. Ibid., s.v., [*hypagō*], 3, "used esp. of Christ and his going to the Father, characteristically of J[ohn].... J[ohn] 7:33; 16:5a, ... 10, 17; ... 13:3; ... 8:14a, ... 21b, 22; 13:33; ... 16:5b."

64. Brindle, "Imminence of the Rapture, 140–41.

5

Paul and the Rapture: 1 Corinthians 15

BY MICHAEL G. VANLANINGHAM

Behold, I tell you a mystery; we will not all sleep, but we will all be changed, in a moment, in the twinkling of an eye, at the last trumpet; for the trumpet will sound, and the dead will be raised imperishable, and we will be changed. For this perishable must put on the imperishable, and this mortal must put on immortality. But when this perishable will have put on the imperishable, and this mortal will have put on immortality, then will come about the saying that is written, "DEATH IS SWALLOWED UP IN VICTORY. . . . Therefore, my beloved brethren, be steadfast, immovable, always abounding in the work of the Lord, knowing that your toil is not in vain in the Lord.

1 CORINTHIANS 15:51–54, 58

The purpose of this book is to make a case for the pretribulation rapture in the New Testament. But it is difficult to do this in 1 Corinthians 15 since there is no clear mention of the tribulation period. If there were, one could determine the chronological relationship of the tribulation to the rapture and argue in favor of a particular view.

Without mention of the tribulation period, it is nearly impossible to establish in 1 Corinthians 15 where the resurrection takes place in relation to the tribulation. One would need to start first at 1 Thessalonians 4–5, and then harmonize the pretribulation rapture and resurrection described there with the resurrection of believers described in 1 Corinthians 15.[1] Because the text we are dealing with here does not mention the tribulation specifically, my primary purpose in dealing with it is to argue for the common premillennial understanding of the passage.

1 CORINTHIANS 15:23–28

But each in his own order: Christ the first fruits, after that those who are Christ's at His coming, then comes the end, when He hands over the kingdom to the God and Father, when He has abolished all rule and all authority and power. For He must reign until He has put all His enemies under His feet. The last enemy that will be abolished is death. For HE HAS PUT ALL THINGS IN SUBJECTION UNDER HIS FEET. But when He says, "All things are put in subjection," it is evident that He is excepted who put all things in subjection to Him. When all things are subjected to Him, then the Son Himself also will be subjected to the One who subjected all things to Him, so that God may be all in all. (vv. 23–28)

The typical nondispensational and nonpremillennial understanding approaches the features of the above paragraph of 1 Corinthians 15 in the following ways.[2] First, there is no time gap that exists between 15:23 and 15:24.[3] If there is no lapse of time, then the resurrection of believers takes place at the same time as "the end" and there is neither room nor necessity for an earthly millennial kingdom.[4] An earthly reign of Christ after the second coming is the typical premillennial and dispensational view.

Second, "the end" will not occur until after Jesus abolishes His opposition prior to His return. This end includes the destruction of "all rule and all authority and power" (15:24). The overthrow of "death," the last opponent vanquished (15:26), will occur at the time of the second coming when the resurrection will take place. Put differently, the resurrection of believers and Christ's coming is "the end," since death is conquered at their resurrection. There cannot be a subsequent earthly kingdom since Jesus' coming marks the end of history, including the abolishing of death.[5]

Third, many nondispensationalists see the reign of Jesus described in verses 25–28 fulfilled entirely during the church age.[6] In Colossians 2:15, Paul affirms the conquest of rulers and authorities, which was accomplished at the cross. In Romans 8:38, Christ's death renders unbreakable God's love for the believer over principalities (the same word as "rule" in 1 Cor. 15:24) and powers. If this understanding of Jesus' reign is correct, then it precludes the premillennial view that an earthly reign takes place after the second coming during which Christ finally dispatches all enemies.

Fourth, the events presented in the second "when" clause ("when He has abolished all rule and all authority and power") in 15:24 transpire prior to "the end" when Jesus hands over His kingdom to the Father. Christ will not deliver to the Father an unsubdued kingdom. This "handing over" of Jesus' kingdom must include the eradication of all rulers, all authority and power, as well as death.[7] If this is the case, then there is no theological need for an earthly kingdom after the second coming and the resurrection of believers during which a final destruction of all opponents takes place.

Four questions arise in considering the timing of events in this passage of 1 Corinthians 15. Let's consider each.

Is There a Time Gap between 1 Corinthians 15:23 and 15:24?

In response to the first argument above that there is no time gap suggested by "then" in 15:24, it should be pointed out that rarely does this word have a nonsequential, nonchronological concurrent force in the New Testament. The use of "then" in John 13:4–5 indicates some time has elapsed between Jesus girding Himself with a towel and washing the feet of the disciples. How could He wash their feet while at the same moment gird Himself with the towel? In John 19:26–27, Jesus' two statements about Mary's care could not have been spoken at the same moment. How could Jesus have said two statements in the same utterance? One statement followed the other. There was some lapse of time, no matter how short or long it might have been.

Paul's use of "then" in 1 Corinthians 15:5 and 7 are more reasonably understood to suggest an interval as well, an interval between Jesus being seen in His resurrection body by Peter, then by the remaining disciples (v. 6), and then (another interval) between James and all the apostles (v. 7). If Paul meant that Peter and the disciples, or James and the apostles, saw Jesus at the same time, why would Paul have used "then" at all? Why not simply say, "He appeared to Cephas and the twelve" or "to James and all the apostles"?[8] The only other places Paul uses "then" (*eita*) outside of 1 Corinthians 15 are in 1 Timothy 2:13 ("It was Adam who was first created, and *then* Eve") and 1 Timothy 3:10 ("These men must also first be tested; *then* let them serve as deacons"). In both passages, *eita* is better understood in a sequential sense that depicts a temporal pause between the events. If Paul usually uses "then" with such a force, then it's likely that between the resurrection of believers at Christ's coming in 15:23 and "the end" in 15:24 there is a span of time that could accommodate a literal earthly rule of Christ.[9] If the sequential force of "then" is valid, the resurrection "of those who are Christ's at His coming" is not "the end." "The end" is a distinct event that follows this resurrection. Wilber Wallis develops the implications of this when he writes,

> At the point marked by the *tote* ["then"] of verse 28, whenever all things have been subjected to Christ, at that time the Son will subject Himself to the Father. The two events are close enough together to come under the limits of the *tote*, and yet there is a sequence implied. . . . The parallelism would suggest that the *tote* of verse 28 brings together in relatively close sequence not only the events of verse 28, but also the same two parallel events as are discussed in the two *hotan* ["when"] clauses of v. 24.
>
> Therefore, since there is a sequence clearly marked, the *telos* ["end," v. 24] cannot be simultaneous with the Parousia [the second coming of Jesus]. Because the *telos* is preceded by the destruction of enemies, and the destruction of enemies cannot be put before the Parousia, the *telos* must stand beyond the Parousia and judgment.[10]

A nondispensationalist might argue that the brief interval between Jesus girding Himself and then washing the disciples' feet (John 13:4–5), or between His words to Mary and then to the beloved disciple (John 19:26–27), may be the same amount of time (mere moments) between the second coming and rapture, and the end including the undoing of death. But nondispensationalists do not argue this way. They maintain that the second coming and rapture of the church is what makes up "the end," and that the second coming, the rapture, and "the end" are preceded by the subduing of all enemies, including death. Even if they claimed that there is an interlude between the rapture and the end, it is an argument from silence to assert that it is a *brief* interlude. Paul gives no indication of the span of time. But if there is *any* interval, the possibility exists that it is long enough to include an earthly kingdom, just as there clearly is between Jesus' resurrection and that of Christians. And the details of the text seem to support this likelihood.

Is the Total Destruction of Death in 1 Corinthians 15:26 at the Second Coming?

To review, the first nondispensational argument, addressed above, holds that there is no time gap suggested by "then" in 15:24 and thus there is no earthly kingdom.

The second argument used by nonpremillennialists suggests that "the end" (v. 24) occurs immediately after Jesus abolishes His opposition prior to His return. So, the second "when" clause in 15:24 ("when He has abolished all rule and all authority and power") occurs prior to the second coming and the resurrection. The last enemy, "death" (v. 26), is conquered at the same time as the second coming when believers are resurrected. Therefore, this viewpoint also concludes there is no earthly kingdom.

In response, it is understandable why many scholars locate the timing of the total destruction of death (which they consider to be "the end") at the same time as the coming of Jesus and the resurrection of believers. Verses 54–57 appear to describe the apparent finality of death's defeat. A case can be made that Paul is talking about the victory of *believers* over death in 15:22–23, which takes place at the rapture/resurrection described in 15:54–57. Paul does not address the resurrection of unbelievers.

The final destruction of death as an independent event, distinct from the rapture, is Paul's topic in verse 26. Edwards notes rightly, "Death has not, it appears from this [the sequence found in vv. 24–26], been destroyed at the second coming and at the resurrection of those that are Christ's."[11] The final elimination of death is distinct from, and sequentially after, the resurrection of all believers.

If this is at all valid, then there is some parallel between what Paul presents and what one finds in Revelation 20–21. Revelation 20:4–6 presents the resurrection of those who were martyred during the tribulation. Their resurrection precedes the destruction of death at the end of the millennial kingdom in 20:14 and 21:4. In other words, their resurrection does not coincide with the final elimination of death. That apparently comes 1,000 years later. Paul appears to envision a similar situation. Believers conquer death at the rapture because of the work of Jesus (15:23, 54–57). But Paul appears to preserve a distinction between their triumph and the final elimination of death in 15:26. Believers are made alive (15:23) *before* the end when death is destroyed, and 15:51–57 refers to that victory of *Christians* over death rather than the final abolition of death altogether.[12] Paul uses first person plural verbs and pronouns ("*we* [believers] will not all sleep [v. 51] . . . *we* will all be changed" [vv. 51, 52] . . . God "gives *us* the victory" [v. 57]; italics added). These first person plurals suggest that his emphasis is on the victory (resurrection) of believers over death, though not necessarily the final complete purging of death from the universe. So Paul's scenario parallels what John presents in Revelation 20:14 and 21:4.[13]

Is Jesus' Reign in 1 Corinthians 15:25–28 Fulfilled during the Church Age?

In response to the third argument above about Jesus reigning during the present era, there may be a better way to understand the texts than many nondispensationalists propose. The subduing of all rule, authority, power, and death is associated with "the end" (v. 24) when "all things are subjected to Him" (v. 28). This is an event that is more likely to be future than past or present since it is demonstrable that not all things are yet in subjection to Him. This makes it unlikely that the reign of Christ Paul has in mind *in this passage* is being presently discharged. Gordon Fee writes,

> The present passive [the verb translated "will be abolished" in v. 26] is best understood as referring to what takes place at the time of v. 24; that is, it refers to Christ's destroying "every dominion, authority and power." In a sense death, the final enemy to be subdued, is already being destroyed through the resurrection of Christ; but Paul's concern here is with its final destruction, which takes place when Christ's own resurrection as firstfruits culminates in the full harvest of the resurrection of those who are his.[14]

Paul, in this passage, appears to invoke a future reign of Christ, or perhaps better, a future phase of the current reign of Christ, that follows His second coming and lasts until the end when His victory is absolute and universally recognized, all enemies are undone, death is vanquished, and the kingdom is turned over to the Father.[15]

Additionally, one can challenge the understanding of nondispensationalists that the rule of Jesus mentioned in 15:24–25 is exhausted at the cross. Is there no allowance in Paul's thought for the possibility of an as-yet future earthly reign? Harold Hoehner writes,

> There are some who think Ephesians is talking about a realized eschatology whereby the cosmic powers also have been subjected as a consequence of Christ's exaltation. Hence, the destruction of the cosmic powers is not at the

parousia but at the exaltation of Christ. Yet, in 6:12 [where both *archē*, trans-lated "rulers," and *eksousia*, translated "powers" are also used as they are in 1 Cor. 15:24] Paul warns believers of the evil powers that presently war against them and urges them to put on the armor of God, which indicates that the cosmic powers are still active. In reality Christ is at the right hand of the Father and everything has been subjected under his feet, but the full exercise of that power will not be evident until his return. This corresponds to 1 Cor. 15:24–28 where it states that God has subjected everything under Christ's feet and in the end, Christ will subject all enemies and will hand the kingdom over to God the Father. At the present, the manifestation of this control is not always evident to us, for there are many inequities, injustices, disasters, unholy actions, and evidences of outright defiance against Christ and God. However, Christ is ex-ercising control without it being obvious to humankind. . . . Hence he has the right to exercise his control but chooses not to fully exercise it immediately in every instance of violation against God's holy character.[16]

Granting Jesus' victory over all rule, authority, and power at His death and resurrection, there is as yet a component of His reign and authority that awaits a full and final consummation after His coming and that culminates in the end.[17]

When Does the Elimination of All Other Rule Take Place?

There is a different way to understand the fourth point above related to the chronological and logical relationship of the second "when" clause to "the end."[18] Gentry and others argue that the second *when* clause ("when He has abolished all rule . . .") takes place before "the end," so that Jesus is ruling and reigning and subduing His enemies now, to be finalized at His coming. In Gen-try's view, the chronological order would be:

1. He abolishes all rule, all authority, and power (v. 24b)
2. The resurrection of "those who are Christ's" at the second coming when death is abolished (vv. 23c–24a, 26)
3. Then "He hands over the kingdom to the God and Father" (v. 24c)

What seems more likely is that the second "when" clause should be under-stood to denote action that transpires before the first "when" clause, though not before "the end." In this understanding, the chronological order would be:

1. The resurrection (rapture) of "those who are Christ's" (15:23)
2. An unspecified amount of time (indicated by the force of "then") (15:24a)
3. "Then comes the end" (v. 24a) . . .
   - "when He has abolished all rule and all authority and power" (v. 24c)
   - and "when He hands over the kingdom to the God and Father (v. 24b)

One support for the second interpretation is the parallel between the two subordinate clauses. Both utilize "when," and both have subjunctive verbs, though this is the usual construction following "when." (However, a *when* clause need not always take a subjunctive verb; e.g., Mark 3:11.) Also, this is the only New Testament verse with dual *when* clauses. In all other verses that have the action of the "when" clause unfolding before the main part of the sentence, the *when* clause stands alone. Here there is a parallel structure involving two *when* clauses, and this parallel suggests that the temporal relationships they depict should be understood in connection with each other, rather than between the second *when* clause and "the end."

Furthermore, it is possible that if Paul wanted to convey the subduing of all enemies (the second *when* clause) as taking place before the end, he may have put the second *when* clause before the words "then comes the end." Thus, "Christ the first fruits, after that those who are Christ's at His coming, when He has abolished all rule and all authority and power. Then comes the end when He hands over the kingdom to the God and Father." As it stands, the word order does not support the view that the action of the second *when* clause takes place before "the end." "The end" is immediately followed and defined by the first *when* clause, and employs a present-tense verb "hands over," suggesting that this phrase is the more prominent of the two, and that the second *when* clause with its aorist verb adds a slightly background feature to the event.[19] The idea is that the conspicuous aspect of "the end" is when Jesus hands over the kingdom to the Father, and of course this presupposes the abolishing of all opposition.

As noted above, the phrase "when all things are subjected to Him" in verse 28 is the functional parallel to "when He has abolished all rule and all authority and power" in verse 24. "Then the Son Himself also will be subjected to the One who subjected all things to Him, so that God may be all in all" in verse 28 is the functional parallel to "when He hands over the kingdom to the God and Father" in verse 24. This suggests that the second *when* clause might be better understood as happening before the first *when* clause rather than before "the end," and that both clauses describe conditions associated with "the end." This yields the chronological order in this manner:

The end comes . . .

1. when all rule, authority, and power is abolished (v. 24b) = all things subjected to Christ during His reign (vv. 25, 28a)
2. when He delivers the kingdom to the Father (v. 24b) = all things subjected to God (vv. 27–28)

Another clue is found in the "for" that introduces 15:25. It probably introduces an explanation of the second *when* clause in 15:24. Jesus' "reign" (*basileuō*, v. 25) is over a "kingdom" (*basileia*, v. 24) that is in place before "the end." That "reign" continues to "the end," which is characterized by bringing to an end "all rule and all authority and power," that is, "all His enemies" are placed "under His feet" (v. 25), and when this has transpired, He "hands over the kingdom" to the Father.[20] This makes it unlikely that the abolishing of all enemies transpires before the end as nonpremillennialists argue.

Another problem with the fourth argument offered by many nondispensationalists is Paul's use of Psalm 110:1 in 15:25a and Psalm 8:6 in 15:27a. There is a similar usage of the two psalms in Hebrews 1–2 where the writer cites them in the same order as Paul (Ps. 110:1 in Heb. 1:13, and Ps. 8:6 in Heb. 2:8). Wallis notes several parallels between 1 Corinthians 15 and Hebrews 1–2. Both writers present the victory and exaltation of the Son by drawing upon Psalm 110 (1 Cor. 15:25a with Heb. 1:13). Both writers advance and confirm this exaltation by citing Psalm 8:6 (1 Cor. 15:27a with Heb. 2:8). Both cite Psalm 8:6 to emphasize the comprehensiveness of the subjugation of all things to Christ ("All things are put in subjection" in 1 Cor. 15:27 parallels "For in subjecting all things to him, He left nothing that is not subject to him" in Heb. 2:8). In 1 Corinthians 15, the conquest of Jesus is a conquest that comes through death, similar to Hebrews 2:9–15. But regarding what might be the most important parallel for our discussion, Wallis writes,

> There is yet another parallel between the Corinthians passage and Hebrews. In Hebrews 2:8, the corrective "not yet" is introduced. The promise of subjugation is universal, and all things will be put under the Son's feet, but "not yet" do we see the subjugation completed. The perfect participle ["subjected"]. . . looking at both ends of the action, would imply that the subjugation has not been begun

nor has it been completed. Jesus Christ has resumed His place at the Father's right hand, and is waiting until His enemies shall be made His footstool, Hebrews 10:13. Parallel to and identical with the subjugation not yet begun nor accomplished is the subjugation of the world to come mentioned in verse 5, which in turn had its antecedent in the promise of 1:13, "Sit at my right hand, until I make your enemies the footstool of your feet."

Hebrews emphasizes the fact that the subjugation of all things is yet future, though a decisive point in the total redemptive plan has been reached in the suffering and death of the Son. Hebrews calls the situation in the future "the world to come." On the other hand, 1 Corinthians makes it clear that that situation is a time when Christ reigns and overcomes His enemies. 1 Corinthians also makes it clear that the time of reigning and conquest is *prior* to the stupendous eschatological end, . . . and *after* the Parousia.[21]

The futurity of the subjugation of all things to Christ in Hebrews 2:5 (in "the world to come") and 2:8 ("But now we do not yet see all things subjected to him," where "him" actually refers to all of mankind restored through the ministry of Christ) seems to support a premillennial interpretation of 1 Corinthians 15. The reign of Jesus that Paul describes is not the one proposed by nondispensationalists—taking place during the present era with His enemies subdued in the wake of the cross. It awaits a future fulfillment in an earthly kingdom following His second coming.

Finally, in support of the premillennial interpretation of this passage, the concept of an intermediate earthly kingdom is found in the literature of early Judaism[22] so that it is not without warrant to see Revelation 20 and 1 Corinthians 15:23ff. as possibly having such a sense. Craig L. Blomberg writes, "Pictures of the twelve apostles judging the twelve tribes of Israel and reigning with Jesus upon his return to earth or of the establishment of his kingdom (Matt. 19:28; Luke 13:29–30; 22:28–30) arguably fit most naturally with such a millennial kingdom."[23]

Still, the question remains: Why does this matter? Who cares who wins this theological brawl? Actually, a considerable amount is at stake in this dispute, especially as it relates to God's faithfulness. Dispensationalists and some nondispensational premillennialists have long maintained that God's intent has always been to bless the world in both spiritual and material ways through the seed of Abraham, including Israel (see Exod. 19:6; Isa. 43:7; 44:23; 60:7, 13, 21; Ezek. 39:13; Zech. 2:5). God's plan was to radiate His magnificence to the world through His restoration and prospering of the nation (see Lev. 26:43–44; Isa.

11:11–12; 48:9; Jer. 30:3, 10, 11; 31:8; Ezek. 20:33–44; 34:11–16; Amos 9:11–15). Ultimately this restoration of Israel comes through the supreme seed of Abraham, the Messiah, Jesus (see Rom. 11:25–32). But if there is no future earthly kingdom in which this can find fulfillment, God's faithfulness and sovereignty can be called into question.[24]

1 CORINTHIANS 15:50-58

As I mentioned at the beginning of this chapter, it is nearly impossible to argue for any tribulational position from this section of Scripture since there is no clear mention of the tribulation. There are, however, two features of the passage that some scholars explore in order to specify the timing of the rapture. Those features are the last trumpet in 15:52 and the citation of Isaiah 25:8 in 1 Corinthians15:54.[25]

The Last Trumpet (15:52)

In the Old Testament, trumpets functioned to call God's people to observe a holy day and new months (Num. 10:10), to come to a solemn assembly or announce a call to war (Num. 10:2–3; Josh. 6:4–6, 8–9, 13–16, 20; Judg. 3:27–30; 6:34; 7:8–9, 13–16, 20, 22; Neh. 4:19–20), and to announce the day of the Lord (Joel 2:1; Zeph. 1:14–16). A trumpet is found in eschatological contexts in Zechariah 9:14; Isaiah 27:13; Joel 2:15; Revelation 8:2, 6, 13; and in Revelation 11:15, which concludes the seven trumpet judgments.[26] Sometimes it accompanies a theophany as well (Ex. 19:13, 16, 19). Trumpets also signaled the commencement of the Year of Jubilee (Lev. 25:9) and the return of exiles in Isaiah 27:13.[27]

But there is no consensus on the identity of "the last trumpet" in 1 Corinthians 15:52. Gundry defends the common posttribulational view that the last trumpet is the same as the seventh trumpet in Revelation 11:15. He argues that it is doubtful the last trumpet of 1 Corinthians 15 sounds *before* all seven of the tribulation trumpets in Revelation as pretribulationism requires. It must sound *after* the seven trumpets, or actually be the seventh trumpet that sounds. At the conclusion of the tribulation, Christ comes rapturing His people and subduing all His enemies (Rev. 11:15–18) and establishing His kingdom. "We may well equate the 'great trumpet' at the posttribulational advent in Matthew 24:31, the last trumpet in 1 Corinthians 15:52, the trumpet of God in 1 Thessalonians 4:16, and perhaps the seventh trumpet in Revelation 11:15–18 as well."[28]

In response to Gundry, Arnold G. Fruchtenbaum points out that it is unlikely the Corinthians could have understood the last trumpet as the seventh trumpet of Revelation since the book of Revelation had not yet been written at the time the Corinthians received 1 Corinthians from Paul. There is no hint in 1 Corinthians 15, nor in Matthew 24 or 1 Thessalonians 4, of a sequence of trumpets, yet it seems reasonable to think that the Corinthians would have understood what Paul meant when he referred to the *last* trumpet (for the suggestions, see below).[29]

Other posttribulationists approach the last trumpet differently. It is the last trumpet not because it is the last in a series of trumpets but because it ushers in the last day.[30] Trumpets were an aspect of the Old Testament day of the Lord when Israel experiences final salvation and judgment (cf. Isa. 27:13; Joel 2:1; Zeph. 1:16; Zech. 9:14). In Isaiah 27:12–13, the great trumpet is sounded in connection with God's gathering up of Jewish people individually, probably in connection with the gathering of Israel in preparation for entrance into the restored kingdom, an event that is always posttribulational. This is probably also the same trumpet as in Matthew 24:31. Moo writes,

> For when one finds only one reference throughout Jesus' teaching to a trumpet, and it is associated with the gathering of the elect into the kingdom, and further finds Paul making reference to the transformation of saints in preparation for the kingdom when he mentions a trumpet, the parallel can hardly be ignored. But the trumpet sound in Matt. 24:31 is manifestly posttribulational. Thus, while dogmatism is unwarranted, the reference to "the last trumpet" in 1 Corinthians 15:52 would suggest that the "transformation" Paul describes takes place at the time when the Jewish nation experiences its eschatological salvation (Isa. 27:12–13) after the final tribulation (Matt. 24:31).[31]

There is a lack of consensus among posttribulationists regarding the identity of the last trumpet.

In response to Moo's paralleling of the last trumpet in 1 Corinthians 15 with the trumpet in Matthew 24:31, it will suffice here to say that the trumpet sounded in Matthew 24 is not to signal a posttribulational rapture. Instead, the trumpet of Matthew 24 is for the regathering of the Jewish people in natural bodies to their homeland *after* the second coming, not during it as required by posttribulationism.[32] The second coming occurs in Matthew 24:30, but this gathering follows it in 24:31. Elsewhere I have written,

The phrase [in Matt 24:31] **will gather** (*episynago*) is used in the LXX in Ps 105:47 (English translations 106:47) and 146:2 (English translations 147:2) for the regathering of the Jewish people to the Holy Land following God rescuing them (also the point of the sounding of the trumpet in Is 27:13, cited by Matthew in v. 31). In the OT, this regathering was not a "rapture" in which God's people would receive their resurrected, glorified bodies, but appears to be an event experienced in natural bodies in which God gathers them into the millennial kingdom.[33]

There is no consensus among pretribulationists either. Drawing strictly from pretribulationists, the "last trumpet" could be the fulfillment of the Feast of Trumpets,[34] the signal that the church is about to experience a theophany much as Israel did in the Old Testament (see Ex. 19:16) but with eternal duration,[35] the alarm that calls the church to relocate to heaven much as a trumpet called Israel in the wilderness to pack and move, or a trumpet sound of deliverance.[36]

A strong case can also be made for the "last trumpet" referring to a military signal. Paul refers to a trumpet with a military sense in 1 Corinthians 14:8 (the same Greek word for "trumpet" as in 15:52).[37] In a Roman army context, the trumpet could be "used to signal the retreat . . . , to end the battle . . . , to gather the scattered . . . , and for the march back to camp."[38] And although it is used with a variety of meanings, the word "order" in 1 Corinthians 15:23 often has been used in a military context for a squad, a corps, or company of soldiers organized for a particular task.[39] This use, coupled with the repeated uses of "victory" in 15:54, 55, and 57, supports the possibility that the "last trumpet" signals that the war is over and the victory won so that we can come home.

However, it is impossible to be certain, and this view can be harmonized with any of the major views of the timing of the rapture. The trumpet could sound as a signal that the war is over for the church before the tribulation, midway through it, during the tribulation but before the wrath associated with the day of the Lord is poured out (the prewrath view), or at the end of the tribulation when the church is raptured and the second coming has transpired. The two points on which there is greater certainty among pretribulationists is that the last trumpet should probably not be equated either with the trumpet in Matthew 24:31 or with the seventh trumpet of Revelation 11:15, both common posttribulational positions.

The Citation of Isaiah 25:8 in 1 Corinthians 15:54

Paul refers to Isaiah 25:8 in 1 Corinthians 15:54. In its Old Testament context, Isaiah 25:8 says,

> He will swallow up death for all time,
> And the Lord GOD will wipe tears away from all faces,
> And He will remove the reproach of His people from all the earth;
> For the LORD has spoken.

Gundry makes a case for a posttribulational understanding of the rapture based on Paul's use of this verse. He writes,

> A perusal of Isaiah 23–26 reveals that the resurrection spoken of in 25:8 and 26:19 will occur after the tribulational anguish of Israel and the nations (24:1–13, 16b–22; 26:18–19, 20, 21) and the establishment of the Messianic kingdom and conversion of Israel (24:14–16a, 22–25:12). Paul quotes Isaiah 25:8 as fulfilled at the resurrection and translation of the Church (1 Cor. 15:54). If the defeat of death for the Church will fulfill the posttribulational defeat of death prophesied by Isaiah, the translation and rapture will likewise be posttribulational.[40]

However, it is unlikely that Isaiah 25:8 is about a posttribulational rapture. Isaiah 25 appears to address God's victory over death at the end of the earthly kingdom period, not the start of it as required by posttribulationism. This is not unlike what one finds in Revelation 20:11–21:4, and Isaiah 25:8 is cited in Revelation 21:4 as taking place at the conclusion of the millennial kingdom. There is still death in the kingdom period (see Isa. 65:20; Rev. 20:9), and it is done away with in the ultimate sense only at the conclusion of that period, later than the church's victory over death at the rapture.

In other words, the final end of death for the universe as a whole is not just posttribulational, it is postmillennial. In this regard Gundry seems to be mistaken, since he ascribes Isaiah 25 to the time of the second coming after the tribulation.[41] In addition, Isaiah contains a statement of finality that does not seem to square with conditions that exist at the time of the rapture of the church, whenever it is, nor during the bulk of the millennial kingdom. Isaiah 25:8 says God will swallow up death "for all time" (lit., "for the duration").[42] It is intriguing to consider that Paul purposefully shifted "for all time" in Isaiah 25 to "victory" in 1 Corinthians to avoid the idea that death is undone forever at the time of the rapture. If Paul should be harmonized with Revelation 20 and 21, then for him to claim that death is banished forever at the rapture would put him at odds with Revelation 21:4 where it seems that death is banished at the end of the millennium. That contradiction is avoided in his use of "victory."

Finally, Paul is probably applying Isaiah 25:8 to the rapture without invoking every aspect of the Old Testament context. For example, there is a comprehensiveness of God's erasing of death that does not fit with the rapture of the church regardless of when it happens. Isaiah 25:6–8 is emphatic about "all peoples" (vv. 6, 7), "all nations" (v. 7), and "all faces" (v. 8) benefiting from God's action, while Paul appears to apply the rapture only to the church.[43] What this implies is that 1 Corinthians 15:54–57 needs to be harmonized with 15:23–28. They can be harmonized with each other, and with Revelation 20 and 21, by preserving the distinction between the rapture and the subsequent final undoing of death. At the rapture, all "in Christ" will be made alive (15:23) and will have victory over death (15:54–57). This precedes and is distinct from "the end" when death is forever and universally destroyed (1 Cor. 15:26; Rev. 21:4).

In other words, 1 Corinthians 15:23 and 54–57 are about the victory of *Christians* over death at the time of the rapture. But the final destruction of death is later than the rapture (15:24–26; Rev. 21:4),[44] and is better understood as happening at the conclusion of the millennium rather than at the second coming as posttribulationism requires.[45]

CONCLUSION

The evidence of the text of 1 Corinthians 15:23–28 supports a premillennial understanding of the relationship of the second coming of Christ, the resurrection of believers, and the final eradication of all His enemies including death. That evidence includes the observation that "then" in 15:24 requires a lapse of time between the rapture of believers and a later abolishing of death. The reign of Jesus during which this conquest takes place is unlikely to occur during the present era but is an as-yet future dramatic phase of His current reign. The use of Psalms 8 and 110, paralleling that of Hebrews 1–2, supports the idea of the futurity of this reign. These points support the common premillennial understanding of 1 Corinthians 15:23–28.

While it is nearly impossible to argue for any approach to the timing of the rapture in 1 Corinthians 15:50–58 since the tribulation is not mentioned, the posttribulational view is not especially defensible since "the last trumpet" in 15:52 probably cannot be equated either with the trumpet of Matthew 24:31 or with the last of the trumpet judgments in Revelation 11:15–18. Posttribulationism also flounders on the better view of Isaiah 25:8 as indicating a postmillennial timing of the final universal removal of death in keeping with its Old Testament contextual sense and its citation in Revelation 21:4. To be more precise regarding the validity of the pretribulational, midtribulational, and prewrath views is difficult since there is no mention of the tribulation. For greater precision, the reader should consult chapter 6 on 1 Thessalonians 4–5, where there is abundant evidence in favor of a pretribulational rapture.

NOTES

1. I will use the terms *resurrection* and *rapture* interchangeably throughout this chapter. Both terms describe the same phenomena—the raising of dead believers and the change living believers will undergo (cf. 1 Thess. 4:14–17).

2. What is summarized here are common amillennial and postmillennial interpretations of this paragraph. There is a remarkable consensus among premillennialists regarding what it means, regardless of their view of the timing of the rapture.

3. Nondispensationalists often argue that the word "then" used in 15:24 (*eita*, a different word from "after that" in v. 23) is used elsewhere in the New Testament to refer to two events that transpire without any interval of time. See John 13:4–5; 19:26–27; 20:27; Hebrews 12:9. In 1 Corinthians 15:5 and 7, in the immediate context of 15:24, it also indicates no time gap. It is this evidence that leads many to see the synchronized occurrence of the resurrection of "those who are Christ's at His coming" and "the end" without the possibility of an intervening kingdom on earth as claimed by premillennialists. If this view is correct, then the rapture takes place at the same time as Christ's coming at the end of the tribulation. There are some, however, who do allow for a lapse of time implied by "then." See, for example, H. A. A. Kennedy, *St. Paul's Conception of the Last Things* (London: Hodder and Stoughton, 1904), 323, and W. D. Davies, *Paul and Rabbinic Judaism: Some Rabbinic Elements in Pauline Theology* (London: SPCK, 1955), 293.

4. For this view, see Geerhardus Vos, *The Pauline Eschatology* (Grand Rapids: Eerdmans, 1952), 245; Herman Ridderbos, *Paul: An Outline of His Theology* (Grand Rapids: Eerdmans, 1975), 557–58; Murray J. Harris, *Raised Immortal: Resurrection and Immortality in the New Testament* (Basingstoke, UK: Marshal Morgan & Scott, 1983), 180; Joseph A. Fitzmyer, *First Corinthians*, Anchor Yale Bible Commentaries (London: Yale, 2008), 572; Raymond F. Collins, *First Corinthians*, Sacra Pagina (Collegeville, MN: Liturgical Press, 1999), 552; Richard H. Bell, *The Irrevocable Call of God: An Inquiry into Paul's Theology of Israel*, WUZNT, 184 (Tübingen: Mohr Siebeck, 2005), 386–90; C. K. Barrett, *The First Epistle to the Corinthians* (New York: Harper & Row, 1968), 357; Robert B. Strimple, "Amillennialism," in *Three Views on the Millennium and Beyond*, ed. Darrell L. Bock (Grand Rapids: Zondervan, 1999), 111.

5. For this common view, see Kenneth L. Gentry Jr., "Postmillennialism," in *Three Views on the Millennium and Beyond*, ed. Darrell L. Bock (Grand Rapids: Zondervan, 1999), 48–49; Harris, *Raised Immortal*, 180; Heikki Räisänen, "Did Paul Expect an Earthly Kingdom?" in *Paul, Luke and the Graeco-Roman World: Essays in Honour of Alexander J. M. Wedderburn*, JSNTSS, 217, ed. Alf Christophersen, Carsten Claussen, Jörg Frey, and Bruce Longenecker (Sheffield: Sheffield, 2002), 10–11; Strimple, "Amillennialism," 111.

6. The words Paul uses in 1 Corinthians 15:24 for "rule" (*archē*), "authority" (*exousia*), and "power" (*dynamis*) are used together also in Ephesians. 1:21. Elsewhere he uses together "rule" and "authority" (Eph. 3:10; 6:12; Col. 1:16; 2:10, 15; Titus 3:1), and in Romans 8:38 he connects *archē* (translated "principalities" there by the NASB) with *dynamis* ("powers"). In all but Titus 3:1, these words most likely refer to demonic structures rather than human political ones.

7. This is the view of Gentry, "Postmillennialism," 49; Fitzmyer, *First Corinthians*, 572; Frederic Louis Godet, *Commentary on First Corinthians* (Edinburgh: T & T Clark, 1889; repr., Grand Rapids: Kregel, 1977), 787–88; Archibald Robertson and Alfred Plummer, *A Critical and Exegetical Commentary on the First Epistle of St. Paul to the Corinthians*, ICC (Edinburgh: T & T Clark, 1978), 355.

8. In addition, there is a manuscript problem in 15:5 and 7 not easily reproduced in English. "Then" (*eita*) is used in 15:24. It is found in 15:5 also. But some manuscripts replaced *eita* in verse 5 with a different word, *epeita*. *Epeita* occurs in 15:23 where it is translated by the NASB as "after that," and in verse 23 it denotes a time gap between Christ's resurrection and that of believers. What this indicates is the similarity in meaning between these terms and the ease with which scribes could substitute one for the other. If *epeita* ("after that" in 15:23) can suggest a chronological interlude, it is likely that *eita* ("then" in 15:24) can as well. There is "little practical difference" between the meanings of the two words (according to Anthony C. Thiselton, *The First Epistle to the Corinthians: A Commentary on the Greek Text*, NIGTC [Grand Rapids: Eerdmans, 2000], 1207). In addition, in other manuscripts, "then" (*eita*) in 15:5 is replaced by an even more explicit "and after these things" (the phrase *kai meta tauta*), again suggesting that some scribes understood "then" (*eita*) to imply a temporal interlude.

9. For this understanding of "then" (*eita*), see Thomas Charles Edwards, *A Commentary on the First Epistle to the Corinthians* (1885; repr., Minneapolis: Klock & Klock, 1979), 414; Godet, *First Corinthians*, 785; George Eldon Ladd, *A Theology of the New Testament* (Grand Rapids: Eerdmans, 1974), 369, 558–59, 567, 629–30; Ladd, *Crucial Questions about the Kingdom of God* (Grand Rapids: Eerdmans, 1952), 178; Robertson and Plummer, *First Epistle*, 354. Sadly, W. D. Davies, *Paul and Rabbinic Judaism*, 293 n. 2, misrepresents Robertson and Plummer, claiming that they argue for a nonsequential concurrent force of "then."

10. Wilber Wallis, "The Problem of an Intermediate Kingdom in 1 Corinthians 15:20–28," *Journal of the Evangelical Theological Society* 18 (1975): 231; similarly Robert H. Gundry, *The Church and the Tribulation* (Grand Rapids: Zondervan, 1973), 141 n. 1.

11. Edwards, *First Corinthians*, 417.

12. Some scholars argue that "the end" refers to a third group that is resurrected along with Christ and Christians, so that "the end" is understood as "the last" group to be raised, namely, unbelievers (see Craig A. Blaising, "Premillennialism," in *Three Views on the Millennium and Beyond*, 204). But this is an unlikely meaning for *telos*, "the end" (so says Harris, *Raised Immortal*, 175). Nevertheless, if "the end" includes the final abolition of death, then the resurrection of martyred tribulation saints and unbelieving mankind might very well take place at that time, even if *telos* does not mean "the final stage of resurrection."

13. For this connection between 1 Corinthians 15 and Revelation 20–21, see Alva J. McClain, *The Greatness of the Kingdom* (Winona Lake, IN: BMH, 1959), 495–96.

14. Gordon D. Fee, *The First Epistle to the Corinthians*, NICNT (Grand Rapids: Eerdmans, 1987), 757.

15. See Godet, *First Corinthians*, 790.

16. Harold W. Hoehner, *Ephesians* (Grand Rapids: Baker, 2002), 284. Similarly Douglas J. Moo, *The Letters to the Colossians and to Philemon* (Grand Rapids: Eerdmans, 2002), 130; George Eldon Ladd, *A Theology of the New Testament* (Grand Rapids: Eerdmans, 1974), 558.

17. The tension between Christ's present reign and His climactic future reign is an illustration of what theologians call "the now and not yet." Jesus has obtained the victory over all His enemies and in a very real sense is reigning over them now. But this is also "not yet"; it awaits a future fulfillment. For this understanding of the now and not yet in 1 Corinthians 15, see Oscar Cullman, "The Kingship of Christ and the Church in the New Testament," in *The Early Church: Studies in Early Christian History and Theology* (Philadelphia: Westminster, 1956), 112–14; Cullman, *Christ and Time: The Primitive Chris-*

tian Conception of Time and History, trans. Floyd V. Filson (Philadelphia: Westminster, 1950), 151–54; H. Bietenhard, *Das tausendjärige Reich: Eine biblisch-theologische Studie* (Zurich: Zwingli-Verlag, 1955), 82–88; Martinus C. de Boer, *The Defeat of Death*, JSNTSS 22 (Sheffield: JSOT Press, 1988), 117–20, though de Boer rejects the idea that Paul teaches the futurity of Jesus' reign in 1 Corinthians 15; N. T. Wright, *The Resurrection of the Son of God* (Minneapolis: Fortress, 2003), 336; C. Marvin Pate, *The End of the Age Has Come: The Theology of Paul* (Grand Rapids: Zondervan, 1995), 67; Thomas R. Schreiner, *The King in His Beauty: A Biblical Theology of the Old and New Testaments* (Grand Rapids: Baker, 2013), 544–45.

18. The ESV does not translate the second *when* clause. It has "after destroying" when the Greek is literally "when He has destroyed."

19. For this understanding of the aorist tense, see Stanley E. Porter, *Idioms of the Greek New Testament*, Biblical Languages: Greek (Edinburgh: T & T Clark, 1992), 23.

20. For the points related to the sequential relationship of the two *when* clauses and their relationship both to *the end* and to 15:25, see D. Edmond Hiebert, "Evidence from 1 Corinthians 15," in *The Case for Premillennialism: A New Consensus*, ed. Donald K. Campbell and Jeffrey L. Townsend (Chicago: Moody, 1992), 232; L. J. Kreitzer, *Jesus and God in Paul's Eschatology*, JSNTSS, 19 (Sheffield: JSOT Press, 1987): 145; G. G. Findlay, "St. Paul's First Epistle to the Corinthians," in *The Expositor's Greek Testament*, ed. W. Robertson Nicoll (repr., Grand Rapids: Eerdmans, 1979) 2:927; Wallis, "The Problem of an Intermediate Kingdom," 133.

21. Wilber B. Wallis, "The Use of Psalms 8 and 110 in 1 Corinthians 15:25–27 and in Hebrews 1 and 2," *Journal of the Evangelical Theological Society* 15 (1972): 27–28. For a similar understanding of the futurity of the fulfillment of Psalm 110 and Psalm 8 in 1 Corinthians 15, see Kreitzer, *Jesus and God in Paul's Eschatology*, 147. Others who see a parallel between the uses of Psalms 8 and 110 in Hebrews 1–2 and 1 Corinthians 15 though without necessarily holding to the futurity of their fulfillment in 1 Corinthians 15, see E. Earle Ellis, *Paul's Use of the Old Testament* (Eugene, OR: Wipf & Stock, 2003; repr., Grand Rapids: Baker, 1981), 96; David M. Hay, *Glory at the Right Hand: Psalm 110 in Early Christianity* (New York: Abingdon, 1973), 60–63, 123–25; George H. Guthrie, "Hebrews," in *Commentary on the New Testament Use of the Old Testament*, ed. G. K. Beale and D. A. Carson (Grand Rapids: Baker, 2007), 946–47.

22. See 4 Ezra 3–14; *2 Apoc. Bar.* 27–40, 53–72, both probably written between AD 70–90; *1 Enoch* 91 and 93, which is BC; *2 Enoch* 32, 33, and 65, probably second century AD.

23. Craig L. Blomberg, "The Posttribulationism of the New Testament: Leaving 'Left Behind' Behind," in *A Case for Historic Premillennialism*, ed. Craig L. Blomberg and Sung Wook Chung (Grand Rapids: Baker, 2009), 69. Harris complains that "the end" "need point to nothing more than the termination of the age or the consummation of world history. It seems speculative to read into a single term several stages of traditional Jewish eschatology" (Harris, *Raised Immortal*, 180; so also Davies, *Paul and Rabbinic Judaism*, 295–97). Yet Paul's background was that of traditional Jewish eschatology, and it might be inadvisable to insist on discontinuity between it and Paul.

24. For a recent defense of the premillennial understanding of the future for national Israel in the eschatological kingdom of God, see *The People, the Land, and the Future of Israel: Israel and the Jewish People in the Plan of God*, ed Darrell L. Bock and Mitch Glaser (Grand Rapids: Kregel, 2014).

25. Robert Thomas, in his chapter 1 of this book, addresses the phrase "we will all be changed, in a moment, in the twinkling of an eye" (1 Cor. 15:51–52). He supports the interpretation that an event that happens in a moment of time is an imminent event, and imminent future events take place at the pretribulation rapture. See his chapter.

26. In the literature of early Judaism, see also 2 Esdras 6:23; 1QM 7:13–14.

27. For the presence of a trumpet at the appearing of a theophany, see Thiselton, *1 Corinthians*, 1296. For the sounding of trumpets heralding the Year of Jubilee as well as the return of the exiles, see Leviticus 25:8–10.

28. Gundry, *The Church and the Tribulation*, 148.

29. Arnold G. Fruchtenbaum, *The Footsteps of the Messiah: A Study of the Sequence of Prophetic Events* (Tustin, CA: Ariel, 1982), 101. Fruchtenbaum proposes that Paul was referring to the trumpets sounded during the Feast of Trumpets associated with *Rosh Hashanah*, the Jewish New Year (Lev. 23:24; Num. 29:1–6). While typical contemporary Jewish practice may be to sound a series of trumpet blasts concluded by a great blast, there is no suggestion that this is required in any biblical passage, making it problematic that Paul had this in mind. Fruchtenbaum says candidly, for a dispensationalist, that Paul's reference to the Feast of Trumpets "says nothing concerning the time of the Rapture" (ibid., 101).

30. Garland, *1 Corinthians*, 744; Fee, *1 Corinthians*, 801–2.

31. Douglas J. Moo, "A Case for the Posttribulation Rapture," *TVR1*, 198; see also 222. Moo notes further that trumpets were an aspect of the OT day of the Lord when Israel experiences final salvation and judgment (cf. Isa. 27:13; Joel 2:1; Zeph. 1:16; Zech. 9:14). In Isaiah 27:12–13, a great trumpet is sounded in connection with God's gathering up of Jewish people individually, probably in connection with the gathering of Israel in preparation for entrance into the millennial kingdom, an event that is always posttribulational. In response, the regathering in Isaiah 27 is not a resurrection. It involves God bringing back the Jewish people dispersed during the eschatological woes.

32. See also the treatment of Moo's argument on Matthew 24 in chapter 2 of this book, "Jesus' Teaching and the Rapture: Matthew 24."

33. Michael G. Vanlaningham, "Matthew," in *The Moody Bible Commentary*, ed. Michael Rydelnik and Michael Vanlaningham (Chicago: Moody, 2014), 1501. One might claim that the verb *episynagō* ("gather") in Matthew 24:31 has a different sense, referring to the rapture, than it does in the LXX where it refers to Israel's regathering to the Holy Land in natural bodies. This is possible. But the parallel passage, Mark 13:26–27, which also uses *episynagō*, provides a more specific chronology than Matthew, and Mark places the gathering after the second coming (note the sequential occurrences of "then" in Mark 13:27 rather than Matthew's two uses of the indefinite "and" in 24:31), not during it as a posttribulational view requires. In addition, Matthew 23:37 also uses *episynagō* to reflect Jesus' wish to gather the Jewish people safely into their land ("the way a hen gathers [*episynagō*] her chicks under her wings"), and it does not appear there that He intended to do this by means of the rapture. The functional opposite of the gathering is the desolating judgment that would befall Jerusalem and all Israel, and this is experienced in natural bodies. For more on the pretribulation rapture in Matthew 24, see chapter 2 in this book, "Jesus' Teaching and the Rapture: Matthew 24." Other arguments against a midtribulational and posttribulational view of the last trumpet can be found in J. Dwight Pentecost, *Things to Come* (Grand Rapids: Zondervan, 1958), 188–92; and John F. Walvoord, *The Rapture Question* (Grand Rapids: Zondervan, 1979), 123–26.

Another argument that makes it unlikely the seventh trumpet in Revelation 11 is the last trumpet in 1 Corinthians 15 is seen in the distinctions between the rapture and second coming. At the rapture, life on earth is normal, believers are removed from the earth, Jesus does not come with His heavenly armies, and believers return with Him to heaven (cf. 1 Thess. 4:16–17; 5:3; John 14:2–3). But at the second coming, Jesus will come to His people on earth, there will be intense hardship on earth due to the seal, trumpet, and bowl judgments, He comes with His armies for battle, and He remains on earth (Zech. 14:4–5; Acts 1:11–12; Matt. 24:30–31; 25:31–32; Rev. 19:11–21).

34. As already noted above, see Fruchtenbaum, *Footsteps*, 101.

35. David K. Lowery, "1 Corinthians," BKC, vol. 2, ed. John F. Walvoord and Roy B. Zuck (1983; repr., Colorado Springs: Cook, 1996), 545–46.

36. On the trumpet call to pack and move, see Pentecost, *Things to Come*, 191–92; on the trumpet sound of deliverance, see Leon J. Wood, *The Bible and Future Events* (Grand Rapids: Zondervan, 1973), 43–44.

37. Renald E. Showers, *Maranatha: Our Lord, Come!* (Bellmawr, NJ: Friends of Israel, 1995), 266.

38. Gerhard Friedrich, "Trumpet," TDNT, vol. 7, ed. Gerhard Friedrich, trans. Geoffrey W. Bromiley (Grand Rapids: Eerdmans, 1971), 74. Consult Friedrich's article for the ancient sources. See also Showers, *Maranatha*, 265–68.

39. de Boer, *The Defeat of Death*, 122; also Kennedy, *St. Paul's Conception of Last Things*, 321; Wright, *The Resurrection of the Son of God*, 336; Thiselton, *1 Corinthians*, 1229; see *1 Clement* 37:1–3; 40:1; Numbers 2:2 LXX; Polybius, *History*, 2.69, 5. BDAG, 988, however, maintains that the word means nothing more than a class or group of individuals without a military sense.

40. Gundry, *The Church and the Tribulation*, 146.

41. A posttribulationist might argue that the lavish banquet, the eradication of death, and the deliverance and vindication of Israel would happen after the tribulation—early in the millennial kingdom as suggested by the themes in Isaiah 25:6–12. Surely Israel's deliverance happens at the second coming, which in Isaiah 25 seems to happen around the same time as the banquet and defeat of death. This makes it appear that the defeat of death is as posttribulationists say, namely, at the time of a posttribulational rapture. But Alan Hultberg ("A Prewrath Response" [to the posttribulational views of Douglas Moo], in *TVRI*, 264–65) draws attention to an important feature in Isaiah's view of the relationship of the restored kingdom to eternity. He writes,

> Certainly the context of Isaiah 25:8 and 26:19 (Isa. 24–27) is associated with God's restoration of Israel, but the temporal relationship of the events is not clear, let alone the relation of the events to other "kingdom" prophecies in Isaiah, not least Isaiah 65:17–20. This latter is instructive, since, on the one hand, Isaiah posits an eschatological period when Zion will be the center of God's favor and the nations will no longer be under the pall of death (Isa. 25:6–8), while on the other he sees a similar period when death and perhaps sin are still possible (Isa. 26:10[?]; 65:20, 22; cf. Zech. 14:16–21). Though some understand these passages as irreconcilable visions of the kingdom, others see in them two phases of the kingdom along the lines of Revelation 20:4–21:8, an initial phase under the mediation of the Messiah (cf. Isa. 11:1–10; 65:25) and a final phase in which God himself reigns and all his enemies have been vanquished (Isa. 25:6–8; cf. Rev. 20:10, 14; 21:1–8). Though Isaiah conflates these two phases, John distinguishes them. It is possible, then, that the resurrection in Isaiah 26:19 is part of the latter phase, when death has been defeated, what in Revelation is the second resurrection.

Hultberg is heavily dependent on Craig A. Blaising, "The Kingdom of God in the New Testament," in *Progressive Dispensationalism*, 274–76. This means Isaiah does not lend to an exact timing of the banishment of death in relationship to the deliverance of Israel and the establishment of the kingdom. But in light of Revelation 21:4, it is possible to be more specific. The abolition of death is at the end of the millennial kingdom, not at the time of, or immediately following, the second coming at the end of the tribulation. For this, see Alva J. McClain, *The Greatness of the Kingdom: An Inductive Study of the Kingdom of God* (Winona Lake, IN: BMH, 1959), 495–96.

42. There is a complicated issue associated with how the LXX, and possibly Paul, deals with the Hebrew. The Hebrew word *lāneaḥ* (a noun with a preposition) is derived from the verb *nāṣaḥ*, which means "to overcome, prevail over." This may account for Paul's use of "victory" (Fee, *First Corinthians*, 803–4 n. 36). It is also possible Paul draws upon Theodotion's LXX version, which tended to translate *lāneṣa* ("forever") with *nikos* ("victory"), or assigns to the Hebrew word the Aramaic sense "victory" (for the latter suggestion, see HALOT, 716).

43. One of the ways NT writers cite the Old Testament is in an applicational sense. Applicational citations do not foist novel interpretations upon the OT. Rather, the NT writers find a theme or principle in the OT that connects with their contemporary situation. But this should not be construed as suggesting that everything in the OT context of the citation is invoked by the NT writer. Michael Rydelnik writes, "Applicational fulfillment recognizes that ancient texts have continuing relevance. By quoting these texts, the writers understood a principle in a biblical passage and then applied it to their contemporary situation"; Michael Rydelnik, *The Messianic Hope* (Nashville: Broadman & Holman, 2010), 108. The principle of Isaiah 25:8 applied by Paul in 1 Corinthians 15 relates to God's promise to conquer death. But in 1 Corinthians 15, the principle is applied quite narrowly to the church, not the entire world. There is no clear indication that he sees a more universal scope of the fulfillment of Isaiah 25:8 at the time of the rapture. That appears to await conditions at the end of the millennial kingdom, on the basis of Revelation 20:6–21:4.

44. Note the occurrences of first person plural verbs and pronouns in 15:51–52: "we" will not all sleep but will all be changed. And God gives "us" the victory in 15:57. And it is not arguing from silence to say this, as if the final destruction of death not being mentioned opens up the possibility that the final abolition of death and the rapture takes place at the same time. As I have argued above, this is an unlikely understanding of *then* and the *when* clauses in 15:24, and does not fit with the apparent chronology of Revelation 20:6–21:4.

45. For this view, see also Hultberg, "A Prewrath Response," 266–67.

6

Paul and the Rapture: 1 Thessalonians 4-5

BY KEVIN D. ZUBER

For if we believe that Jesus died and rose again, even so God will bring with Him those who have fallen asleep in Jesus. For this we say to you by the word of the Lord, that we who are alive and remain until the coming of the Lord, will not precede those who have fallen asleep. For the Lord Himself will descend from heaven with a shout, with the voice of the archangel and with the trumpet of God, and the dead in Christ will rise first. Then we who are alive and remain will be caught up together with them in the clouds to meet the Lord in the air, and so we shall always be with the Lord. Therefore comfort one another with these words.

1 Thessalonians 4:14–18

Whether in conversations in the church lobby or in the seminary hallway, one is likely to hear the charge that teaching on subjects of eschatology generally and on the rapture of the church specifically is "irrelevant to the practical needs of people," or that it is "too nebulous and imprecise to be helpful," or that it is "controversial and divisive." The apostle Paul's letters to the Thessalonian church prove those perceptions to be shortsighted and unwarranted.

In 1 Thessalonians the apostle makes virtually constant reference to future things but always with a pastoral tone and an objective. In particular, the Scripture passages to be addressed in this chapter have been called two of the most "outstanding prophetic or eschatological passages of the New Testament."[1]

THE RAPTURE AS PRACTICAL AND PASTORAL TEACHING

Paul's teaching about the rapture of the church in 1 Thessalonians 4:13–18 is one of the most practical and pastorally helpful passages in all of Paul's letters. Actually, this entire letter is a pastoral missive, written to the apostle's beloved "brethren" (cf. 1:4; 2:1, 9, 14, 17; 4:9, 10, 13; 5:1, 4, 12, 14, 26). These key eschatological passages, especially the instruction about the rapture (4:13–18), contain some very practical instruction in the New Testament. This was written to believers who were dealing with one of the most traumatic and difficult eventualities in life—the death of a loved one. Furthermore, Paul's teaching here is not as nebulous and unclear as many would want to suggest, even though it does consider an event that is strange, and even implausible (because it is supernatural), to many modern and naturalistically minded twenty-first century readers.

It is true that Paul's instruction here does require a certain degree of familiarity with basic biblical eschatological teachings (e.g., the day of the Lord). It is fair to assume that Paul had provided the Thessalonian believers with that teaching during his relatively brief stay in Thessalonica (cf. Acts 17:1–9; and note how Paul reminds them of what they already knew—1 Thess. 5:1). It is simply a false dichotomy to suggest that because this passage is an attempt to comfort the grieving (4:13), it is therefore not meant to teach in detail about eschatology (i.e., the end times). The claim that this is "not a passage about the parousia but a passage about grieving for the dead"[2] simply will not do. It is clearly about both. This false dichotomy must be challenged, for it is when the believer has the firmest grasp of the eschatological certainties taught in Scripture that he or she finds the greatest practical comfort and practical encouragement (see 4:18; 5:11).

While it may be true that the doctrine of the rapture is divisive due to the controversial element of its timing, the rapture ought not to be ignored for that reason. Indeed, the arguments ought to be made, clearly articulated, and conclusions drawn. For it is surely better for the church as a whole to keep studying and debating important doctrines than to ignore them and possibly lose them altogether due to a lack of consideration.[3]

WHY PAUL WROTE 1 THESSALONIANS 4:13–5:11

As noted above, it seems that during his ministry in Thessalonica, along with other matters of doctrine, Paul had taught the relatively new believers certain matters relating to the end-time events and the parousia, i.e., the coming of the Lord Jesus Christ. From there, Paul traveled to Corinth, but soon sent Timothy back to Thessalonica to learn of the welfare of the Thessalonian believers. The interim was brief between the time of Paul's ministry in Thessalonica and Timothy's report upon his return to Paul in Corinth (cf. 3:2, 5). Nevertheless, some of the believers in Thessalonica had died and the church was enduring persecution (cf. 3:3–4). These circumstances caused some concern among the brethren. So Paul wrote a letter to the Thessalonians.

The precise reason for the Thessalonians' grief has generated much debate. Just why did the Thessalonians grieve? I. Howard Marshall notes five different ways this question has been answered.[4] Of these, the view that has received "the greatest support," writes Wanamaker, "has claimed that Paul's belief in the imminent return of Christ meant that he had given no systematic instruction about the resurrection."[5] As a result, when Christians began to die, this raised a question about their fate. Thus Paul offers this instruction on the resurrection to fill in a gap in the doctrinal and practical understanding of the Thessalonians.

However, it is very unlikely that the Thessalonians had a deficient understanding of the resurrection, or entertained a less than robust hope in the resurrection, or that while Paul was with them he had failed to include that crucial doctrine in his eschatological teaching (much less his gospel teaching, cf. 1 Cor. 15:3–4). Charles A. Wanamaker lists several reasons why this "explanation fails to carry conviction." Paul's own "full-fledged understanding of the resurrection" is clearly reflected in what he wrote in 1 Corinthians 15, and it is highly doubtful that a "shift occurred in Paul's thought between [the writing of] 1 Thessalonians and [the writing of] 1 Corinthians."[6]

Considering that Paul was "as to the Law, a Pharisee" (Phil. 3:5), he most certainly would have believed in the general resurrection of the dead. Furthermore, it is inconceivable to suppose that he had not included the teaching of Christ's resurrection in his preaching and his basic teaching about Jesus Christ (i.e., in preaching the gospel; cf. Acts 13:30, 34–36; 1 Cor. 15:20). Indeed, Paul's reference to the death and bodily resurrection of Jesus in 1 Thessalonians 4:14 implies that this was something they already knew, understood, and believed.[7] That being the case, it is nearly certain that Paul would have also included instruction about the resurrection and the hope of believers in Christ (cf. 1 Cor. 15:3–5, 20–23, 35–49). Thus, the suggestion that Paul's instruction in 1 Thessalonians 4:13ff. is simply to establish the fact of the resurrection of believers itself is untenable. In other words, Paul's letter to the Thessalonians is much more than just an introduction or even a simple reminder of the believer's hope of resurrection.

As noted, Paul "had taught them about end-time events, such as Christ's return to gather believers to Himself (e.g., 1:9–10; 2:19; 3:13). They also knew about the day of the Lord (5:1–3)."[8] So the question is, if the Thessalonians already had an expectation of the resurrection, and they had already been taught about the return of Christ and understood the nature and purpose of the day of the Lord, what was their concern? What doctrinal and practical questions are the apostle addressing? It seems the best answer is this: the issue of the way these future events fit together. In other words, the Thessalonians needed to know when the resurrection of the saints was going to happen with respect to the return of the Lord. The question really was a matter of timing.

Why would the Thessalonians have such a question? As noted already, some of the believers in Thessalonica had died, and this caused their loved ones to question whether those who died would therefore miss out on the blessing of the Lord's return for His bride, the church (cf. John 14:1–3; Eph. 5:27). It seems the Thessalonians did not doubt their loved ones' future resurrection. But they were concerned that their deaths meant they would miss out on the wonder and elation of "being there" when the Lord returned for His own (cf. John 14:1–3).

Still others began to think that the persecution they were facing (cf. 1 Thess. 1:6; 2:1ff.) meant that perhaps they had already entered the time of tribulation known as "the day of the Lord" (cf. Joel 2:30–32; Zech. 14:1; Mal. 4:1, 5). Perhaps others were so convinced that the "end times" Paul had spoken of were upon them that they could just "sit back and relax" and wait in passive indifference (cf. 5:6; 2 Thess. 3:11). Furthermore, it seems that the Thessalonians had been exposed to some false teaching on these issues (which prompted Paul's exhortation in 2 Thess. 2:1–2 that they "not be quickly shaken").

In sum, it seems best to understand that the concern, grief, and ignorance (4:13) of the Thessalonians were not about the fact of the resurrection of believers, nor about the full nature of the parousia and related events (the day of the Lord) but about the timing of these eschatological events. As for their loved ones who died, the Thessalonians certainly knew they would be raised. But those deaths led to several questions: (1) when would the resurrection of the saints happen relative to the events of the tribulation; (2) did those deaths mean their loved ones would miss the great day of the Lord's return for His bride (cf.

John 14:1–3); and (3) did those deaths (perhaps due to persecution) mean that the day of the Lord had begun and the living Thessalonians now had to endure that day of judgment and wrath before they experienced the Lord's deliverance, when He would gather His own to Himself?

PAUL'S INSTRUCTION ON THE RAPTURE: 1 THESSALONIANS 4:13–18

The Purpose of Paul's Teaching on the Rapture

In 1 Thessalonians 4, Paul makes it very clear that his teaching was designed to instruct the Thessalonian believers so that they would not be "uninformed" (4:13a). There is no hint of rebuke in this phrase. Paul knows nothing of a dichotomy between doctrinal teaching and practical instruction. Paul introduces his subject with the phrase "But we do not want you to be uninformed, brethren." The use of this phrase is typical of Paul, either as a formula to introduce a new matter (e.g., Rom. 1:13; 1 Cor. 10:1; 12:1) or as an expansion on a topic previously, but somewhat marginally, discussed (e.g., 2 Cor. 1:8). Here, "the formula probably did not introduce totally new material but explained or elaborated on teachings previously shared with the church (cf. 5:2)."[9]

Furthermore, Paul writes so that they would "not grieve [about those who are asleep] as do the rest who have no hope" (4:13b). The expression "those who are asleep" (v. 13a) was a common euphemism for the dead. While the term "sleep" was known as a euphemism for the dead in both Jewish (Old Testament) and Greek writings,[10] it was especially suited to a Christian view of death. The term *koimao* ("asleep") was often used to refer to believers who had died (cf. Matt. 27:52; John 11:11; Acts 7:60; 13:36; 1 Cor. 11:30; 15:6, 18, 20, 51; 2 Pet. 3:4). This was because, as far as their bodies were concerned, the deceased looked as if they were only in the repose of sleep and they had the expectation of "awakening"—that is bodily resurrection. Thus Thomas concludes, "This sleep refers to the physical body and not to a man's spirit."[11]

What does Paul mean by "the rest who have no hope"? Clearly, "the rest" are the unbelievers. Many in the pagan world were bereft of any real comfort in the face of the death of a loved one. As Green notes, in general "at the popular level desperation in the face of death reigned."[12] However, the Greeks did have some notions of the immortality of the soul (cf. Plato, *Phaedo*, 70b; 78b–80b), and a vague sense of "life after death" could be found in the ancient myths (e.g., the view of Hades in Greek myths) and the mystery religions that were current in the first century.[13] But these esoteric notions did not generally reach to the common man and all unbelievers lacked "the one true hope, the Christian hope, which Christ validated by his resurrection"[14]—namely, the hope of bodily resurrection and the hope of the return of Christ (cf. Titus 2:13).

The Thessalonians had this hope not just as a vague aspiration but as a confident expectation.[15] Thus, while they would experience the normal grief of loss and separation from a loved one, their grief was not to be of the same kind as the unbelievers. "Their grief should be tempered and informed by the hope they held."[16] And that hope was in the resurrection of the body at the return of Jesus Christ.

The Warrant for Paul's Teaching on the Rapture

The guarantee of the rapture of the church is the death and bodily resurrection of the Lord Jesus Christ (4:14). The expression "For if [*gar ei*] we believe that Jesus died and rose again" does not imply any uncertainty or question about the matter being addressed and could legitimately be translated, "For since. . . ."[17] This would then indicate that Paul is appealing to a doctrine or teaching that he had taught them and that they had accepted as true.[18] When he mentions the resurrection in 4:16 ("the dead in Christ will rise first"), it seems that the issue is not whether there will be a bodily resurrection of believers (that seems to be something the Thessalonians already believed and expected). Instead, the issue seems to be the timing of it relative to the experience of those who have not "fallen asleep" (i.e., "we who are alive and remain") and relative to the day of the Lord (cf. 5:1–2).

In other words, the apostle's point is not simply "the dead in Christ will rise" (for that they already understood—that was, and is, the believer's hope). But his point is that they "will rise *first*" (emphasis added). Thus, two truths (Christ's bodily resurrection in history and their bodily resurrection in promise) that they already believed were restated to assure them that this new instruction—regarding the timing of the Lord's coming—was also true. This new instruction would assure them that their loved ones had not missed the wonder and blessing of the Lord's coming for His own (cf. John 14:1–3).

The Source of Paul's Teaching on the Rapture

To further assure the Thessalonians of the verity of this teaching, Paul asserts that his teaching is "by the word of the Lord" (4:15a). As to the source of this "word of the Lord," several views have been suggested. Some commentators have suggested that Paul is referring to the Lord's teaching in the Gospels (perhaps Matt. 24:31ff.).[19] Others propose this was a part of the oral tradition of Jesus' teaching that made its way through the early church but that was not recorded (as seems to be the case with the quotation in Acts 20:35). Still others posit the possibility that this was a direct word from the Lord to Paul (or another prophet). This last view has much to commend it.

First, in the parallel text on the same subject matter (1 Cor. 15:51–54, the rapture), Paul speaks of a "mystery." A "mystery" in Paul's use of the term refers to "divine truths that had not been revealed in previous ages but have been made known to the Lord's people by the New Testament (cp. Eph. 3:1–5, 9; Rom. 16:25)."[20] Hiebert is confident that "this 'mystery' [was] undoubtedly a direct revelation to Paul."[21] Therefore, this "word of the Lord" was the source of Paul's knowledge of the "mystery" of the rapture. Also, this "view is in full accord with the scriptural records that Paul did receive direct communications from the risen Lord from the very beginning of his ministry (cf. Acts 9:5–6; 22:17–21; Gal. 1:12; 2:2; 1 Cor. 11:23)."[22]

However one resolves the question of the source of Paul's teaching, the import of the statement is clear: to establish the authority and certainty of his teaching, Paul affirms it has the warrant and assurance of the very "word of the Lord." The Thessalonians can be confident that this teaching is truth.

The Substance of Paul's Teaching on the Rapture

The substance of Paul's teaching on the rapture deals with the two groups of believers (the dead and the living) involved in this event, and the nature of the event itself. In essence, Paul is about to explain how each of the two groups in view will experience the rapture. It should be noted that this explanation of the rapture is precisely how Paul answers the doctrinal and existential questions of the Thessalonians! The question of the Thessalonians was—on the premise that the living will certainly experience the wonder and blessings of the Lord's return (described in 1 Cor. 15:50–57 and John 14:1–3)—will those who have died miss the Lord's return (or perhaps even the resurrection)? Paul's answer here is to say, in effect, "Neither group is going to miss it for here is how it will unfold. Here is what you need to know about the nature and the timing of this glorious event."

The first group of those who will experience this event are described as both those "who have fallen asleep in Jesus" (4:14c) and "the dead in Christ" (4:16c). Hiebert notes, "The chief difficulty of the verse is the significance of the phrase translated 'in Jesus,' [which is] quite literally, 'through Jesus' (*dia tou Iēsou*)."[23] The issue is complicated by the question of whether the phrase "in/through Jesus" goes with the verb "will bring"—hence, the idea would be something like "God will bring with Him and through Jesus (as an agent of action) those who have fallen asleep" (cf. ESV—"even so, through Jesus, God will bring with him those who have fallen asleep"). Or does the phrase go with "those who have fallen asleep"—in which case this translation in the NASB is most likely—"those who have fallen asleep in Jesus"?

The problem is the first rendering is awkward and unlikely. But, the second rendering is problematic because the Greek preposition *dia* does not mean "in"—it means "through." If one opts for the second translation (again, essentially the NASB), one must determine what might be the meaning of "through Jesus." Some have suggested it means they "fell asleep," that is, died "through or by" their testimony to Jesus—i.e., they were martyrs. This, however, is taking the interpretation in a rather speculative direction; there is no other indication that these deaths were anything other than that normal eventuality of life—namely, loved ones die.

It seems best to take the preposition "in the sense of accompaniment, with the resultant meaning 'those who have died as Christians,' perhaps 'in contact with Jesus.'"[24] Hence, the translation "in Jesus" is meant to emphasize that it is not just "any who sleep" but only those who sleep "in Jesus"—only those who died while in relationship to Him will accompany Him when He returns. So, in effect, it means something very like the other description "the dead in Christ" (4:16c; cf. 1 Cor. 15:18).

In any case, Paul's point is clear: this group will certainly be present at the coming of Jesus, for "God will bring" them to the event. Here is the word that the Thessalonians needed: "No, they will not miss it, they will certainly be there, and that by divine appointment!" This is the thrust of "God will bring with Him":

That those who have fallen asleep "God will bring with him" is the fundamental declaration in Paul's reply to the unenlightened sorrowing of the Thessalonians. They have not cause to sorrow for their departed loved ones because when God acts to bring back the risen Christ at the *parousia* they will return with Him. The verb rendered *bring* is frequently translated "lead" and serves to picture the departed saints as following the lead of their Lord in His triumphal train in His return from heaven. The verb stresses the "blessed association of the departed Christians with their Lord at the *parousia*, in which part the Thessalonians feared their sleeping brethren would have no part."[25]

How can this group be "with Him" at the moment of His coming and then also be the ones who "will rise first"? For a few interpreters, this appears to be a rather speculative question. Therefore, it may be dismissed as more specific than necessary, given the purpose of the apostle to simply offer pastoral comfort to the Thessalonians with respect to their deceased loved ones. Such interpreters suggest that to address such questions is to go beyond Paul's purpose.

Actually, this interpretation of Paul's teaching does not go beyond what Paul likely taught the Thessalonians about the death of the saints and the truth of the resurrection. We can safely assume that the Thessalonian believers already understood that for those who have died "in Christ," there is the promise that "to be absent from the body" is "to be at home with the Lord" (cf. 2 Cor. 5:8). So, this was not their question. The question of the Thessalonians concerned what happens to their loved ones, the "dead in Christ," when the Lord returns. Paul's teaching here explains that those loved ones in their "absent-from-the-body" state will accompany Jesus (this truth was a new part of Paul's teaching) to be reunited with their resurrected bodies (this truth they already understood and anticipated). It is a false dichotomy to choose between a practical over against a prophetic purpose of Paul's teaching in 1 Thessalonians.

It may be observed that after Paul had mentioned the resurrection of Jesus, it would have seemed appropriate to highlight the resurrection of the departed believers. "The use of 'bring' rather than 'raise' [in 4:14] shifts the focus of the saying from a resurrection like Christ's (the emphasis one would expect after v. 14a) to involvement along with the living saints in the parousia brought about by the Father's initiative (Mark 13:32)."[26] In other words, had Paul simply wanted to reassure the Thessalonians about the resurrection of the saints, he could have done so immediately after mentioning Christ's resurrection. Instead, "he speaks of their association with Jesus at His coming." According to Hiebert, this shows "that the worry of the Thessalonians was not whether those who had died would rise, but whether they would share in the glories of Christ's return."[27] Paul's assurance is, "They certainly will."

The second group to be involved in this event is identified by Paul as "we who are alive and remain until the coming of the Lord" (4:15b; cf. 4:17a). In this brief comment the apostle offers three key affirmations. First, by the simple use of the first person pronoun "we," he indicates that he saw himself among those who would be living at the time of the Lord's return. He looked for the return of the Lord to take place at any moment, i.e., "Paul believed the coming of Christ to be imminent."[28] This was a perspective he maintained consistently throughout his life and ministry (cf. 1 Cor. 15:51–52; 2 Cor. 5:1–10; Phil. 3:20; Titus 2:11–13; cf. 2 Tim. 4:8). Although he could readily acknowledge that he might die in service to Christ (Phil. 1:20–21; 2 Tim. 4:6–7), nevertheless "Paul lived in constant expectation of the Lord's return."[29]

Second, the apostle expected this group to "remain until the coming of the Lord" (4:15). This, obviously, is the coming he has been referring to, namely, the coming that will accomplish the reunion with those departed saints. It was the anticipation of this reunion of the living with the dead that was to give the Thessalonians comfort for their loved ones and for themselves. However, it would be odd to think that Paul understood the time remaining until the Lord returns as a time that would extend through the day of the Lord (the tribulation, see the discussion below). How would it be comforting to realize that they, the living, would have to endure the terrible trials of the tribulation? If that was the case, Paul should have offered a more pertinent form of comfort! If Paul believed that the Thessalonians would "remain" through the tribulation, he should have comforted the Thessalonians regarding their departed loved ones by telling them that it was actually a blessing that, their loved ones, being dead, had missed that terrible time. Furthermore, he should have alerted them that they should take some thought and concern for themselves, for they themselves might soon be facing the hardships of the tribulation, should it come.

Indeed, it seems clear that part of their fear and concern was that they perhaps had entered into the day of the Lord. But Paul's instruction (as will be seen below in the discussion of 1 Thess. 5:1–11) is that they were not in those days (that day will not "overtake you," 5:4), that they would not experience what those days held in store (i.e., they would not suffer God's wrath, 5:9; cf. 1 Thess. 1:10; Rev. 3:10), and that they should remain vigilant in constant expectation of Jesus' return. In short, Paul teaches that those who "remain until the coming of the Lord" should be comforted (4:18) by looking forward with anticipation and expectation for that part of the coming of the Lord that brings about their blessed reunion with the "dead in Christ." He does not tell them they should be looking for the signs that they are in the day of the Lord (in actuality, a *discomforting* thought). In other words, the "remaining" time is *up to* but not *into* the day of the Lord.

Third, Paul is emphatic that this second group (i.e., those who are alive and remain at the time of the coming of the Lord) will not precede the first group— the ones "asleep." For emphasis he employs a double negative—"by no means, not at all."[30] This note strongly indicates that the concern of the Thessalonians was not that they feared their departed loved ones would miss the resurrection but that they were somehow disadvantaged in that they had died before His second advent. Wanamaker renders this phrase "we shall certainly have no advantage over those who have fallen asleep."[31] The Thessalonians apparently "feared that the dead would be raised at some time after the parousia and so miss the glories of that day."[32] Paul affirms here that will not be the case. In fact, the living will have no advantage or precedence over the "dead in Christ" at the Lord's return for them. The living "will not meet the returning Christ ahead of the dead, nor will they have any precedence in the blessedness of His coming."[33] Thus the fears and concerns of the living—that those who had died would miss out on the glory of the Lord's return for His own and thereby be somehow deprived of blessing or joy—were alleviated.

The Nature of the Event according to Paul's Teaching on the Rapture

Paul might have left his assurance and comfort of the Thessalonians with what he had just said. Instead, he adds a description of the event of the Lord's return for His own so that the Thessalonians might better appreciate how it is that the living Christians will not have an advantage over the "dead in Christ." Paul notes at least seven features of this event.

First, it will be a personal manifestation of the Lord—"the Lord Himself" (4:16a). Paul mentions no angelic entourage—the focus is on "the Lord Himself" (contrast the second coming described in Mark 13:26–27). This small detail points to the promise He made to His disciples in John 14:1–3 ("I will come again and receive you to Myself," v. 3).

Second, it will be a cross-dimensional event—"will descend from heaven" (4:16a). The emphasis here is not merely on the direction the Lord will travel as it is on the realm from which He begins His journey. He will indeed travel from (or through) the atmospheric heavens to earth, but more significantly He "will descend" from the heavenly realm (the presence of God) to the physical earth. The disciples who watched Jesus return to heaven (cf. Acts 1:9–11) were told "This Jesus, who has been taken up from you into heaven, will come in just the same way as you have watched Him go into heaven" (Acts 1:11b). Paul had already alluded to this in 1 Thessalonians 1:10 where he commended the Thessalonians for their faithful patience and expectation because they were waiting "for His Son from heaven."

Third, it will be accompanied by celestial sounds—"a shout, with the voice of the archangel and with the trumpet of God" (4:16b). These three details, since they each describe sounds, have been taken by some as describing one sound or perhaps two sounds.[34] But it seems better to understand them as three successive sounds. The first sound here is the "shout." This "shout" is not qualified or described further: who utters the shout, those to whom it is directed, or what is said is not specified. The term itself seems to be a military term, "a cry of command,"[35] or "'shout of command' and implies authority and urgency."[36]

In the original Greek of the phrase "the voice of the archangel," there are no articles. So it literally reads, "a voice of an archangel" or even "an archangelic [like] voice." Since the term "archangel" appears only one other time in the New Testament (Jude 9), and since that is the only texts that identifies an archangel by name, it would seem best to be cautious about what this sound is and who is making it.[37]

The last celestial sound is "the trumpet of God." Again, there is no article in the original, so it reads "a trumpet of God." "The trumpet of God is an image occurring frequently in the Old Testament in contexts of theophany and eschatological judgment . . . as well as in both Jewish and Christian apocalyptic traditions. . . ."[38] This trumpet is almost certainly the same as that mentioned in 1 Corinthians 15:52 and some see the same trumpet in Matthew 24:31. But the trumpet of 1 Thessalonians 4:16 is not to be equated with Matthew 24:31 or any in Revelation 8–11. Instead, this trumpet "seems to have a twofold purpose: to assemble God's people (cf. Ex. 19:16–19) and to signal His deliverance of them (cf. Zech. 9:14–16)."[39]

It seems best to acknowledge that the events noted so far will be simultaneous—the shout, the voice, the trumpet, and the appearance of the Lord will happen all at once at the outset of the event. However, it is possible that the shout will be sustained through the sound of the voice of the archangel, and both of those sounds will be sustained throughout the sounding of the trumpet. With the shout and the voice of an archangel and the trumpet of God, a grand fanfare will be heard over the entire earth. "Clearly the rapture does not seem to be a silent affair. It seems that a tremendous reverberating sound will actually encircle the earth."[40] And Martin adds, "No one will be able to miss the event. No one will fail to realize that something remarkable is about to occur."[41] But how much of this cacophony will the unsaved world understand? The world will not miss that something supernatural is occurring. But in all likelihood they will not realize what the noise is, nor grasp the magnitude of the event (at least at first).[42]

Fourth, it will be an orderly event: "the dead in Christ will rise first. Then we who are alive and remain" (4:16b–17a). As noted above, Paul did not need to explain what he meant by "will rise," for the Thessalonians already knew of and expected the bodily resurrection of the saints. The new information here—and what was intended to comfort the living—was that the "dead in Christ" will rise "first." This "first" is not the first resurrection in history, nor is this intended to distinguish the resurrection of the redeemed as over the unsaved— the unsaved are not in view here. "*First* means that the dead believers will be resurrected before the living are caught up."[43] Significantly, Paul does not say the ones who are "alive and remain" will be raised; rather they will experience something entirely unique.

Fifth, it will happen in the temporal atmosphere—"in the clouds . . . in the air" (4:17c). The "clouds" in view here should be understood as the same sort of clouds that the disciples witnessed when they watched Jesus ascend into heaven (cf. Acts 1:9). The reference to "air" here clearly indicates the atmosphere that surrounds the earth. "In five of its seven occurrences in the New Testament the word *air* (*aera*) means the atmosphere. Nor does it seem necessary to depart from that meaning here."[44] This event will take place in the same elements and in the same (literal) manner as did the ascension of Jesus in Acts 1.

Some commentators and critics have questioned whether Paul's language should be taken literally. Marshall, for instance, claims that if the language is taken literally, it will "lead to antinomies and contradictions."[45] Others suggest that the type of literature and the language here is "apocalyptic" and hence not intended to be taken literally.[46] However, such a view does not seem to fit Paul's language here, nor his own perspective—he seems to take this information (and he expects his readers to take this information) literally. Wanamaker concedes that, "While a literal realization of Paul's symbolic depiction of the coming of Christ seems implausible for many people today. . . . [i]n all probability Paul did believe in some type of historical realization of his description of the end."[47]

Actually, the point can be made even more emphatically—Paul surely meant this description of the event to be taken literally. First, the very details he provides would be superfluous unless he intended to describe a literal event. In other words, if these details do not describe an actual event but are meant only to provide a "sense or feeling about the world" and a vague "hope" for some future deliverance, then they are unnecessary and potentially misleading. Second, it seems unlikely to suppose that a "symbolic hope" would have been sufficient to answer the fears and concerns of the Thessalonians. Third, the real basis for seeing the event in literal terms is the experience of Jesus Himself—He was literally and bodily raised from the dead. He literally and bodily ascended into heaven. The same terms used to describe His experience are the terms used here to describe this future experience of those who are His. If His experiences of resurrection and ascension were literal, one can be sure these events will happen in just the same literal manner.

The sixth feature of this event is its suddenness. People are "caught up" (4:17; cf. 1 Cor. 15:52). The term here is *harpazō*, which means "to grab or seize suddenly so as to remove or gain control, *snatch* . . . [or] *take away*."[48] MacArthur concludes this describes "a strong, irresistible, even violent act,"[49] a "taking by force" (cf. Matt. 11:12; John 10:12; Acts 8:39). Thus the experience of those living when this event occurs is not resurrection but transformation, i.e., an instantaneous change from an earthly physical body to a heavenly physical body. The transformation and change here appears to be identical to the one in view in 1 Corinthians 15:51–52, where Paul notes "we will not all sleep, but we will all be changed," and so "the dead will be raised imperishable," and at the same instant "we [the believers living at that moment] will be changed."

Finally, it will be a reunion. This is the great note of comfort for the living believers that should replace grief for their lost loved ones. There are three aspects to this reunion. It will be mutual—"together with them" (4:17b). It will be grand—"to meet the Lord" (4:17c). It will be lasting—"and so we shall always be with the Lord" (4:17d). The first feature reinforces the main point of Paul's encouraging instruction. He wanted to reassure and comfort the Thessalonians concerning those who have died. Not only will those who have departed not miss the Lord's return for His own, they will be reunited with the living—but then transformed—saints.

The second aspect contains a note of grandeur. This reunion will have a "ceremonial element" about it, for it will be an arranged meeting. Many commentators have proposed that the term *apantēsis* ("to meet") has a technical meaning pertaining to a specific type of meeting. It is suggested that at such a meeting, an official delegation proceeds out of the city to greet a visiting dignitary outside the city walls and then escorts that dignitary back into the city.[50] Actually, although it is widely held and frequently referenced, this view is mostly based on a single work by Erik Peterson written in 1929–30.[51] Through simple multiplication of citation, the view that this term in 1 Thessalonians 4 refers to this technical meaning has achieved the status of "common knowledge."

However, a study of Peterson's work and an analysis of the use of the term "to meet" in ancient Greek literature demonstrates that the term *apantēsis* ("to meet") does not have such a technical meaning. Michael R. Crosby notes:

A computer search of the literature written during the several centuries surrounding Paul's era using the *Thesaurus Linguae Graecae* (*TLG*) [a comprehensive digital database of all surviving ancient Greek texts] produced 91 pages of citations of passages that employ forms of [*apantēsis* and related forms, and] only a minority of the uses of these terms describes formal receptions. For example, Philo Judaeus uses these words 27 times, but not once to describe the meeting of a dignitary. Similarly, Josephus employs them 92 times but only ten times in descriptions of formal receptions. In the LXX the noun [often a form of *apantēsis*] . . . designates the hostile meeting of armies, although it also describes virtually any kind of meeting.[52]

It is surprising, then, even after acknowledging the validity of Crosby's analysis, that Green concludes, "There remains little doubt that this custom formed the background of this teaching."[53] Furthermore, in the two other uses of this Greek term in the New Testament—in the parable of the ten virgins (Matt. 25:6, 10) and in describing Paul's reception by the Christians in Rome (Acts 28:15)—*apantēsis* does not fit with its supposed technical meaning. Neither the meeting with Paul in Acts 28 nor that of the bridesmaids and bridegroom in Matthew 25 have any of the "formal features" of the Hellenistic formal reception of a visiting dignitary.

Here, in effect, is a case of choosing between two metaphors to describe the event. One metaphor describes this event in terms of a "visiting dignitary" wherein a group of citizens and officials go out to greet an honored guest or conquering hero and return to the city with pomp.

A better metaphor is that of the bride and bridegroom. In this view 1 Thessalonians 4:13ff. pictures a bridegroom coming to retrieve his bride (in fulfillment of His promise—John 14:3). This is a bride who has been made ready for her reception at the groom's home (cf. Eph. 5:26–27). Once the groom meets the bride, He takes the bride to His Father's house (cf. John 14:2–3) where the wedding feast will complete the formal union of marriage (cf. Rev. 19:7–9). The first metaphor pictures an event based on elements found nowhere else in the New Testament to describe Christ's relationship with His church. But the second metaphor correctly incorporates several other key texts and provides a richer explanation of the event, using a recognized biblical metaphor—bride/church and Bridegroom/Christ.

Paul highlights the last—and lasting—feature of this reunion with the promise "and so we shall always be with the Lord" (v. 17). Here Paul does not specify just what happens after the reunion. The text ends with the meeting "in the clouds . . . in the air." He only says that the saints—both those raised and those changed (cf. 1 Cor. 15:51–52)—will be "always . . . with the Lord." If any implication is to be made, it seems most plausible to conclude that the saints remain with Jesus *wherever He happens to be*. Wanamaker comments, "Those who meet the Lord in the air . . . are caught up to a heavenly ascent by the clouds without any indication that they then return to earth." Indeed, he concludes that whatever the supposed connotations of *apantēsis* ("to meet") might be, "the rest of the imagery (the clouds and being caught up to the Lord) are indicative of an assumption to heaven of the people who belong to Christ." And the final phrase, "and so we shall always be with the Lord" (v. 17), "suggests that both dead and living Christians will return to heaven with the Lord, not only to enjoy continuous fellowship with him, but in terms of 1:10, to be saved from the coming wrath of God."[54]

PAUL'S INSTRUCTION ON THE DAY OF THE LORD:
1 THESSALONIANS 5:1–11

The Purpose of Paul's Teaching

Having assuaged the angst of the Thessalonians concerning their loved ones who had died, Paul moves on to another matter of concern for the believers in Thessalonica. The apostle is clearly considering a new subject "yet not one completely distinct from the previous one."[55] This is indicated by the transitional expression "Now as to" (*peri de*). Quite clearly both of these paragraphs have to do with eschatology, and Paul considers them to contain a related topic. However, he is answering a different question than he did in chapter 4. He is observing events from a wider angle, and here his intent is not to offer the believers comfort but to impart to them a needed exhortation. In the previous passage, Paul was addressing the concern of the Thessalonians about their departed loved ones and their part in the Lord's return for His own. In chapter 5, he is addressing matters that concerned the living Thessalonians themselves. The circumstances and experiences of the believers in Thessalonica were causing some to ask if the day of the Lord had already begun and even to wonder if they were fated to suffer the fury, sorrows, and troubles of that day (cf. 2 Thess. 2:2).

Thus Paul is taking a wider view and considering not just the rapture but the broader end-times picture. This is seen in his use of the phrase "the times and the epochs" and in his reference to the day of the Lord. The terms "times" (*chronos*) and "epochs" (*kairos*) have reference "in a general sense to the end times."[56] The first connotes "chronological time" as measured by a clock or calendar, and the second refers to events or eras of time. Used together, "the two [terms] apparently formed a stock phrase in the church's teaching about the end times (cf. Acts 1:7)."[57] "Taken together, the two terms suggest that the Thessalonians were curious about the timing of the end-time events. . . . Specifically, the congregation wanted to know when the rapture and the day of the Lord would take place."[58]

In the previous passage (4:13–18), Paul was informing the Thessalonians about matters over which there was some confusion, clarifying those matters so that they might not be "uninformed" (4:13). In chapter 5, he is reminding the Thessalonians of information they already possessed ("For you yourselves know," 5:2a) and exhorting them to apply that knowledge in practical Christian living.

The Substance of Paul's Teaching (5:2–3, 4b)

It seems likely that since Paul references the day of the Lord and indicates that the Thessalonians had some familiarity with the concept, they understood the broad sweep of this prominent biblical teaching either through Paul's own teaching or their familiarity with the Old Testament. The expression "day of the Lord" is found in both the Old and New Testaments: Isaiah 13:6, 9; Ezekiel 13:5; 30:3; Joel 1:15; 2:1, 11, 31; 3:14; Amos 5:18 (2x), 20; Obadiah 15; Zephaniah 1:7, 14 (2x); Zechariah 14:1; Malachi 4:5; Acts 2:20; 2 Thessalonians 2:2; 2 Peter 3:10. The more general expressions of "the day," "that day," or "the great day" occur more than seventy-five times in the Old Testament.[59]

Assuming the Thessalonians had something more than a passing understanding of the extensive biblical teaching concerning the day of the Lord, they would have known that that day will be a day of wrath, distress, destruction, desolation, darkness and gloom, and of battles (cf. Zeph. 1:5–16). It will be a day of judgment and vengeance (Isa. 34:8; 61:2; 63:4). It will begin with judgments against the nations (Isa. 2:12ff.; Ezek. 30:3; Joel 3:1ff.; Obad. 15; cf. Zech. 9:1–8; cf. Matt. 24:6–8), it will progress to judgments on the nation of Israel (Joel 1:15–20; 2:1; Amos 5:18; Zeph. 1:7ff.; see Matt. 24:9ff.), and will continue with the total destruction of the nations that oppose God's people. It will end with the blessing of the nation of Israel at the appearance of their Messiah (Zech. 14:1ff.).

Clearly, the day of the Lord is not limited to that last feature (the second coming) but includes the whole time of judgment on the nations. The day of the Lord also includes the seal judgments of Revelation 6:1–17 (i.e., the "birth pangs" of Matt. 24:6–8), which judgments are identified as the wrath of God and of the Lamb in Revelation 6:16–17. So the whole time—from the "birth pangs" to the final battle (cf. Zech. 9:10f; 14:3)—is rightly identified as the day of the Lord. "This time of trial at the outset of the earthly day of the Lord will thus not be brief."[60] That time is also called the tribulation (cf. Matt. 24:9, 21; cf. Mark 13:19).[61]

The Status of Unbelievers (5:3)

Apparently, Paul could have confidence that the Thessalonians were cognizant of these most prominent features of the day of the Lord, as well as its overall nature, so that here he needed only to remind them of one feature: the imminence of that day. Specifically, he noted that that day "will come just like a thief in the night."

This metaphor is employed in other texts (e.g., Matt. 24:36–43; Luke 12:35–40; 2 Pet. 3:10; Rev. 3:3; 16:15), and in each case the point is that the event at hand will come—as a thief does—unexpectedly and threateningly. This metaphor highlights the "suddenness," the "unexpected and threatening" nature of that day (cf. Zeph. 1:14). Paul adds another metaphor at the end of 5:3—that of "labor pains" coming upon a pregnant woman; he explicitly identifies the pertinent feature of this metaphor—"labor pains" come "suddenly." Furthermore, such pains are not merely painful, but they come on inexorably and they are increasingly intense and severe as they progress. Thus, the objects of this judgment will find that "their destruction will come upon them suddenly" and "they will not escape." That Paul has unbelievers in view here is clear by his careful use of pronouns: when addressing the Thessalonians he uses the second person plural "you." But in verse 3 he switches to the third person plural "they" in describing those who are caught unaware by that day. Furthermore, "the contrast expressed in verse 4 makes it clear that the reference ['they'] is to the unbelieving world, not the church."[62]

Another indication that unbelievers will be overtaken by the bewildering suddenness of the onset of the "day of the Lord" is the fact that it will happen "while they are saying, 'peace and safety!'" "'Peace' characterizes their inward repose," notes Thomas, "while 'safety' reveals their freedom from outward interference."[63] In other words, they will have a sense of calm and security and will be experiencing the prosperity, security, and confidence that comes from the absence of conflicts (wars) and enjoyment of social accord (domestic tranquility). While it is conceivable that there could be some who might make disingenuous pronouncements of "peace and safety" in times of genuine conflict and danger (as in Jeremiah's day when false prophets cried "'Peace, peace' when there is no peace," Jer. 6:14 ESV), it seems unlikely that this is what Paul has in mind here.

It seems better to understand that Paul meant that these people actually believe they enjoy, and indeed have a genuine sense of "peace and safety." That being the case, it seems unlikely that this is describing conditions at the end of the day of the Lord or at the time just prior to the second coming.[64] Rather, these are expressions that indicate that the perception of many at that time, both with respect to their personal conditions and the state of the world, that things are just fine. The sense of security and even optimism will be characteristic of many (if not most) in the unbelieving world just prior to His coming for His own (the rapture) and the arrival of the day of the Lord. They will be completely taken by surprise and will be utterly unprepared for the cataclysmic events to follow.

The Status of the Thessalonians (5:4b)

In stark contrast, Paul affirms that the day of the Lord will not be the experience of the living Thessalonians (and by extension to any believers who are living in the days prior to the rapture and onset of the day of the Lord). That day will not "overtake you [i.e., believers in the church at Thessalonians] like a thief." This begins to fill in the whole picture and to provide a fuller answer to the Thessalonians' questions.

As Paul wrote to the Thessalonians, the day of the Lord was clearly yet future. It was an event that "will come" (5:2). The verb here is "a vivid futuristic present" that indicates "the day is already on its way."[65] Its arrival is certain, but it has not yet arrived. Paul's statements regarding the unpreparedness of the unbeliever makes this clear as well ("then destruction *will* come . . . they *will* not escape"). This then would assure the living Thessalonian believers that they had not entered the day of the Lord; the tribulation was indeed coming, but it had not yet arrived.

Might some future generation of believers actually suffer what the Thessalonians had feared—and find themselves in the day of the Lord? Here it may be observed that both the rapture and the day of the Lord are portrayed as imminent events; that is, they could take place at any moment. But how can two events be equally imminent? As Thomas argues, "Were either the rapture or the day of the Lord to precede the other, one or the other would cease to be an imminent prospect." He adds, "Only if the rapture coincides with the beginning of the day of the Lord can both be imminent and the salvation of those in Christ coincide with the coming of wrath to the rest (v. 9)."[66]

Here, then, is not only an answer to the Thessalonians' concern but also a promise to the succeeding generations of believers. Since the rapture will take all living saints to be with the Lord at the same time that the day of the Lord commences, no believer need fear that he will be found in the day of the Lord. Hiebert concludes, "Believers have nothing to fear from that day. They will have been taken up in the rapture (4:13–18), the event which inaugurates the day of the Lord as the day of judgment on the world."[67]

The Application of Paul's Teaching on the Day of the Lord (5:4a, 5, 9–10)

Here Paul offers three reasons why he is so confident of his declaration to the Thessalonians that "the day would not overtake you" (5:4)—and why neither they nor any saint will enter the day of the Lord.

First, they live in a realm outside the realm of the unbelievers who are liable to the judgments of, and unwittingly in danger of, the terrors of that day. The Thessalonians are not "in darkness" (5:4a); Christians "are not of night nor of darkness" (5:5b) and they do not live in that realm. "The repeated negative with the genitive, 'not of the night, nor of darkness' indicates the domain to which they do not belong."[68] The connotation of darkness is a realm or domain opposed to God, disposed to sin, and characterized by rebellion (cf. Acts 26:18; Eph. 6:12; Col. 1:13). This is not where believers live (since they have been rescued from that domain "to the kingdom of His beloved Son," Col. 1:13). So they are not liable to the judgments that will befall those who live in that realm. Since believers are nonparticipants in the realm of darkness, they have "the promise of non-participation in 'the day' of the Lord."[69]

Second, they enjoy a status (or relationship) of "sons of light and sons of day" (5:5a). The expression "son of" was often used in the New Testament not to identify a man's paternal relationship but to indicate some "personal characteristic" of that individual. "'Son of . . .' was a Hebraism commonly found in the New Testament to ascribe some quality to the person named (cf. Mark 3:17; Luke 10:6 ESV; 16:8; John 17:12; Acts 4:36)."[70] Thus, the expression "sons of light" describes the believers' new understanding (John 1:8–9; as the "enlightened," cf. 2 Cor. 4:6), who have a "new nature (cf. John 12:36; Eph. 5:7–8), new relationship (cf. 1 Pet. 2:9; 1 John 2:8), and new destiny since they will become 'partakers of the inheritance of the saints in light' (Col. 1:12)."[71]

The expression "sons of day" is unique. It is "not attested anywhere else and so may have been a Pauline neologism."[72] The "doubling up" of the expression ("sons of . . . sons of . . .") emphasizes the point that believers have a different status and the day/night contrast is once again the contrast of two realms.[73] "Day is the realm in which [the believers] are now living as light-possessed men."[74] As such the believers "are not to be counted as belonging to either night or darkness, that is, the realm where God is neither present nor acknowledged."[75] Those who are in the realm of the day/light need not fear that they will suffer the fate of those in the realm of night/darkness. Believers "are not in darkness"; they possess an entirely different nature. The day of the Lord is a "day of darkness" (Joel 2:2; Zeph. 1:15); "the day of the Lord . . . will be darkness and not light" (Amos 5:18; cf. v. 20). MacArthur concludes the day of the Lord "is for night people; thus day people need not fear the Day of the Lord; they will not be a part of it."[76] This is borne out in the third reason for Paul's confidence.

Third, they have a promise of deliverance, salvation, and life (5:9–10). Paul makes the clearest statement he can to assure the living Thessalonians that they had not entered the day of the Lord—an assurance that rightly extends to all who are living in the realm of day/light (i.e., all who are believing in Christ at the time of His coming). He states, "God has not destined us for wrath." Some take the reference to "wrath" as something generic—God's displeasure with the wicked and ultimate judgment on the unbelieving.

However, in 1 Thessalonians 1:10 Paul made reference to something more specific, namely, "the wrath to come." Wanamaker suggests that this wrath to come "is the wrath that will come on the day of judgment."[77] There is some merit to that view. The New Testament frequently speaks of God's wrath being poured out on the wicked and unbelieving (cf. Matt. 3:7; John 3:36; Rom. 1:18; 2:5, 8; 3:5; 4:15; 5:9; 9:22; 12:19; Eph. 5:6; Col. 3:6; Rev. 14:9–11). But the only "day" Paul mentions in this letter is the day of the Lord. If the "wrath" in 1:10 is the same "wrath" referred to here in 5:9, it would seem obvious that "wrath to come" will arrive not on some undefined "day of judgment" but on and with *the* day of the Lord. So Thomas concludes, "Without question this wrath is future and specific, being identified with the messianic era just prior to his reappearance ([1 Thess.] 1:10; 2:16) and with the sudden destruction mentioned in v. 3" [i.e., 5:3].[78]

This is a deliverance to which believers have been "destined" or "appointed" (*etheto*, 5:9). When used of persons, *etheto* means "'to place, to appoint' to a position or service or 'to destine' them *unto* (*eis*) [translated here "for"] the realization of a definite goal."[79] So the idea here is believers have been definitely *not* "destined" for the day of the Lord. "When God vents his anger against earth dwellers (Rev. 6:16, 17), the body of Christ will be in heaven as the result of the happenings outlined in 4:14–17 (cf. 3:13)."[80] Thus, Paul is assuring the Thessalonians that they will "face neither temporal 'wrath' on the day of the Lord (cf. Rev. 6:17), nor eternal 'wrath' in hell."[81]

This deliverance is not just negative but also positive—it is "for obtaining salvation." The term "obtaining" (*peripoiēsin*) means something like "gaining," "winning," or "acquiring." There is no thought of "procuring one's salvation by works." This "salvation"[82] is provided by the grace that comes "through our Lord Jesus Christ, who died for us" (5:9b–10a). "The simple, yet profound phrase 'who died for us' (cf. Rom. 5:8) expresses the sole basis for believers' salvation."[83] The Greek word "for" (*hyper*) means "on our behalf," "in our place," or "as our substitute." No greater assurance of deliverance could be offered (cf. Rom. 8:31ff.). And this deliverance is for all believers—"whether we are awake or asleep."

The contrast here cannot be between those "who sleep [and] do their sleeping at night" (5:7a), for that would extend the promise of life ("we will live together") to those in the realm of night/darkness. Although it is conceivable, it is highly improbable that Paul has in mind actual physical sleep as over against the physical state of being awake, as if the promise is that believers will be delivered by the rapture even if they happen to be asleep in bed when He comes for His own.[84]

It is possible Paul has another sense in mind: the ones in view are all believers but some may be "sleeping believers" (i.e., those believers who are spiritually unprepared or distracted, acting like night people) and some may be "awake believers" (i.e., those believers who are prepared for the rapture and are living like day people should). But this imports a sense for the terms that is not found in this context. It seems better to return to the discussion back in 4:13–18 and understand Paul's promise here to include those who are "awake" as those "who are alive and remain" (4:15), and those "asleep" as those who "have fallen asleep in Jesus" (4:14), who are the "dead in Christ" (4:16). "The marvelous reality," MacArthur concludes, "is that all believers 'will live together with Him' as Jesus Himself promised" (cf. John 14:1–3) and Paul has revealed (cf. 1 Thess. 4:17).[85]

The Admonition and Encouragement of Paul's Teaching on the Day of the Lord (5:6–8, 11)

Paul does not leave his teaching at the theoretical level but applies this eschatological instruction to practical concerns. Paul's admonitions here (5:6–8) are introduced by the words "let us." Those who are in the realm of day/light must be alert ("not sleep"); they must be "sober,"[86] and they must be equipped with the believer's armor—"breastplate" and "helmet." Even this speaks to the believer's confidence and expectation of deliverance from the day of the Lord, as Paul explains these items in terms of "faith," "love," and "hope." Faith is "trust in God's power, purposes, and plan. It is the unwavering belief that God is completely trustworthy in all that He says and does."[87] Love is the believer's proof that he or she is "born of God and knows God" (1 John 4:7). Hope is the confident expectation that produces perseverance (Rom. 8:24–25).[88] "These three (faith, love, and hope) strengthened [the Thessalonians] for their present trials (1:3) and doubts (5:14)," writes Thomas. "[They] could confidently anticipate a future deliverance not to be enjoyed by those in darkness (v. 3), but assured to those in the realm of light (vv. 4–5)."[89]

Thus Paul concludes with this note of encouragement: "Therefore, encourage one another and build up one another, just as you also are doing" (1 Thess. 5:11). "Based on the truth he had given them, they were to reassure the anxious and fearful that they would not experience the Day of the Lord."[90] It seems rather obvious that, far from being nebulous or impractical or divisive, this is clear, practical, and unifying eschatological truth.

CONCLUSION

Paul clearly believed that he might be among those who would experience this wonderful event, this blessed hope of the rapture, when Jesus, the Bridegroom, returned (as He had promised in John 14:1–3) to retrieve His bride, the church. Paul believed the rapture was imminent (it could happen at any time). He taught the Thessalonians that their deceased loved ones would not miss this event, and that they would join one another in a wonderful, joyful reunion in the air with the Lord (1 Thess. 4:17). His teaching included the reassuring truth that they were not destined for the wrath of the day of the Lord, the future tribulation period (5:9), but for the joy of being with Jesus (4:17; 5:9). In light of Paul's belief and expectation, and his teachings and admonitions to the Thessalonians, it may be fairly concluded that in 1 Thessalonians Paul taught a pretribulation rapture of the church.

NOTES

1. John F. Walvoord, *The Thessalonian Epistles* (Grand Rapids: Zondervan, n. d.), 38.

2. D. Michael Martin, *1, 2 Thessalonians*, NAC (Nashville: Broadman, 1995), 143. Green attempts to draw the same dichotomy when he proposes that this "passage has suffered much ill as it has been mined to provide clues concerning the timing of the 'rapture' of the church. . . . This is not the stuff of speculative prophecy." Rather, "the text is located at the funeral home, the memorial service, and the graveside." Gene L. Green, *The Letters to the Thessalonians*, Pillar New Testament Commentary (Grand

Rapids: Eerdmans, 2002), 229. However, this fails to appreciate the simple point that Paul's purpose is to provide clear teaching (not speculation) about the timing of the believer's eschatological expectation precisely because that is where he finds comfort, assurance, and hope in the face of the stark reality of death.

3. See Alan Hultberg, "Introduction," *TVR1*, 24.

4. I. Howard Marshall, *1 and 2 Thessalonians* New Century Bible Commentary (London: Marshall, Morgan and Scott, 1963), 120–22.

5. Charles A. Wanamaker, *The Epistles to the Thessalonians*, New International Greek New Testament (Grand Rapids: Eerdmans, 1990), 165.

6. Ibid.

7. "In the Greek text, this [first class conditional] clause is the *protasis* of a conditional sentence that presents an assumption that is considered to be certain, 'For since we believe that Jesus died and rose . . .' (NRSV)." Green, *The Letters to the Thessalonians*, 220. A first-class conditional clause assumes that the condition stated in the "if" clause is a reality. James A. Brooks and Carton L. Winbery, *Syntax of New Testament Greek* (Lanham, MD: University Press of America, 1979), 163.

8. John MacArthur, *1 & 2 Thessalonians* (Chicago: Moody, 2002), 124.

9. Martin, *1, 2 Thessalonians*, 143.

10. Cf. Martin (ibid., 143 n 63) and Wanamaker (*The Epistles to the Thessalonians*, 167) both cite Homer (*Iliad* 11:241) and Sophocles (*Electra* 509) as well as Genesis 47:30; Isaiah 14:8; and 2 Maccabees 12:45.

11. Robert L. Thomas, "1, 2 Thessalonians," *Expositor's Bible Commentary*, ed. Frank E. Gaebelein, vol. 11 (Grand Rapids: Zondervan, 1978), 276. There is nothing here or anywhere in Paul's writings (or the New Testament) to suggest a doctrine of "soul sleep" or "unconscious existence" after death. The New Testament clearly indicates that believers when "absent from the body" are "at home with the Lord" (2 Cor. 5:8) not "asleep with the Lord." "To read the term as an ontological assertion regarding the state of believers in the interim between death and resurrection is to import ideas not supported by this context." Martin, *1, 2 Thessalonians*, 143–44.

12. Green, *The Letters to the Thessalonians*, 218; among others, Green cites Theocritus, "'Hopes are for the living; the dead are without hope' (*Idyll* 4.42)." William Barclay adds, "In the face of death the pagan world stood in despair. They met with grim resignation and bleak hopelessness." Barclay, *The Letters to the Philippians, Colossians, and the Thessalonians*, rev. ed. (Louisville: Westminster, 1975), 203.

13. Howard F. Vos, "Religions: Greco-Roman," *International Standard Bible Encyclopedia*, ed. Geoffrey W. Bromiley, rev. ed. (Grand Rapids: Eerdmans, 1988), 4:113–14. "These religions are commonly known as mystery religions because they had a secret initiatory ritual . . . and [offered] a promise of living in bliss with the deity beyond the grave" and "assured the initiate of eternal bliss in companionship with the deity." However, these notions were almost exclusively platonic and offered a "spiritual," indeed, "mysterious" relationship with the deity—notions far removed from that of "bodily resurrection."

14. Martin, *1, 2 Thessalonians*, 144.

15. "The majority of the NT writers invest *elpis*, 'hope,' with the nuance of 'confident expectation' or 'solid assurance.'" The verb form of this term conveys "the firm conviction that because of Jesus' resurrection from the dead we can have confidence as we face the future (Rom. 8:24–25; 1 Cor. 15:19)." William M. Mounce, ed., "Hope," *Mounce's Complete Expository Dictionary of Old and New Testament Words* (Grand Rapids: Zondervan, 2006), 340.

16. Green, *The Letters to the Thessalonians*, 219.

17. See again endnote 7.

18. It could be that Paul is referring to "a creedal formula that summarized Christian proclamation." Martin, *1, 2 Thessalonians*, 145. If so, this would indicate that belief in Jesus' bodily resurrection was an early and consistent part of Paul's gospel proclamation and very likely a significant part of his previous instruction to the Thessalonians.

19. In support of the view that Paul is drawing much of his teaching about the rapture and the day of the Lord from portions of the Olivet Discourse, see chapter 2, "Jesus and the Rapture: Matthew 24."

20. Floyd H. Barackman, *Practical Christian Theology* (Grand Rapids: Kregel, 2001), 519.

21. D. Edmond Hiebert, *The Thessalonian Epistles* (Chicago: Moody, 1971), 195.

22. Ibid., 196. Also, this view renders moot the question of where the "quotation" from the Lord begins and ends (cf. the discussion of Martin, *1, 2 Thessalonians*, 147–48).

23. Hiebert, *The Thessalonian Epistles*, 196.

24. Robert Hanna, *A Grammatical Aid to the Greek New Testament* (Grand Rapids: Baker, 1983), 379; citing C. F. D. Moule, *An Idiom Book of New Testament Greek*, vol. 1 (Edinburgh: T. & T. Clark, 1908), 57.

25. Hiebert, *The Thessalonian Epistles*, 194.

26. Martin, *1, 2 Thessalonians*, 146.

27. Hiebert, *The Thessalonian Epistles*, 195.

28. Wanamaker, *The Epistles to the Thessalonians*, 172. Wanamaker adds that Paul's "parenetic instruction in 1 Cor. 7:25–31 is determined by his belief that the adult generation at the time of his writing was the last generation before the end."

29. MacArthur, *1 & 2 Thessalonians*, 133.

30. Hiebert, *The Thessalonian Epistles*, 197; in the original Greek *ou mē* with the aorist subjunctive.

31. Wanamaker, *The Epistles to the Thessalonians*, 172.

32. Martin, *1, 2 Thessalonians*, 149.

33. Hiebert, *The Thessalonian Epistles*, 197–98.

34. See Hiebert, *The Thessalonian Epistles*, 198–99.

35. Wanamaker, *The Epistles to the Thessalonians*, 173.

36. Hiebert, *The Thessalonian Epistles*, 198. Perhaps the instance of Jesus calling out Lazarus's name in John 11:43 is a good analogy. See MacArthur, *1 & 2 Thessalonians*, 134.

37. MacArthur, *1 & 2 Thessalonians*, 134. "It is impossible to say who the archangel whose voice will be heard at the Rapture is."

38. Wanamaker, *The Epistles to the Thessalonians*, 173. The references cited by Wanamaker: "(Ex. 19:16, 19; Isa. 27:13; Joel 2:1; Zeph. 1:14–16; Zech. 9:14); (cf. . . . Matt. 24:31; Rev. 8:2, 6, 13; 9:14)."

39. MacArthur, *1 & 2 Thessalonians*, 134.

40. Hiebert, *The Thessalonian Epistles*, 201.

41. Martin, *1, 2 Thessalonians*, 152.

42. There are instances recorded in Scripture when a heavenly voice was heard on earth and although those to whom it was not directed did indeed hear the sounds, they failed to discern any meaning from it or to understand its significance. See Acts 9:7; 22:9; John 12:28–30.

43. Hiebert, *The Thessalonian Epistles*, 201. "The picture is not to be equated with Revelation 20:1–10."

44. Ibid., 202. In a footnote, Hiebert cites Acts 22:23; 1 Corinthians 9:26; 14:9; Revelation 9:2; 16:17 as support for *air* (*aera*) meaning the atmosphere.

45. Marshall, *1 and 2 Thessalonians*, 128. Just what those "antinomies and contradictions" would be he does not specify.

46. J. J. Collins, *The Apocalyptic Imagination* (New York: Crossroads, 1984), 214, who argues, "The language of the apocalypses is not descriptive, referential newspaper language, but the *expressive* language of poetry, which uses symbols and imagery to articulate a sense or feeling about the world. Their abiding value does not lie in the pseudo-information they provide about cosmology or future history, but in their affirmation of a transcendent world"; as cited in Wanamaker, *The Epistles to the Thessalonians*, 172–73.

47. Wanamaker, *The Epistles to the Thessalonians*, 173.

48. BDAG, 3rd ed. (Chicago: University of Chicago Press, 2000), 134.

49. MacArthur, *1 & 2 Thessalonians*, 136.

50. Those who appeal to this meaning are many: cf. Ernest Best, *The First and Second Epistles to the Thessalonians* (London: Hendrickson, 1986), 199; Green, *The Thessalonians*, 226, 228; Anthony A. Hoekema, "Amillennialism," in *The Meaning of the Millennium: Four Views*, ed. Robert G. Clouse (Downers Grove, IL: InterVarsity, 1977), 183, 216 n. 19; Abraham J. Malherbe, *The Letters to the Thessalonians* (New York: Doubleday, 2000); Martin, *1, 2 Thessalonians*, 153 n. 86; Wanamaker, *The Epistles to the Thessalonians*, 175; and many others. See also Justin Taylor, "9 Reasons We Can Be Confident Christians Won't Be Raptured before the Tribulation," *The Gospel Coalition*, August 5, 2014: http://www.thegospelcoalition.org/blogs/justintaylor/2014/08/05/9-reasons-we-can-be-confident-christians-wont-be-raptured-before-the-tribulation/, accessed January 6, 2015.

51. See Erik Peterson, "Die Einholung des Kyrios," *Zeitschrift für Systematische Theologie* 7: 1929-30 (682-702).

52. Michael R. Crosby, "Hellenistic Formal Receptions and Paul's Use of *APANTHSIS* in 1 Thessalonians 4:17," *Bulletin for Biblical Research* 4 (1994): 19.

53. Green, *The Letters to the Thessalonians*, 228.

54. Wanamaker, *The Epistles to the Thessalonians*, 175.

55. Thomas, "1, 2 Thessalonians," 11:280.

56. MacArthur, *1 & 2 Thessalonians*, 136.

57. Martin, *1, 2 Thessalonians*, 156. "The pair may have been stereotyped to the point that they were used as a couplet without regard to the meaning of the individual words."

58. MacArthur, *1 & 2 Thessalonians*, 142. Green notes, "Preoccupation with the timing of the day of the Lord arose frequently in biblical and Jewish literature; thus the question the Thessalonians raised is hardly surprising." See Daniel 12:6; Matthew 24:3; Acts 1:6. Green, *The Letters to the Thessalonians*, 231.

59. For added detail on the day of the Lord, see chapter 3.

60. Thomas, "1, 2 Thessalonians," 11:281.

61. See Leon J. Wood, *The Bible and Future Events* (Grand Rapids: Zondervan, 1973), 55.

62. Hiebert, *The Thessalonian Epistles*, 212. Hiebert adds, "The vast masses of mankind will be preoccupied with the things of this earth and will show no interest in preparing for the Lord's coming." See also Matthew 24:37-39; Luke 17:26-27.

63. Thomas, "1, 2 Thessalonians," 11:282.

64. This is especially so when one realizes that if the day of the Lord is understood as the second coming itself, these pronouncements are being made in the throes of the "great tribulation, such as has not occurred since the beginning of the world until now, nor ever will" (Matt. 24:21).

65. Thomas, "1, 2 Thessalonians," 11:281.

66. Ibid.

67. Hiebert, *The Thessalonian Epistles*, 215.

68. Ibid., 215, 217. "*Night* and *darkness* are again figurative; *night* being the state of man's alienation from God who is light, and *darkness* the realm of sin and iniquity." Ibid., 217.

69. Thomas, "1, 2 Thessalonians," 11:283.

70. Martin, *1, 2 Thessalonians*, 163; cf. F. Blass and A. Debrunner, *A Greek Grammar of the New Testament and Other Early Christian Literature*, trans. and rev. Robert W. Funk (Chicago: University of Chicago, 1961), §162.6; Nigel Turner, *A Grammar of New Testament Greek*, vol. III, *Syntax* (Edinburgh: T. & T. Clark, 1963), 207-8.

71. Hiebert, *The Thessalonian Epistles*, 217.

72. Wanamaker, *The Epistles to the Thessalonians*, 182.

73. See Hiebert (*The Thessalonian Epistles*, 217–18) who suggests that there may be an intentional chiastic structure here. Whether there is or not, it seems that Paul meant to emphasize the uniqueness of the believer's status by the use of the expression "sons of" for them but not for the corresponding status of the unbeliever—they are not called "sons of darkness . . . sons of night."

74. Ibid., 217.

75. Wanamaker, *The Epistles to the Thessalonians*, 183.

76. MacArthur, *1 & 2 Thessalonians*, 158.

77. Wanamaker, *The Epistles to the Thessalonians*, 183; cf. Hiebert, *The Thessalonian Epistles*, 223.

78. Thomas, "1, 2 Thessalonians," 11:285.

79. Hiebert, *The Thessalonian Epistles*, 222.

80. Thomas, "1, 2 Thessalonians," 11:285.

81. MacArthur, *1 & 2 Thessalonians*, 163.

82. While the whole of the believer's salvation—justification, sanctification, and glorification—was accomplished by Christ's sacrificial death, Paul likely has the final phase, glorification, in mind here.

83. MacArthur, *1 & 2 Thessalonians*, 164.

84. Thomas cites this view and rightly rejects it. Thomas, "1, 2 Thessalonians," 11:285.

85. Cf. MacArthur, *1 & 2 Thessalonians*, 164.

86. The aside or parenthetical comment in verse 7 seems to indicate that Paul meant this admonition to be taken in more than a metaphorical sense. Those who are living in the realm of day/light must never be counted among those who drink so as to literally "get drunk." To do so would belie their claim and status as people of the day/light realm.

87. MacArthur, *1 & 2 Thessalonians*, 161.

88. See note 15 above.

89. Thomas, "1, 2 Thessalonians," 11:284.

90. MacArthur, *1 & 2 Thessalonians*, 164.

7

Paul and the Rapture:
2 Thessalonians 2

BY NATHAN D. HOLSTEEN

Now we request you, brethren, with regard to the coming of our Lord Jesus Christ and our gathering together to Him, that you may not be quickly shaken from your composure or be disturbed either by a spirit or a message or a letter as if from us, to the effect that the day of the Lord has come. Let no one in any way deceive you, for it will not come unless the apostasy comes first, and the man of lawlessness is revealed, the son of destruction, who opposes and exalts himself above every so-called god or object of worship, so that he takes his seat in the temple of God, displaying himself as being God. Do you not remember that while I was still with you, I was telling you these things?

2 Thessalonians 2:1–5

I've never been a big fan of jigsaw puzzles. Oh, sure, there have been times when I've been sucked into a family-focused task of putting together a ten-million-piece puzzle. But I've never gotten "the bug." It's interesting enough, but not addictive.

It's rather ironic, then, that one of the central interests of my professional career has revolved around the principle of *coherence*. In engineering and in theology, the question "how do the various pieces fit together?" is critical. It's the difference between success and failure. It's the difference between compelling sense and utter nonsense.

In this chapter I plan to approach the text of 2 Thessalonians 2 as if it were a jigsaw puzzle. When people put together a jigsaw puzzle, they typically seek out the "corner pieces" first, and then they begin to assemble the "edge pieces." This is commonplace, precisely because the shape of a corner or edge piece—the shape of the piece itself—makes it clear where the piece belongs in the puzzle.

When we take this approach to the text of 2 Thessalonians 2, a surprising picture comes into focus. The rapture must be pretribulational. There is no other way to put the pieces of the puzzle together. When someone who believes in a posttribulation rapture comes to the puzzle of 2 Thessalonians 2, he or she will always end up leaving out a piece or two. (By the way, don't you *hate* it when you get to the end of a five-thousand-piece jigsaw puzzle only to discover that *one piece* is missing?) The other option the posttributionist may choose is to pull out a pair of theological scissors and trim the offending piece to match the hole they have left in their puzzle. Either way, the rest of us know immediately that the rules of jigsaw puzzledom[1] have been violated. The principle of *coherence* has been destroyed. We have encountered nonsense rather than compelling sense.

In keeping with the theme of solving a jigsaw puzzle, I intend to approach the text of 2 Thessalonians 2 by identifying first the corner pieces and edge pieces. Once we have figured out how these pieces "frame" the overall picture provided by 2 Thessalonians 2, we will turn our attention to the pieces in the center of the puzzle—the ones most difficult to place. Every step of the way, my desire is to keep the *shape* of each piece in mind. Only in this way can we hope to arrive at a completed puzzle.

ASSEMBLING THE PUZZLE: THE CORNER PIECES

Virtually all commentators agree on certain ideas in the text of 2 Thessalonians 2. Whether they are conservative or liberal, whether they affirm a pretribulation rapture or a posttribulation rapture (or indeed some other flavor), the overwhelming majority of commentators agree on several points in the text. Those common points are what I call the "corner pieces." The shape of those pieces is so distinctive and so clear that few are willing to challenge their placement.

Specifically, very few will argue against these two ideas that frame the text of 2 Thessalonians 2: (1) the Thessalonian believers had received a message, one purported to have its origin in the Pauline entourage; and (2) this message was, according to Paul, a deception.

1. "A Spirit or a Message or a Letter as if from Us"

Commentators agree that the setting of Paul's second letter is the church in Thessalonica. This is because Paul provides valuable contextual clues as to this setting. Paul urges them not to be "quickly shaken from [their] composure or . . . disturbed either by a spirit or a message or a letter as if from us, to the effect that the day of the Lord has come" (v. 2). The Thessalonians had received a message, somehow purporting to be authoritative. Perhaps they thought that the message came from God by means of a spirit, or perhaps they thought that it came from a letter from Paul and his entourage. We do not know. But what we do know is that Paul clarified the situation for the Thessalonians. He had heard of such a message, and he wanted to set the record straight.

While it may seem pedantic, I think that it is critically important that we start with this observation if we want to construct our jigsaw puzzle correctly. It is a point of significant agreement among commentators, and one that is determinative in shaping our understanding of the entire passage. The Thessalonian believers, after having been instructed by Paul in his first letter (1 Thessalonians), had encountered a message that they *thought* was authoritative. This message, as we are going to discover shortly, was erroneous. The conflict between what Paul had already taught and what the new message was suggesting was the source of trouble in the Thessalonian church.

2. "Let No One . . . Deceive You"

The second corner piece that we encounter in 2 Thessalonians 2 is the observation that the message received by the Thessalonian church was, in fact, erroneous. It was a deception, not in accord with the truth previously taught by Paul.

Once again, the overwhelming majority of commentators agree. That's why I consider this a corner piece. The passage itself makes no sense whatsoever if we ignore this observation. It is explicit in the text, and commentators who disagree on a host of other issues find themselves in stunning agreement here.[2]

The crucial point here is that the Thessalonians had received a message they thought was authoritative, but the message, according to Paul, was deceptive. This point cannot be brought into doubt by any suggestion arising from the consideration of other pieces in the puzzle. It is *always* a mistake to ignore the corner pieces in a jigsaw puzzle. Once you recognize them and what they contribute to the recognition of the picture, they stand unmoved.

As we proceed, we are going to encounter certain puzzle-solvers who, without denying that this is a corner piece, are going to attempt to give this piece a slightly different coloring. This, too, is unacceptable. Here's the truth one more time. The message received by the Thessalonians was a *lie*. It was *wrong*. It was a *deception*. We will encounter the reasons for this forceful language shortly.

THE EDGE PIECES

The second step in solving a jigsaw puzzle is to arrange the edge pieces appropriately. In the case of 2 Thessalonians 2, there are a number of phrases that occasion some degree of debate and yet are absolutely critical in determining the way the rest of the passage fits together. These phrases, then, I will call "edge pieces." Their shape *should* be enough to bring about agreement from the majority of interpreters, but in certain cases the shape of the piece is subjugated to some interpreter's desire to change the picture painted by the passage. The result, of course, is confusion. One cannot change an edge piece without destroying the integrity of the picture.

I suggest that there are several edge pieces. Each one of them ought to be clear as to how they fit into the overall picture, and each ought to be clear as to how it helps bring clarity to the rest of the picture. In this case, the argument of this chapter is simple: we ought to consider these pieces in the light of how they fit within this passage. The concept of coherence is our guide.

"The Coming of Our Lord Jesus Christ and Our Gathering . . . to Him"

The phrase "with regard to the coming of our Lord Jesus Christ and our gathering together to Him" (2 Thess. 2:1) has occasioned significant debate in discerning its meaning. The point in question is simply this: Does Paul envision Christ's coming here as synonymous—or at least contemporaneous—with "our gathering together to Him"?

The first point that one ought to observe is that there is no basis for claiming that the two events are synonymous on the basis of Greek grammar. Some have attempted to apply the Granville Sharp rule to this passage,[3] which would make the "coming" and the "gathering together" apply to the same event. But such an application is invalid.[4] Any discussion of the identity of "the coming of our Lord" and "our gathering together to Him" must be held on the basis of the context, not simply on the basis of the erroneous application of a principle from Greek grammar.[5]

If the two terms are not, textually speaking, required to pertain to one event, the question that arises immediately is this: To what do the phrases "coming of our Lord Jesus Christ" and "our gathering together to Him" refer?

It should be admitted up front that determining the referents of these two phrases is going to be an exercise in correlation—connecting the ideas presented here with similar ideas encountered elsewhere in Scripture. As a result, the interpreter's theological bias is likely to become visible, at least to some extent, in the process. No one is immune to this; we can only do our best to identify the links that are most probable in view of the variety of passages that come to bear on this subject. We must also, in view of the main point of this chapter, assess the overall fit of our hypotheses within the main thrust of this passage. In other words, if our correlation with other passages leads us to suggest a meaning for "the coming of our Lord" that mars the basic picture painted by this passage, we must conclude that we have done the job of correlation poorly; we have erroneously imported meanings from other passages of Scripture that do not belong here in 2 Thessalonians 2.

With that said, let's tackle the first phrase. The meaning of "the coming of our Lord Jesus Christ" seems reasonably straightforward, because the context of 2 Thessalonians 2 is in agreement with one well-attested usage of this terminology elsewhere in Scripture.[6] The referent seems to be the second coming of our Lord.

This suggestion is bolstered first by the preceding context of 2 Thessalonians 2. In 2 Thessalonians 1:9–10, Paul describes the justice that will be meted out when Jesus comes (note that this is a different word in Greek; *erchomai* is the word used here, whereas *parousia* is the word used in 2 Thess. 2:1). But in chapter 2, our understanding of the coming of Jesus to which Paul refers there is enhanced by the description Paul offers. He refers to this coming as the "revelation" (Gk. *apokalupsis*) of our Lord, accompanied by mighty angels and flaming fire. What this means is that as we read Paul's second letter to the Thessalonians, the idea of our Lord's second coming is firmly in our mind as we reach the beginning of chapter 2. Consequently, it seems very natural (and highly probable) that Paul's use of the phrase "the coming of our Lord Jesus Christ" refers to the second coming.

This suggestion is further corroborated by the very passage we are examining. In 2 Thessalonians 2:8, Paul explains that the lawless one (the man of lawlessness) will be brought to an end by the appearance of Christ's coming (again, this is the Greek word *parousia*). It seems virtually unmistakable in this context that Paul is using the phrase "the coming of our Lord Jesus Christ" to refer to the second coming.

The situation is very different when we come to the second phrase, "our gathering together to Him." There is nothing at all in the preceding context to help us figure out the referent of "our gathering together to Him." Nor is there anything in the succeeding context to help us figure out what the referent is. This is true, of course, unless one sees the *apostasia* in verse 3 as a reference to the rapture. We will discuss this shortly.

As a result, most commentators look elsewhere in Scripture for candidates in determining the referent of "our gathering." And this, as it turns out, is a very easy task. Paul provided a compelling parallel to this kind of language in his first letter to the Thessalonians. Looking at 1 Thessalonians 4:17, we find these words: "Then we who are alive and remain will be caught up together with them in the clouds to meet the Lord in the air, and so we shall always be with the Lord."[7] This passage, the famous source of our term *rapture,* correlates very nicely with the idea we find in the phrase "our gathering together to Him."

It is entirely relevant at this point to observe the significant biblical and contextual basis in support of this correlation. In 2 Thessalonians 2:5, Paul, in correcting the erroneous teaching that the Thessalonians had encountered, interjects a reminder: "Do you not remember that while I was still with you, I was telling you these things?" We can legitimately infer, then, that Paul's teaching in 2 Thessalonians 2 was not entirely new to the Thessalonians; Paul had already taught them these things.

By logical extension, then, we should not be surprised if we find a correlative concept in 1 Thessalonians 4 that helps us understand 2 Thessalonians 2. The rapture in 1 Thessalonians 4 reasonably provides the concept that Paul intends when he uses the phrase "our gathering together to Him" in 2 Thessalonians 2.

The result of this discussion of the two phrases is this: we have identified very strong candidates for both referents. Both are supported by the immediate context, and by usage outside 2 Thessalonians. It is no wonder, then, that these identifications find broad support from commentators, even when those commentators disagree strongly on the overall teaching of 2 Thessalonians 2.

Of course, the mere appearance of these two phrases together does not answer the question "Is the rapture simply a part of the second coming?" Those commentators who read these phrases as an indication that the second coming *includes* the rapture are not getting that idea from this text.[8] If such an idea is to be affirmed, it must be coming from somewhere else in Scripture, or from the presuppositions of the commentator—and therefore should be subjected to intense scrutiny. In all honesty, this teaching can only be mentioned in 2 Thessalonians 2 if it is imported from elsewhere. Again, the idea of one event with two different "faces" is not found in this passage.

An example might help here. If, in speaking to a friend, I say that "I am looking forward to my mother's coming, and to our attending the concert," I am *not* implying that my mother's arrival and the concert are two sides of the same event. Rather, the natural implication is that they are two distinct events that are somehow conceptually connected. I suggest that this is exactly the case with "the coming of our Lord" and "our gathering together to Him."

This is where the main focus of this chapter comes into play once again. When we ask the question "How do all the pieces in this passage fit together?" we are actually led by the passage to conclude that "the coming of our Lord" and "our gathering together to Him" are two separate events. This is because the subject matter of 2 Thessalonians 2 is simple to determine. Nobody disagrees with the subject matter of 2 Thessalonians 2, for to do so would call into question one's ability to read reasonably simple texts. The subject matter of 2 Thessalonians 2 is *not* the second coming. Instead, the subject matter is, broadly speaking, the day of the Lord—which culminates in the second coming.[9]

When we observe the actual subject matter of the passage, we are led to a significant question for those who suggest that "the coming of our Lord Jesus Christ" and "our gathering together to Him" are two aspects of the same event. Granting the posttribulational perspective (for the sake of argument), the question is this: Why would Paul start this passage by mentioning *one event* (a posttribulation rapture at the time of the second coming), and then proceed to discuss the entire breadth of the seven-year tribulation? This is not unlike a sportscaster advertising a show in which she plans to discuss the San Antonio Spurs' epic Game 5 victory over the Miami Heat to win the NBA Championship in 2014. But when you tune in to the broadcast, you find that she actually talks about the entire Spurs season. You tuned in to hear about Game 5 but instead you hear a long story about the whole season.

You know what many listeners would do? They would change channels, because what was advertised and what was delivered were two different things.

My conviction is that we should expect nothing less from the inspired writer of Scripture. We *should* expect a significant fit between what a biblical writer says he's going to talk about, and what he actually talks about.

In this case, just such a fit is apparent here in 2 Thessalonians 2—as long as one does not bring with him preconceived notions that the second coming and the rapture are two sides of the same coin. As it turns out, they are not two sides of the same coin. They are completely different events. Paul's introductory statement creates a conceptual space within which he offers the doctrinal correction contained in the rest of the chapter. Paul's introductory statement brings to the reader's attention a time span *from* the rapture *to* the second coming (even though Paul reverses the order here, listing the second coming first). Then, using the remainder of the chapter, Paul fills in the salient events (but not all of them, obviously) that are to occur within this time span.

When we recognize this, Paul's words ring out clear and true. They fit. When Paul writes, "with regard to the coming of our Lord Jesus Christ and our gathering together to Him" (2 Thess. 2:1), he actually means "with regard to the second coming [which occurs at the end of the day of the Lord] and the rapture [which occurs at the beginning of the day of the Lord]." This understanding provides a much better fit with the content of the passage.

The Day of the Lord

The second of our edge pieces has to do with the phrase "the day of the Lord" in 2 Thessalonians 2:2. As we have already seen, this phrase is critical in that it must fit with one of our corner pieces. The deceptive message received by the Thessalonian believers is clarified here. The deception was that someone claimed the day of the Lord had come. Our understanding of what the day of the Lord is will shape our understanding of this passage. That's why this is an edge piece. Not everyone agrees on what "the day of the Lord" means, and as a result very different pictures are imagined.

However, this is where our approach to 2 Thessalonians 2—the idea of completing a jigsaw puzzle—really helps us. As we will see, there are some suggestions as to the meaning of the phrase "day of the Lord" that do have *some* biblical support from other passages. But when one brings those suggestions into *this* passage, the result is confusion. Such suggestions ought to be rejected, simply because they do not work in the context of 2 Thessalonians 2.

One such view—a view that is doomed to failure because it simply cannot be forced into 2 Thessalonians 2—is offered by Robert H. Gundry. Gundry's view is that the day of the Lord is a reference to the second coming, and not a reference to any part of the tribulation. Gundry writes, "The identification of that day [the day of the Lord, mentioned in his previous sentence] with the hope of Christians once more points to a posttribulational rapture since, as we have already seen, the day of the Lord will not begin until after the tribulation."[10]

This view causes devastation to the text of 2 Thessalonians 2. Why? Because of the shape of the lie that the Thessalonian believers had been told. They had been told "the day of the Lord has come." But if the day of the Lord *is identified as* a posttribulation rapture at the second coming (as Gundry suggests), the fact that the day of the Lord had already come could hardly be believed by the Thessalonians. They could certainly know they were not raptured and resurrected yet. Since the nature of the deception in 2 Thessalonians is the subject of the next puzzle piece, I will forego any further discussion here.

A far better option for understanding "the day of the Lord" in 2 Thessalonians 2:2 is affirmed by Wanamaker. Even though Wanamaker holds to a posttribulation rapture,[11] the shape of this passage forces him to suggest that the Thessalonians most likely understood the day of the Lord "not as a literal twenty-four-hour period but as the final period of the present order culminating in the coming of the Lord Jesus."[12] In other words, Wanamaker suggests that the day of the Lord is "something similar to the Jewish idea of the 'messianic woes,' a period of severe distress before the appearance of the messiah, who would usher in the period of salvation."[13]

This view, which considers the day of the Lord as mentioned in 2 Thessalonians 2:2 to be a part of what many would call "the tribulation," has much to commend it. First, it coheres well with the context of 2 Thessalonians 2. As we have already seen, the view that the day of the Lord is a reference to the second coming of our Lord is completely incompatible with the context; such a view renders the whole message meaningless. But the view that the day of the Lord is the tribulation—or some particular part of the tribulation—has great merit. Secondly, this view has widespread support among commentators. As a matter of fact, commentators who take a posttribulational view of the rapture and commentators who take a pretribulational view have affirmed this perspective on the meaning of the day of the Lord.[14]

The reason for this agreement even across pretribulational/posttribulational lines is simple: the text of 2 Thessalonians forces the reader in this direction if the reader wishes to make any sense of the passage. Reading "the day of the Lord" as "the second coming" does not work, as we have already mentioned. In addition, there are very few who would be willing to allow that the day of the Lord refers to anything *prior* to the rapture/tribulation time period. Consequently, many commentators agree. The day of the Lord here is a reference to the future seven-year tribulation, or some particular part of the tribulation. In a stunning display of coherence, Paul has chosen a term that fits precisely with his introductory statement, "with regard to the coming of our Lord Jesus Christ and our gathering together to Him" (2 Thess. 2:1). The day of the Lord is a term that refers generally to the same time period. It all fits . . . again![15]

"It Will Not Come"

The third of our edge pieces is demonstrably connected to one of our corner pieces and another one of the edge pieces. In the NASB, the phrase is "it will not come." In context, this phrase in 2:3 is connected with the edge piece we called "the day of the Lord," for the phrase "the day of the Lord" is the antecedent of the pronoun "it" in the phrase "it will not come." This third edge piece is also connected to a corner piece—the one we called "let no one deceive you in any way." That's because "it will not come" is the divine truth that stands in correction to the lie the Thessalonians had heard. They had heard that the day of the Lord had come, but the divine truth is that the day of the Lord will not have come unless two things are seen first. More about this later.

For now, we should start by observing that this edge piece in 2 Thessalonians 2:3 presents an interesting challenge with respect to the grammar of the passage. Paul makes use of a conditional statement, but only provides the reader with the first part. Paul writes, "Unless the apostasy comes first, and the man of lawlessness is revealed," leaving the "then" part of the conditional statement unexpressed.

In order to follow the flow of Paul's argument, we are going to need to fill in the blank of the missing apodosis (the "then" part of the conditional statement). Most commentators agree that the best way to do this is to connect the missing apodosis to the previous context. Likewise, most familiar translations of the Bible in English follow this pattern—connecting the apodosis to the previous statement in verse 2, "that the day of the Lord has come."[16]

This is where the fun begins. The verb that most commentators look to for guidance in filling in the missing apodosis, *enestēken*, is in the perfect tense. That is why most translations use a phrase something like "shaken from your composure or . . . disturbed either by a spirit or a message or a letter as if from us, to the effect that the day of the Lord *has come*" (2 Thess. 2:2). The words "has come" in that phrase represent the translators' choice in rendering the word *enestēken*.[17] But what, then, is the opposite of "has come"? It would seem that this meaning is the one we seek when we fill in the missing apodosis.

I asked a colleague, who is both a graduate of the University of Notre Dame and a skilled thinker, to fill in the blank in the following story: Do not believe it if someone tells you that the final reign of Notre Dame football has come. For I tell you the truth, unless LSU wins a national championship first . . .

Now as our conversation unfolded, this colleague correctly identified the form of the verb that is implied by the structure of the story. The missing phrase is this: *the final reign of Notre Dame football has not come.*

The point, I believe, is clear. The missing apodosis in Paul's text is this: *the day of the Lord has not come.*

Putting this back into the flow of Paul's thought, here is a paraphrase clarifying the meaning we find in Paul's text: "I urge you not to be shaken or disturbed by any message to the effect that the day of the Lord has come. Do not be deceived in that way, for I tell you that the day of the Lord has not come unless the apostasy comes first and the man of lawlessness is revealed."

Many commentators and translators subtly shift the tense of the supplied verb when they fill in the missing apodosis. The NASB, for example, supplies the phrase "*it [the day of the Lord] will not come* unless. . . ." This choice, it seems to me, is not driven by the text or the structure of the text—it is driven by other, unidentified factors. My conviction is that we ought to make exegetical choices that are driven first by the text, considered in its grammatical, literary, and historical contexts. When we do that in this passage, it seems reasonable that our preference in filling in the missing apodosis will be "the day of the Lord has not come."

What is the point? Simply this. Second Thessalonians does *not* say that the apostasy and the revealing of the man of lawlessness *precede* the day of the Lord. The text itself is ambiguous on this point; it does not say whether these two events precede the day of the Lord, or whether these two events form the initial stage of the day of the Lord.[18] What the text says is this: you can know that you are not in the day of the Lord unless you have seen the apostasy and the revealing of the man of lawlessness.[19] The day of the Lord will not have come unless you see the apostasy and the revealing of the Antichrist.

THE CENTER PIECES

The final stage in solving a jigsaw puzzle is to wrestle with the fit of the center pieces. These are pieces that may at first seem to fit in a number of different ways, and as a result there is great debate over exactly what their shape is. However, at the end of the day, there is only one fit that completes the picture in the precise way the picture was intended. Any other approach is forced, and creates a degree of incoherence in the picture that the puzzle was not meant to present.

At the same time, we should recognize that not all center pieces affect the picture in exactly the same way. As we are about to discover, some center pieces play a much more integral role in completing the picture. Others may allow for a little ambiguity.

In the case of 2 Thessalonians 2, two phrases fit the description of a "center piece." Both have been the subject of significant disagreement. For the first center piece, we will discover that some degree of ambiguity is tolerable. For the second center piece, once we examine the nature of this disagreement—and how this phrase fits into the overall picture that we have already come to see with abundant clarity—we will conclude that there is only one possible placement for this piece. And when we see that placement, the puzzle will be complete.

The Greek Word Apostasia

The first of the center pieces we should consider is the single word *apostasia*. In the NASB, this word is rendered "apostasy."

In the context of 2 Thessalonians 2, this word's place is easy to decipher. Paul, by the inspiration of the Holy Spirit, teaches the Thessalonians that the day of the Lord will not have come unless the *apostasia* comes first and the man of lawlessness is revealed (2 Thess. 2:3). But exactly what is the *apostasia*?

The vast majority of interpreters suggest that the *apostasia* is a religious or political defection—a falling away from the faith, which is an action typically associated with the Antichrist himself. To be sure, the text gives plenty of reasons for this suggestion.

Gundry agrees with this suggestion—that the *apostasia* in 2 Thessalonians

2:3 is a "religious apostasy or political defection."[20] But beyond this, he actually denies that the immediate context ought to help us understand the meaning of the word. Gundry writes:

> There is a measure of truth in the statement that the idea of defection comes from the context. However, when the word appears exclusively or predominantly in such contexts—in the NT, the LXX, the *koine*, and classical Greek— defection becomes inherent to the meaning. Where a question [raised by the context] arises, therefore, we are bound to recognize the prevailing connotation of the word.[21]

Gundry—despite the fact that he has overlooked the context—maintains, to his credit, a sense of consistency in linking his understanding of the day of the Lord with his understanding of the *apostasia*. Recall that Gundry views the day of the Lord as a reference to Christ's second coming, not to the tribulation. Therefore, it becomes clear that the chronological relationships articulated by the passage are viable when using Gundry's understanding of what the day of the Lord is and what the *apostasia* is. To simplify, his position becomes this: the rebellion against God led by the Antichrist during the tribulation (that is, the *apostasia*) will precede the second coming (i.e., will precede the day of the Lord).

That does not prove that Gundry's view of this passage overall is correct, nor does it prove that his understanding of *apostasia* is correct.

Let me be clear. It is entirely possible that Gundry's understanding of *apostasia* is correct. It is held by a significant number of scholars.[22] It *does* fit into the picture presented by 2 Thessalonians 2, even when we recognize the pretribulation rapture as Paul intended. Indeed, this is the "safe" call to make when wrestling with the meaning of *apostasia*.

There is another possibility. It does not change the overall picture but fits well with it in very significant ways. The possibility to which I refer is the suggestion that *apostasia* may mean "the departing" and thus be a reference to the rapture, not to a religious defection.

This suggestion has appeared on a number of occasions within the ranks of pretribulational commentators. Most recently, H. Wayne House has argued rather cogently for this view, and his arguments remain very persuasive.[23] His defense of *apostasia* as a possible reference to the rapture boils down to these observations: (1) the idea of a departure is clearly within the semantic range that lexicographers admit for the word *apostasia*; (2) lexical studies show that *aposta-*

sia and its cognates do often refer to a spatial separation rather than a conceptual separation (this usage is also found in the LXX and in other Greek texts); and (3) the context of 2 Thessalonians 2 makes a reference to the rapture possible.

It should be noted here that House makes a very reasonable claim based on this evidence. His conclusion to the matter is this: "I have sought to demonstrate that the departure of the church may be the proper understanding found in the Greek word *apostasia* in 2 Thessalonians 2:3. Certainly the case is not conclusive, but it should not be dismissed out of hand as many have done."[24]

House's claim is worth revisiting, especially in light of this chapter's approach. It is absolutely true to suggest that the meaning "rapture" for the word *apostasia* creates a much more compelling fit with the content of the entire chapter. Since Paul opens the chapter by referring to "our gathering together to Him," one ought to be alert to additional references to the rapture. As we hinted earlier, this is a weakness of the posttribulation view; when we attempt to force 2 Thessalonians 2 into the posttribulational mold, there are *no* additional references to the rapture. The rest of the chapter must be read as references to the second coming. Consequently, posttribulationism is a view that offers a less compelling fit with the shape of 2 Thessalonians 2.

On the other hand, there is no *incontrovertible* evidence that the word *apostasia* was intended by the Holy Spirit to mean "departure" here. All we have is the argument from coherence. This is why I am happy to conclude this little section with Gundry's words. Gundry, in trying to squash all notions of pretribulationism in 2 Thessalonians 2, says that "Paul should have quieted the agitation of the Thessalonians by telling them that a pretribulational rapture will absent them long before the arrival of the day of the Lord."[25] In recognition of the deep irony, I respond, "It's very possible that Paul did just that <u>in his use of *apostasia*</u>." I don't want to be emphatic on this perspective, but it is most assuredly a possibility that demands consideration.

Shaken from Your Composure or Disturbed

Our final puzzle piece is a gem. It's not really the place I would have expected to end up in an attempt to put the pieces of 2 Thessalonians 2 together, but as things turn out, this piece is the capstone of our work. This puzzle piece is the simple little phrase "shaken from your composure or . . . disturbed" (v. 2). In the text of 2 Thessalonians 2:1–2, the phrase looks like this:

Now we request you, brethren, with regard to the coming of our Lord Jesus Christ and our gathering together to Him, that you not be quickly *shaken from your composure or be disturbed* either by a spirit or a message or a letter as if from us, to the effect that the day of the Lord has come. (italics added)

This phrase captures the response that the Thessalonian believers were experiencing in the face of a deceptive message that they thought was true. They were shaken. They were disturbed.

Again, I never would have suspected that this would be the phrase that would tie all the pieces together. But here it is: if you cannot paint a picture in which the disturbance of the Thessalonians makes sense, then you have not accurately understood the passage.

It is instructive to start with Gundry once again. Gundry's clearest answer to the question "What does the phrase 'shaken from your composure or . . . disturbed' mean?" is this:

If the Christians mistakenly thought that they were experiencing the tribulation and believed posttribulationism because of Paul's previous teaching, they would have been rejoicing, we might suppose, rather than troubled at the prospect of quick deliverance. But that line of reasoning sets up false alternatives, joy versus sorrow. Paul mentions neither. Instead, he directs his remarks to the problem of agitation among the Thessalonians, agitation at the prospect of an immediate return of Christ.[26]

In essence, Gundry understands the Thessalonian believers to have been suffering from an "agitation at the prospect of an immediate return of Christ." Let's subject this view to a little analysis.

My first question is, Why? Why would the prospect of an immediate return of Christ cause any agitation whatsoever? (I am granting here for the sake of argument Gundry's contention that Paul had previously taught the Thessalonians a posttribulational view of Christ's return—not because it is defensible from the text but simply to show the faulty nature of Gundry's argument.) If Paul had taught the Thessalonians that Christ's return would follow the tribulation, and then they received some form of communication suggesting that they were in the midst of the tribulation, what would their response be? Certainly it would not be agitation. How can one be agitated when what one believes to be true actually begins coming true? It is not agitation.[27]

This view encounters a very inconvenient objection: the biblical text itself.

Paul entreats the Thessalonians not to be "quickly shaken from your composure or be disturbed either by a spirit or a message or a letter as if from us, to the effect that the day of the Lord has come" (2 Thess 2:2). If Gundry's view is correct, how could this admonition make sense? According to the text, some of the Thessalonians were shaken by a report that the day of the Lord had come! If, in this context, the day of the Lord is equivalent to the second coming, then being shaken in mind is impossible.[28] It is as if you and I were standing in the middle of downtown Dallas, and I were to say to you, "Please don't be upset by any reports to the effect that Dallas has been obliterated by a nuclear missile." Since a glance around you would immediately invalidate my concern, you would not be shaken in your composure—you would be concerned for my mental state! In a similar way, Paul's admonition in 2 Thessalonians 2:2, when viewed according to Gundry's prescription, is meaningless. The only possible disturbance would be a concern about Paul's impossible understanding of future events!

By the way, this is what often happens when a well-intentioned interpreter of Scripture brings his or her preexisting theological *demands* to the text. He or she will find a way—no matter what kind of damage to the text might occur—to impose those demands on the text. But when you and I consider carefully the import of those demands and the stress fractures they cause in the text, we can see them for what they are. Such demands represent *eisegesis*, a reading *into* the text, rather than leading the meaning out of the text to a Bible-believing readership (that's exegesis).[29]

Now I have to admit that Gundry is not the only author who struggles with the fit of this piece of 2 Thessalonians 2. Even noted Bible scholar F. F. Bruce struggles with finding a way to make this piece fit into his understanding of the picture presented by the text. In his famed commentary on 2 Thessalonians, Bruce quotes the fourth-century church historian Eusebius [*Historia Ecclesiastica* 6.7] in suggesting that the persecution under Septimius Severus (Roman emperor, AD 193–211) "disturbed the minds of many" and resulted in the thinking that the Antichrist had come.[30] Bruce dismisses this idea, but he does mention that other biblical commentators defend the argument that the disturbance is simply the recognition that Antichrist has arrived.

This suggestion that the "disturbance" is the Antichrist's arrival is indeed flimsy. If Paul had already taught the Thessalonians that the rapture is posttribulational, then surely the phrases "shaken" and "disturbed" represent a poor fit for the state of mind experienced by those who should be expecting the events of the tribulation. When such believers see the arrival of Antichrist, there would be no "disturbance." There would be a sober recognition that the plan of God was unfolding before the believers' eyes.

Further, notice that Paul's counterargument does not fit with this hypothesis. Instead of correcting a mistaken idea that the Antichrist had been revealed in the time of the Thessalonians, Paul's argument focuses on the day of the Lord. The day of the Lord is the subject of Paul's correction, because the erroneous teaching that had upset the Thessalonians was about the day of the Lord. Paul's corrective said simply that the day of the Lord has not come unless the *apostasia* comes first and the man of lawlessness is revealed. This counterargument is a complete failure if the Thessalonians thought that they were seeing the revelation of the man of lawlessness.

After considering a number of alternatives, Bruce concludes that our only hope of understanding the disturbance in the minds of the Thessalonians is by examining the content of Paul's encouragement to them—an encouragement that, in view of the text, leads Bruce to conclude that Paul "judged that it would help them to be told something about the sequence of events leading up to the day of the Lord. They had been taught about the actual events, but they needed to have them set in their chronological relationship."[31]

In the final analysis, Bruce does much better than most posttribulationists—precisely because he turns to the actual text of 2 Thessalonians 2 in order to determine the shape of this particular puzzle piece. But his conclusions are marred by his misunderstanding of two "edge pieces" we have already considered ("the day of the Lord," and "it will not come"). It is almost as if Bruce recognizes that his perception of the disturbance experienced by the Thessalonians is going to lead him to deny his view of these two edge pieces, and consequently he chooses to remain agnostic about the disturbance.

This, then, renders the ultimate verdict on Bruce's view untenable. According to Paul as inspired by the Holy Spirit, there was an erroneous teaching that had caused the Thessalonian believers to be shaken from their composure and disturbed. But Bruce, because of his errant understanding of the day of the Lord and his subtle misreading of "it will not have come," cannot figure out what the disturbance is. So, in effect, Bruce says, "Whatever the disturbance is, it has to fit the text." But then he ignores the whole picture presented by the text. Consequently, the shape of the puzzle piece suggested by F. F. Bruce simply does not fit the text of this passage, nor the picture that the passage is presenting.

Let's consider one more. Wanamaker's view of the disturbance is clarified by these words: "If I am correct that Paul was not well-informed about the situation when he wrote 2 Thessalonians, then the real problem disturbing his converts may have involved the participation of deceased Christians in the parousia and assumption to heaven as discussed in 1 Thess. 4:15–18."[32]

Again, does this fit the context? Paul recognizes that the Thessalonians are disturbed by a lie. So he corrects that lie. But nowhere does Paul mention the "real problem," according to Wanamaker. The "real problem" involves the participation of deceased Christians in the parousia?

The answer, once again, is no. This is an unconvincing way of reading our final puzzle piece. It simply does not fit. Because of a preconceived notion of posttribulationism, Wanamaker has to recast the passage in implausible ways, only to arrive at a possibility. This is just not the way to read Scripture.

This center piece in the puzzle is absolutely determinative in either appreciating the picture presented by this passage or defacing it beyond recognition. No amount of hand-wringing or wishful thinking will make this center piece disappear. No pulling out of the theological scissors in hopes of trimming this piece to fit in a preconceived posttribulational scheme will work. There is simply no way around it: if the Thessalonians had understood Paul to have previously taught them a posttribulation rapture, then their erroneous acceptance of the lie that the day of the Lord had come would not have disturbed them. They would have expected the events of the tribulation to precede the supposed single event known as the rapture/second coming (i.e., a posttribulation rapture).

Instead, the text itself provides a compelling fit when we put the pieces together. That fit is simply this: The Thessalonians had previously been taught that the rapture would precede the day of the Lord. The lie that they heard just prior to Paul's writing the second letter to them suggested that the day of the Lord had come; and being told that the day of the Lord had come necessarily implied that they had missed the rapture. *That* would most certainly be disconcerting. *That* would have had shaken the Thessalonians from their composure.

CONCLUSION

Our puzzle is now complete. By starting with the corner pieces and then proceeding to place the edge pieces, the final placement of the center pieces became much clearer. What we discovered along the way is this—the Thessalonians had received a message that seemed authoritative. We do not know if they thought it came from God directly, or from Paul—but the Thessalonians thought that the message was reliable, when in reality it was a lie. It was deceptive. These observations framed our discussion as the corner pieces of our puzzle.

Next, we observed that the edges of our puzzle were defined by several concepts. First, the "coming of our Lord" refers to the second coming, and "our gathering together to Him" refers to the rapture. But these two events do not necessarily occur at the same time. The text does not force us to see them as two sides of one coin. On the contrary, our developing understanding of the picture presented by this puzzle leads us to suggest that, subject to further corroboration, these two events form the beginning and ending of a time span about which Paul desires to offer additional instruction.

An additional edge piece clarified our understanding of the day of the Lord, which is presented as an extended time of judgment—messianic woes, if you will—that leads up to the second coming. Also, we learned that the divine truth presented by Paul teaches us that the day of the Lord will not have come unless the *apostasia* comes first.

The framework of the corner pieces and the edge pieces then allowed us to wrestle much more effectively with the center pieces. We realized that *apostasia* does indeed have a semantic range that will allow either the meaning "defection" or "departure," and that the primary reason for choosing between these two alternatives ought to be found in the context of 2 Thessalonians 2.

Then we came to the final piece. This is the piece that confirms or denies the entire process of putting a puzzle together. And we discovered that posttribulational interpretations consistently fail to find a way to make this puzzle piece fit. They trim it, they force it into a differently shaped spot, or they paint a new image on it—but they cannot account for 2 Thessalonians as it stands written.

As a consequence, the conclusion is simple: The only coherent picture that can be defended as arising from 2 Thessalonians 2 is that of a pretribulation rapture.

NOTES

1. Yes, I realize that "puzzledom," unlike "kingdom," is not a word. *Mea culpa.*

2. R. C. H. Lenski provides a reasonable example. He treats this fact as a given, hardly even needing comment. It is a framing observation so foundational to his work that he jumps directly into a discussion of the grammar of the phrase. He even finds a literary connection to Paul's description of how the message came to the Thessalonians. Lenski writes: "'Do not let anyone deceive you in any way!' re-echoes Jesus' warning given in Matt. 24:4. It brands the allegation as a 'deception,' and 'in any way' refers to the three

forms of the allegation already indicated as well as to any other forms that may yet appear." Lenski, *The Interpretation of St. Paul's Epistles to the Colossians, to the Thessalonians, to Timothy, to Titus and to Philemon* (Columbus, OH: Lutheran Book Concern, 1937), 406.

3. See, for example, Gordon D. Fee, *The First and Second Letters to the Thessalonians*, NICNT (Grand Rapids: Eerdmans, 2009), 272. Fee says that the two events are listed as "two sides of a coin," and in footnote 10 he indicates that this description "seems to be made certain by the fact that a single definite article controls both nouns ['coming' and 'gathering together']."

   See also Leon Morris, who says, "The subject of his [Paul's] request is twofold, but the use of the single article shows that the coming of the Lord . . . and the gathering of the saints are closely connected. Indeed, they are two parts of one great event." Morris, *The First and Second Epistles to the Thessalonians*, NICNT, 213.

4. See Daniel B. Wallace, *Greek Grammar beyond the Basics* (Grand Rapids: Zondervan, 1996), 290. Since [this] TSKS construction [a TSKS construction is a Greek phrase that contains a definite article, a substantive, the Greek word *kai,* and another substantive] involves impersonal substantives, the highest degree of doubt is cast upon the probability of the terms referring to the same event. This is especially the case since the terms look to concrete temporal referents (the parousia and the gathering of the saints), for the identical category is unattested for concrete impersonals in the NT.

   This is not to say that one could not see a posttribulational rapture in the text, for even if the words do not have an identical referent, they could have simultaneous ones. Our only point is that because of the misuse of syntax by some scholars, certain approaches to the theology of the NT have often been jettisoned without a fair hearing.

5. It is worth noting that a number of posttribulation scholars are careful to avoid the erroneous application of the Granville Sharp rule to this passage in 2 Thessalonians 2:1. Gundry is one such careful scholar. See Robert H. Gundry, *The Church and the Tribulation* (Grand Rapids: Zondervan, 1973), 113.

6. One attested usage of the phrase "the coming of the Lord" in the New Testament appears to refer to the rapture (see, for example, 1 Thess. 4:15 and 1 Thess. 5:23). But the usage here seems to take the phrase "the coming of our Lord" to mean "the second coming." This usage is attested in 2 Thessalonians 2:8 (as we shall see shortly); 2 Peter 1:16; and 2 Peter 3:4.

7. The reader will want to review the previous chapter in this book for a discussion on how the text of 1 Thessalonians 4 and 5 affirms a pretribulation rapture. That perspective, defended ably in that chapter, is simply assumed here.

8. One example of a scholar who views the two events as part of one occurrence is D. Michael Martin, who writes, "Paul juxtaposed Jesus' coming and the gathering of the saints as coincident events that are part of a single happening." Martin, *1, 2 Thessalonians*, NAC (Nashville: Broadman, 1995), 223.

9. Even the most cautious commentators implicitly agree with this. Lenski provides one example; in his respected commentary, he titles the entire section on 2 Thessalonians 2, "The Great Apostasy and the Revelation of the Antichrist Precede the Parousia." See Lenski, *Epistles to the Colossians, to the Thessalonians, to Timothy, to Titus and to Philemon*, 400.

10. Gundry, *The Church and the Tribulation*, 114.

11. Charles A. Wanamaker writes, "Paul's theme is not merely the public manifestation of the Lord but also the disposition of Christians with respect to it. On account of this he proceeds to write the words 'and our assembling with him.' This is the only instance in Paul's letters of [*episunagōgē*] or its cognate verb, but the idea is parallel to the one found in 1 Thess. 4:16f. The emphasis of the word lies on the act of the community's gathering together with the Lord at the time of his coming." See Wanamaker, *The Epistles to the Thessalonians: a Commentary on the Greek Text,* New International Greek Testament Commentary (Grand Rapids: Eerdmans, 1990), 238.

12. Ibid., 240.

13. Ibid.

14. One example of a pretribulational commentator is Thomas L. Constable, "2 Thessalonians," BKC, vol. 2, ed. J. F. Walvoord and R. B. Zuck (Wheaton: Victor Books, 1985), 717. One example of a posttribulational commentator is Wanamaker, *Epistles to the Thessalonians*, 238.

15. For further information on the day of the Lord, see chapter 3 in this book.

16. I am aware of Robert Thomas's strong argument for rendering this Greek word, *enestēken*, as "is present" instead of "has come" (see Thomas's chapter in this present work). While I agree with his thinking in essence, I am less inclined to render *enestēken* as "is present" for a very simple reason. I believe that the truth toward which Thomas is pointing is visible without rendering *enestēken*, a verb in the perfect tense, as a present tense in English. This will become clear shortly.

17. Wanamaker provides one example of a renowned commentator who affirms the propriety of his position. He writes, "The available evidence for the use of *enestanai* ['to be present,' the aorist infinitive form of *enistēmi*, which is the verb that shows up in our text as *enestēken*, 'has come'], however, indicates that the word never has this sense ['to be about to take place'] when used in the past tenses, and so, with a majority of recent commentators, I accept that the word must have the meaning 'has come.'" See Wanamaker, *Epistles to the Thessalonians*, 240.

18. Once again, Gundry's treatment of 2 Thessalonians 2 exhibits a carelessness with the text, apparently because of Gundry's focused intent to make the text say what he wants it to say. Gundry writes, "Paul writes that the day of the Lord cannot have come already because two outstanding events, which have not yet taken place, must take place *before* that day (2 Thess. 2:1–4). These events, the revelation of the man of lawlessness and the apostasy, which will culminate in his self-deification, will fall within the tribulation. It is self-evident that since these two events will occur *before* the day of the Lord, the day of the Lord cannot include the tribulational period during which they occur [emphasis in the original]." See Gundry, *The Church and the Tribulation*, 93. It is clearly *not* self-evident that the day of the Lord comes *after* the two events mentioned in 2 Thessalonians 2, as we have seen.

19. As you can tell, I agree significantly with Robert Thomas's observations in his chapter in this present work.

20. Gundry, *The Church and the Tribulation*, 116.

21. Ibid., 117. It is very problematic for any scholar to actually argue against context in the process of discerning the meaning of a word. This appears to be the result of Gundry's devotion to the concept of posttribulationism. Posttribulationism is a nonnegotiable for Gundry, and the biblical text dare not stand in the way of it—nor, for that matter, can any recognized principle of biblical interpretation.

22. Wanamaker is once again illustrative. He writes, "In the apocalyptic context of 2 Thessalonians 2, the rebellion referred to is a religious one directed against God. In all probability we may identify those whose rebellion is mentioned in v. 3 with those who are to be deceived in vv. 10–12." See Wanamaker, *Epistles to the Thessalonians*, 244.

23. See H. Wayne House, "*Apostasia* in 2 Thessalonians 2:3: Apostasy or Rapture?" in *When the Trumpet Sounds*, ed. Thomas Ice and Timothy Demy (Eugene, OR: Harvest House, 1995).

24. Ibid., 286.

25. Gundry, *The Church and the Tribulation*, 96.

26. Ibid., 114.

27. Remember that Gundry identifies the day of the Lord as being equivalent to the second coming. So how is it that he changes that identification here? Now, confronted with the biblical phrase "the day of the Lord has come," he equates the day of the Lord with the tribulation. We examine this subject more completely in subsequent paragraphs.

28. It is interesting that Gundry never attempted to correct his problematic interpretation of identifying the day of the Lord with the second coming. The publication of his work *The Church and the Tribulation: A Biblical Examination of Posttribulationism* in 1973 brought this problem to light. But when he had the chance to correct the flaw (twenty-four years later), he did not do so; see Robert H. Gundry, *First the Antichrist* (Grand Rapids: Baker, 1997), Kindle Location 180. Therein, Gundry says, "So in context the Day of the Lord is the day of his coming and of Christians' meeting him then." The day of the Lord is still, for Gundry, the day of the second coming.

29. In all fairness to Gundry, he has a number of reasons that, in his estimation, justify the conclusion that the day of the Lord *is* the second coming. See chapter 6, "The Day of the Lord," in Gundry, *The Church and the Tribulation*. However, it should be noted that all of the passages cited by Gundry therein have reasonable explanations that fit their respective contexts, without causing a fatal flaw in the logic of 2 Thessalonians 2. Actually, this is one of the central tenets of responsible biblical interpretation: when you find a biblical passage that contradicts a hypothesis you brought to it from other passages, you must revise that hypothesis.

30. F. F. Bruce, *1 & 2 Thessalonians*, WBC (Waco, TX: Word, 1982), 165.

31. Ibid., 166.

32. Wanamaker, *Epistles to the Thessalonians*, 241.

8

John and the Rapture: Revelation 2-3

BY ANDREW M. WOODS

P*retribulation rapturism* is the belief that the rapture of the church will take place before (*pre*) a seven-year tribulation period begins. *Imminency* figures prominently in pretribulational thinking and indicates that Christ's return for His church through the rapture is the very next event on the prophetic horizon. Since the rapture is a signless event, no predicted sign must first transpire before the rapture can occur.

If the rapture is imminent, then it logically follows that it must precede the tribulation period, also known as Seventieth Week of Daniel. The church is never exhorted to look for the signs of the tribulation period but is instead commanded to look for Christ's return. Thus, pretribulationists are quick to point to the numerous New Testament passages conveying the idea that the rapture is the next event on the prophetic horizon (James 5:8; 1 Thess. 1:10; 4:15; 1 Cor. 1:7; 15:51; Titus 2:13; Phil. 3:20; John 14:3; 1 John 2:28; 3:2–3).

Imminency supports pretribulationism since it is the only rapture position contending that the rapture could take place today. Prophecy scholar John F. Walvoord had a plaque in his office that read "perhaps today." Only pretribulationists can confidently assert "perhaps today." The other rapture positions that place the rapture either in the middle of the tribulation (midtribulation rapturism), three-quarters into the tribulation (prewrath rapturism), or at the end of the tribulation period (posttribulationism) must, by their very definition, point to a series of prophetic events in the tribulation that first must take place before the rapture can occur.

Christ conveyed to John the *Apocalypse*, which is also known as the book of Revelation. If the New Testament teaches that the rapture is imminent, then it stands to reason that this concept would also occur in Revelation 2–3, in which Christ addressed seven struggling churches in Asia Minor. These two chapters represent Christ's final word to His church. If imminency is a New Testament idea, then it is reasonable to expect that this concept would also be found in this section of Scripture. This expectation is heightened given the fact that Revelation in general emphasizes Christ's imminent return (Rev. 1:1a, 3b; 22:7a, 12a, 20a).

Indeed, the imminent return of Christ for His church through the rapture is clearly taught in Revelation 2–3, as it is elsewhere in the New Testament. Rather than surveying the imminency passages in the order in which they appear in Revelation 2–3, this analysis will examine them in their order of clarity. Admittedly, some passages in these chapters convey imminency with greater clarity and certainty than do others. In the comments that follow, some explanation will be provided as to why this is so. The clearest passages will be given the earliest and most comprehensive treatment.

REVELATION 3:10

In Revelation 3:10, Christ promised the church at Philadelphia: "Because you have kept the word of My perseverance, I also will keep you from the hour of testing, that hour which is about to come upon the whole world, to test those who dwell on the earth." Commentators of all stripes readily acknowledge that this verse represents the most significant verse in the debate over the timing of the rapture. In fact, posttribulationist Robert Gundry concedes, "Probably the most debated verse in the whole discussion about the time of the Church's rapture is Revelation 3:10."[1] Therefore our analysis will give this verse the first and most thorough treatment.

Is this verse a promise of divine preservation through the events of the tribulation period, as posttribulationists contend, or is it a promise of divine protection by being kept out of this time period altogether, as pretribulationists contend? Much of the debate centers around the phrase *tēreō ek*, translated as "keep [you] from." According to posttribulationist George Ladd, "the promise of Revelation 3:10 of being kept *from* [*ek*] the hour of trial need not be a promise of removal from the very physical presence of tribulation. It is a promise of preservation and deliverance in and through it."[2] Gundry echoes the same perspective:

Essentially [ek], a preposition of motion concerning thought or physical direction, means *out from within*. [ek] does not denote a stationary position outside its object, as some have mistakenly supposed in thinking that the [ek] of Revelation 3:10 refers to a position *already* taken outside the earthly sphere of tribulation. . . . If [ek] ever occurs without the thought of emergence, it does so very exceptionally.[3]

Charles Ryrie sums up the controversy:

Posttribulationists say that "from" (ek) refers to protection of the church within the Tribulation. Pretribulationists understand it to mean preservation by being absent from the time of tribulation. One is internal protection (while living through the Tribulation); the other is external protection (being in heaven during that time). Which meaning does "from" (ek) support? The answer is either, if the preposition is considered alone. But for the record, let it be said that ek does denote a position outside something without implying a prior position inside and then emergence from within. The pretribulationist understanding of ek is supported by a number of verses that have nothing to do with the rapture and therefore do not beg the question.[4]

As will be demonstrated, the weight of the evidence favors the pretribulational understanding. This evidence will be examined in the following four areas: (1) some initial problems with the posttribulational interpretation of the passage, (2) the meaning of "keep you from," (3) a brief analysis of what exactly the church is promised to be kept from, and (4) how the pretribulational understanding of this verse harmonizes well with the rest of Revelation's contents (Rev. 4–22).

Initial Problems with the Posttribulation Interpretation

There are at least *three* general problems with the posttribulational understanding that Revelation 3:10 teaches that God will preserve the church through the tribulation period. *First*, if this is a divine promise, then God does a poor job keeping it since Revelation also records numerous martyrdoms of believers during the tribulation period. This posttribulational assumption of preservation in the midst of the tribulation period exists largely because the book of

Revelation often portrays God's people as being supernaturally protected from many of the apocalyptic judgments during the tribulation period. For example, Revelation 9:4 says, "They were told not to harm the grass of the earth, nor any green thing, nor any tree, but *only the men who do not have the seal of God on their foreheads*" (italics added). Revelation 16:2 similarly says, "The first angel went and poured out his bowl on the earth, and it became a loathsome and malignant sore broke out *on the people who had the mark of the beast and who worshiped his image*" (italics added).

Thus, according to posttribulationism, just as God supernaturally protected national Israel from the various plagues of the book of Exodus (Ex. 8:22, 24; 9:4, 6; 11:4–7), God will do the same thing for His church in the midst of the tribulation period. True, both Revelation 9:4 and 16:2 teach that believers on earth during the tribulation will be exempted from the fifth trumpet and the first bowl judgments. However, these are the only verses that specify God's people will be spared from any tribulation judgments. The implication is that believers will still experience the rest of the suffering described in the book of Revelation. Thus, it is inaccurate to suggest that if the church is on the earth during the tribulation period, it will enjoy divine protection.

If this were so, then the countless martyrdoms during this time period are inexplicable.[5] Notice how Revelation consistently portrays the frequent martyrdoms that tribulation believers will endure as a consequence of Christ's opening the first seal judgment, which will usher in the reign of the Antichrist (Rev. 6:1–2; 2 Thess. 2:9–12). Revelation 6:9–11 says,

> When the Lamb broke the fifth seal, I saw underneath the altar the souls of those who had been slain because of the word of God, and because of the testimony which they had maintained; and they cried out with a loud voice, saying, "How long, O Lord, holy and true, will You refrain from judging and avenging our blood on those who dwell on the earth?" And there was given to each of them a white robe; and they were told that they should rest for a little while longer, until the number of their fellow servants and their brethren who were to be killed even as they had been, would be completed also.

Similarly, in Revelation 7:13–14 when an elder asks who are those appearing in white robes, the Lord answers, "These are the ones who come out of the great tribulation, and they have washed their robes and made them white in the blood of the Lamb."

Revelation 13:10 echoes, "If anyone is destined for captivity, to captivity he goes; if anyone kills with the sword, with the sword he must be killed. Here is the perseverance and the faith of the saints." See also Revelation 13:15 and 20:4 for descriptions of killings of those who "do not worship the image of the beast" and of those "beheaded because of their testimony of Jesus." These prophesied wide-scale martyrdoms simply cannot be reconciled with any prophetic theory arguing for the church's preservation during the tribulation.

Second, since Christ's promise in Revelation 3:10 was given to comfort the Philadelphia church, how would such a promise of selective preservation (i.e., a "protection" that still includes widespread persecution and massive martyrdom) serve as any real source of comfort to this church? Townsend asks, "It must be questioned whether this kind of 'preservation' would be of any comfort and encouragement to the persecuted Philadelphians."[6]

The third problem with this preserving of the church through the tribulation period is this: If God had intended to communicate preservation in the midst of the tribulation, there were far more effective ways of expressing this idea. English notes:

> The usual Greek for "through" is *dia*, and for "in," *en, eis, epi,* and *kata*. It would seem that, if the Spirit of God intended to convey to the readers of this passage that the Lord would keep His own *through* or *in* the hour of trial, He would have used *dia*, or *eis*, or *epi*, or *kata* and not *ek*, which surely implies *out of* rather than *through* or *in*.[7]

Showers also explains:

> The idea of the saints being shielded from the testing while living within and through this time period also would have been expressed more clearly through the use of another preposition, either *en* (meaning "in") or *dia* (meaning "through") [thus, "I will keep you *in* or *through* the time period of testing"] rather than *ek*.[8]

"Keep You From"

The Greek preposition translated "from" in Revelation 3:10 is the word *ek*, which can carry the idea of separation from something. This is the same preposition translated "out of" in Matthew 7:5, which says, "You hypocrite, first take the log *out of* your own eye, and then you will see clearly to take the speck *out of* your brother's eye" (italics added). Thus, by the use of this identical preposition in Revelation 3:10, the idea is conveyed that the church at Philadelphia will be kept entirely out of the tribulation in the same way a log must be completely removed from someone's eye before he has the ability to completely remove the speck that is in his brother's eye. In other words, if this is also how *ek* is used in Revelation 3:10, then the idea expressed here is total removal from rather than sustenance or protection in the midst of.[9]

Townsend has produced a helpful word study demonstrating that the preposition *ek* often denotes total removal from its object.[10] He explains, "Sufficient evidence exists throughout the history of the meaning and usage of [*ek*] to indicate that this preposition may also denote *a position outside its object with no thought of prior existence within the object or of emergence from the object.*"[11] Examples from the standard Greek lexicon include being kept beyond the range of missiles or outside of the harm of smoke as well as standing completely aside of something.[12]

Examples also abound in the Septuagint, the Greek translation of the Hebrew Old Testament, produced two centuries before Christ. Proverbs 21:23 says, "He who guards his mouth and his tongue, *Guards* his soul *from* troubles" (italics added). Here, the Septuagint employs *ek*, which is translated "from." Interestingly, the word translated "guard" here is *diatēreō*, which is almost identical to *tēreō*, rendered "keep" in Revelation 3:10. The only real difference between the two verbs is that the former adds intensification. Thus, the combination of the preposition *ek* coupled with the nearly identical verb makes Proverbs 21:23 and Revelation 3:10 linguistically parallel. Guarding one's tongue obviously causes him to escape trouble entirely rather than merely sustaining him through trouble.[13] Josephus also furnishes examples where the preposition *ek* coupled with the verb *rhyomai* ("to rescue") is used to convey a totally outside position. "He *delivered* them *from* those dire consequences which would have ensued from their sedition but for Moses' watchful care" (italics added).[14]

The New Testament also furnishes numerous examples where the preposition *ek* coupled with a verbal expression conveys a position completely outside of something.[15] Acts 15:29 says, "Abstain from things sacrificed to idols and from blood and from things strangled and from fornication; if you *keep* yourselves *free* from such things, you will do well" (italics added). Here *ek* translated as "from" communicates to Gentile believers to abstain from these practices, or keep themselves away from them entirely, so as not to avoid an unnecessary offense for the Jew. Interestingly, the word translated "keep" here is again *diatēreō*, which is nearly identical to *tēreō*, translated "keep" in Revelation 3:10. As noted earlier, the only real difference between the two verbs is that the former adds strength to the notion of keeping. Thus, like Proverbs 21:23, the combination of the preposition coupled with the nearly identical verb makes Acts 15:29 and Revelation 3:10 linguistically parallel.

John 12:27 also uses *ek* alongside *sōzō* to convey complete removal from its object when it says, "Now My soul has become troubled; and what shall I say, 'Father, *save* Me *from* this hour?'" (italics added). Here, Christ prays for a complete exemption from the ordeal of the cross. This verse also bears substantial similarity to Revelation 3:10 in that John is the author, Jesus is speaking, and reference is made to a future hour of divine wrath (John 7:30; 8:20). The same preposition and verb combination shows up again in Hebrews 5:7, which says, "In the days of His flesh, He offered up both prayers and supplications with loud crying and tears to the One able to *save* Him *from* death . . ." (italics added). If this is a reference to Christ's Gethsemane prayer (Matt. 26:39, 42; Mark 14:32–36), then Christ is again portrayed as praying for a complete exemption from the ordeal of the cross. The same combination again shows up in James 5:20, which says, "let him know that he who turns a sinner from the error of his way will *save* his soul *from* death and will cover a multitude of sins" (italics added). Here, *ek* translated "from" is used to communicate that turning someone away from sin will help him entirely escape the consequences of that particular sin, which is death.

In Colossians 1:13, Paul also furnishes yet another example where the preposition *ek* coupled with the verb *rhyomai* ("to rescue") is used to convey a total outside position: "For He *rescued* us *from* the domain of darkness, and transferred us to the kingdom of His beloved Son" (italics added). Here *ek*, translated "from," is used to convey that the believer's citizenship and domain is positionally transferred entirely out of Satan's domain at the point of faith in Christ. At the point of faith, believers are not positionally kept in the domain of darkness only to be removed from it at some later point in time. On the contrary, believers are kept positionally and entirely out of Satan's realm when they trust Christ.

First John 5:18 illustrates and buttresses this very point depicted in Colossians 1:13 of the complete positional removal and escape from the domain of darkness that the Christian enjoys at the point of personal faith in Christ. This verse says, "We know that no one who is born of God sins; but He who was born of God keeps him, and the evil one does not touch him." Once again, the idea expressed in all of these passages through the Greek preposition *ek* is total removal from rather than sustenance or protection in the midst of. Likely, the same idea is found in Revelation 3:10.

John 17:15, "I do not ask You to take them out of the world, but to *keep* them *from* the evil one" (italics added), deserves special attention since it represents the only other occurrence of *tēreō* coupled with *ek* in all of classical Greek, the Septuagint, and New Testament Greek.[16] Because Christ specifically stated here that the believers are to be left in the world, posttribulationists interpret this verse to mean that the believer is to be preserved in the moral sphere of Satan.[17] This is the view of posttribulationist John Piper, who "believes that the main Scripture which some believe supports the pretribulational rapture viewpoint (Revelation 3:10) does not necessarily mean that believers will be taken away from the earth . . . ; rather, it could mean that God will keep or protect His people from evil during the tribulation (see also John 17:15)."[18]

However, although the disciples were still in the world, they were not within the sphere of the evil one when Christ prayed. In actuality, Jesus prayed that the disciples would be kept completely out of Satan's domain. His prayer has been answered, as Paul later wrote, "For He rescued us from the domain of darkness, and transferred us to the kingdom of His beloved Son" (Col. 1:13). This truth of the believer's protection from Satan's jurisdiction is also borne out in 1 John: "We know that no one who is born of God sins; but He who was born of God keeps him, and the evil one does not touch him" (5:18). Thomas Ice explains, "I am sure Piper would agree Christ's prayer has been answered since all genuine believers are protected from Satan. In the same way, all Church-Age believers will be kept out of the time of the tribulation via the rapture before that seven-year event."[19]

Interestingly, the context of John 17:15 has nothing do with preservation from Satan's attacks as the posttribulationist presumes. Rather, it pertains to God's preservation of His own. Townsend notes:

> Gundry interprets John 17:15b as a prayer for the preservation of the disciples in the moral sphere of Satan, since they are to be left in the world (John 17:15a). In the context of John 17:11–16, the idea of keeping is related to salvation and the possession of eternal life, not preservation from the moral assaults of Satan. The issue is the keeping of salvation (i.e., the perseverance of the saints) not progression in sanctification (which is taken up in 17:17).[20]

Thus, when considered in this light, far from supporting posttribulationism, John 17:15 actually becomes a pretribulational proof text. In sum, when the preposition *ek* is coupled with either *tēreō* or equivalent verbs throughout classical Greek, the Septuagint, Josephus, and the New Testament, a strong case can be made that when the same or a nearly identical combination is employed in Revelation 3:10, the Philadelphians would also be kept in a position completely outside of its object.

KEPT FROM WHAT?

Now that we have surmised that the promise of Revelation 3:10 indicates that the church at Philadelphia will be kept completely outside of its object, the next question to consider is, what is the object? In other words, what is the Philadelphia church promised to be kept from? The remainder of the verse answers, "the hour of testing, that hour which is about to come upon the whole world, to test those who dwell on the earth" (Rev. 3:10b). Further questions must be answered in order to understand what the Philadelphians are promised to be exempted from. *First*, what is meant by "the hour"? *Second*, what is meant by the expression "the whole world"? *Third*, what is meant by "the testing of the earth dwellers"? *Fourth*, what is meant by "which is about to come"?

1. Kept from the Hour

First, what is meant by "the hour"? In Johannine literature, the term "hour" (*hōra*) is often used to convey an extended period of time as opposed to a specific twenty-four-hour cycle (John 2:4; 4:21, 23; 5:35; 7:30; 8:20; 12:23, 27; 13:1; 16:25, 32, 42; 17:1; 19:27; 1 John 2:18; Rev. 14:7; 17:12). In Revelation 3:10, the term "hour" is preceded by a definite article in the Greek text, indicating that it is referring to a specific period of time already well known to the audience. Showers notes, "The fact that Christ's statement placed the definite article 'the' before the words translated 'hour' and 'about [about to come]' indicates that He had a specific or definite period of testing in mind. He was not referring to history in general with its sporadic testings."[21] Because the hour in view is not specifically identified in the immediate context, it is likely something already defined by prior Scripture. Newell notes, "There is no reasonable doubt that it *must* refer to The Great Tribulation of which Daniel wrote (12:1), and to which our Lord referred in Matthew 24:15–21."[22] Understanding this hour as the trib-

204 | Evidence for the Rapture

ulation period fits well with the extended context of the book, which examines this time period in Revelation 6–18.

The term "hour" is helpful in ascertaining exactly what the church is promised deliverance from. It is common for nonpretribulational rapture perspectives to postulate that because the wrath of God will not actually begin until a later point in the tribulation period, the church must be present for part of this period. Although the premise that God's wrath does not begin until later can be challenged (see chapter 3), let's assume for argument's sake that the wrath of God will not begin until some later point. Even so, pretribulationism is still not overthrown, since the promise of Revelation 3:10 is that the church will be kept from the *time* of the tribulation period and not merely from God's wrath. According to Rhodes:

> The posttribulational view, expressed in the writings of George Eldon Ladd, Robert Gundry, and others, is the view that Christ will rapture the church after the tribulation period at the second coming of Christ. This means the church will go through the time of judgment prophesied in the book of Revelation, but believers will be kept from Satan's wrath during the tribulation (Revelation 3:10). Pretribulationalists . . . respond, however, that Revelation 3:10 indicates that believers will be saved out of or separated from (Greek: *ek*) the actual time period of the tribulation.[23]

Geisler similarly observes, "In context, the statement about being saved 'out of' (Gk: *ek*) the time of trial does mean saved from it (not through it). One cannot be saved from an entire hour by being in any part of it."[24] Thiessen notes that the promise "holds out exemption from the period of trial, not only from the trial during that period."[25] Showers explains:

> Christ promised to keep these church saints from the *time period* characterized by the testing Christ had in mind. If the Lord had meant that He would keep them from just the testing itself, He could have made that very clear by omitting the words "the hour" and simply saying, "I will keep you from the testing." . . . If people live within a time period, they are not separated from it. . . . The only way to keep people from an entire time period is to prevent them from entering it.[26]

Ryrie comments, "It is impossible to conceive of being in the location where something is happening and being exempt from the time of the happening."[27] Again, Ryrie explains how understanding this time component of the divine promise significantly undermines posttribulationism and promotes pretribulationism:

> However, the promise of Revelation 3:10 not only guarantees being kept from the trials of the Tribulation period but being kept from the time period of the Tribulation. The promise is not, I will keep you from the trials. It is I will keep you from the hour of the trials. . . . But how clear and plain is the promise. "I . . . will keep you from the hour of testing." Not just from any persecution, but from the coming time that will affect the whole earth. (The only way to escape worldwide trouble is not to be on the earth.) And not just from the events, but from the time. And the only way to escape the time when the events take place is not to be in a place where time ticks on. The only place that meets those qualifications is heaven.[28]

Despite Christ's plain statement that the church will be exempted from the actual time of the future tribulation period, posttribulationists sometimes counter this perspective by employing Jeremiah 30:7. "Alas! for that day is great, there is none like it; and it is the time of Jacob's distress, but he will be saved from it." Gundry notes that Israel was given a promise similar to Revelation 3:10 of being saved from "the hour of testing" or "the time of Jacob's distress." In the Septuagint translation of this verse (Jer. 30:7), *sōzō* ("save") is used alongside *apo* ("from"), which conveys the notion of separation even more forcibly than does *ek*. Consequently, Gundry argues, "If a pretribulational rapture was not or will not be required for deliverance from the time of Jacob's distress, neither will a pretribulational rapture be required for preservation from the hour of testing."[29] In other words, just like with God's dealings with Israel, all that Revelation 3:10 promises is that the church will be *sustained through* or ultimately *rescued out of* the tribulation period rather than *kept from* the time of the tribulation period.

However, this argument fails to distinguish that Israel and the church represent separate programs of God. They are two trains running on separate railroad tracks. Chafer notes twenty-four differences between Israel and the church.[30] While the church's program involves preservation from God's wrath (1 Thess. 1:10; 5:9; Rom. 5:9; 8:1), Israel's program involves the incorporation of divine distress to awaken the unbelieving Jewish remnant to their need to trust in Jesus or *Yeshua* for personal and political salvation (Dan. 9:24–27; Matt. 23:37–39). Since the patriarch Jacob's name was changed to Israel (Gen. 32:28; 35:10), the designation "Jacob's distress" in Jeremiah 30:7 leads to the realization that God's program for Israel, rather than the church, is in view here.

206 | Evidence for the Rapture

Because Revelation 3:10 was given to the church in Philadelphia (Rev. 3:7) and because Jeremiah 30:7 is describing God's program for Israel, the two verses should not be conflated. Newell clarifies this point in his treatment of Revelation 3:10: "It cannot mean merely, preserved *in* and through *it*: for the remnant of Israel, God's earthly people, will have that preservation (Jeremiah 30:7; Daniel 12:1), whereas this is a promise given by a *heavenly* Christ to His *heavenly* saints."[31] In sum, Revelation 3:10 indicates that the church will be exempted from the actual time period of the coming tribulation.

2. Kept from the Whole World

Second, what is meant by the expression "the whole world"? An argument used by those contesting that Revelation 3:10 speaks of a pretribulation rapture is to suggest that this expression is not really referring to a global tribulation of the future. Rather, the expression is merely describing a past, localized event. After all, if this expression is not referring to a future worldwide tribulation but only to a historical, localized event, then Revelation 3:10 obviously cannot be speaking of a pretribulation rapture prior to the future tribulation period.

In this regard, critics of pretribulationism make much of the Greek word *oikoumenē*, which is translated "earth" in Revelation 3:10. They suggest that *oikoumenē* refers merely to the habitable and known world of the Roman first-century world.[32] Some posttribulationists, such as William Bell, contend that *oikoumenē* shrinks the hour of testing to the known Roman world of the apostle John's generation. He writes, "The seemingly universal terms are used elsewhere in the New Testament to mean the civilized world of that day, i.e., the Roman Empire. . . . The several empire-wide persecutions of Christians could easily satisfy the universal terminology."[33]

Although *oikoumenē* can at times refer to a limited realm (Luke 2:1; Acts 11:28; 17:6; 24:5), it is not a technical word meaning the exact same thing every time it is employed. Rather, its meaning must be determined by its surrounding context. Clearly, in other contexts, *oikoumenē* can take on a global meaning. Most would ascribe to *oikoumenē* a global nuance in Matthew 24:14 given the global and futuristic import of this chapter (Matt. 24:21–22, 29–31). It certainly has this same universal meaning in both Luke 4:5 and Revelation 12:9 if indeed Satan is the "god" of the entire world (1 John 5:19). It would also take on a global nuance in passages describing the final judgment of all of mankind (Acts

17:31). It also seems to have a global interpretation in Revelation 16:14 as the kings of the entire world are gathered together for the battle of Armageddon at the conclusion of the tribulation. In fact, standard lexical works readily acknowledge how *oikoumenē* can at times have a global meaning.[34]

A future global meaning rather than a past local understanding of *oikoumenē* better fits the immediate context of Revelation 3:10. *First*, the adjective *holos* translated "whole" is used to modify "earth" (= "the whole earth"), thereby giving *oikoumenē* a global understanding. Surely most would assign the same global nuance to the same adjective attached to the word "world" (*kosmos*) in one of John's other writings found in 1 John 5:19 ("the whole world lies in the power of the evil one"). Why cannot this nearly identical combination have the same global nuance in Revelation 3:10?

Second, understanding *oikoumenē* in its global sense fits well with the extended context of the entire book of Revelation, which provides an in-depth look at this time period in Revelation 6–18. For example, when studying Revelation 16:18b, it is quite clear that John is describing global future events in this section: "and there was a great earthquake, such as there had not been since man came to be upon the earth, so great an earthquake was it, and so mighty." Ice observes, "The 'hour' or 'time' of testing is what we will be kept from. Further, the hour of testing is said to be something that will in the future come upon the whole earth. Thus, it is clear that it is not something that happened in the days of the early church, since no one knows of a global testing that came upon the whole earth in the first century."[35] Thomas further notes, "This is not merely a local time of troubling the community at Philadelphia. It will encompass 'the whole inhabited earth' (*tēs oikoumenēs holēs*)."[36]

By defining *oikoumenē* of Revelation 3:10 based upon how *oikoumenē* is used in foreign contexts (Luke 2:1; Acts 11:28; 17:6; 24:5), pretribulation opponents are committing a hermeneutical error known as "illegitimate totality transfer." The error arises when the meaning of a word as derived from its use elsewhere is then automatically read into the same word in a foreign context.[37] For example, we would not transfer the total meaning of "world" in the phrase "the ancient world" into our understanding of the phrase "the animal world." One is a time period; the other is a group of living things. Words only have meanings based upon the contexts in which these words are found. *Oikoumenē* of Revelation 3:10 means something entirely different than *oikoumenē* of localized settings (Luke 2:1; Acts 11:28; 17:6; 24:5) since these uses of the same word transpire in completely different contexts than Revelation 3:10. In sum, the church is promised an exemption from the global test of the future tribulation period.

3. Kept from the Testing of the Earth Dwellers

Third, what is meant by the testing of those who dwell upon the earth? The words translated "testing" and "to test" in Revelation 3:10 are the Greek noun *peirasmos* and the Greek verb *peirazō*. Constable explains, "The Greek word translated 'testing' (*peirasai* [a form of *peirazō*]) means to test to demonstrate the quality of a thing, not to purify its quality."[38] For example, the church at Ephesus tested (*peirazō*) false apostles for the purpose of revealing them to be liars (Rev. 2:2). James 1:13–14 similarly explains, "Let no one say when he is tempted, 'I am being tempted by God'; for God cannot . . . tempt anyone. But each one is tempted (*peirazō*) when he is carried away and enticed by his own lust." Showers concludes, "Christ was declaring that the purpose of the future period of testing will be for God to test 'them that dwell on the earth' to demonstrate or expose the kind of people they are."[39] In secular Greek, *peirazō* conveys the notion of a test for the purpose of exposing someone's true character, typically with the negative intent to test to demonstrate a failure.[40]

Furthermore, the concept of earth dwellers as used by John in Revelation speaks specifically and exclusively of unbelievers. For example, in Revelation 13:8 and 17:8, John uses the expression "those who dwell on the earth" to refer to those who worship and follow after the Beast whose names are not written in the Lamb's Book of Life. Ice observes:

> This phrase "earth dwellers" is used eleven times in nine verses in Revelation (3:10; 6:10; 8:13; 11:10 2xs; 13:8, 12, 14 2xs; 14:6; 17:8). As you examine each individual use, except 3:10, you will see that all refer to a special class of stubborn sinners who are set in their rebellion against the God of heaven. You will also find that the phrase is *only* used to refer to those during the tribulation period. Therefore, since the future hour spoken of . . . in 3:10 is set in contrast with the present set of believers in the church age, and the future "earth dwellers" will be active during the time period in which believers are said to be kept from, it is clear that John speaks of the time or hour of the tribulation. This is why 3:10 is a clear promise that Christ will keep believers from the time of the seven year tribulation.[41]

An analysis of the phrases "testing," "to test," and "those who dwell upon the earth" in Revelation 3:10 indicates that the coming time to test the earth dwellers as depicted in Revelation 3:10 represents a period when unbelievers rather than believers will be tested (Rev. 6:12–17; 9:20–21; 16:1, 7, 8–11, 21). Thus, the clear inference is that this test is not for the church, which is already in faith, but rather is aimed specifically at unbelievers.

Although the church will be exempted from this test depicted in Revelation 3:10, this does not mean the church will be spared other kinds of tests beforehand. For example, members of the church remain candidates for the ordinary trials of life (James 1:2–4). In John 16:33, Jesus said, "In the world you have tribulation, but take courage; I have overcome the world." Moreover, today's Christians are also not exempted from the wrath of man. "Indeed, all who desire to live godly in Christ Jesus will be persecuted" (2 Tim. 3:12), the Scripture says. Nor is the modern Christian exempted from Satan's wrath. To the church at Smyrna, Christ said, "Do not fear what you are about to suffer. Behold, the devil is about to cast some of you into prison, so that you will be tested, and you will have tribulation for ten days. Be faithful until death, and I will give you the crown of life" (Rev. 2:10).

Members of the church are obviously targets of satanic wrath as we regularly struggle, "not against flesh and blood, but against the rulers, against the powers, against the world forces of this darkness, against the spiritual forces of wickedness in the heavenly places" (Eph. 6:12). In addition, believers of today are not spared from the wrath of the world system. Jesus explained, "If the world hates you, you know that it has hated Me before it hated you. If you were of the world, the world would love its own; but because you are not of the world, but I chose you out of the world, because of this the world hates you" (John 15:18–19).

While it remains a biblical truism that the church is not spared from various forms of suffering, it will be spared from the test depicted in Revelation 3:10. Trials as well as the wrath of man, Satan, and the world are an ongoing reality for today's Christians. But according to Revelation 3:10, they will have no part in the coming worldwide test of the unbelieving earth dwellers. Simply put, although trials (little "t") are a daily reality, we are not candidates for the Trial (capital "T"). While Jesus never promised the church at Philadelphia an exemption from tests (little "t"), He did promise them an exemption from the Test (capital "T"), known as the great tribulation period, which is coming upon the whole earth to test the unbelieving earth dwellers.

Interestingly, it appears that the very reason why the church will be exempted from the ultimate test of the tribulation is because the church has faithfully undergone other tests already. The promise of Revelation 3:10 is preceded by the phrase, "Because you have kept the word of My perseverance. . . ." Showers notes, "Christ based His promise on the fact that the church saints had already passed their test. In light of that, . . . Christ promised that He would not put them into the period that . . . will have the purpose of testing a very different group of people."[42]

4. Kept from What Is about to Come

Fourth, what is meant by "which is about to come"? This phrase conveys the idea of imminency or an any-moment expectation. In other words, the hour of testing mentioned in Revelation 3:10 could transpire momentarily. The natural question arises: How will Jesus make good on His promise to the church at Philadelphia to keep them completely out of the hour of testing that is about to imminently come to pass? Christ's answer is found in the subsequent verse, "I am coming quickly; hold fast what you have, so that no one will take your crown" (Rev. 3:11). Thus, He explains, the promise of being kept out of the imminent coming (*erchomai*) of the tribulation period (Rev. 3:10) will be fulfilled at the similarly imminent coming (*erchomai*) of Christ (Rev. 3:11).

That Revelation 3:11 is speaking of the rapture is strengthened by the reference to a crown or reward in the latter part of the verse. Rewards are associated with the Lord's coming for the church. First Corinthians 4:5 links Christ's return for the church to rewards, saying, "Therefore do not go on passing judgment before the time, but wait until the Lord comes who will both bring to light the things hidden in the darkness and disclose the motives of men's hearts; and then each man's praise will come to him from God" (cf. 2 Tim 4:8 on the reward for those who love Christ's coming).

The implication seems to be that if the imminent return of Christ (Rev. 3:11) is the means by which the Lord will fulfill His promise to keep the church from the coming time of tribulation designed to test unbelievers, then the rapture of the church must precede this time of tribulation. Townsend explains:

> This connection indicates a relationship between the promise of keeping in 3:10 and the coming of the Lord in 3:11. There will be preservation outside the imminent hour of testing for the Philadelphian church when the Lord comes. This, in turn, indicates that although . . . [*tēreō ek*] in 3:10 does not refer directly to the rapture of the church, rapture as the means of preservation is a proper deduction from the context.[43]

Showers similarly concludes, "Thus, the more specific implication of Christ's exclamation in Revelation 3:11 is that [by] the rapture of the church saints from the earth in conjunction with His imminent coming from heaven . . . Christ will keep or separate them from the entire period of testing."[44]

Revelation 3:10 in Summary

In Revelation 3:10 the Philadelphia church is promised complete removal from a specific time well established in prior Scripture as the tribulation period, otherwise known as Daniel's Seventieth Week. This time period is both future and global in scope. This time period is also divinely designed to "test" or reveal the lack of spiritual quality of unbelieving humanity. Moreover, this time period will come at any moment. In order to fulfill His promise of keeping the Philadelphians totally out of this time period, Christ promises to return during an even earlier or more imminent time to rapture His church to heaven.

Is Revelation 3:10 only a promise to the Philadelphian church or is it something that is promised to the entire universal church? The latter alternative seems preferable given the fact that the identical promise is also made to other New Testament churches besides Philadelphia (1 Thess. 1:10; 5:9). Interestingly, Christ's promise to Philadelphia seems applicable to the other churches as well, since Christ concludes His comments to Philadelphia with the following phrase, "He who has an ear, let him hear what the Spirit says to the churches."

Notice the plurality of the concluding noun, "churches." Such plurality seems to broaden the promise to the universal church as opposed to isolating it specifically to the church at Philadelphia. Showers observes, "Revelation 3:13 indicates that the Holy Spirit intends Christ's message to the Philadelphia church to be applicable to all churches; therefore, Christ's promise to the Philadelphia church saints is a promise to all church saints."[45] Ice further explains:

> The promise in Revelation 3:10 is a universal promise that is applicable to all the churches, which says in 3:13: "He who has an ear, let him hear what the Spirit says to the churches" (see also 2:7, 11, 17, 29; 3:6, 22). While our Lord's promise in 3:10 is to the Philadelphia church, it is also a promise to the universal church as well. The same is true, for example, in the Book of Colossians when Christ tells them in 3:1 to "keep seeking the things above;" or to "set your mind on the things above, not on the things that are on earth" (3:2). It is true that the Epistle was written historically to the Colossian believers and there are no passages that specially say these are universal passages for all be-

lievers, but what Christian does not take them to be universal of all believers throughout the church age? Is only Philadelphia (and only those alive at the time of writing) to "hold fast what you have, in order that no one take your crown," since Christ is coming quickly (3:11)? Is only Philadelphia to receive the name of God, the name of God's city, and a new name at our Lord's coming (3:12)? Or, will all believers benefit from all the promises made to the seven churches? Certainly these promises made to first-century, Philadelphia believers are universal for the whole church. Therefore, 3:10 is a promise to the universal church. It is rare indeed for a posttrib[ulationist] to try to argue this point. They rather argue against other points, knowing that this issue is clear.[46]

HARMONIZATION WITH REVELATION 4-22

If the above pretribulational interpretation of Revelation 3:10 is accurate, then this interpretation would find itself in harmony with the rest of Revelation's contents. How well does the pretribulational interpretation of Revelation 3:10 fit with the futuristic section of the book (Rev. 4–22)? Revelation 1:19 furnishes the book's three-part structure. It says, "Therefore write the things which you have seen, and the things which are, and the things which will take place after these things." "The things which you have seen" consist of John's interaction with the glorified Christ as recorded in Revelation's first chapter. "The things which are" comprise the seven letters to the seven churches of Asia Minor as recorded in Revelation 2–3. "The things which will take place after these things" constitute the futuristic section of the book as recorded in Revelation 4–22. That Revelation 4:1 begins this third and futuristic section is evident from the twofold repetition of the expression "after these things" (*meta tauta*), which is the same phrase used to describe this final section of the book in Revelation 1:19. This final section of the book contains the most vivid description of the tribulation period in the Bible (Rev. 4–19).

Yet, this section contains no single clear reference to the church on the earth during this time period. While the Greek word *ekklēsia*, translated "church," is found nineteen times in Revelation 1–3, which comprises the first two sections of the book, the word is not found a single time in the book's futuristic section (Rev. 4–22). In fact, the only time in this section where *ekklēsia* is used is in the benediction, reminding the readers of Christ's exhortation to preach these truths in the churches (Rev. 22:16). Other than this scant reference, the word "church" is totally absent from the book's futuristic section. We might inquire why? The obvious answer lies in the fact that the church will not be on the earth during this horrific time period having already been raptured to heaven before the tribulation begins just as the Lord promised in Revelation 3:10.

Moreover, in the book's second section, the following exhortation occurs seven times: "He who has an ear, let him hear what the Spirit says to the churches" (Rev. 2:7, 11, 17, 29; 3:6, 13, 22). It is noteworthy that the nearly identical expression occurs in Revelation 13:9, which is given to encourage those experiencing persecution from the Beast during the tribulation period. This verse says, "if anyone has an ear, let him hear." Notice that the familiar expression "what the Spirit says to the churches" is omitted from Revelation 13:9 despite the fact that it is attached to the same expression seven times in Revelation 2–3. We might ask why the clause "What the Spirit says to the churches" is left off in Revelation 13:9 despite its sevenfold prominence in Revelation 2–3. Once again, the answer lies in the fact that the church will not be on the earth during this seven-year time period, having already been raptured to heaven before the tribulation begins as promised in Revelation 3:10.

Not only is the word "church" (*ekklēsia*) absent from the section of John's Apocalypse directly pertaining to the tribulation period, but the concept of the church is missing as well. Paul routinely described the church, or the body of Christ, as consisting of all people from all nations on equal footing as joint heirs in one new man or spiritual organism. According to Galatians 3:28, in the church age, "There is neither Jew nor Greek, there is neither slave nor free man, there is neither male nor female; for you are all one in Christ Jesus." Ephesians 2:14 similarly explains, "For He Himself is our peace, who made both groups into one and broke down the barrier of the dividing wall." Thus, national barriers or boundaries no longer positionally divide believers from one another in the church age. Today, the preeminent servant of God is no longer national, ethnic Israel but rather the church, or the body of Christ, consisting of believers in Jesus from all nations.

Yet, chapters 4–22 of the book of Revelation describe a time when national barriers will once again be erected as God will again use national Israel as His special instrument to bless the world. Prominent among them will be the 144,000 Jews from the twelve tribes of Israel (Rev. 7:1–8) who will evangelize the world (Rev. 7:9–16). Similarly, during the future tribulation period, God will appoint two Jewish witnesses, most likely Moses and Elijah (Rev. 11:3–14). Moreover, despite the fact that the church is the object of satanic opposition in the present age (Eph. 6:10–20), during the coming tribulation, Satan will relentlessly attack national Israel (Rev. 12:1, 13; cf. Gen. 37:9–10). Thus, not only is the word "church" absent from Revelation's depiction of the future tribulation, the Pauline concept of the church as a body with no national barriers is also absent from this time period. Unlike today, the singular national entity Israel will be the object of not only divine blessing but also satanic wrath in the futuristic section of the Apocalypse. The only logical explanation for this abrupt transition is that the church has already been raptured to heaven before the events of the tribulation period unfold as predicted in Revelation 3:10.

If the church is ever hinted at or mentioned at all in Revelation's description of the tribulation period, it is always portrayed as being in heaven and never on the earth. For example, Revelation 1:20 symbolizes the church as seven lampstands. These lamps or lampstands are described as already being in heaven once the events of the tribulation period begin (Rev. 4:5). Thus, there is no reference to the church either in word or concept in Revelation 4–22. This deafening silence corroborates with a pretribulational interpretation of Revelation 3:10.

Looking at Revelation 4–21 alongside Revelation 3:10 teaches readers the imminent return of the Lord for His church. As has been demonstrated, there are awkward initial problems with the nonpretribulational interpretations of Revelation 3:10, making them untenable. The church will be kept from the well-known future tribulation period whose major purpose is to test unbelieving humanity. This understanding harmonizes well with the remainder of Revelation's prophetic content.

LESS CLEAR IMMINENT-RETURN PASSAGES IN REVELATION 2–3

In addition to Revelation 3:10, a number of remaining passages found in the seven letters to the seven churches (Rev. 2–3) may also contribute to the doctrine of Christ's imminent return. However, they should be held with less dogmatism and certainty since whether they are actually speaking of the second coming of Christ or a special coming of Christ is a matter of debate. These include promises of deliverance (2:25; 3:20) and judgment (2:5, 16, 22; 3:3, 16).

Robert Thomas presents a case arguing that the rapture and the beginning of Daniel's Seventieth Week are simultaneous events (see chapter 1). Because relief for the believer through the rapture and judgment for the unbeliever through Daniel's Seventieth Week are concurrent events, imminence is used to depict both occurrences. While believers in these churches of Revelation 2–3 will be raptured, unbelievers in these same churches will face the judgment of the tribulation period.[47] Thomas explains how such *dual imminence* supports the pretribulational rapture:

> Six of the seven messages of Christ in Rev 2–3 contain references to His coming. . . . His coming is imminent, whether for deliverance or for judgment. The only way this can happen is for the deliverance—the rapture of the church—and the judgment—the beginning of Daniel's seventieth week—to occur simultaneously. . . . A survey of other relevant NT passages reflects the same dual imminence for the two events. The phenomena surrounding these predicted comings lead inevitably to the conclusion that Christ's return for His church must be pretribulational, because this is the only way to explain satisfactorily how the two future events can be simultaneous.[48]

While this thesis has much to commend it and should not be dismissed too quickly, the imminency passages considered under this rubric should be advocated with less dogmatism than Revelation 3:10, since the thesis is built around four assumptions that are a matter of debate. Before exploring these remaining passages, let us first note the *four* assumptions that first must be embraced before these passages can be touted as clearly promoting imminency.

Questionable Assumptions

1. Believers and Unbelievers Comprise the Churches of Revelation 2–3

The dual imminency idea for both the believer through the rapture and the unbeliever through the beginning of the tribulation period is predicated on the notion that the Asia Minor churches of Revelation 2–3 are comprised of both believers and unbelievers. Although this is a view held by many, it must also be conceded that it is at least possible that only a regenerated, believing audience is addressed in Revelation 2–3. John seems to identify with the spiritual status of his immediate audience when he says, "I, John, your brother and fellow partaker in the tribulation" (Rev. 1:9). Notice how John here uses the expression "your brother." Thus, the argument can be made that just as John was a believer, then so were those he addressed, which would be the congregations of the Asia Minor churches.

Moreover, not only are the ones John addresses within the churches (Rev.

2:1, 8, 12, 18; 3:1, 7, 14), they are also depicted as overcomers (2:7, 11, 17, 26; 3:5, 12, 21), an expression that John uses elsewhere to describe the regenerate (1 John 4:4; 5:4–5). In fact, the specific promises granted to these overcomers, such as eating from the tree of life (Rev. 2:7; 22:2, 14), not being hurt by the second death (Rev. 2:11; 20:6, 14; 21:8), and having their names recorded in the Book of Life (Rev. 3:5; 20:12, 15) seem germane to all believers.

While it is often assumed that the deplorable spiritual status of five of the seven churches reveals the unregenerate state of many within these churches, we should remember that the worst offender is Laodicea. In fact, to this wayward church Christ offers no word of positive affirmation as He does with all of the other churches. However, to Laodicea, Jesus offers no threat of eternal retribution but rather says, "Those whom I love, I reprove and discipline" (Rev. 3:19). Jesus' promise of discipline is a reminder of this church's believing status since such discipline is a mark of God's love and spiritual ownership (Heb. 12:5–11). Even the references to satanic influence among the churches (Rev. 2:24) need not disqualify the audience's regenerated status since believers have the ability to open the door to satanic influence in their lives by pandering to the old nature (Eph. 4:26–27).

2. The Return of Christ Is Conditioned on a Human Response

The coming of Christ mentioned in these chapters is often conditioned upon a human response (Rev. 3:3, 20). If the coming of Christ spoken of here is instead often a reference to the rapture, then the difficulty lies in understanding how the return of Christ can ever be conditioned upon a human choice of some kind rather than uniquely upon God's sovereignty (Acts 1:6–7). Of Revelation 3:3 ("Therefore if you do not wake up, I will come like a thief, and you will not know at what hour I will come to you"), Ladd, a posttribulationist, observes:

> However, in the present context, the warning is far more suitable to some historical visitation when the Lord will bring upon a lethargic church an unexpected experience which will mean a divine judgment. This interpretation is supported by the fact that this visitation is posited upon the failure of the church to repent—a condition which is not primarily related to the Lord's return.[49]

In other words, how can the timing of a divinely determined sovereign eschatological event, such as the rapture, ever be conditioned in any way on any sort of human response, such as repentance within a church? While Thomas does attempt an explanation to this conundrum of whether Christ's coming is a rapture or historical "coming" in divine judgment on the Laodicean church,[50] suffice it to say that this issue persists as a genuine debate among interpreters.

3. A Special Coming of Christ to Discipline Local Churches

Many of the coming judgments spoken of in these chapters (Rev. 2:25, 16, 22; 3:3, 16) may not be references to the beginning of the tribulation period but rather to a special coming of Christ in discipline to these individual churches. Such discipline would be akin to the discipline experienced by Ananias and Sapphira in the Jerusalem church (Acts 5:1–11) as well as by the Corinthians for the unworthy manner in which they were partaking of the Lord's Supper (1 Cor. 11:30). However, a special coming interpretation would be improbable regarding Revelation 3:10–11 due to the contextual modifiers of a worldwide tribulation (3:10) and a reward (3:11). Such modifiers are absent in the above judgment-coming texts.

4. A Gap between the Church's Rapture and the beginning of the Tribulation Period

The assumption that the rapture is an event that will occur simultaneously with the beginning of Daniel's Seventieth Week[51] is an assumption not embraced by the majority of interpreters. Most see a gap of some undisclosed duration between the church's rapture and the Antichrist's signing of the peace treaty with unbelieving Israel, which initiates the tribulation period (Dan. 9:27a).[52] Grant Jeffrey summarizes, "There may be an interval of time, however small, between the rapture and the signing of the seven-year treaty with Israel. Whether this interval occupies a few days, months or years, it must be short because God will not leave the earth without a witness to His truth."[53]

While trying to explain how his view of a rebuilt Babylon poses no threat to the rapture's imminency, Bullinger notes, "There is only one conclusion, that in the interval of, say some 30 or more years between the removal of the church and the last 'week' of Daniel's prophecy, it will be revived, and exceed all its former magnificence."[54] Larkin similarly observes:

> But I hear a protest. How, you say, can we be expecting Jesus to come at "any moment," if the city of Babylon must be rebuilt before He can come? There is not a word in Scripture that says that Jesus cannot come and take away His

Church until Babylon is rebuilt. The Church may be taken out of the world 25 or even 50 years before that.[55]

This critique of these *four* assumptions is not offered for the purpose of rejecting the dual imminency position. Rather, it is given simply to demonstrate that interpreting the subsequently analyzed passages from Revelation 2–3 as eschatologically oriented needs to be held with less dogmatism and certainty, and more reservation in comparison to an eschatological interpretation of Revelation 3:10.

PROMISES OF DELIVERANCE

With this acknowledgment that some imminency passages in these chapters are less clear than others, let us now examine the passages in Revelation 2–3 that seemingly support imminency. Let us first explore the promise of divine deliverance (Rev. 2:25; 3:20).

Revelation 2:25

Christ's exhortation to the church of Thyatira in Revelation 2:25 says, "Nevertheless what you have, hold fast until I come." Here Christ exhorts believers at Thyatira to endure by reminding them of the imminent and signless event of His return to rescue them. Thomas explains:

> The incentive to do so was the nearness of Christ's return. No matter how severe enemy pressures might become, the followers of Christ had the hope that His return was imminent. All they had to do was hold out a little longer, and their Lord would rescue them from the clutches of evil. . . . The truth of His coming provides motivation for moral action here.[56]

Revelation 3:20

To the church at Laodicea, Christ said, "Behold, I stand at the door and knock; if anyone hears My voice and opens the door, I will come in to him and will dine with him, and he with Me" (Rev. 3:20). Many use this verse for evangelistic purposes in order to invite the unbeliever to trust Christ for initial salvation. Yet this approach is fraught with problems,[57] not the least of which is that Christ addressed an audience that is already in faith. As previously noted, in the immediately prior verse (Rev. 3:19), the Laodicean church is described as beloved and warned of the prospect of divine discipline (Heb. 12:5–11). Perhaps a better view interprets Revelation 3:20 as a divine call to a wayward church for the reestablishment of divine fellowship.[58] The dining imagery of Revelation 3:20 fits this fellowship theme well since it is reminiscent of the Last Supper, when Christ enjoyed an intimate time of fellowship with His disciples just prior to His crucifixion.[59]

Some contest that Revelation 3:20 is eschatological on the grounds that in other eschatological contexts where door imagery is used, Christ is portrayed either as a judge or rewarder of faithfulness at His return rather than calling for repentance as this passage does.[60] However, important reasons remain as to why interpreters should be open to an imminency understanding of the verse.[61] First, such door imagery is common in biblical eschatological contexts (Matt. 24:43; Mark 13:29; Luke 12:36; James 5:9). Second, supper imagery is commonly associated with the yet future messianic kingdom (Matt. 26:29; Mark 14:25; Luke 12:35–38; 22:30; Rev. 19:9).[62]

PROMISES OF JUDGMENT

In addition to promises of imminent deliverance, promises of imminent judgment also abound in Revelation 2–3 (Rev. 2:5, 16, 22; 3:3, 16). These must also be considered when developing a perspective on Christ's imminent return.

Revelation 2:5

To the church at Ephesus, Jesus gave this warning: "Therefore remember from where you have fallen, and repent and do the deeds you did at first; or else I am coming to you and will remove your lampstand out of its place—unless you repent." Since no worldwide crisis is in view here[63] and an interpretation involving a special coming of Christ in discipline is prominent in letters to other churches (Rev. 2:22),[64] many interpret Revelation 2:5 as a predicted removal of the Ephesian spiritual sphere of influence (Matt. 5:13–16). Jesus spoke of something similar in the Sermon on the Mount—the possible loss of spiritual influence, when He said, "You are the salt of the earth; but if the salt has become tasteless, how can it be made salty *again*? It is no longer good for anything, except to be thrown out and trampled underfoot by men" (Matt. 5:13).

This view seems bolstered by the fact that only one of the seven lampstands is threatened with extinction, and the Ephesian church ultimately did go out of existence.[65] However, imminency of the tribulation judgments is also a viable interpretation of Revelation 2:5. Revelation's theme relates to Christ's return (Rev. 1:7), the extended context refers to the future (Rev. 4–22), and the present tense verb "come" (*erchomai*) is used frequently throughout the book to denote Christ's return (Rev. 1:7; 3:11; 16:15; 22:7, 12, 20).[66]

Revelation 2:16

To the Pergamum church, Jesus sent this warning: "Therefore repent; or else I am coming to you quickly, and I will make war against them with the sword of My mouth" (2:16). This statement could be a prediction of a special coming of Christ in discipline, especially since the Balaamites and Nicolaitans condemned in the Pergamum letter have ceased to exist. However, imminency of coming tribulation judgment could also be in view since the combination of the present tense verb "come" (*erchomai*) coupled with "quickly" (Greek adverb *tachy*) as used here is also employed in the Apocalypse to communicate Christ's return (3:11). *Tachos* (Greek noun "quick") is also used to depict Christ's return in the book's opening verse (Rev. 1:1). Moreover, the sword protruding from Christ's mouth also is a reminder of how John would later describe Christ's return (Rev. 19:15; cf. 2 Thess. 2:8; Isa. 11:4).[67]

Revelation 2:22

To the church at Thyatira, Jesus said, "Behold, I will throw her on a bed of sickness, and those who commit adultery with her into great tribulation, unless they repent of her deeds." Many interpret this verse as a reference to a special coming of Christ in discipline due to the previously described problem of conditioning the return of Christ to a human response. However, the imminent tribulation may also be in view. Interestingly, the expression "great tribulation" as used here is used in only one other place in the book of Revelation, in a context that clearly speaks of Daniel's Seventieth Week (Rev. 7:14). We also find the expression "great tribulation" in reference to Daniel's Seventieth Week in Matthew 24:21. In fact, this time of unequaled distress is universally understood throughout Scripture as the coming tribulation period (Joel 2:2; Jer. 30:7; Dan. 12:1).

Revelation 3:3

To the church at Sardis, Jesus addressed this warning, "So remember what you have received and heard; and keep it, and repent. Therefore if you do not wake up, I will come like a thief, and you will not know at what hour I will come to you." Once again there exists the previously described problem of conditioning Christ's return upon the human response of repentance. Thus, many instead embrace the notion that this verse is talking about a special coming of Christ to discipline. Constable explains, "Failure to heed these warnings would result in Jesus Christ sending discipline on the believers that would surprise them."[68] However, understanding this verse as speaking of the imminent judgment of the tribulation period upon unbelievers within the church remains a distinct possibility. Thief-in-the-night imagery is frequently associated with eschatological events in Scripture (Matt. 24:42–43; Luke 12:39; 1 Thess. 5:2; 2 Pet. 3:10; Rev. 16:15).[69]

Revelation 3:16

To the church at Laodicea, Jesus said, "So because you are lukewarm, and neither hot nor cold, I will spit you out of My mouth." Perhaps this verse is speaking of a special coming of Christ in discipline. As noted previously, in Christ's subsequent remarks to this church (Rev. 3:19), He describes them as beloved but also warned them of the prospect of divine discipline, which is a reality only for the believer (Heb. 12:5–11). However, others point out that the five adjectives used to describe the church in verse 17 could only be describing those who never came to know Christ personally.[70] Thus, they instead interpret this verse as predictive of imminent tribulation judgments about to come upon unbelievers within the church. They note how the phrase "about to" (*mellō*) as used in this verse to depict imminent regurgitation is also used to depict eschatological events elsewhere in Revelation (Rev. 3:10).

Thus, the numerous verses found within Revelation 2–3 contribute to the argument for the imminent return of Christ. Although not as clearly expressed as the promise of the Lord's return for His church as found in Revelation 3:10, promises of imminent deliverance of believers are arguably found in Revelation 2:25 and 3:20. Moreover, promises of imminent tribulation judgment for unbelievers within these churches are also found among the letters to the Asia Minor churches (Rev. 2:5, 16, 22; 3:3, 16).

CONCLUSION

The concept of imminency lends further support to the doctrine of the pretribulation rapture. Not only is the imminent appearing of Christ taught consistently throughout the pages of the New Testament in general, but it also finds specific support in Revelation 2–3, which constitutes Christ's final word to His church. Of these, Revelation 3:10 represents the clearest and most certain promise of Christ's imminent return. Other passages from these chapters also appear to teach imminency. These include Christ's promises of relief to the struggling Asia Minor churches (Rev. 2:25; 3:20) as well as warnings of imminent judgment (Rev. 2:5, 16, 22; 3:3, 16). While the contribution of these other passages to imminency deserves careful consideration, they should be qualified, given the fact that their impact upon imminency is based upon certain debatable presuppositions.

Given the pervasiveness of imminency in the New Testament, the church should eagerly await the very next event on the prophetic horizon, which is the rapture of the church.

NOTES

1. Robert H. Gundry, *The Church and the Tribulation* (Grand Rapids: Zondervan, 1973), 54.

2. George Eldon Ladd, *The Blessed Hope* (Grand Rapids: Eerdmans, 1956), 85–86.

3. Gundry, *Church and the Tribulation*, 55–56.

4. Charles C. Ryrie, *What You Should Know about the Rapture* (Chicago: Moody, 1981), 114–15.

5. Robert L. Thomas, *Revelation 1–7: An Exegetical Commentary*, ed. Kenneth Barker (Chicago: Moody, 1992), 286.

6. Jeffrey L. Townsend, "The Rapture in Revelation 3:10," *BibSac* 137 (July 1980): 253.

7. E. Schuyler English, *Re-Thinking the Rapture: An Examination of What the Scriptures Teach as to the Time of the Translation of the Church in Relation to the Tribulation* (Neptune, NJ: Loizeaux Brothers, 1954), 89.

8. Renald Showers, *Maranatha: Our Lord, Come!* (Bellmawr, NJ: Friends of Israel, 1995), 212.

9. What is important to understand is the general idea that the Greek preposition *ek* can carry the idea of separation from something. Although "take the speck out of your brother's eye" in Matthew 7:5 does imply the speck was originally in the eye and then removed in seeming support of posttribulationism, more linguistic evidence will be produced in the subsequent discussion indicating that this is not the meaning of the same term in Revelation 3:10.

10. Townsend, "The Rapture in Revelation 3:10," 254–59.

11. Ibid., 254.

12. In classical Greek literature, Liddell and Scott list several instances where *ek* means "of Position, *outside of, beyond*." See Henry George Liddell and Robert Scott, *An Intermediate Greek-English Lexicon* (Oxford: Clarendon Press, 1968), 498–99. Examples include Homer's *The Iliad*, 2.14.130 (*ek beleōn*: "Thereafter will we hold ourselves aloof from the fight, *beyond the range of missiles*, lest haply any take

wound on wound. . . ."), Homer's The *Odyssey*, 2.19.7 (*ek kapnou*: "out of the smoke"), and Herodotus's *The Histories*, 2.3.83 (*ek mesou katēsato*: "stood aside").

13. Ryrie, *What You Should Know*, 115–16. For other examples throughout the Septuagint where *ek* (or sometimes a synonym) is used with synonyms of *tēreō* also conveying a complete removal, see Townsend, "The Rapture in Revelation 3:10," 254–55.

14. Josephus, *Antiquities*, 4.2.1. See also Josephus, *Antiquities*, 12.10.5; 13.6.3.

15. Ryrie, *What You Should Know*, 115–16. For an example of *ek* coupled with a nonverbal expression also conveying something completely outside of its object, see 1 Corinthians 9:19.

16. Harald Riesenfeld, "*Tēreō*," TDNT, ed. Gerhard Kittel (Grand Rapids: Eerdmans, 1965), 8:142. See also Gundry, *Church and the Tribulation*, 58.

17. Gundry, *Church and the Tribulation*, 59.

18. Lauren Leigh Noske, "Nine Reasons Why John Piper Disagrees with Nicolas Cage's 'Left Behind' Movie's View of Rapture," *The Gospel Herald*, August 6, 2014; www.gospelherald.com. See also John Piper, "Definition and Observations concerning the Second Coming of Christ," Desiring God Ministry, August 30, 1987; www.desiringgod.org.

19. Thomas Ice, "John Piper and the Rapture," 3; Pre-Trib Research Center, online: www.pre-trib.org.

20. Townsend, "The Rapture in Revelation 3:10," 258.

21. Showers, *Maranatha*, 214.

22. William R. Newell, *Revelation: A Complete Commentary* (1935; repr., Grand Rapids: Baker, 1987), 71. This future tribulation period is well attested to throughout both the Old and New Testaments (Deut. 4:26–31; Isa. 2:10–21; 13:6–13; 17:4–11; Jer. 30:4–11; Ezek. 20:33–38; Dan. 9:27; 12:1; Zeph. 1:14–18; Zech. 14:1–4; Matt. 24:9–31; 1 Thess. 5:1–4; 2 Thess. 2:1–12).

23. Ron Rhodes, *The End Times in Chronological Order: A Complete Overview to Understanding Bible Prophecy* (Eugene, OR: Harvest House, 2012), 50.

24. Norman L. Geisler, *Systematic Theology*, vol. 4 (Minneapolis: Bethany, 2004), 654.

25. Henry Clarence Thiessen, "Will the Church Pass through the Tribulation Period?," *BibSac* 92 (April–June 1935): 202–3.

26. Showers, *Maranatha*, 211–12.

27. Charles C. Ryrie, *A Survey of Bible Doctrine* (Chicago: Moody, 1972), 170.

28. Ryrie, *What You Should Know*, 116–17. See also Charles C. Ryrie, *Come Quickly Lord Jesus. What You Need to Know about the Rapture* (Eugene, OR: Harvest House, 1996), 135.

29. Gundry, *Church and the Tribulation*, 60.

30. Lewis Sperry Chafer, *Systematic Theology*, vol. 4 (1948; repr., Grand Rapids: Kregel, 1993), 47–53.

31. Newell, *Revelation*, 71.

32. For example, Kenneth L. Gentry, "The Great Tribulation Is Past: Exposition," in *The Great Tribulation: Past or Future?*, ed. Thomas Ice and Kenneth L. Gentry (Grand Rapids: Kregel, 1999), 44.

33. William Bell, "A Critical Evaluation of the Pretribulation Rapture Doctrine in Christian Eschatology" (Ph.D. diss., New York University, 1967), 304.

34. Johnston notes that *oikoumenē* "may have a very wide reference. . . . Sometimes it is synonymous with . . . [*aiōn*, 'age, world'] and . . . [*kosmos*, 'world'] . . . . Hence, *oikoumenē* may mean also mankind as a whole . . . ." See George Johnston, "*Oikoumenē* and *Kosmos* in the New Testament," *New Testament Studies* 10 (April 1964): 353. Of the use of *oikoumenē* in Matthew 24:14, Michel similarly writes, "It is certainly not to be linked here with political imperial style. The reference is simply to the glad message which is for all nations and the whole earth." See Otto Michel, "*Oikoumenē*," TDNT, ed. Gerhard Kittel (Grand Rapids: Eerdmans, 1965), 5:158.

35. Thomas Ice, "Kept from the Hour," Pre-Trib Research Center, www.pre-trib.org/articles/view/kept_from_hour2 .

36. Robert L. Thomas, "The 'Comings' of Christ in Revelation 2–3," *The Master's Seminary Journal* 7 (fall 1996): 173.

37. James Barr, *The Semantics of Biblical Language* (London: Oxford University Press, 1961), 218.

38. Thomas L. Constable, "Notes on Revelation," 2015 edition, 49, www.soniclight.com/constable/notes/pdf/revelation/pdf.

39. Showers, *Maranatha*, 215.

40. Heinrich Seesemann, "*Peirazō*," TDNT, ed. Gerhard Kittel (Grand Rapids: Eerdmans, 1965), 6:23.

41. Ice, "Kept from the Hour," 2. See also Thomas Ice, "The Meaning of 'Earth Dwellers' in Revelation," *BibSac* 166 (July–September 2009): 350–65; Showers, *Maranatha*, 216.

42. Showers, *Maranatha*, 212.

43. Townsend, "The Rapture in Revelation 3:10," 261.

44. Showers, *Maranatha*, 213.

45. Ibid., 217–18.

46. Ice, "Kept from the Hour," 2–3.

47. Thomas, "The 'Comings' of Christ in Revelation 2–3," 153–81.

48. Ibid., 153.

49. George Eldon Ladd, *A Commentary on the Revelation of John* (Grand Rapids: Eerdmans, 1972), 57.

50. Thomas, "The 'Comings' of Christ in Revelation 2–3," 158–59, 165.

51. Ibid., 173–74.

52. John F. Walvoord, *The Prophecy Knowledge Handbook* (Wheaton: Victor, 1990), 485, 487, 492; Showers, *Maranatha*, 59; Charles C. Ryrie, *Basic Theology* (Wheaton: Victor, 1986), 465.

53. Grant Jeffrey, *Apocalypse: The Coming Judgment of the Nations* (Toronto: Frontier, 1992), 125.

54. E. W. Bullinger, *Commentary on Revelation* (Grand Rapids: Kregel, 1984), 577. See also page 559.

55. Clarence Larkin, *The Book of Revelation* (Glenside, PA: Larkin, 1919), 162.

56. Thomas, "The 'Comings' of Christ in Revelation 2–3," 155.

57. Dennis M. Rokser, *Seven Reasons Not to Ask Jesus into Your Heart"* (Duluth, MN: Grace Gospel Press, 2012).

58. Robert H. Mounce, *The Book of Revelation*, NICNT, ed. Gordon D. Fee, rev. ed. (Grand Rapids: Eerdmans, 1997), 113.

59. In John 13:30, Judas, the only unbeliever in the group, left the upper room early on.

60. R. H. Charles, *A Critical and Exegetical Commentary on the Revelation of St. John*, ICC, 2 vols. (Edinburgh: T. & T. Clark, 1920), 1:101.

61. Thomas, "The 'Comings' of Christ in Revelation 2–3," 158–59.

62. Bullinger, *Commentary on Revelation*, 208.

63. G. B. Caird, *The Revelation of Saint John*, Black's New Testament Commentaries, ed. Henry Chadwick (London: Black, 1966), 32.

64. Isbon T. Beckwith, *The Apocalypse of John* (New York: Macmillan, 1919), 450.

65. Henry Barclay Swete, *Commentary on Revelation,* 3rd ed. (1911; repr., Grand Rapids: Kregel, 1977), 28.

66. Thomas, "The 'Comings' of Christ in Revelation 2–3," 160.

67. Ibid., 162.

68. Constable, "Notes on Revelation," 44.

69. Thomas, "The 'Comings' of Christ in Revelation 2–3," 164.

70. For example, see Alan F. Johnson, "Revelation," *Expositor's Bible Commentary*, ed. Frank E. Gaebelein et al. (Grand Rapids: Zondervan, 1981), 12:458.

9

What Child Is This? A Forgotten Argument for the Pretribulation Rapture

BY MICHAEL J. SVIGEL

And she gave birth to a son, a male child, who is to rule all the nations with a rod of iron; and her child was caught up to God and to His throne.

REVELATION 12:5

In the middle of the 1800s, with no baby shower and no frilly "It's a Boy!" announcements, the modern pretribulation rapture doctrine was born. As it grew and matured over the next several years, some embraced the newborn doctrine while others rejected it. Nevertheless, through the vehicle of popular preaching, teaching, and writing, the pretribulation rapture became a fixture in many churches and institutions, still enjoying a high degree of popular support today.[1]

However, interest in and support for the pretribulation position among evangelical scholars seems to have declined in recent years. The perception among interested scholars appears to be that the doctrine rests on flimsy inferences drawn from unclear passages dependent upon peculiar presuppositions.[2] In short, many today believe that the doctrine of the church's rapture from the earth prior to a future seven-year tribulation simply has no clear exegetical basis.[3]

In this chapter I want to revisit a forgotten argument for the pretribulation rapture that accompanied the birth of the rapture doctrine itself. In fact, I will suggest that John Nelson Darby, the earliest clear proponent of the modern pretribulation rapture doctrine, actually rested his view on what many at the time believed to be a strong exegetical foundation: the catching up of the "male child"—identified by early pretribulationists as the body of Christ—in Revelation 12:5.

In preview, I will show that during the 1830s to 1850s, Darby moved from a more general prewrath rapture view to settle on a strictly pretribulation perspective. Though he continued to use numerous corroborative arguments to defend his pretribulation position, the load-bearing pillar for the timing of the rapture was the argument from Revelation 12:5. As Darby's associates and followers adopted and strengthened this exegetical argument in their own teaching, the doctrine grew in popularity.

However, in the generations following the original formulation and popularization of the pretribulation rapture, supporters eventually dropped the exegetical argument from Revelation 12:5 while maintaining the corroborative arguments. The result? Most defenders of the pretribulation rapture doctrine have actually forgotten the original exegetical argument that once underpinned their view. In turn, many who had once supported the pretribulation position have changed to a midtribulation, posttribulation, or prewrath perspective.[4]

In short, I will make the case that Darby's early defense of the pretribulation rapture based on Revelation 12:5 should never have been abandoned. In fact, I will argue that this passage, when examined closely, provides a strong foundation for a pretribulation rapture of the church.

DARBY'S LOST ARGUMENT FOR THE PRETRIBULATION RAPTURE

Irving's Partial Prewrath Rapture

Contrary to some popular treatments of the subject, including those of MacPherson and Reid,[5] the doctrine of the pretribulation rapture in the modern era did not actually begin with Edward Irving and his followers. Irving seems to have held a partial prewrath secret rapture view, not a pretribulation position.[6] That is, not all believers would be rescued prior to the pouring out of God's wrath ("prewrath") but only those who are among the spiritually mature and holy ("partial"). This rapture would be both unannounced and perhaps even unnoticed by most ("secret"), since the remnant of the holy was thought by the Irvingites to be relatively small compared to the large mass of nominal or carnal Christians.

In 1831, only three years before his death, Irving advanced such a partial prewrath rapture, and this only ambiguously and with great hesitation. At one point he closely associated the event of 1 Thessalonians 4:17 with "the second coming of Christ, with all his saints, to establish his kingdom over all the nations under the whole heaven."[7] Later, however, he clarified that this event, though constituting a single return, is actually complex, including a rapture of the church prior to Christ's execution of wrath.[8] Did Irving understand a secret rapture for the faithful as a rescue from wrath? Yes. Did he understand a catching up of the whole church prior to the seven-year tribulation? No.

Darby's Pretribulation Rapture

As far as I can tell, based on the evidence available, the first person to articulate a true pretribulation rapture was John Nelson Darby.[9] In that early articulation, Darby appealed to an argument based on the identification of the "male child"—or more literally "male son"[10]—in Revelation 12:5 as the corporate body of Christ and his catching up to God as the rapture of the church. Prior to arriving at this conclusion, however, Darby first had to have four convictions in place:

1. A consistent futurist interpretation of the book of Revelation and of the Seventieth Week of Daniel 9:27—these prophecies pointed to future, not past, present, spiritual, or ideal realities;
2. A strong doctrine of the mystical union between Christ and the body of Christ, the church;
3. An openness to distinguish Old Testament Israel from the New Testament church—especially allowing for different symbols in Revelation to refer to these two different groups of saints; and
4. A literal understanding of the order of events and chronological indicators in Revelation 11–13—if the prophecy says something will last 1,260 days, then it will last 1,260 days.

With these four chair legs firmly in place, Darby concluded that the rapture of the church described in 1 Thessalonians 4:17 and alluded to in 1 Corinthians 15:51–52 would occur prior to the seven-year tribulation. But these legs were built only gradually in Darby's doctrinal development.

In the year 1839, Darby published his *Notes on the Book of Revelations*. In this early edition Darby was not completely clear about the identification of the woman and the child in Revelation 12 or of the precise timing of the rapture. However, like Irving, he clearly held to a "secret rapture" view that took place "at least" prior to the final three and a half years of "great tribulation."[11] At that time, Darby understood the vision of Revelation 12:5 to refer not to historical or prophetic events but to a general picture of the relationship of various participants in God's plan. This was more of an idealist rather than futurist interpretation of the vision.[12] That is, it represented spiritual truths or principles true in every age and applicable to all Christians rather than events that would happen during the tribulation of the future.

Darby's Move to a Complete Rapture of the Church

In a letter dated 1843, Darby still seemed to vacillate between a complete rapture of all believers or a partial rapture of only the faithful: "It may be some will pass through, but I am more than ever confirmed . . . that the faithful will be kept from it."[13] Thus, the uncertainty and lack of clarity expressed in his 1839 edition of *Notes on the Book of Revelations* had not yet solidified into a clearly pretribulation rapture of the whole body of Christ even by 1843.

However, five years later, in a letter dated May 1, 1848, Darby clearly placed the period of the church between the sixty-ninth and seventieth week of Daniel 9:27. He also noted, "The church is never, properly speaking, seen at all" in the book of Revelation from chapter 4 through chapters 21 and 22. This, he wrote, "is the interval between the removal of the church from the place of testimony, and the manifestation of it in a glorious testimony."[14] Here we have the workings of a clear pretribulation rapture view.

What changed in Darby's thinking to solidify these convictions?

In another letter that same year, Darby walked through his interpretation of Revelation 12. He identified the woman as Israel, no longer idealizing her as the spiritual church as he had done in the previous decade. With regard to the identification of the "male son," Darby argued that the church is brought into the symbol "as being identified with Christ Himself," as already indicated in Christ's promise to overcoming believers in Thyatira.[15] In this promise in Revelation 2:26–27 to the church at Thyatira, Christ quoted Psalm 2 and extended His messianic rule described in the psalm to include those who overcome (i.e., church saints), forming a oneness by which they rule together. The passage reads, "He who overcomes, and he who keeps My deeds until the end, TO HIM I WILL GIVE AUTHORITY OVER THE NATIONS; AND HE SHALL RULE THEM WITH A ROD OF IRON, AS THE VESSELS OF THE POTTER ARE BROKEN TO PIECES, as I also have received authority from My Father."

Thus, Darby made a corporate connection between the "son" in Revelation 12:5 and His body, the church, applying the same promise of Psalm 2 both to Christ and to the church. This is more explicit later in his letter, when he placed the catching up of the son "out of the scene" prior to the war in heaven and the casting down of Satan. Thus, the catching up of the male son in Revelation 12:5 also corresponds to the removal of the church from the "historical course of events."[16] The power of the kingdom is established, but not until after the final judgments and the second coming will it take its place in the earthly realm.

In 1852, Darby delivered a series of lectures on the letters to the seven churches in Revelation. Three years later these published lectures had gone through several editions, one-third of which included his straightforward argument for the pretribulation rapture. Having concluded that Revelation primarily deals with events yet future, Darby saw in the vision of Revelation 12 a description of events associated with either the birth of the church or the future seven-year tribulation period. He therefore identified the woman in labor at the opening of the vision as a corporate symbol for the nation of Israel (Rev. 12:1). The dragon, desiring to devour her child, is Satan working through the evil world powers against God's people (12:2–4). Finally, Darby identified the male son in Revelation 12:5 as the mystical body of Christ, the church. Having been born from the woman (Israel), the male son (the church) is described in terms of the king Messiah in whose image this corporate body is to be conformed. Before the dragon is able to devour this mystical male son, however, he is "caught up" to God and to His throne.

In Darby's understanding, then, this catching up of the male child portrays the future rapture of the church described in 1 Thessalonians 4:17. According to the chronology embedded in Revelation 11–13, the catching up will be followed by war in heaven, Satan's banishment to the earth, the devil's attempt to destroy the remnant of Israel, and finally the flight of Israel into the wilderness for three and a half years. All together, the events following the male son's rapture to heaven include the future seven-year tribulation period. Thus, in Darby's interpretation, the rapture of the male son (the church) in Revelation 12:5 occurs before the tribulation. Darby wrote:

> If the mighty man, the mystic man, the man-child of Revelation xii. is to act [judging the world with a rod of iron], He must first be complete. . . . The head and the body must be united before He can act as having this title before the world; because the mystic man as a whole cannot take it until the Church is taken up to Him. For not until then—until the Church, the body, is united to the Head, Christ, in heaven—is the mystic man in that sense complete; and therefore, the Church must be taken up before Christ can come in judgment.[17]

In another lecture Darby dealt with Revelation 12, in which he intended to address "the gathering up of the Church of God, the heavenly saints, to be with Christ."[18] He noted that "the taking up of the saints is the taking them out of the way of those judgments" that will come upon the whole world. He then interpreted Revelation 12:5 explicitly as the rapture of the church: "In the chapter we have read, you have first Christ Himself and the church, figured in the man-child; and then in the woman who flees from persecution for 1260 days you have the Jewish remnant, those who are spared in the time of judgment but are not yet brought into glory."[19]

Darby also nuanced the idea of the absence of the church in the book of Revelation this way: "But you never find in prophecy, until the end of Revelation—you never find the church revealed in prophecy, except in connection with Christ."[20] Thus he noted:

> I have no doubt that the "man child" spoken of in the chapter that we have been reading includes the church as well as Christ. But it is Christ that is principally meant, for the church would be nothing without Christ; it would be a body without a head. It is Christ who has been caught up; but the church is included, for whenever He begins to act publicly, even as regards Satan being cast down, He must have His body, His bride, with Him; He must have His brethren, His joint-heirs.[21]

Darby not only cited Revelation 2:16–17 but also Daniel 7, when the "saints of the Highest One" (vv. 18, 27) receive judgment from the Ancient of Days— "the saints who will be in the heavenly places with Christ, when Christ comes."[22]

Thus, Darby relied on both Old and New Testament passages to establish the corporate identification of the saints with Christ.

So, we can see that Darby's mature doctrine of the pretribulation rapture was accompanied by a clear identification of the woman in Revelation 12:1–2 as Israel.[23] He interpreted the birth of the male son in 12:5 as Christ, but he also associated the church with Christ so intimately that he could say, "Thus we get the church, united with Christ, taken up to God, and the woman fled into the wilderness."[24] In fact, because of the catching up of the church and its spiritual warfare in heaven, Satan will be cast down to the earth (12:5, 7–9).[25] So it is the church of God—the inhabitants of heaven—who are called to rejoice at the casting down of Satan (12:12).[26]

In sum, four elements came together for Darby to construct his pretribulation rapture teaching. The first was a consistent futurist interpretation of the book of Revelation, so the catching up of the male son described a future event. Secondly, he held to a strong doctrine of the mystical union between Christ and the church, found stunningly exemplified in the vision of the male son in Revelation 12:5. The third element was an openness to distinguishing Old Testament Israel from the New Testament church, found envisioned in the woman (Israel) giving birth to the male child (the church)—two distinct entities with separate, but intertwined, destinies both past and future. The fourth element helpful in supporting the pretribulation rapture view was a literal understanding of the chronological indicators in Revelation 11–13. Though all of these ingredients were individually present in other works on Revelation in the centuries and decades leading up to the nineteenth-century prophecy movement,[27] not until Darby did they come together to provide the fertile soil within which his biblical argument for the pretribulation rapture of the church could sprout.

REVISITING THE ARGUMENTS
FOR THE RAPTURE IN REVELATION 12:5

All of this may be interesting for the history of the pretribulation rapture doctrine, but was Darby right in his understanding of the rapture in Revelation 12:5? Were his followers correct in reading the passage the same way?

I think they were.

Years ago, my own persuasion to the pretribulation rapture doctrine came as a result of reading this same passage in Greek, finding it filled with oddities beckoning the reader to dig deeper, and finally realizing that the author intended for us to understand the passage to refer not merely to Christ but to Christ in union with His body, the church. Thus, when the male son is caught up to God prior to the unfolding of the events of the tribulation, we're meant to understand this as a reference to the long-expected rapture of the glorified church described in 1 Thessalonians 4:17. It was only later, through my historical studies, that I learned that not only had others seen the rapture in Revelation 12:5 but that this was the view of the earliest supporters of the pretribulation rapture doctrine.

In fact, I was astonished to learn that the earliest advocates of a pretribulation rapture (Darby, William Kelly, William Blackstone, H. A. Ironside, etc.) pointed to *this* passage as exegetical evidence for a pre-seven-year rapture. The problem is this is a symbolic vision that needs to be carefully interpreted, and the interpretational issues are somewhat complicated and require a working knowledge of the original Greek.

However, I think the time has come to turn back the clock, give Darby, Kelly, and other early pretribulation rapture teachers a voice at the table. Perhaps their identification of Revelation 12:5 as the rapture—to some, laughable at first glance—is, in fact, true. In the remainder of this chapter, I intend to show that Darby and others were right after all. I will argue afresh that the symbol of the male son in Revelation 12:5 is best identified as the body of Christ, the church, and the male son's catching up to God is best identified as the rapture of the church that takes place prior to the events of the seven-year tribulation.

The six following considerations persuaded me of this interpretation.

1. The Consistency in Symbolism

Summary Statement. Identifying the male son as the body of Christ is fully consistent with the symbolism of the vision recorded in Revelation 12:1–6. If the woman represents a corporate entity (Israel through the ages), and if the dragon represents a corporate entity (the satanic world system through the ages, with Satan at its head), then it is entirely consistent with the apocalyptic symbolism of the vision for the male son to represent the church as the body of Christ through the ages, with Christ as its head.

Closer Examination. Three symbolic figures appear in Revelation 12:1–6—the woman, the dragon, and the male son.[28] What does each of these three symbolic images represent?

Introduced in Revelation 12:1, the woman is "clothed with the sun, and the moon under her feet, and on her head a crown of twelve stars" (12:1). Her condition follows: "She was with child; and she cried out, being in labor and in pain to give birth" (12:2). Some have identified this woman as the church of both the Old and New Testaments.[29] Others, especially those who assert a distinction between Israel of the Old Testament and the church of the New, see the woman as representing national Israel alone.[30] Still others lean toward the Israel view but with a caveat: the woman is "ideal" Israel.[31]

Recognizing that the woman is, in fact, a symbol, rather than a literal individual female in cosmic clothing, it seems most probable that the symbol represents the remnant of Israel. That is, she is the body of Israel incorporate, whose members are not merely the physical seed of Jacob but that smaller, spiritual elect Israel, which Paul calls the "remnant chosen by grace" (Rom. 11:5 NIV).[32] When we compare the Greek of Revelation 12:1 and the Septuagint (ancient Greek) translation of Genesis 37:9, we see a strong correspondence. Revelation 12:1 ESV reads: "And a great sign appeared in heaven: a woman clothed with the sun [*ton hēlion*], with the moon [*hē selēnē*] under her feet, and on her head a crown of twelve stars [*asterōn*]." In Genesis 37:9, Joseph relays the symbolic dream he had to his brothers: "As it were the sun [*ho hēlios*], and the moon [*hē selēnē*], and the eleven stars [*asteres*] did me reverence."[33] The sun, moon, and stars correspond to the symbols in Joseph's dream, where they represented the patriarch, matriarch, and the sons of Jacob, i.e., the father, mother, and twelve tribes of the nation of Israel respectively[34] (LXX). In further support of this interpretation, the symbol of a woman for the nation of Israel is found throughout the Old Testament's prophetic literature.[35]

Though Revelation 12:9 calls the dragon "the serpent of old who is called the devil and Satan, who deceives the whole world," the symbolism in the vision points to more than merely an individual. Because the dragon and the beast of Revelation 13 are clearly distinguished (Rev. 13:3–4; 16:13), the symbolism of the seven heads and ten horns is not intended to identify him as the Beast of the next chapter. Rather, the Beast is later created in the image of the dragon; he is not identical to him. The dragon's symbolism leads to a corporate identification as the nations of the world opposed to God and His people. This is indicated by the correspondence between the seven heads and ten horns of the dragon and the same gruesome anatomy of the four beasts of Daniel 7:1–8.

In that Old Testament symbolic vision, Daniel sees fours beasts that have a total of seven heads and ten horns. The first beast (representing the Babylonian Empire) has one head (7:4); the second beast (Medo-Persia) has one head (7:5); the third beast (Greece) has four heads (7:6); and the fourth beast (Rome) has one head and ten horns (7:7). All of these beasts, incidentally, are corporate identities, referring both to characteristics of the empires' leaders and incorporating the historical-political system as well. So, in Revelation 12:9, drawing on this principle of corporate identity in Daniel 7, the vision of the dragon sums up the totality of Satan's political opposition to God and His people throughout history. That's the meaning of the seven heads and ten horns.

Thus, the symbol of the dragon in Revelation 12 is best seen as Satan *working through* world empires. In the second half of the tribulation, the Beast from the sea looks like the dragon, having seven heads and ten horns, and also sharing some physical features of the four world powers of Daniel 7:1–7 (cf. Rev. 13:1–2). So, the dragon symbolizes a corporate entity—both the world system as the great enemy of God's people throughout history and the secret ruler of that world system, Satan himself.

Finally we come to the symbol of the male son. Because both the woman and the dragon are described with Old Testament symbols that point us to corporate identities, the consistent interpreter should consider whether the male son, too, is more than just an individual. Now, it's possible that the male son refers to Jesus and Jesus alone. God can do what He wants in His visions! But the responsible interpreter shouldn't rush to a hasty judgment. A corporate interpretation of the male son, if it fits a careful examination of the text, would be more consistent with the symbolism of the passage.[36]

Of course, as was the case with the dragon—and even with the original beasts of Daniel 7—the corporate interpretation of the male son would not deny the likelihood that the individual, Jesus Christ, is also part of the symbol. However, if the symbolism is consistent in the vision, Jesus Christ is not alone; the church, the body of Christ in spiritual union with Him by the baptism of the Holy Spirit (1 Cor. 12:13–14), would be part of the intended meaning of the symbol.[37] This mysterious spiritual union of Christ with His body, the church, is one of the great, unique doctrines of the New Testament (e.g., Acts 9:4; Rom. 12:5; 1 Cor. 12:27; Eph. 4:15–16). Therefore, the corporate identification of the male son in Revelation 12:5 does not discount the notion that Christ is also in view but allows for consistency in interpretation.

2. The Allusion to Isaiah 66:7

Summary Statement. Revelation 12:5 contains an allusion to Isaiah 66:7. Identifying the male son as the body of Christ best explains this allusion. The use of the neuter Greek adjective *arsen* ("male") modifying the masculine noun *huios* ("son") and the image of Israel giving birth points careful readers back to Isaiah 66:7–8, where a corporate body, Israel, gives birth to another corporate body. The image of Israel giving birth is parallel to Revelation 12:5, and John explicitly breaks the rules of Greek grammar (modifying the masculine "son" with the neuter "male") to point us back to this passage in Isaiah 66. The child in both cases is a corporate body, not an individual.

Closer Examination. Revelation 12:5 reads: "And she gave birth to a son, a male . . . [*huion arsen*], who is to rule all the nations with a rod of iron."[38] True, most modern commentators identify the male son as none other than Jesus Christ.[39] And we must admit that a cursory reading of the passage (especially in English) lends itself to this interpretation. However, the following considerations lessen the likelihood that Jesus Christ alone is in view here while at the same time strengthening the notion that the child symbolizes the entire body of Christ.

In Revelation 12:5 the neuter adjective *arsen* ("male") modifies the masculine noun *huion* ("son"). Now, Greek grammar dictates that adjectives match the gender of the nouns they modify. Masculine adjectives modify masculine nouns. Neuter adjectives modify neuter nouns. But what John does with the grammar in 12:5 is like somebody saying, "She had a son; it's male," instead of something more natural: "She had a son, he's male."

At this point another obvious question arises: Why would John point out that the son is male anyway? Is it not self-evident that all *sons* are male? But in the book of Revelation, such strange, unexpected use of grammar and imagery is meant to point us to interpretive keys, usually parallel passages from the Old Testament. This is precisely what John is doing in Revelation 12:5. The discordant grammar and the strange phrase "male son" should cause the reader to slow down, pay attention, and proceed carefully to catch what the vision is trying to communicate.

So, to what passage is John pointing us and, more importantly, *why*?

There's no question that John's use of "bad grammar" in Revelation 12:5 is intended to point the reader back to the images of Isaiah 66:7.[40] That passage reads, "Before she travailed, she brought forth; before her pain came, she gave birth to a boy (*arsen*)." The next verse demonstrates that the woman and child of Isaiah 66:7–8 are not intended to represent individuals but rather corporate bodies: "Who has heard such a thing? Who has seen such things? Can a land be born in one day? Can a nation be brought forth all at once? As soon as Zion travailed, she also brought forth her sons [*ta paidia,* plural]" (Isa. 66:8). The parallelism in the passage identifies the "male" in verse 7 with the plural "children" in verse 8, describing Zion giving birth not to an individual but to "a land" and "a nation."

Now the question is, why does John point us to Isaiah 66:7–8? He usually uses Old Testament imagery in the book of Revelation in one of two ways: either to say, "This *is* that," or to say, "This *is like* that." John either makes an exact equation:

$$\text{Old Testament image} = \text{Image in Revelation}^{41}$$

Or John draws a meaningful parallel between the two:
$$\text{Old Testament image} \parallel \text{Image in Revelation}^{42}$$

It seems that John alludes to Isaiah 66:7–8 not to *equate* (=) the passages but to draw an important parallel (||) necessary for us to properly interpret the image of Revelation 12:5. [43] (This will be clearer in light of other considerations of the birth of the male son in Revelation 12:5, which we will discuss shortly.) The point of the parallel is that the male son is *not* an individual. Instead, like the corporate "male" born to corporate "Zion" in Isaiah 66:7–8, the male son in Revelation 12:5 should be interpreted as a corporate body.

3. The Allusion to Daniel 7:13

Summary Statement. Identifying the male son as the body of Christ best explains the allusion in Revelation 12:5 to Daniel 7:13. John uses the term *huios* ("son") and the image of the son receiving a kingdom before the throne of God. This reminds John's readers of the vision of the "Son of Man" in Daniel 7:13–14 receiving a kingdom from the Ancient of Days. This vision in Daniel 7 is actually interpreted corporately by the interpreting angel. This further supports the view that the male son is the church in union with Christ, not simply Christ alone.

Closer Examination. In Isaiah 66:7 the woman gave birth to a male: *eteken arsen* ("she bore a male"). This is interpreted in verse 8 as Zion giving birth to her children: *eteken Ziōn paidia autēs* ("Zion bore her children"). Nowhere in verses 7–8 is the word *huios* ("son") used; but John inserts this word in Revelation 12:5—"And she bore a son" (*eteken huion*). But if John is pointing his readers back to Isaiah 66:7, why didn't he simply use the exact phrase, *eteken arsen* ("she bore a male")? Instead, he inserted *huios* ("son") into the quotation: *eteken huion arsen* ("she bore a son, a male").

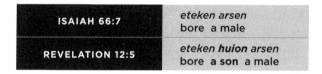

ISAIAH 66:7	*eteken arsen* bore a male
REVELATION 12:5	*eteken huion arsen* bore a son a male

This raises the question: Why the insertion of *huios* ("son")? The best explanation for John's insertion of *huios* in the quotation is to point the reader back to yet another vision from the Old Testament—the "Son of Man" (*huios anthrōpou*) in Daniel 7:13–14. The passage reads:

I kept looking in the night visions,
And behold, with the clouds of heaven
One like a Son of Man was coming,
And He came up to the Ancient of Days
And was presented before Him.
And to Him was given dominion,
Glory and a kingdom,
That all the peoples, nations and men of every language
Might serve Him.
His dominion is an everlasting dominion
Which will not pass away;
And His kingdom is one
Which will not be destroyed. (Dan. 7:13–14)

The imagery of Daniel 7:13–14 has several similarities with what we see in Revelation 12:5. In both places the "son" (*huios*) is destined to rule the nations, He is brought into the presence of God, and He is presented before His throne (see Dan. 7:9, where the Ancient of Days is seated on a throne). It shouldn't seem strange that John would intentionally allude to Daniel 7 by means of these parallel images and the use of the word *huios* ("son") to describe the child. Remember, John had already clearly alluded to Daniel 7 in Revelation 12 when he described the dragon as having seven heads and ten horns (Dan. 7:1–8). Thus, Daniel 7 imagery and language is already present in Revelation 12.

It is likely, then, that John inserted the term *huios* ("son") into his quotation of the phrase *eteken arsen* ("she bore a male") from Isaiah 66:7 in order to make a further connection between the male child and the "Son of Man" in Daniel 7:13–14. Some might see this as a clear proof that Jesus, the "Son of Man," is therefore the sole referent in the image of the male son. Actually, the allusion to Daniel 7 strengthens the corporate identification of the male son.

The fact is, when Daniel's interpreting angel (7:16) gives the meaning of the vision of the Son of Man approaching the throne of the Ancient of Days and receiving authority to rule, he does not interpret it simply as a future messianic king or heavenly Savior. Instead, the angel interprets the vision *corporately*.[44] He says, "But the saints [plural] of the Highest One will receive the kingdom and possess the kingdom forever, for all ages to come" (Dan. 7:18). Then, in verse 22, the "saints [plural] of the Highest One" are given the kingdom; and in verse 27 both the corporate and individual rulers are indicated together: "Then the sovereignty, the dominion and the greatness of all the kingdoms under the whole heaven will be given to the people of the saints [plural] of the Highest One; His kingdom will be an everlasting kingdom, and all the dominions will serve and obey Him." Thus, the "Son of Man" figure in the vision is interpreted *corporately* as the Messiah *and His saints* in Daniel 7:18, 22, 26–27, not as a lone individual. One commentator notes, "If the humanlike figure [the Son of Man] balances the [four] creatures [of Daniel 7], it would not be surprising if, like them, it could have both individual and corporate reference."[45] And Seow puts it simply: "The one is the many; the many are the one."[46]

For this reason, John uses the term "son" (*huios*) in Revelation 12:5 to point readers back to the "Son of Man" vision of Daniel 7 and its corporate identification as Messiah and His saints, which we know from the New Testament to be the church.[47] Thus, John's subtle allusion to the vision of the Son of Man in Daniel 7 further strengthens the identity of the male son in Revelation 12:5 as the body of Christ, the church, which is to rule over the nations with their head, Jesus Christ, after being presented before the throne of God to receive the reward of the kingdom.

4. The Language and Imagery of "Snatching" (Harpazō)

Summary Statement. Identifying the male son as the body of Christ best explains the use of *harpazō* ("snatched") in Revelation 12:5. Regardless of context, *harpazō* always indicates a sudden removal or snatching. In contrast, for the ascension of Christ to the throne of God, the New Testament uses terms such as "to be lifted up" ([*epairō*] Acts 1:9), "to ascend" ([*anabainō*] John 20:17; Eph. 4:8–10), and "to take up" ([*analambanō*] Mark 16:19 NIV; Acts 1:11). These are less dramatic terms, meaning a simple removal from one place to another. Revelation 12:5, on the other hand, describes the male son being suddenly snatched away from the dragon, who wanted to devour the child. The ascension of Christ was gradual (Acts 1:10), not sudden.

Also, Revelation 12:5 is a context of "rescue" from the threat of the dragon. In His ascension to heaven, Christ was not rescued but ascended victoriously. He was in no danger from the devil or anybody else. The term "rapture," *harpazō*, is never used elsewhere of Christ's ascension to heaven. Thus, the use of *harpazō* in a rescue context like Revelation 12:5 is completely inappropriate to describe the ascension of Christ. But it is completely appropriate to describe the rapture of the church as a rescue from Satan's intensifying efforts to destroy the church as it approaches the end times.

Closer Examination. John describes the destiny of the male son in the following way: "And her child was caught up [passive of *harpazō*] to God and to His throne" (12:5b). Most readers who interpret the male son as Jesus Christ identify the catching up of the child to the throne of God as the ascension. However, such a view creates an insurmountable problem. Simply put, the verb *harpazō* ("to snatch") is wholly inappropriate for describing the ascension of Christ.

The word *harpazō* always includes the notion of "snatching," not merely relocating from one physical location to another.[48] In every usage in the Greek version of the Old Testament (the Septuagint), as well as in the New Testament and the first-century writings of Josephus, *harpazō* brings to the passage this connotation of sudden snatching. Of the thirty-nine occurrences in the Septuagint, all refer to a sudden, unexpected removal, often in the context of robbery or violent attack. Never does *harpazō* refer to a neutral relocation from one place to another. In the New Testament, the word occurs fourteen times. Setting Revelation 12:5 aside, every occurrence in the New Testament refers to the same type of sudden, unexpected removal as in the Septuagint. In no instance does it refer to a neutral relocation.

Finally, after examining all eighty-six occurrences of *harpazō* in the works of Josephus, Ernest Moore concluded that *harpazō* "is most often used in a bad sense—of seizing or snatching the persons or property of others."[49] When used in a good sense, it is used often in contexts of rescuing something or someone from a perilous situation (e.g., Josephus, *Jewish War* 2.291; 4.71; 5.522; *Antiquities* 12.113). Thus, it is clear that in all occurrences in the Septuagint, New Testament, and Josephus, *all* of them refer to a sudden or violent snatching away.

Simply put, *harpazō* ("to snatch") does not at all fit the descriptions of the ascension of Jesus to the Father. For the ascension of Christ, the New Testament authors consistently use neutral terms of spatial relocation in an upward trajectory. Some of these terms are used with Jesus as the actor (John 20:17; Eph. 4:8–10), not simply as a passive object of the action. Jesus was actively involved in His own ascension, which is portrayed as a gradual upward action.[50]

John himself was well aware of these ascension terms. Besides using the word *anabainō* ("to ascend") for the ascension of Christ in John 20:17, he also used the exact word some twelve times in Revelation itself. Especially noteworthy is that John used *anabainō* just twelve verses earlier in describing the ascension of the two resurrected witnesses to heaven (Rev. 11:12). With this ascension vocabulary fresh in his mind, John instead used *harpazō* ("to snatch") in Revelation 12:5. If the removal of the male son to heaven was meant to represent the ascension of Christ, why didn't John use the ascension terminology, especially since it would have made the most sense and identified most clearly that the male son was, in fact, Jesus Christ alone? The simplest solution to this puzzle is that the catching up of the male son was not, in fact, intended to refer to the ascension of Christ but to the rapture of the church.

Some have tried to solve this problem by suggesting the snatching away is not the ascension but some other event in Christ's life. For example, Caird suggests the snatching away is unto *death*, that the entire scene in Revelation 12:1–6 is a recasting of Psalm 2, while Osborne argues that the snatching away is an image of the resurrection, snatching Jesus from the grave.[51] The problem with such views is that the destination of the sudden snatching is "to God and to His throne," an event which took place, according to the New Testament account, some forty days after the resurrection (John 20:17; Acts 1:1–11). These views also fail to fully consider the corporate identification of the male son supported by the allusions to Isaiah 66:7, Daniel 7:13, and (as we will see in the next section) even Psalm 2. If the corporate identification defines the symbol, identifying this with any specific event in the life of Christ (death, resurrection, or ascension) fails.

Yet another factor to be considered is the fact that *harpazō* is used in a rescue context in Revelation 12:5—a rescue from the jaws of the dragon in order to prevent being devoured. Elsewhere in the New Testament, the term *harpazō* is used to connote rescue (Acts 23:10; Jude 23). In fact, in his study of the term in Josephus's writings, Moore concludes, "The rare occurrences of [*harpazō*] in a good sense serve to emphasize the general meaning of 'robbery with violence,' for they are usually in a context of violence. Even in a good sense, the suddenness of the action which [*harpazō*] denotes, and which is conveyed in the word 'snatching,' is rendered necessary by the violence of others."[52] That is, the term tends to be used positively as a rescue from a dangerous situation.

Revelation 12:1–4 sets up such a perilous situation in which the dragon stands with open jaws, ready to devour the male son when he is born. Thus, the term *harpazō* is used in a rescue context. Such a rescue nuance is incompatible with the New Testament portrayal of the ascension of Christ, not to mention His crucifixion. Jesus Christ was not snatched away to God to escape any threat, either real or imagined, either from Satan or from any other.[53] Ladd emphasizes this problem when he writes, "This can hardly be an allusion to the ascension of Christ, for his rapture did not have the purpose of escaping Satan's hostility."[54]

At this point, the problems associated with identifying the male son as Jesus Christ alone and the catching up of the child to the throne as Christ's death, resurrection, or ascension are insurmountable. The interpretation that the male son represents only Jesus Christ is not only *unsupported* by the use of *harpazō*— that interpretation is, in fact, *contradicted*. For the snatching up of the child to the throne of God clearly rescues the child from the dragon's desires to harm it. At His ascension Jesus was certainly *not* snatched up to the throne of God as a rescue from danger.

We summarize our findings in the following chart. Clearly, only the final interpretation passes the four tests.

CHART 6

Interpretations of the Snatching of the Male Son Evaluated

INTERPRETATION	LANGUAGE PASS/FAIL?	RESCUE PASS/FAIL?	DESTINATION PASS/FAIL?	IDENTIFICATION PASS/FAIL?
The male son is Christ alone; the snatching is Christ's ascension.	**FAIL** *Harpazō* is wrong for describing the ascension, which was gradual.	**FAIL** Christ's ascension was not a rescue from any danger.	**PASS** Destinations are the same for male child and Christ: God and His throne.	**FAIL** Christ alone does not account for corporate allusions to Isa. 66:7 and Dan. 7:13.
The male son is Christ alone; the snatching is Christ's death.	**PASS** *Harpazō* can mean a violent attack, like the crucifixion.	**FAIL** Christ's crucifixion was not a rescue from harm.	**FAIL** The destination of Christ's death was the grave.	**FAIL** Christ alone does not account for corporate allusions to Isa. 66:7 and Dan. 7:13.
The male son is Christ alone; the snatching is Christ's resurrection.	**PASS** *Harpazō* could indicate a sudden, unexpected snatching from the grave.	**PASS** Christ's resurrection was a rescue from the death instigated by Satan.	**FAIL** Christ's resurrection was not suddenly to God's throne but to the earth.	**FAIL** Christ alone does not account for corporate allusions to Isa. 66:7 and Dan. 7:13.
The male son is Christ in union with the church; the snatching is the resurrection and rapture of the church (1 Thess. 4:17).	**PASS** *Harpazō* indicates a sudden, unexpected snatching both from the grave and the earth; it is the same word used of the rapture in 1 Thess. 4:17.	**PASS** The church's resurrection and rapture is a rescue from coming wrath, including the wrath of the devil and the wrath of God.	**PASS** The church's resurrection and rapture is to God's throne in heaven, where they will receive the reward of the kingdom.	**PASS** Christ in union with the church accounts for the corporate allusions to Isa. 66:7 and Dan. 7:13.

5. The Allusions to Psalm 2:9

Summary Statement. Identifying the male son as the body of Christ best explains the three allusions to Psalm 2:9 in Revelation. In Psalm 2:9, God tells the Messiah, "You shall break them [the nations] with a rod of iron, You shall shatter them like earthenware." Revelation alludes to this verse three times. In the first allusion, Revelation 2:26–27, Christ expands and enlarges this promise to include *the church*, the body of Christ. In the final allusion, Revelation 19:14–15, Christ and the heavenly armies come to earth, fulfilling the promise when they begin to reign. And in Revelation 12:5, the psalm is applied to the male son. Thus, understanding the male son as Christ in union with His body, the church, is most consistent with how the application of the promise of Psalm 2:9 in the book of Revelation incorporates both Christ and the church.

Closer Examination. J. Dwight Pentecost attempted to argue that the quotation of Psalm 2:9 offers undeniable proof that the male son is Jesus Christ: "Since this child is born 'to rule all nations with a rod of iron' (Rev. 12:5), it can only refer to Christ, the one whose right it is to rule. The Psalmist confirms this interpretations in Psalm 2:9, which is admittedly Messianic."[55] In fact, however, the quotation of Psalm 2:9 actually *strengthens* the identification of the male son as the body of Christ rather than as Christ alone. This is demonstrated by an examination of the other two occurrences of the quotation of Psalm 2:9 in Revelation.

Psalm 2:9 is first quoted in Revelation in 2:26–28, where Christ broadens or extends the promise of the psalm to believers: "He who overcomes, and he who keeps My deeds until the end, TO HIM I WILL GIVE AUTHORITY OVER THE NATIONS; AND HE SHALL RULE THEM WITH A ROD OF IRON, AS THE VESSELS OF THE POTTER ARE BROKEN TO PIECES, as I also have received authority from My Father; and I will give him the morning star." At the vision of Christ's return to earth recorded in Revelation 19:14–15, the passage is quoted once again, this time applied to Christ: "And the armies which are in heaven, clothed in fine linen, white and clean, were following Him on white horses. From His mouth comes a sharp sword, so that with it He may strike down the nations, *and He will rule them with a rod of iron*; and He treads the wine press of the fierce wrath of God, the Almighty" (italics added).

This dual application of the promise of Psalm 2:9 harmonizes perfectly with the identification of the male son as the church in union with Christ.[56] It is simply not true that quoting Psalm 2:9 limits the interpretation of the male son to Christ alone. In fact, it strengthens the corporate identification of the male son as the church, as chart 7 shows.

CHART 7

Interpretations of the Allusion to Psalm 2:9 Evaluated

INTERPRETATION	REV. 2:26–28 PASS/FAIL?	REV. 12:5 PASS/FAIL?	REV. 19:14–15 PASS/FAIL?
The male son is Christ alone; Ps. 2:9 refers to His reign.	FAIL Christ expands the promise of Ps. 2:9 to include the saints.	FAIL The male son is best interpreted corporately based on allusions to Isa. 66:7 and Dan. 7:13.	PASS Christ is identified as the fulfillment of Ps. 2:9 at His return as Judge and King.
The male son is Christ in union with the church; Ps. 2:9 refers to Christ's reign with His saints.	PASS Christ expands the promise of Ps. 2:9 to include the saints.	PASS The male son is best interpreted corporately based on allusions to Isa. 66:7 and Dan. 7:13.	PASS At His return as Judge and King, Christ is accompanied by the armies of heaven, identified as the saints (Rev. 17:15) who reign with Him (20:6).

6. The Omission of Death and Resurrection

Summary Statement. Identifying the male son as the body of Christ best explains the omission of the death and resurrection of Christ. The sudden shift from the male son's birth to his place in heaven has often puzzled interpreters who see this as a reference to Christ alone, since the death and resurrection of Christ—not His birth and ascension—are of "first importance" with regard to the gospel of Christ (1 Cor. 15:3–5). The identification of the male son as the body of Christ explains the omission and resolves the problem.

Closer Examination. If we identify the male son in Revelation 12:5 as Christ alone, how do we explain the omission of His death and resurrection?[57] Often, the idea of foreshortening is invoked.[58] However, it still seems strange that the essential elements of the work of Christ—His death and resurrection—would be missing without a hint. This is especially problematic because Paul called the death and resurrection of Christ "of first importance" (1 Cor. 15:3). As we have seen earlier, some have identified the snatching away of the male son as either Christ's crucifixion or resurrection, but the problems with those interpretations have been addressed.

So the puzzle remains: If the intent of Revelation 12:5 is to identify the male son as Jesus Christ alone, why are the death and resurrection of Christ absent from the vision?

This puzzle is solved if the male son refers not to Christ alone but to the body of Christ, the church. The intent of the vision is to symbolize the catching up of the body of Christ from the earth to heaven at the rapture. When this occurs, not all believers will have experienced physical death; some will still be alive and will experience not death but transformation (1 Cor. 15:51–52; 1 Thess. 4:15–17). The reason, then, why the death and resurrection of the male son are missing from the vision is simple: the male son refers not primarily to Christ at His ascension but to the church at the rapture.

CONCLUSION: THE MALE SON AND THE RAPTURE

Considering all of the evidence set forth above, my conclusion is this: The best interpretation of Revelation 12:5 is the rapture of the church described in 1 Thessalonians 4:17. This conclusion is based on the following arguments:

1. *There is no good exegetical reason to reject the view that the male son represents the church in union with Christ.* Nothing in the corporate identification contradicts the text.
2. *The common identification of the male son as Christ alone does not actually account for all of the evidence.* The "Jesus only" interpretation tends to ignore the allusions to Isaiah 66:7–8 and Daniel 7:13–14, which support a corporate identification. The interpretation of the catching up of the son as Christ's ascension actually contradicts the basic meaning of *harpazō*, and the interpretation of the catching up as Christ's resurrection contradicts the destination of the action as the throne of God.
3. *The identification of the male son as the body of Christ in union with Christ Himself incorporates all of the evidence.* No evidence is ignored and all evidence is satisfied by the interpretation of the male son as the body of Christ and the snatching up as the rapture.

THE TIMING OF THE RAPTURE IN REVELATION 12:5

Having identified the male son as the body of Christ and his snatching away as the rapture, the next question we have to answer is whether this vision presents a pretribulation rapture.[59] A close examination of the chronological indicators and an understanding of the events that follow the snatching away of the male son reveal that this is a pre-seven-year event.[60]

After the male son is caught up (Rev. 12:5), i.e., immediately after the rapture and at the beginning of the tribulation, we are told that there is war in heaven. Michael the archangel and his army fight the dragon, who is cast down to the earth (12:7–9). We should recall that 1 Thessalonians 4:16 says that the archangel is also associated with the rapture of the church, which, given the identification of the male son, just occurred prior to the outbreak of this heavenly war. Now, we can safely assume that the war in heaven takes some amount of time. It should not necessarily be understood as an instantaneous event simply because it takes place in the spiritual realm.

An intriguing episode in Daniel 10 reveals that conflict between angelic and demonic forces takes real time.[61] The interpreting angel told Daniel, "From the first day that you set your heart on understanding this and on humbling yourself before your God, your words were heard, and I have come in response to your words. But the prince [a demonic force] of the kingdom of Persia was withstanding me for twenty-one days; then behold, Michael, one of the chief princes [i.e., angels], came to help me, for I had been left there with the kings of Persia" (Dan. 10:12–13). Conflict between only two angelic/demonic beings delayed angelic activity for three weeks. We may reasonably assume that a final battle between the forces of Satan and the forces of the archangel Michael described in Revelation 12:7–9 will take some amount of time as well.

One unspecified period of time elapses in the narrative following the catching up of the church to God and the casting down of the devil and his angels to the earth. In the context of Revelation 12, this unspecified period of time follows the rapture, but takes place before the woman's (the righteous remnant of Israel's) 1,260 days (i.e., three and one-half years) of protection from the dragon. So the war in heaven must take place during the first half of the future tribulation period.

When the dragon is at last cast down after the prolonged conflict, there is a song of victory in heaven (Rev. 12:10–12). If we read this in light of the church having recently been resurrected/transformed and raptured, now dwelling in heaven, the song makes perfect sense:

> Now the salvation, and the power, and the kingdom of our God and the authority of His Christ have come, for the accuser of our brethren has been thrown down, he who accuses them before our God day and night. And they

overcame him because of the blood of the Lamb and because of the word of their testimony, and they did not love their life even when faced with death. For this reason, rejoice, O heavens and you who dwell in them. Woe to the earth and the sea, because the devil has come down to you, having great wrath, knowing that he has only a short time.

Those who dwell in heaven, then, are the recently raptured saints (symbolized earlier in the catching up of the male son). In this action, the kingdom of Christ begins to manifest itself in the heavenly realm; finally the judgments of the day of the Lord described in the book of Revelation are beginning to affect both the spiritual and physical realms. Note also that those who had once been accused by the devil "day and night" are now said to have overcome him. No longer is there a basis for accusation against the saints, for they have been transformed immortal, resurrected, and glorified at the rapture of the church (1 Thess. 4:17; 1 Cor. 15:52). Those left behind on the earth, however, are about to face the "great wrath" of the devil, whose time is now short. The church, though, has been saved not only from the wrath of God but also from the wrath of the devil (1 Thess. 1:10; 5:9).

After the dragon is cast down, he turns to attack the woman, the faithful remnant of Israel, which has been reconstituted at the beginning of the tribulation period (see Rev. 7:1–8). Before the woman is preserved in the wilderness for 1,260 days, however, the dragon, working through the world powers, launches an attack on Israel with an army (Rev. 12:13–16). The image of the flood in Old Testament prophecy is likely that of an invasion (Ezek. 1:24; Dan. 9:27). The dragon first attempts to destroy the woman with an invasion during the first half of the tribulation after the war in heaven, but the army is defeated. Then, the woman flees to be protected in the wilderness for 1,260 days during the second half of the tribulation. This invasion, or earthly warfare, also takes time, during which the woman is protected from the fierce wrath of the dragon.

Utterly frustrated at his repeatedly failed plans, the dragon next turns his attention to the "rest of the offspring" of the woman—those who are saved during the tribulation (likely seen earlier in the vision of the "great multitude" of Rev. 7:9–17, which many call the "tribulation saints"). In order to accomplish his worldwide persecution of the tribulation saints, the dragon turns to a different means of combating the people of God: the Beast from the sea, commonly known as the Antichrist (Rev. 13). It is at the midpoint of the seven-year tribulation period that the forty-two months of the Beast's authority begins (Rev. 13:5).

To sum up, the catching up of the male son is immediately followed by time-consuming events before the midpoint of the tribulation: spiritual warfare in heaven resulting in the casting down of Satan (Rev. 12:7–12) and warfare on earth by which the dragon attempts to destroy Israel (12:13–16). All of this must take place during the first half of the tribulation, during which the remnant of Israel is saved and sealed (7:1–8), the temple in Jerusalem is rebuilt (11:1–2), and the two witnesses carry out their ministry prior to the rise of the Beast and their martyrdom (11:3–7). The reign of the Beast and False Prophet, then, take place during the second half of the tribulation (Rev. 13). These events are depicted in chart 8.

Thus, given the chronological indicators in Revelation 11–13, the catching up of the male son, the church, takes place prior to the seven-year tribulation.

CHART 8

Events Prior to and During the Tribulation

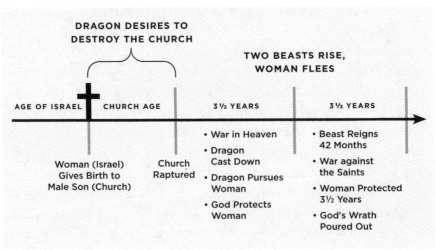

CONCLUSION

C. S. Lewis, arguing for the absurdity of concluding that an old idea had been discredited simply because it had "gone out of date," once urged his readers, "You must find why it went out of date. Was it ever refuted (and if so by whom, where, and how conclusively) or did it merely die away as fashions do? If the latter, this tells us nothing about its truth or falsehood."[62]

In this chapter I've tried to give new life to an old argument—indeed, an original argument—for the pretribulation rapture of the church. Darby and several other early teachers of the pretribulation rapture continued to use many corroborative arguments to defend their position. However, the catching up of the male son in Revelation 12:5 provided a key element many other passages lacked: a clearer ordering of events in relation to the seven-year tribulation.

Admittedly, the argument can be a little complicated. It requires the interpreter to deal with the original Greek text, the use of the Old Testament in the book of Revelation, and several symbols and allusions important to deciphering the puzzling elements of the drama of Revelation 12. In fact, the complexity of the argument may be one of the reasons why it fell into disuse and was eventually forgotten.

Nevertheless, in a church climate in which support for the doctrine of the pretribulation rapture seems to have weakened, the original argument from Revelation 12:5 deserves a closer look. I believe when serious students of Scripture give attention to the details of this passage, they will see a reasonable biblical case for the pretribulation rapture and renew their hope in that day when the church, the body of Christ, will be "caught up to God and to His throne" (Rev. 12:5).

The substance of this chapter has appeared in different forms in two articles in the Trinity Journal: *Michael J. Svigel, "'What Child Is This?' Darby's Early Exegetical Argument for the Pretribulation Rapture of the Church," 35.2 (fall 2014): 225–51; and Michael J. Svigel, "The Apocalypse of John and the Rapture of the Church: A Reevaluation," 22.1 (spring 2001): 23–74.*

NOTES

1. For a look at the early history of the doctrine, see Clarence B. Bass, *Backgrounds to Dispensationalism: Its Historical Genesis and Ecclesiastical Implications* (Eugene, OR: Wipf & Stock, 2005), 40, 76–77; Richard Reitner, "A History of the Development of the Rapture Positions," in *TVR* (Grand Rapids: Zondervan, 1996), 13–21. On the popularity of the pretribulational position today, see Tim LaHaye, *The Rapture: Who Will Face the Tribulation?* (Eugene, OR: Harvest House, 2003); Hal Lindsey, *Vanished into Thin Air: The Hope of Every Believer* (Los Angeles: Western Front, 1999); and Amy Fryckholm Johnson, *Rapture Culture: Left Behind in Evangelical America* (New York: Oxford Univ. Press, 2004).

2. Gary DeMar, *End Times Fiction* (Nashville: Nelson, 2001), 36; Robert H. Gundry, *First the Antichrist* (Grand Rapids: Baker, 1997), 140–41; Douglas J. Moo, "Response to 'The Case for the Pretribulational Rapture Position,'" *TVR*, 87–101.

3. See Barbara R. Rossing, *The Rapture Exposed* (Cambridge, MA: Westview, 2004), 21–22; N. T. Wright, "Farewell to the Rapture," *Bible Review* 17 (August 2001): 8, 52.

4. See Marvin Rosenthal, *The Pre-Wrath Rapture of the Church* (Nashville: Nelson, 1990); George E. Ladd, *The Blessed Hope: A Biblical Study of the Second Advent and the Rapture* (Grand Rapids: Eerdmans, 1956).

5. Dave MacPherson, *The Rapture Plot* (Simpsonville, SC: Millennium III, 1995), 55–85. Early critics of the doctrine also mistakenly linked its origins to Irving (William Reid, *Plymouth Brethrenism Unveiled and Refuted* [Edinburgh: Oliphant, 1875], 296; cf. Thomas Croskery, *Plymouth-Brethrenism: A Refutation of Its Principles and Doctrines* [London: William Mullen, 1879], 138).

6. Early rapture critic James Bennett rightly observed that Irving taught "that the whole Church would not escape the great tribulation, but only those who followed his directions. And a modification of this is held by many who are not Irvingites. They say that only some will escape, viz., those who are watching for the Advent." Bennett, *The Second Advent* (London: James Nisbet, 1878), 153–54.

7. Edward Irving, *Exposition of the Book of Revelation*, vol. 1 (London: Baldwin and Cradock, 1831), 160. Irving himself limited the catching up of the saints to faithful believers, not to every Christian (ibid., 1:165–66). This does not appear to be a pretribulation rapture of the entire body of Christ but rather a partial prewrath view (cf. ibid., 771).

8. Ibid., 1:164–65.

9. Present-day dispensationalists note that Darby included both Old Testament and New Testament saints in the resurrection and rapture of the church prior to the tribulation; see John Nelson Darby, *Lectures on the Second Coming* (London: G. Morrish, 1909), 56.

10. The New American Standard Bible (and the ESV, KJV, NKJV, and NIV) translate the phrase "male child." However "male son" is more accurate, as the Greek uses the neuter adjective *arsen* ("male") to modify the masculine noun *huios* ("son"). Therefore, the author's translation "male son" will appear in subsequent references to Revelation 12:5. The implications of "male son" will be detailed in the sections "The Allusion to Isaiah 66:7" and "The Allusion to Daniel 7:13" (235–36)

11. This was a common view among secret rapture advocates, placing the rapture at least before the final three and one-half years of Antichrist's reign. However, early rapture teachers were not entirely clear on whether it might occur even earlier. In 1878, Bennett wrote, "Between these two events, the coming and the revelation of Christ, we are told there is an interval of at least three and a half years" (Bennett, *The Second Advent*, 160). In 1922, Charles Erdman noted the diversity of views among those who held to the "secret rapture." He wrote, "It is taught by some that this Rapture will be in 'secret,' and that it will precede the reappearing of Christ by 'three and one-half years,' or by 'seven years,' or by 'seventy years.'" Charles R. Erdman, *The Return of Christ* (New York: George H. Doran, 1922), 54.

12. Thus, in Darby's early interpretation, the initial vision of the woman in heaven referred to the spiritual, heavenly, positional reality of the church, whose subject is Jesus Christ, while the woman being pursued and fleeing referred to the actual historical experiences of God's people; see John Nelson Darby, *Notes on the Book of Revelations* (London: Central Tract Depot, 1839), 69–93.

13. John Nelson Darby, *Letters of John Nelson Darby* (Oak Park, IL: Bible Truth, 1971), vol. 1, no. 29, "Letter to Gillett, from Lausanne," 1843

14. Ibid, 1:66, "Letter to Major Lacey," May 1, 1848.

15. Ibid., 70, "Letter to Ralph Evans," July 15, 1848.

16. In *Letters*, 1:70, Darby writes, "The setting up the power of the kingdom, though not yet applied to the earth, is when Satan is cast down, on the war in heaven—not saving grace—this is power, but the accuser is cast down. This puts the church, if the man child refers to that (also out of the scene and historical course of events)—out of the scene, nor does it take the warrior power."

17. John Nelson Darby, *Seven Lectures on the Prophetical Addresses to the Seven Churches*, 3rd rev. ed. (London: G. Morrish, 1855), 153–54. Around the year 1860, Darby also noted in a letter to William Kelly, "I admit the man-child to be Christ most fully, though I may bring in the church in Him" (*Letters*, 1:179, "Letter to William Kelly," 1860). Clearly Darby regarded the primary image to refer to Christ, then the church only in virtue of their being "in Him."

18. Darby, *Lectures on the Second Coming*, 54. Though published in 1909, these lectures occurred sometime before 1882, the year Darby died.

19. Ibid., 54–55.

20. Ibid., 60–61.

21. Ibid., 61.

22. Ibid., 62.

23. She is "the Jewish people, nothing else—because Christ is not born of the church, but, looked at as reigning and glorious in the world, was born of the Jews" (ibid., 64).

24. Ibid., 65.

25. Ibid., 65–66.

26. Ibid., 67.

27. See Michael J. Svigel, "'What Child Is This?' Darby's Early Exegetical Argument for the Pretribulation Rapture of the Church," *Trinity Journal* 35, no. 2 (fall 2014): 235–39.

28. For a history of the interpretations of Revelation 12 throughout church history, see Pierre Prigent, *Apocalyspe 12: Histoire de l'exégèse* (Tübingen: Mohr, 1959). For a sampling of eighteenth- and nineteenth-century interpretations of both the woman and the male son, from the sensible to the bizarre, see Svigel, "What Child Is This?," 235–45.

29. G. H. Lang, *The Revelation of Jesus Christ: Select Studies*, 2nd ed. (London: Paternoster, 1948), 198–201.

30. John F. Walvoord, *The Revelation of Jesus Christ* (Chicago: Moody, 1966), 188.

31. George E. Ladd, *A Commentary on the Book of the Revelation of John* (Grand Rapids: Eerdmans, 1972), 167; Robert Mounce, *The Book of Revelation*, rev. ed. (Grand Rapids: Eerdmans, 1998), 23.

32. This does not preclude the possibility that the symbol includes a second referent with Mary as the mother of Jesus fulfilling historically some aspect of the vision. See G. K. Beale, *The Book of Revelation*, New International Greek Testament Commentary, ed. I. Howard Marshall and Donald A. Hagner (Grand Rapids: Zondervan, 1999), 628.

33. Brenton translation of the Septuagint (LXX). Sir Lancelot C. L. Brenton, *The Septuagint with Apocrypha: Greek and English*, repr. ed. (Peabody, MA: Hendrickson, 1986). The only passages in the Old Testament where sun, moon, and stars appear together are Genesis 37:9; Deuteronomy 4:19; Ecclesiastes 12:2; Isaiah 13:10; Jeremiah 8:2; Jeremiah 38:36; Joel 4:15; and the apocryphal *Sir.* 50:6–7. None of these supplies a plausible background for identifying the woman except for Genesis 37:9, which leads to the conclusion that the woman represents the people of Israel.

34. See Jacob B. Smith, *A Revelation of Jesus Christ: A Commentary on the Book of Revelation*, ed. J. Otis Toder (Scottdale, PA: Herald, 1961), 181.

35. See J. Massyngberde Ford, *Revelation*, The Anchor Bible, ed. W. F. Albright and David Noel Freedman (Garden City, NY: Doubleday, 1975), 195: "Although the woman may be an individual, a study of the OT background suggests that she is a collective figure. . . . In the OT the image of a woman is a classical symbol for Zion, Jerusalem, and Israel, e.g. Zion whose husband is Yahweh (Isa. 54:1, 5, Jer. 3:20, Ezek. 16:8–14, Hos. 2:19–20), who is a mother (Isa. 49:21, 50:1, 66:7–11, Hos. 4:5, Baruch 4:8–23), and who is in the throes of birth (Mic. 4:9–10, cf. Isa. 26:16–18, Jer. 4:31, 13:21, Sirach 48:19[21])." See also Mounce, *Revelation*, 231.

36. Lang, *Revelation*, 198.

37. H. A. Ironside, *Revelation*, Ironside Commentaries, rev. ed. (Neptune, NJ: Loizeaux Brothers, 1996), 140.

38. After the word "male," the NASB includes the word "child" in italics, to avoid the phrase "male son," which is an awkward clarification even in English—what other kind of son is there besides a "male" son? Because the word is not part of the original Greek, I have dropped it from this translation.

39. See Prigent, *Apocalyspe 12*, 145. Cf. Mounce, *Revelation*, 231–34; William R. Newell, *Revelation: Chapter-by-Chapter*, rev. ed. (Grand Rapids: Kregel, 1994), 175–76; Ford C. Ottman, *The Unfolding of the Ages in the Revelation of John* (Grand Rapids: Kregel, 1967), 284–85; and J. Dwight Pentecost, *Things*

to Come (Grand Rapids: Zondervan, 1958), 215. Other proponents include Smith, *Revelation*, 183–84; Henry Barclay Swete, *Commentary on Revelation*, repr. ed. (Grand Rapids: Kregel, 1977), 151; Robert L. Thomas, *Revelation 8–22, An Exegetical Commentary*, ed. Kenneth Barker (Chicago: Moody, 1995), 125–26; and Walvoord, *Revelation*, 189–90.

40. For a full discussion, see G. K. Beale, *John's Use of the Old Testament in Revelation*, JSNTSS, 166, ed. Stanley E. Porter (Sheffield: Sheffield Academic, 1998), 341–43.

41. An example would be the allusions to the imagery of the seraphim or cherubim from Isaiah 6:2–3 and Ezekiel 1:10–14; 10:4–14 used in Revelation 4:6–8. The intention is to identify the angelic beings seen in the Old Testament with the angelic beings seen in the throne room of Revelation.

42. An example would be the identity of the two witnesses in Revelation 11:3–6, where the text uses imagery from passages like Exodus 7:14–25; 1 Kings 17:1; and Zechariah 4:2–3. The intention is not to identify the two witnesses as Zerubbabel and Joshua or as Moses and Elijah but to communicate that these two witnesses are *like* these Old Testament figures in some way. Thus, the symbolism informs our interpretation by drawing parallels.

43. Admittedly it is possible that John meant that the birth of the corporate male son in Revelation 12:5 is, in fact, a direct fulfillment of the prophecy of Isaiah 66:7–8. In that original context, God promised Israel a miraculous restoration and renewal (Isa. 66:10–24), as well as an ingathering of people from every nation to see the glory of the Lord (Isa. 66:18–19). It is in this context that God establishes "the new heavens and the new earth" (Isa. 66:22). While this regeneration of the new heavens and new earth is portrayed in Revelation as yet future (cf. Rev. 21:1–22:5), this regeneration is seen in the church in promissory form (Rom. 8:20–22). If the male son of Revelation 12:5 is understood as the body of Christ, and if John is making an equation with the imagery of Isaiah 66:7–8 instead of a parallel, then the point of the allusion would be that Israel is the source of the messianic community (what we know as the church) as well as the relationship between the messianic community and the eschatological regeneration (in the millennium, which will be reigned over by the church).

44. Towner writes, "These three texts [Dan. 7:18, 21–22, 27] make clear that he [the Son of Man] has now been radically interpreted as an identifiable and specific collective entity"; in W. Sibley Towner, "Daniel," *Interpretation: A Bible Commentary for Teaching and Preaching*, ed. James L. Mays, Patrick D. Miller, and Paul J. Achtemeier (Louisville: John Knox, 1984), 105.

45. John E. Goldingay, *Daniel*, WBC, vol. 30, ed. David A. Hubbard, John D. W. Watts, and Ralph P. Martin (Dallas: Word, 1989), 170. Similarly, Towner notes, "In the same way in which the beasts represent both kingdoms and their kings, so the son of man could represent the coming fifth monarchy even though he might remain an individual figure" (Towner, *Daniel*, 106).

46. Choon-Leong Seow, *Daniel*, Westminster Bible Companion, ed. Patrick D. Miller and David L. Bartlett (Louisville: Westminster, 2003), 16.

47. Casey notes, "The corporate interpretation of the man-like figure was in use from the time of the composition of the book of Daniel onwards" (Maurice Casey, "The Corporate Interpretation of 'One Like a Son of Man' (Dan. vii 13) at the Time of Jesus," *Novum Testamentum* 18 [1976]: 179). This means the corporate understanding of the "Son of Man" was common both in Jesus' time and thereafter, making a reference to "Son of Man" imagery from Daniel 7 almost certain to conjure up corporate identifications.

48. One lexicon defines *harpazō* in the following ways: "*snatch, seize*, i.e., take suddenly and vehemently, or take away in the sense of 1. *steal, carry off, drag away*. . . . 2. *snatch* or *take away*—a. forcefully" (BAGD [Chicago: University of Chicago, 1979], 109). Thus Ford writes, "The verb *harpazō*, 'snatch,' is never used of the ascension of Christ, although *anabaino*, 'ascend,' used of the two witnesses in 11:12, does have this connotation, and is used in relationship to the ascension of Jesus." But in our present text there seems to be no Christological reference.

49. Ernest Moore, "[*Biazō, Harpazō*], and Cognates in Josephus," *New Testament Studies* 21 (1975): 525.

50. In fact, in Acts 1:10 the combination of the imperfect of *eimi* ("to be") with the present parenthetical participle *atenizontes* ("as they were gazing") and the present participle *poreuomenou* ("while He was going") makes best sense if the ascension of Christ was seen as a gradual rather than sudden event.

51. George Bradford Caird, *The Revelation of Saint John*, Black's New Testament Commentary, ed. Henry Chadwick, repr. ed. (Peabody, MA: Hendrickson, 1993), 149–59; Grant R. Osborne, *Revelation*, BECNT, ed. Moisés Silva (Grand Rapids: Baker, 2002), 463.

52. Moore, "[*Biazō, Harpazō*], and Cognates in Josephus," 525–26.

53. Lang, *Revelation*, 198.

54. Ibid., 170. It must be pointed out that Ladd does not conclude that the male son is the church but "John's vivid way of asserting the victory of God's anointed over every satanic effort to destroy him."

55. Pentecost, *Things to Come*, 215.

56. The use of Psalm 2:9 in Revelation also argues to some degree for an identification of the "armies of heaven" in Revelation 19:14 with overcoming believers of the church (Rev. 2:26–28). It is the armies who actually break the nations to pieces. This would suggest, then, that the church, the body of Christ, is raptured, resurrected, and glorified before the return of Christ to earth described in Revelation 19:11–21.

57. Cf. J. Ramsey Michaels, *Revelation*, IVP New Testament Commentary Series, ed. Grand Osborne (Downers Grove, IL: InterVarsity, 1997), 149. He explains the difficulty by suggesting that 1) John consistently uses other symbols (such as a Lamb) for the death of Christ; and 2) that the emphasis in Revelation 12:5 is on Jesus' identification with the "seed" of Genesis 3:15.

58. Beale, *Book of Revelation*, 639.

59. If one understands the male son's catching up to be with Christ at His ascension, this event clearly is a pretribulational event. If we understand the male son to be the corporate body of Christ that is caught up at the rapture, the event is still pretribulational. The order of the events in Revelation 12 must be the same whether Christ's ascension or the rapture of the church is in view.

60. This, of course, requires interpreters to hold to a generally futurist view of Revelation and a literal understanding of the chronological indicators. Preterists, idealists, historicists, and allegorists will likely not find these arguments convincing.

61. See Peter R. Schemm Jr., "The Agents of God: Angels," in Daniel L. Akin, Bruce Riley Ashord, and Kenneth Keathley, eds., *A Theology for the Church*, rev. ed. (Nashville: Broadman & Holman, 2014), 252; Henry C. Thiessen, *Lectures in Systematic Theology* (Grand Rapids: Eerdmans, 1949), 207.

62. C. S. Lewis, *Surprised by Joy: The Shape of My Early Life* (New York: Harcourt, 1955), 207–8.

10

Israel: Why the Church Must Be Raptured Before the Tribulation

BY MICHAEL A. RYDELNIK

How awful that day will be! There will be none like it! It will be a time of trouble for Jacob, but he will be delivered out of it.

<small>JEREMIAH 30:7 HCSB</small>

believe Jesus will return someday but I do not know if there will be a rapture, let alone that it will take place before a future tribulation." These were the words of my friend, a theologically educated, committed follower of Jesus, who loves the Bible and holds a PhD from a world-class seminary. Yet I suspect that his agnosticism about prophecy is not unusual in an era when it is considered arrogant to hold convictions about the end times.

What makes my friend's comment even more surprising is that he is clear in seeing a difference between God's plan for Israel[1] and His plan for the church.[2] Generally, people who see this distinction in biblical revelation believe in the pretribulation rapture of the church, and with good reason. Seeing a distinction between Israel and the church inexorably leads to a belief that the rapture of the church will take place before the tribulation, when God refocuses His attention on Israel.

The point of this chapter is to show how understanding God's plan for Israel and the church should affect one's view of the rapture. In a sense, this chapter is my response to my friend (albeit with more details). The distinction between the church and Israel should yield a belief that the rapture of the church will take place before the tribulation[3] of the end of days (a pretribulation rapture). To make this case I will examine three biblical truths about Israel and the church, leading to the conclusion that the rapture will indeed take place before the tribulation.

ISRAEL IS CENTRAL TO THE TRIBULATION

The first biblical truth essential for understanding the timing of the rapture is that the nation of Israel is central to the future tribulation. During the tribulation, God will once again make Israel His primary concern. Although God will certainly express His wrath for sin during the tribulation and ultimately judge the Gentile nations, nevertheless, God's emphasis will once again be on the Jewish people. This is evident in several ways.

Israel Is Central as the Catalyst to the Tribulation

The Scriptures speak of the rapture of the church as an event that could take place at any moment. In chapter 1 Robert Thomas defends the imminency of the Messiah's return as a strong argument for a pretribulation rapture. Jesus taught that His followers must "be on the alert then, for you do not know the day nor the hour" (Matt. 25:13).

In contrast to this, the tribulation is not an imminent ("any-moment") event but one that the Scriptures identify with a precise starting point, when Israel signs a covenant with the future false messiah (more commonly known as "the Antichrist").[4] In Daniel 9:24–27, there is a prophecy of the Seventy Weeks that are destined for Daniel's people, Israel (9:24).[5] Each week represents a period of seven years, with the first sixty-nine weeks culminating in the coming of Jesus the Messiah. After a gap in time, the Seventieth Week will begin with the coming prince (or the Antichrist), who "will make a firm covenant" of peace "with the many" in the leadership of Israel (Dan. 9:27). Although some consider this prince to be Jesus the Messiah, it is inconceivable that the Messiah would be the one who would commit the abomination of desolation described later in the verse. Therefore, the prince of Daniel 9 is more accurately identified as the Antichrist, who will desecrate the future temple in Jerusalem and halt the worship of God there.

This covenant is yet future and will mark the beginning of the tribulation period (Matt. 24:29; Mark 13:24). The key here is that it is Israel's covenant with the coming prince that begins the tribulation. It is a precise and specific time in contrast to the "any-moment" nature of the rapture. Therefore, Israel, in making this covenant, is the catalyst of the future tribulation.

Israel Is Central as the Focus of the Tribulation

The prophet Jeremiah gives the tribulation period a distinctive description. He says of it, "How awful that day will be! There will be none like it! It will be a time of trouble for Jacob, but he will be delivered out of it" (Jer. 30:7 HSBC). This demonstrates that God's focus during the tribulation is on Israel—it is "a time of trouble for Jacob" (suggesting that the church will have already been removed).

Daniel's introductory words to the Seventy-Weeks oracle reveal that the message of the prophecy was intended for Israel (Dan. 9:24). It states, "Seventy weeks have been decreed for your people [i.e., Daniel's people Israel] and your holy city" (Jerusalem). The first sixty-nine weeks culminate with the coming of the Messiah Jesus before the establishment of the church.[6] The Seventieth Week (the tribulation period) begins when God turns His primary attention once again to Israel after the removal of the church. This entire prophecy pertains to Israel and not to the church at all. Therefore, according to Daniel, just as Jeremiah had revealed, Israel is the focus of the tribulation.

Having identified Israel as God's focal point during the tribulation, how does God focus His attention on Israel? There are several specific ways that mark Israel as the center of attention during the tribulation.

First, *the tribulation will be a time of persecution for Israel.* This is evident from Revelation 12, a passage that speaks of Israel in symbolic terms. It describes "a woman clothed with the sun, and the moon under her feet, and on her head a crown of twelve stars" (Rev. 12:1). That this woman represents Israel is evident from her attire. The sun, moon, and stars allude to the story of Joseph's dream (Gen. 37) in which these represented Jacob and his sons. Likewise, the twelve stars allude to the twelve tribes of Israel. Although some have identified the woman as the church, this is unlikely because the woman gives birth to the Messiah. Obviously, the Lord Jesus descended from Israel (Rom. 9:5), not the church. Nor is she the Virgin Mary, for whom the rest of the events in the chapter have no relation. Since it is common in Revelation for women to have symbolic significance such as the harlot of Babylon (Rev. 17–18) and the bride of Christ (Rev. 19:1–10), it makes the most sense to identify the woman of Revelation 12 as Israel.

Later in the vision, the dragon (representing Satan) is cast out of heaven and thrown to the earth (Rev. 12:9, 13). Then "he persecuted the woman" (Rev. 12:13) for three and one-half years (a reference to the second half of the tribulation period). When the dragon sees that God is protecting the woman, he turns his attention to persecuting "the rest of her offspring—those who keep God's commands and have the testimony about Jesus" (Rev. 12:17 HCSB), referring to Satan's persecution of Jewish followers of Jesus in the tribulation.

As mentioned above, Jeremiah depicts the tribulation as a time of trouble for Israel just as is portrayed in Revelation 12. An additional idea in Jeremiah 30 is that Israel's difficulties will be so terrible that the Lord exclaims, "How awful that day will be! There will be none like it. It will be a time of trouble for Jacob, but he will be delivered out of it" (Jer. 30:7 HCSB). Both Revelation 12 and Jeremiah 30 reveal that under God's sovereignty, Satan will persecute the Jewish people during the tribulation period even as God preserves them.

Second, *the tribulation will be a time of war for Israel.* There will be multiple wars during the tribulation, and it appears that Israel will face multiple attacks. The first is a prediction of an invasion of Israel by Magog and its allies (Ezek. 38–39).[7] Identifying these invading nations is possible by comparing them to the biblical record. The book of Genesis lists the nations that descended from Noah's son Japheth (Gen. 10:2–5), and there is considerable overlap with Ezekiel's invading armies. These include Magog, Meshech, Tubal (Ezek. 38:2); Persia, Cush, and Put (Ezek. 38:5); Gomer and Beth-togarmah. Some Bible versions (e.g., NASB) include Rosh as if it were a place name (some have even mistakenly identified it as Russia). However, the Hebrew word actually means "head" or "leader," and refers to the "*chief prince* of Meshech" (as in the HCSB). The invading nations are identifiable as the following modern nations: Magog is from the area between the Black and Caspian Seas; Meshech and Tubal, always listed together, refer to parts of eastern Turkey as does Beth-torgarmah; Persia refers to modern Iran, Cush to modern Sudan, Put to modern Libya; Gomer refers to the Cimmerians from Eastern Asia Minor, near modern Armenia and the various Islamic states from the former Soviet Union. All these nations are Islamic today, so it appears that somewhere near the middle of the tribulation[8] there will be an Islamic invasion of Israel (Ezek. 38:16). Nevertheless, God will defeat all these nations decisively (Ezek. 38:17–23).

Israel will not only experience war in the middle of the tribulation but also near the end, specifically in the campaign of Armageddon. According to the book of Revelation, "the kings of the whole world" will gather together "for the war of the great day of God, the Almighty" (Rev. 16:14). The text also reveals that this mustering of troops will be at "the place which in Hebrew is called Harmagedon" (v. 16) or Armageddon (HCSB, ESV, NIV), referring to the Jezreel Valley spreading out from Mount (Heb. *Har*) Meggido. These massive armies will make their way to Jerusalem and, according to Zechariah, will establish a siege against Jerusalem that "will also be against Judah" (Zech. 12:2).

This is all under the sovereign plan of God since He claims responsibility for bringing these armies there, stating "I will gather all nations against Jerusalem to battle" (Zech. 14:2). As desperation mounts, the Jewish leaders of Jerusalem will lead the nation of Israel to turn in faith to Jesus the Messiah (Zech. 12:10), who will return to the Mount of Olives to "fight against those nations, as when He fights on a day of battle" (Zech. 14:3). Although God will ultimately deliver His people, before He does, the tribulation will include wars of aggression against Israel.

Third, *the tribulation will be a time of godly service for Israel.* During the tribulation, there will be 144,000 Jewish people, from all the twelve tribes (Rev. 7:4–8), who are called "the bond-servants of our God" (v. 3). They are a remnant of Jewish people who come to faith in Jesus after the removal of the church at the rapture. No doubt there will be Bibles and other materials that will enable these 144,000 Jewish people to understand and receive the gospel. This remnant of Israel will be sealed by God and set apart for His service. What they will do in service to God is unstated. However, in the paragraph that follows the description of the 144,000, there is a potential hint. It describes a vast multitude of peoples, "from every nation and all tribes and peoples and tongues [languages]" (v. 9) who are the martyrs of the tribulation period (vv. 14–17). It appears that many people from across the earth will come to faith during the tribulation. This suggests that the role of the 144,000 of Israel will be as the evangelists of the tribulation period, helping people all over the world to put their trust in Jesus the Messiah, even during this time of terrible persecution.

Fourth, *the tribulation will be a time of cleansing for Israel.* A general principle of Scripture is that God uses difficulties, even persecution, to cause people to turn their attention to Him (cf. Ps. 120:1). Thus, it appears that God will allow Israel to be persecuted during the tribulation in order to draw the nation to Himself and to cause many Jewish people to trust in Jesus the Messiah as described in Ezekiel 20:34–38. This passage portrays Israel's restoration to her ancient homeland from a worldwide dispersion (v. 34) after which God will enter into judgment with Israel (vv. 35–36). God promises that these events, taking place during the future tribulation, will have an ultimate purpose: "I will make you pass under the rod, and I will bring you into the bond of the covenant" (v. 37). Once Israel has passed under the rod of discipline, God will "purge from you [Israel] the rebels and those who transgress against Me. . . . Thus you will know that I am the LORD" (v. 38).

A similar description is found in the prophet Zechariah, who depicts the tribulation as a time when Israel will be cleansed from sin. The tribulation will function as a refiner's fire, with the promise that "I will bring the third part through the fire, refine them as silver is refined, and test them as gold is tested. They will call on My name, and I will answer them; I will say, 'They are My people,' and they will say, 'The LORD is my God'" (Zech. 13:9).

Additionally, although Jeremiah identifies Israel's trouble during the tribulation as God's just discipline on Israel (Jer. 30:11), His ultimate purpose is to cleanse Israel. As a result of their difficulties during the tribulation, Israel will turn to the Lord, who will say, "You shall be My people, and I will be your God" (Jer. 30:22). The point of all this is that God will use the persecution of Israel during the tribulation to cause the nation to turn to the Messiah Jesus so that the people of Israel will experience God's cleansing from sin (cf. Zech. 12:10; 13:1).

Clearly, God will once again focus His redemptive plans on Israel during the tribulation. As God's focal point of that time, Israel will be persecuted, face war, and be cleansed during the tribulation. At the same time, a remnant of Israel will serve God throughout the tribulation, proclaiming the message of Messiah Jesus to the world. Plainly, Israel has a special role in the tribulation as the object of God's greatest attention during this period of time.

ISRAEL SETS UP CHRIST'S RETURN

Besides being the catalyst and the focus of the tribulation, Israel is central to the tribulation as the nation that brings it to an end. The nation of Israel will do this by setting up the return of the Lord Jesus. Several passages tied together support this idea.

First, *Jesus said that He would not return until Israel welcomed Him back*. In

Matthew 23:37–39, Jesus speaks to Jerusalem, which represents the leadership of the Jewish people. Then He laments that the Jewish people through their leadership had rejected Him, although He would have gathered them to Him "the way a hen gathers her chicks under her wings" (v. 37). Therefore, Jesus predicts that Israel's "house is being left to [them] desolate." Jesus' lament over Jerusalem culminates with His promise: For I say to you, from now on you will not see Me until you say, 'Blessed is He who comes in the name of the Lord!'" (v. 39). This Old Testament quotation is the ancient Jewish words of welcome and greeting. In essence, Jesus is saying that He will not return until Israel welcomes Him back. This indicates that Israel holds the key to the return of the Messiah Jesus; when the nation, through their leadership, believes in Him and calls for His return, then they will see Him once again.

Second, *the prophet Zechariah foretold an eschatological event when God would pour out His Spirit on Israel.* Then the nation "will look on Me whom they have pierced; and they will mourn for Him, as one mourns for an only son, and they will weep bitterly over Him like the bitter weeping over a firstborn" (Zech. 12:10). God's Spirit will be poured out, conveying grace to Israel's leadership (the house of David) and populace (the inhabitants of Jerusalem), and thereby enabling them to offer supplication. As a result of this divine enablement, Israel will respond with faith. The words "look on" are the same as used when Israel looked upon the bronze serpent in faith to receive healing (Num. 21:9). The object of their look of faith is the Lord Himself ("Me")—the One they have pierced.[9] The reference to God as the pierced One refers to the piercing of a representative of God, namely, the incarnate Messiah.

Israel's national repentance will be great, mourning for their past rejection of the Messiah as intensely as a parent weeps over the loss of an only child. This prediction of Israel's look of faith upon the Messiah and their repentance for their past rejection of Him will accomplish the necessary welcome for the return of the Messiah as foretold by Jesus Himself (cf. comments on Matt. 23:37–39 above).

Third, *Israel will experience spiritual cleansing as a result of believing in the Messiah Jesus.* Having looked upon Him in faith and repented of their rejection of the Messiah, Israel will receive forgiveness just as Zechariah predicted (Zech. 13:1). Using figurative language, the prophet describes Israel's spiritual restoration as the opening of a fountain "to wash away sin and impurity" in the house of David and the residents of Jerusalem (v. 1 HCSB). This is the prophet's depiction of the national salvation of Israel at the return of the Messiah.

The apostle Paul also speaks of this when writing of the day when "all Israel will be saved" (Rom. 11:26a).[10] Israel's welcoming of the Messiah Jesus and turn of faith to Him will result in the Messiah Jesus' return to Jerusalem just as He foretold in Matthew 23:37–39. And having returned, then He will save Israel. Paul uses the words of Isaiah to depict Messiah Jesus saving Israel: "THE DE-LIVERER WILL COME FROM ZION, HE WILL REMOVE UNGODLINESS FROM JACOB. THIS IS MY COVENANT WITH THEM, WHEN I TAKE AWAY THEIR SINS" (Rom. 11:26b–27).

Fourth, Israel will also experience physical deliverance when the Messiah Jesus returns. The climax of the tribulation will be when Israel welcomes the Messiah Jesus back and He forgives their sin. At that time, when all the nations are gathered against Jerusalem for battle (Zech. 14:2), the Lord Jesus will fight for His people and grant them deliverance (v. 3). Then "His feet will stand on the Mount of Olives" and He will deliver Israel from the armies besieging her (v. 4).

These four passages demonstrate that Israel plays the central role in bringing the future tribulation to a close. It is only when Israel welcomes the Messiah Jesus by faith that He will literally return, saving them both spiritually and physically at that time. The Messiah's return to save Israel will bring an end to the tribulation period. At that time, Israel's role will be crucial because the return of the Messiah Jesus is contingent on their turning to Him.

The point thus far has been to show that Israel is central to the future tribulation. During that time, God's attention will once again be almost entirely on the Jewish people. This, by itself, does not necessarily indicate that the rapture will take place before the tribulation. However, the emphasis on Israel would suggest that the church had already been removed once the tribulation is under-way. Therefore, the next aspect of this chapter will be to investigate the church's apparent absence from the earth during the future tribulation.

THE CHURCH IS ABSENT FROM
THE EARTH DURING THE TRIBULATION

The second biblical truth that is crucial is that the church appears to be absent from the earth during the tribulation. At the outset of this discussion, it must be admitted that this is an argument from silence. This is significant in that it is impossible to prove a negative. It is within the realm of possibility for the church to be on the earth during the tribulation, but that is not mentioned in any passage. Nevertheless, the biblical texts that speak of the tribulation period never mention the church on earth. For example, the church is plainly present on earth in the first three chapters of Revelation, being explicitly mentioned nineteen times. However, after the focus in Revelation shifts to the tribulation (chapters 4–19), the church no longer appears on earth. Therefore, it seems extremely unlikely for the church to still be present during the tribulation but never explicitly mentioned, seeming to imply a pretribulation rapture.

The Church Will Be Removed from the Earth before the Tribulation

Early in the book of Revelation, the Lord Jesus promises the church at Philadelphia, "I also will keep you from the hour of testing, that hour which is about to come upon the whole world, to test those who dwell on the earth" (Rev. 3:10). A careful reading of this verse indicates that the church will be removed before the tribulation.

First, although this promise is explicitly made only to the Philadelphian church, more likely it applies to all churches. In fact, the whole book is addressed to seven churches (Rev. 1:4, 11), which seem to be representatives of the universal church. So a promise to one church would be a promise to all. A supporting piece of evidence of this is the recurrent phrase in all the messages to the churches of Asia Minor, "He who has an ear, let him hear what the Spirit says to the churches" (Rev. 2:7, 11, 17, 29; 3:6, 13, 22). The warnings and promises to the individual churches were not limited to those churches but were addressed to the church at large. Thus, the promise of being kept from the hour of testing is not limited to the church at Philadelphia but was a promise for the universal church as well.

Second, the actual promise of being kept from the hour of testing also supports the idea that the church will be removed from the earth before the tribulation. It is true that the words "to keep [you] from" (*tereo ek*) could possibly mean "preserve through," and suggest that the church would be preserved while still in the tribulation. But if that is what the author intended, he would have more likely used a different preposition (*dia* instead of *ek*) so that it would be literally translated "kept through" (*tereo dia*). Also, if this verse only promised the church preservation throughout the tribulation, then the promise was not kept. Plainly, those who understand this as merely promising preservation and not removal view all the believers of the tribulation period as being part of the church. Since many believers will be martyred during the tribulation (cf. Rev. 6:9–11; 12:11), then how could this be a promise of preservation? Those who sacrificed their blood and lives would wonder why God did not keep His promise to preserve them through the tribulation. It makes far more sense to see this as a promise that the church will be removed before the tribulation and to view the martyrs as tribulation saints who come to faith in the Lord after the church has been removed.

Moreover, in the Upper Room Discourse, John uses the Greek words *tereo ek* in a way that supports the idea of removal when Jesus prayed that His followers would be protected "from the evil one" (John 17:15). In this verse, the meaning is not that believers are in the evil one and still preserved but rather that believers are kept apart from the evil one.[11] This is exactly how John uses those words in Revelation 3:10, with the idea that the church will be kept apart (not preserved through) the hour of testing.

Finally, "the hour of testing" is not speaking of a localized persecution of the church at Philadelphia but of a global persecution throughout the tribulation. John frequently uses the word "hour" not of a literal sixty-minute period but of a general period of time (cf. John 2:4; 4:21, 23; 5:25, 28; 7:30; 8:20; 12:23; 13:1; 16:2, 4, 21, 25, 32; 17:1; 1 John 2:18; Rev. 14:7, 15). In fact, the use of the article "*the* hour" seems to indicate a well-known period of testing, such as the tribulation (known from Old Testament passages such as Jer. 30:4–7; Dan. 12:1; Zech. 14:1–4). Furthermore, the testing in Revelation 3:10 will come upon "those who dwell on the earth," indicating a worldwide tribulation (as it is indicated by "all the nations" in Rev. 12:5 and "the whole world" in 16:14).

Revelation 3:10 is a promise for the whole church to be literally removed before the worldwide testing or tribulation period. Therefore, this passage supports a pretribulation rapture and explains why the church is not found in the rest of the book of Revelation's depiction of the tribulation.

The Church Is Present in Heaven during the Tribulation

Although the book of Revelation does not include the church on the earth during the tribulation, it does picture the church in heaven during that time. The twenty-four elders in heaven are representative of the church. Although some believe they are angelic beings, this is unlikely. According to Revelation

4:4, there were twenty-four thrones in heaven and seated upon them were "twenty-four elders sitting, clothed in white garments, and golden crowns on their heads." Their white clothes indicate that these were redeemed people who have exchanged their filthy clothes for white garments. Their golden crowns suggest that they have already been evaluated at the judgment seat of Christ and have received their reward (1 Cor. 3:10–15; 2 Cor. 5:10).

These twenty-four elders also sing of their redemption in Revelation 5:9–10, saying "You were slain, and purchased for God with Your blood men from every tribe and tongue and people and nation. You have made them to be a kingdom and priests to our God; and they will reign upon the earth." According to some versions, they sang "You have made *us* into a kingdom and priests"[12] (emphasis added), supporting the idea that they represent the church as redeemed people. However, if the better reading is "You have made *them*" (rather than "us"), it would not necessarily mean that they are not speaking of themselves. In much the same way, Moses's song of deliverance speaks of Israel in the third person, and he certainly was not excluding himself from that redemption (cf. Ex. 15:13–18). Thus, the church is present in Revelation 4–5, but in heaven and not on earth.

In further support of the above premise, notice that Revelation 6–18, the section that describes the tribulation, excludes any mention of the church on earth. Some have argued that the mention of the 144,000 bond servants of God, 12,000 from each one of the twelve tribes of Israel is a reference to the church (Rev. 7:1–8). However, they are described as part of the twelve tribes of Israel, referring to the descendants of Abraham, Isaac, and Jacob—ethnic Israel—and not the church. (See the next section for more detailed support of this point.) Others maintain that the book of Revelation does include the presence of believers on earth during the tribulation in passages like Revelation 7:14–17; 11:17–18; 12:10–12; 14:12; 15:2–4. Plainly, there are believers on earth during the tribulation, but they are tribulation saints, not members of the church, the body of Christ.

The church does appear again in heaven, in Revelation 19:4–10, at the marriage supper of the Lamb. Once again, the twenty-four elders of the church are present, leading the church in worship of God (Rev. 19:4). The church appears now as a bride, wearing "fine linen, bright and clean" (Rev. 19:8). Evidently the church is in heaven, celebrating the marriage supper of the Lamb. In the very next paragraph, the Lord Jesus is depicted as the rider on a white horse. He is "called Faithful and True" (v. 11) and returns to earth as "KING OF KINGS AND LORD OF LORDS" (v. 16) to deliver Israel and defeat the armies of the Beast. Accompanying Him are "the armies which are in heaven" and they are "clothed in fine linen, white and clean" (v. 14). Based on the description of the church in the previous paragraph (wearing "fine linen, bright and clean," v. 8), these armies are none other than the church, descending to the earth with their Lord Jesus.

Two observations are necessary. First, the church is already in heaven at the marriage supper of the Lamb and therefore not raptured at the end of the tribulation when Jesus returns. The church's presence in heaven during the tribulation at the marriage of the Lamb plainly supports the idea of a pretribulation rapture. Second, the church will finally fulfill one aspect of its destiny, which was to love Israel and not act arrogantly toward her nor act ignorantly concerning God's loving plan for the nation (Rom. 11:18, 25). Finally, the church will become the defenders of Israel, as the army of saints that returns to earth with the Lord Jesus to save Israel. This is quite distinct from the record of the church on earth, which regrettably persecuted Israel for much of its history. That was so contrary to God's heart! Yet in the end, the church will join their Savior in defending His people Israel and saving them from destruction.

Thus far, this chapter has maintained two complementary ideas: (1) Israel is God's central concern during the tribulation, and (2) the church, especially as depicted in the book of Revelation, is not present on earth during the tribulation but rather is seen in heaven during that time period. This leads to the next aspect of this chapter—the examination of the differences between the church and Israel as two generally distinct and separate entities.

ISRAEL AND THE CHURCH ARE DISTINCT ENTITIES

It seems obvious from Scripture that God has distinct plans for Israel and the church. However, some may want to deal with these differing plans by merging Israel and the church into one entity, the collective people of God. Thus, God's two distinct plans become one and it is maintained that God's focus on Israel in the tribulation is actually about the church. However, a careful examination of the evidence will reveal that the merger of Israel and the church into one people of God is not supported by Scripture.

The Church and Israel Have Different Beginnings

The first way to see that Israel and the church are distinct is by recognizing their different beginnings. Israel traces its inception to the call of Abraham and God's covenantal promise to make a people out of Abraham's descendants (Gen. 12:2; 15:3–5). Furthermore, this promise was passed on to Isaac and Jacob (26:3–5; 35:11–12), and then Israel came from the twelve sons of Jacob (Gen. 46:8–27). Thus, the biblical definition of Israel is purely ethnic, referring to the descendants of Abraham, Isaac, Jacob, and Jacob's twelve sons.

The beginning of the church is quite distinct from the beginning of Israel. For example, in Matthew 16:18, Jesus promised that He would build His church, indicating that the church was not yet in existence during His earthly ministry and yet future. Clearly, Jesus saw the church as distinct from Israel, which was already in existence when He made that promise.

A simple reading of Acts also seems to show that the events on Pentecost in Acts 2, with the giving of the Holy Spirit, refer to the birthday of the church. Although Acts 2 does not plainly state this, it seems to be the author's point. However, it is made more explicit later in the book of Acts. After Peter preaches to Cornelius and his household and they believe, Peter is required to justify his baptism of these Gentiles who believed in Jesus the Messiah without first requiring them to be circumcised and thereby adopt Judaism. Peter explains that he witnessed the Holy Spirit fall upon them "just as He did upon us *at the beginning*" (Acts 11:15, italics added). Evidently, Peter is referring to the way the Holy Spirit had previously fallen on the apostles at Pentecost, an event he labels as "the beginning." He could be referring to no other beginning than that of the church. It is clear that the New Testament sees the beginning of the church as quite distinct from the patriarchal beginnings of Israel.

Israel and the Church Are Different Communities

A second way to see the distinctions between Israel and the church is that both groups are made up of differing people. As shown above, the Hebrew Bible had already defined Israel as the descendants of Abraham, Isaac, and Jacob. Although the Scriptures distinguished between national Israel and the faithful remnant of believers within the nation (cf. 1 Kings 19:18), Israel as a nation was always composed of the ethnic descendants of the patriarchs.

The New Testament also affirms an ethnic definition of Israel in several passages. One passage that does so clearly is Romans 11:1–5. Paul's first assertion in that paragraph is that God has not rejected His people Israel, despite their unbelief in Jesus the Messiah (Rom. 11:1). Secondly, as a proof of God's faithfulness to ethnic Israel, Paul maintains that God has drawn a remnant of faithful believers within Israel. In fact, Paul argues that there always was a faithful remnant within ethnic Israel, as seen in the "SEVEN THOUSAND MEN WHO HAVE NOT BOWED THE KNEE TO BAAL" in Elijah's day (Rom. 11:4). He concludes that there is and always will be a faithful remnant of Jewish followers of Jesus, "a remnant according to God's gracious choice" (v. 5). Paul clearly holds to the ethnic definition of Israel as descendants of Abraham, Isaac and Jacob. Moreover, the proof that this definition will not change is found in God's choice for salvation of the remnant of Israel, the Jewish followers of Jesus.

A second NT passage that affirms an ethnic definition of Israel is Romans 2:28–29. Some have maintained that in Romans 2:28–29, Paul redefines the Jewish people to include Gentiles who believe. There Paul defines the meaning of Jewishness as not one who is a Jew "outwardly" (physical circumcision alone) but one who is a Jew "inwardly" with circumcision "of the heart." In the past, many interpreters understood this passage to refer to the church as the new Israel. They assumed Paul to be redefining and expanding Israel from the physical descendants of Abraham, Isaac, and Jacob, to the spiritual followers of Messiah, particularly Gentile believers.

However, this interpretation does not fit the context. From Romans 1:18–3:20, Paul is making the case that all people are sinful. He begins by showing that pagan Gentiles are lost in sin (1:18–32) and then proceeds to demonstrate that even Gentile moralists are separated from God by their sin (2:1–16). Having proven the sinfulness of Gentiles, Paul asserts that Jewish people are also sinful (2:17–3:8), as is all the world (3:9–20). The discussion of the meaning of true Jewishness falls in the section about Jews. Paul is not describing Gentile believers becoming true Jews. Rather, he is defining those who are the truest Jews within the Jewish community. He is not expanding the meaning of "Jew" but narrowing it. Specifically, Paul is referring to Jewish people who believe in Messiah Jesus as the truest Jews.[13] These faithful Jewish people are the remnant among the whole people of Israel. Therefore, even here, the word "Jew" refers to ethnic Jewish people.

Besides the near context, the biblical context also supports this view. The idea of the truest Jews being those who are both physically and spiritually circumcised is found in the prophet Jeremiah. He calls on Israel to "circumcise yourselves to the LORD and remove the foreskins of your heart" (Jer. 4:4). He also warns Israel that those who are merely physically circumcised but not spiritually circumcised will one day face punishment. He laments that "all the house of Israel are uncircumcised of heart" (Jer. 9:26). Jeremiah has recognized that there is a group of Jews within the Jewish community who have circumcised both their flesh and their hearts. These are the truest Jews. Seemingly, Paul is using the same perspective.

McClain's comments on Romans 2:28–29 recognize the ethnic Jewish identity of the "true Jews." "Some people think this statement teaches that every Christian is a Jew, but what it really teaches is that every Jew is not a Jew. No man can be a Jew unless he is born outwardly as a son of Abraham, and also inwardly in spirit; therefore, a man born only outwardly of Abraham is not a true Jew."[14] Although McClain is correct in seeing this as narrowing the meaning of "Jew" to Jewish believers, it is unlikely that Paul meant that the rest of the Jewish people were no longer to be considered Jews. In the next paragraph, speaking of Jews who do not believe, Paul asks what other advantages belong to the Jewish people if automatic salvation is not one of them. By his very question, Paul shows that he thought that these Jewish people were still ethnically Jewish, as did Jeremiah (cf. Jer. 9:26 above). His point in Romans 2:28–29 is that the remnant, the Jewish followers of Jesus, by having fulfilled the full requirements of Jewishness—physical descent and spiritual circumcision—are not the only real Jews, but in reality they are the truest of all Jews.

Objections to an Ethnic Definition of Jews

Arguments against this position are based on three Scripture passages. The first objection points to Romans 9:6. Some object to this ethnic definition of Jews by arguing that Paul has expanded the people of Israel to include Gentiles when he writes, "For they are not all Israel who are descended from Israel" (Rom. 9:6). This approach is exactly the opposite of what Paul is maintaining. As in Romans 2:28–29, Paul is not widening the definition of Israel but narrowing it. He is not saying that Gentile believers are the children of promise and therefore the true Israel. Rather, it is the Jewish believers, as Abraham's children by both physical and spiritual descent, who are the true Israel.

The context actually supports a reference here to Jewish believers. Robert Saucy expresses it well:

> But consideration of the context makes it much more plausible that Paul has reference to a division *within* Israel. Having introduced this major section by declaring his concern for "those of my own race, the people of Israel" (9:3–4), the apostle goes on to elaborate God's elective purpose *within* the physical descendants of Abraham (cf. 9:7–13). The point of the entire section is that while the promises of God to Israel may appear to have failed when one looks at the totality of Israel, which is predominantly unbelieving, there is a remnant within Israel, "an 'Israel' within ethnic Israel."[15]

In addition to the contextual argument, there is a lexical argument for interpreting Romans 9:6–8 as Jewish believers in Jesus. Arnold Fruchtenbaum has done an extensive word study, reviewing each of the seventy-three uses of "Israel" in the New Testament. In each case, the word refers to physical descendants of Abraham, Isaac, and Jacob.[16] Only this passage and one other possible text (Gal. 6:16, see below) are proposed as the exceptions to the rule. But it seems unlikely that Paul would use the word in such an unusual way, particularly because interpreting this passage as speaking of Jewish followers of Jesus fits the contexts far better.

The apostle Paul characterizes messianic Jews as the true Israel by virtue of their physical descent and their appropriation of God's promises by faith in Messiah. According to Paul, God keeps His promises to the Jewish people through the true Israel, the Jewish followers of Messiah Jesus. Paul is not saying the church is the true Israel; rather he is arguing that the truest of all Israel are the Jewish believers in Jesus who are both ethnically part of Israel, and as part of the remnant, spiritually true to the God of Israel.

A second verse used to support viewing the church as having been merged with Israel is Galatians 6:16. The phrase "the Israel of God" has been a source of great contention, with the majority of Christian interpreters taking the expression to refer to the church universal as the true Israel. However, for several reasons a more likely interpretation is that Paul was blessing all who follow his teaching and then added a special blessing for Jewish believers in Jesus.

First, taking this as a special blessing for messianic Jews fits the normal syntax of the Greek conjunction (*kai*) as a continuative or conjunctive usage ("and"). Paul would be blessing those "who follow this standard *and* the Israel of God." This is the most normal way to translate the conjunction. To see this as referring to the church requires an unusual usage, translating the word with an explicative usage ("even"). Then the translation would be a blessing upon those "who follow this standard, *even* the Israel of God." S. Lewis Johnson correctly notes, "We should avoid the rarer grammatical usages when the common ones make good sense."[17]

Second, the usage of the word "Israel" argues on behalf of this being a blessing upon Jewish believers. Of the seventy-three usages of "Israel," this would be the only one that does not refer to physical descendants of Abraham, Isaac, and Jacob (see above).[18] It is unlikely that Paul decided to use the word in a "spiritual" sense when every other time he uses it as literally referring to the people of Israel.

Third, understanding the "Israel of God" to refer to the faithful Jewish remnant would fit the context in a far better way. At the end of the epistle, having rebuked those that were demanding circumcision in addition to faith as a requirement for justification before God, Paul certainly wanted to bless everyone in Galatia that supported his teaching. However, some might have viewed Paul's sharp rebuke as attacking all Jewish believers. Therefore, Paul added a specific blessing, not a general blessing, for those who would accept his teaching—a specific blessing for the Jewish believers who agreed with him. They were "the Israel of God," the loyal Jewish remnant of Israel.

The New Testament definition of Israel is identical to the definition found in the Hebrew Scriptures: the people of Israel are the physical descendants of Abraham, Isaac, and Jacob. However, the composition of the church is quite distinct—it is made up of all true believers in Jesus from every ethnic background, including both Jewish people and Gentiles.

A third passage used to support viewing the church as having been merged with Israel is Ephesians 2:11–22. This is perhaps the foundational passage about the church as composed of all believers of this age, Jewish and Gentile. At the outset of this text, Paul identifies *alienation* as the essential problem that existed between Jews and Gentiles (2:11–12). This estrangement is rooted in the contrast between the people Israel, who were the people of God by covenant, and the Gentiles, who were pagans and therefore called "Uncircumcision" (Eph. 2:11; cf. Gen. 17:2, 9–14). The rift between Jews and Gentiles is also seen in the spiritually bankrupt situation of Gentiles before the coming of Jesus. Gentiles had no standing or position to claim: they were "without the Messiah," referring to their lack of any messianic promise or hope; without any status because they were "excluded from the citizenship of Israel, and foreigners to the covenants of the promise," leaving them without any promises from God to claim; "without hope" for the future but entrenched in a philosophy of despair; and ultimately "without God in the world" because of being bound by the meaninglessness of idolatry (Eph. 2:12 HCSB).

God resolved the alienation between Jews and Gentiles by providing *reconciliation* for them through the Messiah Jesus (2:13–18). In a summary statement, Paul uses a contrast ("but now," v. 13) to remind Gentiles who once were far off (vv. 11–13) that they have been brought near to God and to the Jewish people by the Messiah's atoning death (v. 13). To clarify what he means by this summary statement, Paul gives an explanation of the process whereby God reconciled Gentiles and Jews (vv. 14–18).

First, Messiah Jesus personifies peace for Jews and Gentiles (v. 14a). In an emphatic statement ("He Himself" and no other), Paul declares Jesus is "our peace." He is not merely a mediator or teacher of peace but instead is a Person who embodies peacemaking. Second, Messiah Jesus produces peace for Jews and Gentiles (vv. 14b–16). Paul maintains that Jesus, in His atoning death, broke down the barrier between Jews and Gentiles by abolishing the enmity evident in the Law. He thereby produced reconciliation via the "one new man." This new man is an entirely new entity, the church or "one body" in which Jews and Gentiles are equally reconciled to each other and to God. Third, Messiah Jesus preaches peace to Jews and Gentiles (vv. 17–18). The Messiah's message of reconciliation, preached by Him through the apostles, addressed the Gentiles who were far from God and the Jewish people who were nearer but yet still in need of Messiah Jesus. Thus, as reconciled and equal members of Messiah's body, the church, Jews and Gentiles can now have equal access to God their Father by the Spirit.

Having described the problem of alienation and explained God's solution as reconciliation, Paul presents the result of Messiah's work: *unification* (vv. 19–22). In the body of Messiah, the church, Jews and Gentiles have been unified spiritually. They are now united in God's kingdom in that they both are fellow citizens (v. 19a). This does not mean that Gentiles have become citizens of the nation of Israel but rather that they have joined the citizenship of God's eternal kingdom, to which all true believers ("the saints") belong. Jews and Gentiles are also united in God's family, being equally part of "God's household" (v. 19b). Finally, they are also united in God's holy temple. In this metaphor of a spiritual temple, the Messiah is the chief cornerstone, holding it all together. The apostles and prophets form the foundation, upon which the building is built, and individual believers, Jews and Gentiles alike, are the building blocks cemented together by the Spirit of God (2:20–22).

Unfortunately, some interpreters have misunderstood this pivotal passage. First, some have contended that Gentile followers of Messiah have now been joined to Israel. The passage does not say this. Although initially Paul identified the Gentile problem as separation from Israel, God's solution to that alienation was not to make Gentiles part of Israel. Rather, the text says that the solution was to make Jews and Gentiles into "one new man." Therefore, Gentile alienation was overcome not by making Gentiles into Israel but by forming an entirely new entity, the church, which is the body of Messiah. Paul goes on to say that this entity was unknown in ages past (Eph. 3:5), and that its unique feature is the full spiritual equality of Jews and Gentiles (v. 6).

A second misunderstanding has been to view this passage as teaching that Jewish believers in Messiah Jesus have lost their distinct national identity as Jews. Plainly, Paul has not affirmed that Jews and Gentiles have lost their distinct ethnic identities. For example, he continues to call Gentile believers "Gentiles" (Rom. 11:13) and calls upon them to show their appreciation for their Jewish believing brethren (Rom. 15:26–27).[19] For this reason, John Stott, commenting on Ephesians 2:15, writes, "Not that the facts of human differentiation are removed. Men remain men and women, women; Jews remain Jews and Gentiles, Gentiles. But inequality before God is abolished. There is a new unity in Christ."[20]

The church and Israel are clearly different. They each began at different times and are composed of different people: Israel has an ethnic composition (physical descendants of Abraham, Isaac, and Jacob) while the church has a spiritual composition (all those who have trusted in Jesus the Messiah in this age). And yet, both Israel and the church are, in some sense, elect peoples. How that can be without their being one and the same will be addressed next.

Israel and the Church Have Different Elections

God's choice of Israel has resulted in that nation being called "the chosen people." Similarly, God has also chosen the church as revealed in Ephesians 1:4, "He chose us in Him." As a result, some have concluded that the election of the church has resulted in their becoming part of Israel. However, the passages in the New Testament that affirm the election of Israel and the church indicate that they are separate entities, chosen in different ways.

Israel's election is national, referring to God's choice of Israel as a distinct ethnic people. This is true but is unrelated to their lack of faith (for the most part) in Jesus the Messiah. The New Testament evidence for the continued election of Israel despite unbelief in Jesus is Romans 11:28–29. There, Paul begins by saying that "regarding the gospel, they are enemies for your advantage" (Rom. 11:28a HSCB), expressing Israel's opposition to the message of Jesus the Messiah. As Paul noted previously in Romans 11, this is advantageous to the Gentile believers of Rome because "salvation has come to the Gentiles" as a result of the Jewish rejection of the gospel (v. 11).

Yet, despite the majority of the Jewish people being opposed to the gospel, "from the standpoint of God's choice they are beloved for the sake of the fathers" (Rom. 11:28b). This shows that God views Israel, despite unbelief, as those who are elect or chosen, and as such they remain beloved. The word "loved" in Scripture is frequently associated with choice. For example, the Scriptures say, "I have loved [chosen] Jacob; but I have hated [rejected] Esau" (Mal. 1:2–3; Rom. 9:13). The point Paul makes is that Jewish opposition to the gospel in no way negates God's national election of Israel for "His great name" (1 Sam. 12:22; cf. Deut. 7:6–9; 14:2). The reason is that "God's gracious gifts and calling are irrevocable" (Rom. 11:29 HCSB).

The church has a different kind of election, one that crosses national boundaries and is distinctly spiritual. More than anything else, it is soteric, meaning that it is an election to salvation. In Ephesians 1:4, speaking of individual members of the church, Paul says God "chose us in Him before the foundation of the world, that we would be holy and blameless before Him." This election is linked to God's loving predestination to adoption (v. 5) and redemption through the sacrificial death of Messiah Jesus (v. 7). Members of the church are indeed elect, but God's choice pertains to their forgiveness of sins and not their ethnicity. Therefore, Israel and the church are both elect but in different ways.

According to Scripture, then, Israel and the church are distinct entities. As such, they have different beginnings, are composed of different people, and experience a different category of election. There is no basis for confusing these two entities into one.

CONCLUSION

Israel is God's focus in the future tribulation, while the church appears to be absent from the earth during that time. Although some might try to unite Israel and the church into one entity, according to Scripture they remain distinct and separate. So what does this have to do with the timing of the rapture of the church?

These principles relate to the timing of the rapture as a logical conclusion. If God will focus His attention on Israel during the tribulation and if the church appears to be absent from earth during that time, and if Israel and the church are distinct, then it appears that the rapture of the church must take place before the tribulation. Today, God's primary means of operating in the world is through the church. However, God will complete the church at the rapture, the dead in Christ will be raised, and the surviving church members will be translated into their glorified bodies (1 Thess. 4:13–18). Then during the tribulation God will turn His attention on Israel once again, using the trouble of that time to discipline the nation justly (Jer. 30:11) and cause the nation to turn in faith to their Messiah Jesus. Then, all Israel will be saved (Rom. 11:25).

My good friend of whom I spoke at the opening of this chapter recognizes that Israel and the church are distinct. Although he is an agnostic regarding future things and does not know what he believes about the pretribulation rapture, in my view, he is being inconsistent. If we hold to Israel and the church as distinct, we are compelled to believe that the rapture of the church will take place before the tribulation, when God refocuses His attention on His people Israel.

NOTES

1. The word "Israel" is frequently confused. I am using it here not in the sense of the modern state nor of the land situated on the Mediterranean Sea. Rather I mean ethnic Israel, or the Jewish people. They are the physical descendants of Abraham, Isaac, and Jacob.

2. For a helpful and thorough defense of the biblical distinction between Israel and the church, see Michael J. Vlach, *Has the Church Replaced Israel?* (Nashville: B&H Publishing, 2010).

3. The tribulation refers to Daniel's Seventieth Week (Dan. 9:24–27). It is a seven-year period of time at the end of days when God sends His wrath upon the earth. It culminates with the return of Jesus the Messiah, who will restore the throne of David and rule over a kingdom of peace and justice for a thousand years.

4. He is also known as "the beast" (Rev. 13:1–9), "the coming prince" (Dan. 9:24–27 HSCB), "the man of lawlessness" (2 Thess. 2:3), and "the Antichrist" (1 John 2:18).

5. This is a somewhat detailed and technical prophecy that will not be fully explained here. However, for a more in depth discussion of this passage, see Michael Rydelnik. "Daniel," *The Moody Bible Commentary* (Chicago: Moody, 2014): 1304–8.

6. This remarkable prophecy of the Messiah's coming began its countdown in 444 BC and was fulfilled in AD 33, on the day when Jesus was presented to Israel as Messiah (commonly known as Palm Sunday). See Michael Rydelnik, "Daniel," 1304–8.

7. For an extended discussion of these ancient nations and where they are located in contemporary times, see Michael Rydelnik, *Understanding the Arab-Israeli Conflict,* rev. ed. (Chicago: Moody, 2007), 192–95.

8. For an extended discussion of the timing of this invasion, see ibid., 195–97.

9. Some take this piercing figuratively since it seems impossible for God to be physically pierced. Nevertheless, since all other usages of the verb "pierce" refer to literal piercing (Num. 25:8; Judg. 9:54; 1 Sam. 31:4; Isa. 13:15; Jer. 37:10; 51:4; Zech. 13:3), it is better to take this verse literally as well. As such it refers to the piercing of a representative of God, namely, the incarnate Messiah. About the human responsibility for piercing the Messiah, Kaiser wisely warns: "This is not to add fuel to the fires of those who have castigated our Jewish neighbors by the stigma of being 'Christ killers.' That slur is as unfair as it is untrue! In fact, the Messiah was put to death by the Jews *and the Romans* [italics his]. It is also true that He was put to death for the sins of all the world. So caution must be exercised in this area when describing the roles that were carried out by the first-century participants in the death of Christ" (Walter C. Kaiser Jr., *The Messiah in the Old Testament* [Grand Rapids: Zondervan, 1994], 223). These verses do indicate that at their end-time repentance, Jewish people will recognize that their ancestors were participants in the conspiracy against the Messiah, not that they acted alone or were perpetually guilty (cf. Acts 4:27–28).

10. The words "all Israel" need not mean every single Jewish person. When the phrase is used in the LXX, it refers to a representation of Jewish people *at a given point in time* (e.g., Num. 16:34).

11. For a thorough discussion of the meaning of the words *tereō ek,* see Jeffrey L. Townsend, "The Rapture in Revelation 3:10," *BibSac* (July–Sept 1980): 255–59.

12. This is the reading of the Majority Text, and the King James and New King James versions.

13. Gutbrod links this passage to Romans 9:4–6: "We are not told here that Gentile Christians are the true Israel. The distinction at R. 9:6 does not go beyond what is presupposed at Jn. 1:47, and it corresponds to the distinction between *Ioudaios en tō kryptō* ('a Jew who is one inwardly') and *Ioudaios en tō phanerō* ('a Jew who is one outwardly') at R. 2:28f., which does not imply that Paul is calling Gentiles the true Jews." Walter Gutbrod, "Israel," TDNT, 3:387.

14. Alva J. McClain, *Romans: The Gospel of God's Grace* (Chicago: Moody, 1973), 86.

15. Robert L. Saucy, "Israel and the Church: A Case for Discontinuity," in *Continuity and Discontinuity: Perspectives on the Relationship between the Old and New Testaments,* ed. John S. Feinberg (Wheaton: Crossway, 1988), 245.

16. Arnold G. Fruchtenbaum, *Israelology: The Missing Link in Systematic Theology* (Tustin, CA: Ariel Ministries, 1993), 684–90.

17. S. Lewis Johnson, "Paul and the Israel of God," in *Essays in Honor of J. Dwight Pentecost,* ed. Stanley D. Toussaint and Charles H. Dyer (Chicago: Moody, 1986), 187.

18. Obviously, as stated earlier in the main text, some do hold that Romans 9:6–8 also refers to the church. But many who affirm a replacement theology interpret that passage as referring to the Jewish remnant. It appears that Galatians 6:16 is the one passage that all supersessionists (i.e., those who hold that the church has replaced Israel) insist uses "Israel" to refer to the church.

19. Note also Paul's "we, you" references in Ephesians, by which he means, "we, Jewish believers" and "you, Gentile believers" (1:11–13; 2:1–3).

20. John Stott, *The Message of Ephesians* (Downers Grove, IL InterVarsity, 1979), 101–2.

OTHER **END TIMES** BOOKS FROM MOODY PUBLISHERS

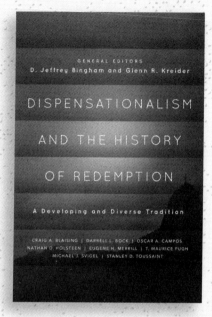

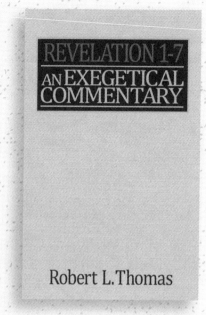

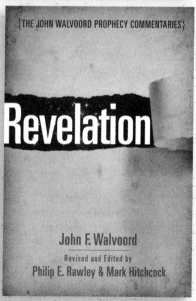

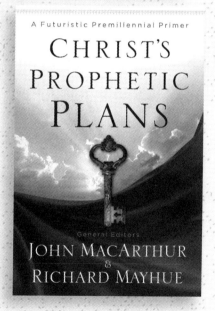

MOODY
Publishers™

From the Word to Life

MORE RESOURCES FROM
MOODY PUBLISHERS

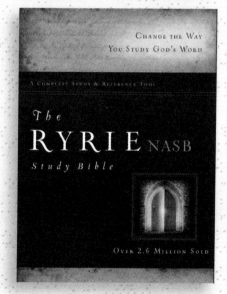

MOODY
Publishers™

From the Word to Life

MOODY Radio™

From the Word ***to Life***

Moody Radio produces and delivers compelling programs filled with biblical insights and creative expressions of faith that help you take the next step in your relationship with Christ.

You can hear Moody Radio on 36 stations and more than 1,500 radio outlets across the U.S. and Canada. Or listen on your smartphone with the Moody Radio app!

www.moodyradio.org